INHERITING THE REVOLUTION

INHERITING THE REVOLUTION

The First Generation of Americans

JOYCE APPLEBY

THE BELKNAP PRESS OF
HARVARD UNIVERSITY PRESS
Cambridge, Massachusetts
London, England

Library of Congress Cataloging-in-Publication Data

Appleby, Joyce Oldham.

Inheriting the revolution: the first generation of Americans/Joyce Appleby.

p. cm.

Includes bibliographical references (p.) and index.

ISBN 0-674-00236-9 (alk. paper)

1. United States–History–1783–1865.

2. United States–Social conditions–To 1865.

3. United States–History–Revolution, 1775–1783–Influence.

I. Title.

E301 .A65   2000

973–dc21   99-049787

To my sons, Mark and Frank, I dedicate this book with love

PREFACE

I BEGAN THIS STUDY inductively following the lives of several thousand American men and women born between 1776 and 1800, but, of course, having studied American history for over forty years, my mind was hardly a *tabula rasa*. My goal was to examine the "inheriting generation," the children and grandchildren of those who participated in the revolutionary break with Great Britain that conferred formal nationhood on a cluster of New World colonies. Much of their collective story will be familiar, but not, I think, the multifarious ways that as individuals confronting a new set of options, they crafted the political style, social forms, and economic ventures of an independent United States.

My research strategy resembled a vacuum cleaner. Reading in primary and secondary sources, I made cards on every member of my cohort whom I encountered. More systematically I looked for records of them in standard encyclopedias, school registers, and manuscript collections. From these leads came information about their associates, writings, and enterprises. I also read over two hundred published autobiographies written by those born between 1776 and 1800, seeking information about persons, places, and things that animated American society during their lifetime, as well as the forms and interpretations that gave meaning to them.

The self-conscious crafting of a life story is a historian's delight and snare, for autobiographies can obscure as much reality as they reveal. Mature authors often put a distorting gloss on youthful decisions. Memory plays tricks, vanity trumps honesty. In the West autobiographies developed as a genre alongside the novel; they often follow the novel's lineal story line, plotting a life around dramatic moments. And like the novel, they usually emphasize individual choices while minimizing the powerful structuring forces of law, property, and custom. There is also the possibility of confounding a first-person narrative with an objective report.

Mindful of these tendencies, I have used memoirs to learn about early childhood, emotional ties, job choices, and the material and social environment in which the lives unfolded. While historians are taught to be suspicious of self-presentations, they ignore the information at a loss. Autobiographies are an unparalleled source of clues about sensibilities—the most evanescent of cultural phenomena—as well as of the values and interpretations that constructed reality for a given generation.

Many people over the last nine years have helped me clarify my thoughts as I have written this book: Joan Waugh, Daniel Howe, Karen Orren, Margaret Jacob, Lynn Hunt, Naomi Lamoreaux, Ann Gordon, Iryne Black, Aimee Lee Cheek, William Cheek, Kirsten Hammer, Ludmilla Jordanova, Anne Sheehan, Christopher Clark, Winifred Rothenberg, Mark Valeri, Carole Shammas, Andrew Robertson, John Majewski, Malinda Alaine, Maggie Brambilla, Elizabeth Townsend, Ruth Bloch, Barbara Packer, Kariann Yokota, Christopher Gantner, Cynthia Cumfer, Eric Altice, Anthony Iaccarino, Gregory Vanderbilt, Sandra Moats, Robert Baker, Andrew Lister, and Gregory Beyrer. I want to give special thanks to Stephen Aron for his trenchant reading of the manuscript and to J. R. Pole for attending to matters of syntax, style, and substance with exquisite care.

I am grateful to the John Simon Guggenheim Memorial Foundation, the UCLA Center for Seventeenth and Eighteenth Century Studies, and the UCLA Senate Research Committee for their support—in some cases sustained support—of this study. I also wish to thank John Hench, Ellen Dunlap, Georgia Barnhill, Nancy Burkett, Thomas Knoles, and Joanne Chaison for opening the riches of the American Antiquarian Society to me.

CONTENTS

ILLUSTRATIONS

INHERITING THE REVOLUTION

I

INTRODUCTION

"Peter Rugg, the Missing Man" enjoyed the reputation of being the most popular short story of the early republic.[1] A phantasmagoric tale, it begins when the title character sets off for Concord one sunny, autumn day in the year of the Boston Massacre. Rugg is on his way home when a violent storm overtakes him. Rather than wait out the bad weather, he swears that he *will see home to-night, in spite of the last tempest, or may I never see home!* Having aroused the fates and furies, Rugg is doomed to traverse the back roads of Massachusetts in his horse-drawn chaise, startling travelers with his mad appearance and the unexpected showers that always accompanied him. A half-century later, Jonathan Dunwell, a New York businessman and the narrator of the story, becomes intrigued by the weird phenomenon he encounters in his frequent trips to Boston and accosts Rugg, wresting from him the facts about a trip to Concord gone awry.

Clearly a desperate man, Rugg turns out to be an opinionated one as well, scoffing when Dunwell tells him that the handsome city he has brought him to is New York. "Poh, New York is nothing; though I never was there," Rugg asserts irascibly. Unperturbed, Dunwell guides Rugg's chaise through Pearl Street, where he observes Rugg's changing countenance: "his nerves began to twitch; his eyes trembled in their sockets; he was evidently bewildered." Awestruck, Rugg exclaims, "This surpasses all human comprehension; if you know, sir, where we are, I beseech you to tell me." Dumbfounded upon passing into Broadway, Rugg insists: "there is no such place as this in North America. This is all the effect of enchantment; this is a grand delusion, nothing real. Here is seemingly a great city, magnificent houses, shops, and goods, men and women innumerable, and as busy as in real life, all sprung up in one night from the wilderness; or what is more probable some tremendous convulsion of Nature has thrown London or Amsterdam on the shores of New England."[2]

William Austin's much-reprinted story, with its contrast between the turbulence on a road to Boston and the majesty of a thriving commercial metropolis, offers an apt introduction to my history of the first generation of Americans—those born after the Revolution. Comparing Rugg's intemperate confusion to the urbane composure of his guide, readers of Austin's tale must have recognized their own good fortune in being the heirs of a revolution they did not have to fight. The narrator's certainty of self acts as a foil for the ambiguity of Rugg's identity—is he a ghost or an aged relic of the colonial era? The transfer of European greatness to the shores of the United States no doubt seemed credible to Americans living in 1825, as did the enormous satisfaction that Dunwell, the buoyant embodiment of American success, took in astounding an old man, trapped in an earlier era. And well might Dunwell boast, considering that between the Boston Massacre and the 1820 census, Boston had tripled in size while New York had grown sixfold, increases without colonial parallels. Dunwell was a modern man; he compared the past to the present and found it wanting. His creator, William Austin, a distinguished member of the Boston bar, registered his own commitment to an egalitarian future when he refused membership in the newly-formed Phi Beta Kappa Society because of its inherent elitism.

The passage of social responsibility from parents to children is always a fascinating interplay of the inherited and the novel. The destruction of much of their elders' world forced the members of this generation to move forward on their own, a necessity that set them apart from earlier and later cohorts. Neither their parents' example nor their communities' tested formulas could guide them in the new situations they encountered. Like Rugg, their mothers and fathers were immured in the past, stuck there at the very time that the pace of change exaggerated the difference between past and present. Many of the new generation became agents of change in an era of change marked by the convergence of political revolutions, commercial expansion, and intellectual ferment that penetrated, as we shall see, the most mundane aspects of life. Never forced, like their parents, to revoke an earlier loyalty to Great Britain, the men and women of the first generation were much freer to imagine what the United States might become. The celebration of Revolutionary events that marked their childhood also made them conscious of not having fought in the war, or run the farm for an absent spouse or parent, or participated in a boycott, or hidden farm produce from marauding British troops.

The very idea of generations resonated with new meaning after the Revolution. As families exerted less influence in the lives of those born after Independence, the young people looked more to their peers for models of behavior. This attachment to one's age group weakened traditional loyalties, but it held out the promise of creating a fresh political will, as the Revolutionary figure Gouverneur Morris discerned when he wrote that a "national spirit is the natural result of national existence; and although some of the present generation may feel colonial oppositions of opinion, that generation will die away, and give place to a race of Americans."[3] In the following decades Morris's "race of Americans" disclosed the creative potential that had long been coiled like a spring within Britain's North American colonies. Engaging with their desires, callings, decisions, and reflections offers an intimate view of how the vibrant new abstractions of democracy—the nation, free enterprise, and liberal society—thickened with meaning during the early nineteenth century.

Highlighting the members of one generation, while largely ignoring those people younger and older who are living alongside them, requires some justification. My correction to this distortion has been to concentrate on the forty years when my cohort predominated in the population, starting when the first of them came of age in the 1790s and ending in 1830 when their juniors, now adults, outnumbered them. A related, more serious problem comes from homogenizing the experience of diverse groups, assigning collective nouns to actions that were really performed by small subsets of the larger society. This would be particularly misleading during the early nineteenth century, when deep political divisions, competing religious insights, and profound disagreements about slavery embroiled the first generation as it assumed responsibility for the nation.

Another conceptual problem when dealing with the early nineteenth century concerns the perception of historic transformations. Since the invention of the printing press and the voyages of exploration, European society has moved through a succession of irreversible developments that have given each generation the strong feeling that theirs has been the great period of change, or even the principal divide between the traditional and modern. The sense of transformative change is no doubt real, but the repetition of such experiences warns us off the notion that there has been one singular period in the long, arduous, and fateful move away from the world of custom. Rather than thinking of a series of ages, each utterly new, it would be better to consider the peculiar mix of innovations and conti-nuities, ruptures and reactions that confronted each cohort. In the case of those born right after Independence, their newfound geographic and social mobility, the novel applications of steam power, and expanding uses of print communicated the sense of the modern that Mr. Dunwell conveyed so effectively to Peter Rugg with a trip to New York City.

Historians talk easily about continuity and change, but in a study that claims so much change for one generation, it is important to be more explicit about the tension between the two. In a very real sense, what Independence brought was an enlarged scope for acting on desires and convictions that had long lain close to the surface of colonial life. The casual oversight of the British government had permitted social experi-ments and encouraged the kind of personal independence that made possi-ble a collective move for political independence. New science, new tech-nology, and new literature had come to the colonies with every boat from Europe. The natural rights philosophy embedded in the Declaration of Independence came from English political thought, radicalized by French philosophers during the eighteenth century. Other novelties that as-tounded contemporaries were but part and parcel of the industrial process affecting all of western Europe.

Where American commentators differed was in attributing their mate-rial accomplishments to the superiority of their political institutions and construing their economic progress as testimony to the soundness of the revolution they had inherited. So much that they saw around them had been newly built, newly ploughed, newly invented that it was possible to think of the United States as having implanted itself on a blank canvas, flourishing because of its good sense in adopting democratic ways. In their eyes, Independence made possible the creation of a distinctive American society that honored individual initiative, institutional restraint, and popular public participation. However inadequate as an explanation of historic change this view might be, the connection between prosperity and democracy sealed the American imagination against a critical stance towards either, a portentous development.

Facing a dramatically different challenge from that of their parents, the men and women born between Independence and 1800 worked out the social forms for the new nation. They—some enthusiastically, others reluctantly—took on the self-conscious task of elaborating the meaning of the American Revolution. Their knowledge of it consisted of passed-on tales rather than first-hand experiences, yet they were the ones to fashion the revolutionary affirmations that gave the United States a national culture replete with purposes, heroes, taboos, prescriptions, symbols, and celebrations. Familiar elements in the colonial world had transmogrified into novelties; Britain changed from a sovereign authority to a rival, and the continent, once at their backs, became a part of a new, national destiny to be faced in the West.

Any study focusing on how a group interprets its shared experience over a specific period of time must confront the vexed relation between the realm of reality—conditions, situations, and decisions—and the constructions bestowed upon it by the participants. My own view is that interpreting reality is the most serious intellectual activity people take part in, but that the process of interpretation—both individual and collective—is always prompted by outside events. Growing to maturity after Independence, my cohort advanced an interpretation of American democracy that included a narrative about the future that left the next generation with far fewer intellectual alternatives. A kind of closure about collective meaning had taken place. Expressed in universal terms, the first generation's understanding of its revolutionary heritage obscured for decades to come the variety of identities and affinities within the nation. Universality was claimed for the qualities displayed by successful white men, throwing other people into the shadows of national consciousness.

Many contemporaries concluded that both democratic and limited government enhanced their free-enterprise economy. Journal commentary, life stories, published gazetteers, and travelers' accounts put into circulation tributes to individual initiative with explorations of risk and venture that contributed discursively to a culture of capitalism. The engagement of

America's first generation with the market provided the intellectual foundations of free enterprise, what we could call the invisible support for material success. This part of the story also abounds with paradoxes. Slave labor produced far higher profits than that from free workers and farm proprietors. Northern indictments of slavery ignored this fact when they promoted free choice and personal liberty as avenues to prosperity. Similarly, religious revivals inspired passionate engagements with God while they enhanced the capacity for disciplined work. By teaching young men and women how to act responsibly and acquire the habits of planning and risk-taking, America's churches furnished the lessons that added moral capital to the entrepreneurs' dollars in the bank.

The decisive events of the 1770s, 1780s, and 1790s structured the world in which the cohort born after Independence took their bearings. The control over information and opinions once exercised by an elite had been wrested away by the articulate critics of that elite in the 1790s. The mobilization of popular will through print campaigns overpowered the tactical advantages that had long accrued to a small, literate upper class. By 1800 a party of reforming democrats had found its voice, a cause, and the strategy for prevailing at the polls. The presidential election of Thomas Jefferson led to the uncoupling of social and political power, drowning in a democratic tidal wave the colonial belief that authority should be exercised through the uncontested leadership of a recognized cadre of families. Jefferson moved swiftly to dismantle the Federalist fiscal program, rushing the land of the national domain into the hands of frontier buyers, reducing taxes, and cutting the size of the civil service. By 1810 a third of the American population lived in a new settlement while even in the older cities the population had more than doubled.

Three European witnesses have left pithy accounts of the perpetual-motion society they discovered in their travels. The Duc de La Rochefoucauld-Liancourt spent thirty-three months in the United States between 1795 and 1797. At every tavern in the rural areas of New England, Pennsylvania, and New York, he encountered farmers moving to some other place. La Rochefoucauld wanted to know if American farmers shared any of the French peasant's attachment to a particular piece of ground, but when he tried to explain this sentiment to them, they invariably told him that such permanence revealed a certain lack of pluck. "It is a country in flux," the duc concluded; "that which is true today as regards its population, its establishments, its prices, its commerce will not be true six months from now."[4]

Thirty years later another perceptive French observer, the young Michel Chevalier, covered much the same territory, geographically and culturally. Responding more philosophically to the constant churning of people in the United States, Chevalier concluded that if "movement and the quick succession of sensations and ideas constitute life, here one lives a hundred fold more than elsewhere; here, all is circulation, motion, and boiling agitation." "Experiment follows experiment; enterprise follows enterprise," he reported, observing that riches and "poverty follow on each other's traces and each in turn occupies the place of the other."[5]

Frederick Marryat, a British naval officer, more laconically commented that "the Americans are a restless, locomotive people: whether for business or pleasure, they are ever on the move in their own country, and they move in masses." "Wandering about seems engrafted in their Nature," he added; they "forever imagine that the Lands further off are still better than those upon which they are already settled."[6] Better than Americans themselves these observers saw the novelty of a society directed almost entirely by the ambitious dreams that had been unleashed after the Revolution in the heated imagination of thousands of people, most of them poor and young.

Although starting from the political moment of Independence, my study ranges back and forth from the public to the personal as it follows the men and women—black and white, immigrant and old stock—of the first generation when they engaged in partisan politics, responded to new market forces, explored the meaning of intimacy in a mobile society, fashioned new social cues for a democracy, and created a network of voluntary associations to take the place of defunct colonial institutions. From these diverse experiences and the welter of intentions that prompted them the autonomous individual emerged as an ideal. For many years we have treated individualism as a natural phenomenon. In the following pages we will see this exemplar taking shape historically, as an ideal, a filter, a measure for invidious comparisons, and the human underpinning for market enterprise and moral reform. By no means reflective of the heterogeneous population of the United States, this autonomous individual came to personify the nation and the free society it embodied, a patriotic icon that differentiated the United States from the savagery at its borders and the tyranny across the Atlantic.

My witnesses are those who did something in public—started a business, invented a useful object, settled a town, organized a movement, ran for office, formed an association, or wrote for publication, if only an autobiography. As they mature we move from the end of traditional society–"the world we have lost"–to the social framework that we are still living within. During their lives, four unexpected developments interacted in unexpected ways: the radicalizing of politics, the revitalization of religion, new opportunities for the young, and the abolition of slavery in the Northern states. All of these changes made public life more spontaneous and fractured, weakening the guards of discretion and restraint that once patrolled the borders between private and public realms. Few in the nation escaped their transforming intrusiveness. The new distinction of free and slave labor with all its social entailments divided the United States in ways that could not have been imagined at the time of the Revolution. Nor could anyone have predicted that the cool, rationalist attitudes of the Enlightenment would be overwhelmed by the warm passions of religious awakening. Economic developments were equally unforeseen, bringing thousands of small opportunities to a cohort of young people eager to break out of the colonial cocoon of their parents.

Not everyone born after the Revolution took part in reconfiguring their society; many stayed at home and replicated their parents' world as closely as they could.[7] Many men and women lacked even the minimal resources to change their lot in life. A majority still found their lives circumscribed by the persisting authority of the man of the house, armed by law and custom with enormous power over his dependents. Nor were changes, which we view in retrospect as progressive, accepted willingly by those who had to endure the disorientation that came with them. Still, revolutions exert unanticipated–often unimaginable–influences. Among African Americans, the emancipation legislation of the Northern states aroused hopes for slavery's end. Free blacks, their numbers swollen by Northern abolition, Southern manumissions, and a much greater scope for self-liberation, gave the lie to slave-owners' dismissive estimates of the capabilities of people of color who now could be found mingling with whites in churches and shops, on the frontier and in the cities of the North and Upper South. Women, largely excluded from citizenship, found ways to participate in the public realm that changed both their histories and the American perception of social participation.

The widening of economic horizons sparked ambitions that ranged from global proselytizing for Christianity to the liberation of the world's enslaved to a dozen other more modest yellow brick roads to self-improvement, as the following six cameos from the first generation will show.

These young people's yearning to give expression to the stirrings of individual ambition epitomized the activists in this generation, sealing the ardent worshipper and inventive manufacturer, the radical reformer and propulsive do-gooder, into a dominant American mold.

⁂

ICHABOD WASHBURN was born in Kingston, Massachusetts in 1798, his seafaring father having died from yellow fever the year of his birth, leaving twins and an infant to be supported by his widow at her loom. At nine Washburn was "put out to live" to relieve his mother of some expense. His wardrobe rolled into a bundle, he walked five miles to Duxbury to work for a harnessmaker. Along the way a windmill excited his curiosity. Jabbering at his companion, he was reproved with the gruff reply, "Don't ask so many questions, boy." By the time Washburn was fourteen he was employed in a cotton factory in Kingston, where he ran the power-loom with an Englishman. All the cog-wheels were made of wood and Washburn reflected that it was probably the first power-loom ever made in America. This experience stirred an interest in mechanics, but his guardian uncle thwarted his wish to go to work for the famous Slater mills in Pawtucket, Rhode Island. The country, he told Ichabod, soon would be so full of factories "that there would be no more machinery to be built."[8]

Washburn described these events in an autobiography, published ten years after his death in 1868. In it he was hailed as the founder and first president of the Washburn & Moen Wire Manufactory, said to be the largest establishment of the kind in the world with eleven acres under one roof.[9] As Washburn shaped his own destiny in the early decades of the nineteenth century, so he helped mold the town, the church, and the nation in which his story unfolded. The accelerating pace of international trade brought an array of opportunities to rural lads in the United States, the nascent textile and machine-making industries calling forth Washburn's latent capacities as a fabricator of wire just as his early acquisition of independent working habits enabled him to respond to the opening.

Far from standing alone, opportunity represents a cultural phenomenon, a complex exchange of information, invitation, assessment, and introspection. When we read a life story, the individuality in the sequential emotions and decisions that carried a young man to success stands out;

hidden are the cultural cues and hints, the social sluices and dams that guided the youth's course. Commerce, so frequently treated as an impersonal, overdetermined force, in fact depended upon personal responses and cultural norms. Washburn enhanced the economy of the United States by pouring his energy into improving productive techniques, as he strengthened the nation's commercial ethic by celebrating his accomplishments in a memoir that detailed his career from a bound-out apprenticeship to ownership of a large plant in industrial America. Washburn could serve as a prototype for the self-made man, appearing as a recognizable type for the first time in this era. He began with nothing, hitched his star to the wagon of industrial development, and watched his talents grease the engine of luck, not the least of those talents being a capacity for hard work.

The motives of self-making among Americans were wondrously broad, comprehending as they did the drive for self-liberation among enslaved Americans, the yearning to reform an erring people, frequently sharpened by an evangelical revival, or the desire for a new beginning on the frontier. Americans had metamorphosed the continent into an empty canvas upon which explorers, settlers, and missionaries could limn their pictures of the future, despite the steady and often violent expulsion of the native population. Almost all in this cohort were born in the country—that grand designation that encompassed the areas outside the America's dozen cities with more than ten thousand people. Most of them grew up in rural penury, for the long and costly War for Independence depleted resources, with farming families paying their share in sons and fathers killed, goods confiscated, crops neglected, and savings lost in depreciated "continental" money.

In no sense typical with his enormous success, Washburn very much belongs to the cohort of men and women coming of age in the 1790s, the ones who sank the footings for a new national identity with their interests, sentiments, and casts of mind. In after hours at the blacksmith's shop, he made hooks, toasting irons, and ploughs. With the proceeds from their sale, he "hired" a seat in the gallery of the Leicester Congregational Church. At age twenty, having bought out the last year of his indenture, Washburn was on his own. It was then that he saw for the first time what he called a "subscription newspaper." As he described the encounter, being "timid and hesitating to subscribe myself, Mr. Melin, a benevolent person standing by said to me, 'Put down fifty cents, young man, and you will soon see it come back to you again.'" Influenced by this advice, Washburn invested fifty cents, and "in a few weeks," he reported, "I received a very large, lucrative order for lead pipe, under circumstances that induced the good Doctor to say, 'I told you so.'"[10] And thus Washburn, like all successful members of this generation, availed himself of the dynamic communication system that was converting a union of localities into a nation of participating readers.

Confronting change in their earliest years—a new constitutional government, an economy bursting out of its geographic and institutional limits, a venerable Protestant faith moving in surprising new directions—Americans born after Independence became the self-conscious shapers of a liberal society, even as it was being transformed by the cumulative forces of economic advance. The structure of their opportunities and the pattern of their responses defined what it was to be an American in the early nineteenth century. A new conception of politics converged with a new appreciation of enterprise, and a new character ideal was created: the man who developed inner resources, acted independently, lived virtuously, and bent his behavior to his personal goals—not the American Adam, but the American *homo faber*, the builder.

The United States offered far more than business opportunities in the early decades of the nineteenth century. As Washburn's renting of the pew with his first earnings suggests, his church, the established Congregational one, played a prominent role in his life. From the sale of toasting irons he made in off-hours, Washburn also purchased *The Memoir of the Life of Harriet Newell*, a book he claimed to have read with more profit than anything except the Bible.[11]

Born sixty miles from Worcester just five years before Washburn, Harriet Atwood Newell found a different avenue for self-fulfillment in her brief life, but like Washburn, she did something unthinkable a decade earlier when she accompanied her husband to India. The *Memoir* that Washburn purchased depicted Harriet as a Christian heroine, celebrated for her piety and lamented for her early death. Her letters and diary, which comprised the *Memoir*, give access to the zeal of a young New England woman at the beginning of America's mission as a missionary country.[12] A wave of religious excitement, cresting in a local revival, washed over Harriet when she was a student at Bradford Academy, leaving her at twelve anxious about the state of her soul.

Harriet Atwood had just turned seventeen when twenty-five-year-old Samuel Newell entered her life, appearing in her journal as an engaged Christian who "expects to spend his life in preaching a Savior to the benighted Pagans." Soon references to his sermons mixed with reports of his visits and then the oblique comment, "he wishes not to influence me;

he would not if he could." Marrying Samuel Newell was a fateful step, for the newly-formed American Board of Commissioners for Foreign Missions was sending him to India along with Adoniram Judson and his wife, Ann Hasseltine Judson. The departure of the two young couples (she accepted Samuel's proposal) stirred the imagination of the evangelical community that was sending them halfway round the world. Family and friends gathered at Salem on a wintry afternoon in February of 1812 to see them off on a merchant brig bound for Calcutta. Mindful of the special roles that the young women would play, Jonathan Allen delivered a special sermon "on the Occasion of Two Young Ladies being about to embark as the wives of ... Missionaries to India."[13]

American enterprise had actually provided the means for the young clergymen and their wives to reach Calcutta, for only twenty years earlier Elias Hasket Derby had pioneered the country's links to India, making himself the first American millionaire along the way. In the United States census of 1790, Salem had been the country's sixth largest city, its flourishing commerce with China and the East Indies augmented by the profits of an extensive coastal trade. It was the widow of another successful Salem merchant, Mrs. Mary Norris, whose munificent gift of $30,000 funded the young couples and their work in India.[14] The Derby firm lost heavily in Jefferson's embargo of 1807–1808, but the second Elias Hasket Derby recovered and established a commercial house on the Isle of France, which also figured in Harriet's story.

After expatiating on the fact that pure religion had sunk deeper roots in England and America than anywhere else in Christendom, Allen in his send-off sermon sketched for his listeners the challenge that lay before the young brides about to set sail. Describing the debased condition of Hindu and Mohammedan women, accounted by their men "an inferior race," he explained that it would be the task of Mrs. Newell and Mrs. Judson to reach them with the Gospel message since their husbands could not possibly gain access to the sequestered women of the East. The devout Christian wives of America's first foreign missionaries, he stressed, had to teach those women that "they are not an inferior race of creatures; but stand on a par with men."[15]

For events after their departure, the *Memoir* drew upon Newell's weekly letters to her mother. In them, she exulted in the joy of having "a most affectionate partner," the dreary speculations about damnation replaced now with vivid descriptions of Calcutta, which they reached by June: "the natives are as thick as bees; they keep a continual chattering ... No English lady is here seen walking the streets." Never had she enjoyed such health, Newell reported; their Mission house in Serampore was spacious, the garden larger and more elegant than any ever seen in America, the mangoes, plantains and guavas an exotic delight. "You will hardly credit me," she told her mother, "when I tell you, that it is fully as expensive living here, as in America." But, alas, the British East India Company used the outbreak of war with the United States as a pretext for expelling foreign missionaries. The couple, with Harriet now pregnant, set sail for a new field of evangelical labor on the Isle of France. A despairing letter from Samuel Newell to his mother-in-law closed the memoir. Crying out against a God who sent them sickness and death instead of success in preaching Christ's gospel, Newell rationed the bad tidings. First he reported God's "taking away the dear little babe which He gave us, the child of our prayers, of our hopes, of our tears," born four days outside the Isle, and then he broke the news that seven weeks later, the consumption that she had undoubtedly carried to India had killed Harriet.[16]

Behind the Newells' departure for Calcutta lay the vaulting spiritual ambition of another young clergyman, Samuel Mills. A few years older than they, Mills had been swept up in a revival in Litchfield County, Connecticut. Sitting on the banks of the Hoosack River, he and two fellow Williams College students dreamed of a great project for their generation— that of carrying the gospel light to the darkest parts of the world. To execute their grand plan, the young men had decided that each should enroll in a different college to recruit fellow missionaries. Mills himself transferred to Yale, from which he graduated in the class of 1809, then continued on to Andover Theological Seminary, where he met Judson and Newell.[17] Andover was exactly the place for such plans to mature, having been established to nurture the flagging evangelical spirit in New England after the Unitarians had taken control of Harvard.[18]

The young seminarians whom Mills mobilized succeeded in turning the attention of their elders towards active proselytizing. Within seven years, the new American Board of Commissions for Foreign Missionaries had sent missionaries to Ceylon, Bombay, and the Sandwich Islands in addition to those working among the Cherokees, Chickasaws, Chocktows, Osage, Senecas, and Tuscaroras.[19] Mills himself embarked with a Dutch Reform minister on a tour of the western and southern states. Trekking through Kentucky, Tennessee, Ohio, and Indiana Territory, they found the inhabitants destitute of religion. As he wrote home, "there are American families in this part of our country, who never saw a Bible, nor heard of

Jesus Christ . . . It is a fact that ought not to be forgotten, that so lately as March, 1815, a Bible in any language could not be found, for sale, or to be given away in New Orleans . . . the whole country, from Lake Erie to the Gulf of Mexico, is as the valley of the shadow of death."[20]

Much given to figures, Mills estimated that the nation at large needed half a million Bibles, with sixty thousand necessary to fill the gap in New York City alone, eighteen thousand in Boston, and upwards to fifty thousand in Philadelphia. He decided that only an ecumenical effort would succeed in such a task and began to organize Episcopalians, Methodists, Baptists, Congregationalists, and Presbyterians into a national Bible society with chapters throughout the states, bending all his efforts to this end from 1814 to 1816. Mills shared the Protestant conviction that the Gospel only flourished where there was political liberty and hence drew Christian Latin America into his missionary plans.

The final resting place in Mills's foreshortened reform career was antislavery. The revolt of slaves and free blacks in French St. Domingue opened up an entirely new vista of human freedom and benevolence to him. When the successful rebels announced the Republic of Haiti, Mills interpreted the event as heralding a new day for all Africans in the New World. He began to raise money for schools for blacks, throwing himself into the activities of the American Colonization Society, founded in 1816 to resettle freed slaves in western Africa. Visiting the schools in Liberia himself, Mills found "a watery grave" at age thirty-five on his return trip home.[21] Like Harriet Newell, he died young, and like her, the memoir of his life inspired those drawn to the evangelical revivals held throughout the country in the early decades of the nineteenth century.

Not all New Englanders had the evangelical spirit of Mills, but a surprising number of those born in the first decades after the Revolution roamed the country in their youth. Thousands of Northerners turned peddler in the winter months, finding in the Southern states ready buyers for the products of Northern industry. Bronson Alcott at sixteen was typical, earning enough money as a subscription book agent to outfit him and his cousin for a winter of peddling in Virginia and North Carolina. The two set off in "the good sloop 'Three Sisters'" with an admixture of youthful peddlers and Connecticut tinmen bound for Norfolk. For the future Transcendentalist philosopher, the South yielded more than profits, for in the libraries of Virginia planters Bronson found totally different reading fare from New England theological tracts, encountering for the first time John

Locke's *Essay Concerning Human Understanding* and William Cowper's letters and poetry.[22]

With taverns even scarcer than good roads, travelers in the early nineteenth century put up at private homes. Yankee peddlers in the Tidewater threw themselves on the hospitality of the great plantation owners, never knowing until they were shown their beds whether they would be put up in the slave quarters or the great house. For many, these travels introduced them to the slave system that differentiated Northern from Southern states. The black presence in the South perplexed and fascinated some, though others left no trace at all of their encounters with enslaved men and women. These Southern rambles struck their elders as adventures of dazzling novelty, for thirty years earlier such youthful initiatives would have been impossible to contemplate, much less execute.

Peace in 1783 had triggered a vast popular migration out of the settled parts of the United States into the pockets of wilderness remaining in the thirteen original states—those undulating forests and valleys of western New York, Pennsylvania, and Virginia, the up country of the Carolinas and Georgia. Through the Cumberland Gap other migrating families poured into Tennessee and Kentucky. Pittsburgh, where the Monongahela and Allegheny rivers join to form the Ohio River, became the provisioning center for thousands more who rafted down the Ohio in search of well-watered acres in the Northwest Territory.

The native population offered fierce resistance to this invasion of their ancestral homes and hunting grounds. The newcomers, aided by the United States Army, met violence with violence. Army victories in 1794 and 1811 opened up vast amounts of new territory while duplicity and diplomacy yielded yet more in purchases. The American migrants believed themselves entitled to the land, even though the Treaty of Paris had recognized the exclusive right of the United States government to negotiate with the native tribes. No longer bound by royal decree to remain east of the Appalachians, families rumbled over the mountains in their heavy wagons, extending as they did the new nation's effective domain, mile after mile.[23] Living at first in fortified enclaves, the land-hungry easterners supplied the manpower for expelling the Indians from the West. Long before the phrase was coined, they treated their march across the North American continent as a manifest destiny. Might eventually made right, or at least the security of title; the native inhabitants moved on or were removed as American migrants brought eleven additional states into the Union by 1821.

Typical of the westward-moving families was that of Daniel Drake, whose parents had migrated to Kentucky with a cluster of relatives from New Jersey. Arriving in a spot near Lexington, they erected a "station" to protect their encroachment from Indian attack. The five families purchased a fourteen-hundred-acre tract, Drake's father paying for his share by selling the horse and wagon that had carried the family west. A wonderful chronicler, Drake retained a vivid memory of corn-husking competitions, frontier weddings, and the details of women's work when he helped his mother. He also remembered the joy of getting his hands on a copy of *Robinson Crusoe* that miraculously found its way to Mayslick, Kentucky. Daniel's father decided to commit his son to the noble profession of medicine as a way of repaying his own good fortune, setting in motion the career of one of the West's principal scholars and spokesmen and an ardent exponent of Enlightenment values in the Ohio countryside.[24]

Opportunity was far from even-handedly dispensed. It came to men before women, whites before blacks, readers and writers before manual laborers, the youthful before their elders. Yet it so abounded in the early decades of the century that it even came to those on the deficit side of luck. Several factors promoted the growth of what had been a miniscule population of free blacks before the Revolution. State legislatures generally granted freedom to those who had fought in the militias and Continental Army, and all states, save South Carolina, had mobilized enslaved men at some point during the war. Many freed blacks were subsequently able to save enough money to purchase their enslaved loved ones.[25] For a few decades, Southern legislatures made it much easier to manumit slaves, a transaction promoted by the depressed state of Southern agriculture. The gradual abolition processes in Northern states liberated thousands of African-American women and men while antislavery sentiment encouraged Northern slave-owners to free their slaves in advance of the legal dates set for gradual emancipation. As some Southerners had feared, the free states became a mecca for those fleeing slavery. Slaves' chances of success increased as the churning of people through the American countryside gave them needed cover.

David Walker, at the same age as Daniel Drake and two years younger than Samuel Mills, made his move from South to North in 1826. Walker was unusual in having been born free, the son of a North Carolina slave and a free mother. Like so many poor young Americans who carved out their careers by moving, Walker left his North Carolina birthplace after traveling throughout the South. He set up his own used clothing store in Boston, where he also served as an agent for Samuel Cornish's New York paper, *Freedom's Journal.* Walker did not find the tolerance he had hoped for in the North, but living in Massachusetts gained him the vote, as well as the means and liberty to publish his ideas. *Walker's Appeal,* a stirring message addressed to black Americans, brought him fame and notoriety. Totally contemptuous of the racial attitudes of most Americans, Walker, who was a member of Boston's African Methodist Episcopal Church, described how he had been "troubling the pages of historians, to find out what our fathers have done to the white Christians of America . . . to merit . . . such punishment." Bold in approach and brilliant in execution, *Walker's Appeal* announced a new voice in the public, that of the angry, articulate African American.[26] The official Southern response to such audacity was swift: Walker was personally denounced with a price put on his head, and the legislatures of Georgia, North Carolina, Mississippi, Louisiana, and Virginia passed laws making it a crime to teach slaves to read and write.[27]

From Virginia to Louisiana those black persons still enslaved—male and female, child or adult—were subject to the abuse of masters because the law defined them as property and permitted their sale to settle debts, sanctioning brutal punishments as well. Never was there a greater disparity between the life situation of one group and the widely advertised ideals of the larger society. Only the contentiousness this fact provoked saved white Americans from the stigma of total hypocrisy.

Walker was readier than most free African Americans to express his anger, but his sense of urgency reflected a common sentiment. The hope for a new era of freedom for black Americans that stirred Samuel Mills oscillated with the despair Walker felt in discovering a racial hatred in the North almost as implacable as the racial tyranny of the South. Northern abolition demonstrated to all that the institution was neither immutable nor permanent; what had yet to be determined was how open to a bi-racial society white Americans would be. The egalitarian pronouncements defending the revolution heartened many free black men and women who acted on their new liberties to form churches, literary clubs, schools, and reform societies. An air of expectancy and anxiety suffused writings on race in the first decades of the nineteenth century as Northerners and Southerners took in the implications of an international antislavery movement. Hanging in the balance was the answer to the question of whether the Northern majority would defer to its principled stand and protect the persons, property, and ambitions of American blacks, or draw back from the demands of justice and identify with the doctrine of racial purity that Southerners urged.

∼✖✿✖∼

LOOKING AT A COHORT of men and women within a larger society pushes to the fore the question of how adults make room for a generation and secure the loyalty of its members. They do so initially in the homes in which newborns are nurtured, for culture is no more nor less than the forms, prescriptions, traditions, and attitudes that are passed through speech and actions from parents to children. In the early nineteenth century, the press became an important conduit of cultural messages as more and more children became literate and literacy itself acted as the matrix for advice, exhortation, example, knowledge, and information. Schools, book-buying clubs, libraries, prayer meetings, and post offices became nodes of literate sociability, slowly separating the participants of this vibrant print culture from those cut off from the circulation of the printed word. Invasive in unprecedented ways, the steady flow of American publications carried ideas and opinions far beyond the reach of the human voice.

Each set of heirs necessarily reworks its cultural inheritance; its members respond selectively, adapting techniques and prescriptions to the exigencies of living, unthinkingly neglectful of some elements, willfully rejecting others, often atavistically spurning its parents' beliefs to revive the tastes and interests of an earlier age. This contrapuntal action of past and present, played out in the intimate and public lives of successive generations, shapes all history. Human beings enter the world wordless and engage with it through the sounds and gestures whose codes slowly become comprehensible. Intuitively and silently the work of reparation and adaptation goes forward, but as one very astute observer has noted: "the values of any new generation do not spring full blown from their heads; they are already there, inherent if not clearly articulated in the older generation. The younger generation makes overt what is covert in the older generation; the child expresses openly what the parent represses."[28]

More than common dates joined the cohort of Americans born between 1776 and 1800. They had to deal with the social experiments and unintended consequences of a war, a revolution, and a fierce partisan battle over the meaning of independence. It had been no part of the colonial resistance movement to abolish slavery, yet Northern judges and legislators over the course of twenty-four years did just that, creating a host of unresolved questions about the relations between slave and free states as well as the status of free blacks, some of them voters. A succession of evangelical Protestant revivals changed the face of American Christianity. At the same time, the bounded world of their parents opened up geographically, intellectually, and socially. New incentives appeared, luring people away from old mores. Similarly, men wondered aloud in published columns how women's position would be fixed in such a fluid society.

Ordinary Northerners, freed from the superior attitudes of an established elite, created a vibrant public realm, charged with the neophyte's energy and roiling with irreconcilable differences. In that contentious and noisy space, those men and women who aspired to do something in public in the first decades of the nineteenth century set the course of the nation. But as they used the new print media to persuade, report, and cajole, they alienated most Southern leaders, which ironically left them freer to follow their "thousand points of light." So we can say that while consciously pursuing economic enterprises, political participation, and revived religion, Northern activists brought into being the civil society of American democracy while Southerners, recoiling from this noisy and intrusive public life, cultivated a more conservative society than that of their revolutionary forebears.

Cultural institutions rest on a particular economic base, and when the base shifts or disappears, venerable institutions can collapse without warning, throwing into high relief the inseparable union of the ideal and the material. This proved to be the case with British authority over the American continental colonies in 1775–1776. After the war, it happened again when many fathers lost control of their maturing sons. Earlier, young adults had depended upon their family's support in an economy that offered them few avenues to independence. When this situation changed and new occupations appeared—as they quickly did after 1789—many parents could not keep their sons—or even some daughters—at home. Similarly, slave-masters discovered the fragility of their peculiar labor system when men and women who had been born into bondage fled for the freedom that the British offered during the Revolutionary War. Exposed for the first time was the skeleton of order without the muscle of enforcement. Families did not shrink in importance; they changed. Fostering early independence, particularly in white teenagers, became one of their new tasks. The political independence of the whole somehow had inspired the personal independence of the parts.

This book follows the trajectory of the liberal society fashioned in the first generation. In chapter 2, I explore the prominence of politics, showing how the democratization of the suffrage influenced the structuring of masculinity. The fierce partisanship that flared up during the bitterly contested presidential elections of 1796 and 1800 cast a long shadow over the lives of the first generation. Parties monopolized political life in a totally unexpected way. Partisanship ran well ahead of people's capacity to explain it, fueled in part by the way that print magnified the invective of conflict. Disputants charged one another with heresy, conjuring up the terror of the Inquisition. Political duels took their toll, North and South. Extending participation to ever greater numbers of voters did more than democratize American government: it thrust politics into every facet of public life, unwittingly educating women and African Americans about the organizational forms and persuasive styles of self-government.

National independence nurtured commercial initiatives as well, fostering westward expansion, manufacturing start-ups and far-flung trading ventures that will be examined in chapter 3. European warfare triggered a long period of prosperity for the United States. At the same time the political defeat of the Federalists removed the restraining hand of the federal government from the American economy. Credit and land became accessible to white men, precipitating the undulating rhythms of boom and bust cycles. Moral issues bounced against economic forces. The European demand for cotton tied the American economy to slavery at the very time that an antislavery movement engaged many Northerners—even some Southerners. Indians became the victims of economic progress. The fertile lands of the Ohio and Mississippi Valleys gave ordinary men a chance to capitalize their family's labor while thrusting the nation into sustained warfare against the native inhabitants. The scope for individual endeavor widened appreciably once the Jeffersonians dismantled Federalist programs that had centralized authority. Chapter 3 follows these developments, highlighting the way that enterprise moved out to the countryside to entice a generation of young men growing up in rural poverty.

Nothing distinguished the United States from other countries in the early decades of the nineteenth century more than the widening scope of opportunity for young people. Chapter 4 explores the careers that men and women pursued, looking at their crucial contribution to the liberalization of old forms with their support for early independence. While most people continued to farm, bringing into cultivation thousands of acres in cotton and grains alongside the orchards, dairies, and gardens near cities, a significant minority of people moved to new jobs in politics, schoolteaching, publishing, manufacturing, preaching, retailing, writing, painting, drawing, exploring, and civil engineering. The very meaning of "career" marked a linguistic innovation in 1800 once young men and women ceased to follow in their parents' footsteps. Formerly used to denote a horse-racing course, career acquired a new reference to a "person's . . . progress through life."[29]

Careers were mostly masculine affairs; women had domestic responsibilities. Replicating their mothers' lives was deemed appropriate, but dramatic changes could not affect one sex without influencing the other, just as the expansion of opportunity to ordinary white men aroused the aspirations of black men. Opportunities even came in ironic packages; a few women carved out successful writing careers extolling traditional virtues for their "fair sex." Where once sons had achieved manhood by emulating their fathers, more and more they were esteemed for carrying a torch into uncharted territory. In time the repeated narrative of the man standing alone, without the superintending authority of minister, magistrate, or father, set a new model for masculinity.

An economic and political liberalization of a society would be but half complete if the taboos, stigmas, and statuses of the earlier era remained intact. Opportunity, mobility, and egalitarian zeal worked together to sap older ways of thinking about social position. A sprawling, inclusive American middle class composed of families known for their respectability, their material competence, and their identification with a progressive model of human endeavor came into power, drawing individuals from all the ranks of colonial society. Chapter 5 follows the elaboration of new discourses about status, merit, and virtue as the first generation sorted through the confusing tropes of revolutionary rhetoric and began self-consciously to rework social distinctions for a liberal democracy.

The reconfiguration of the public realm necessarily impinged upon the affections of men and women. Objects of love, emotional ties to friends, worship of God—all were subject to pressures from unanticipated changes. Chapter 6 looks at the intimate relations elaborated during the early decades of the nineteenth century. The collapse of venerable hierarchies and the scattering of family members caught Americans unawares. Mobility—both geographic and social—cut off young people from the community of their childhood. The new generation sought different avenues of emotional release. Husbands and wives, fathers and mothers, sisters and brothers, friends and lovers became objects of intense concern to those coming of age after the Revolution. An astounding wave of evangelical revivals brought an emotional intensity to the relations between awakened Christians and their God.

Change came at a price. The mobility that carried Americans to new careers and new communities undermined older arrangements for maintaining order, weakening the authority of fathers, ministers, and magistrates. Confronting the irreparable shredding of older ties, members of the first generation discovered their calling as reformers, demonstrating to a skeptical world that uncoerced cooperation and voluntary efforts could do the work of central government and established churches. Chapter 7 looks at the men and women who mobilized temperance societies, foreign missions, antislavery forces, and urban charity while working vigorously for the observance of the sabbath. More literate than their parents, they depended upon printed materials for information and edification, learning how to make persuasion do the work of command. Merging the private with the public in their exertions for a progressive America, the earnest articulators of new goals in the first generation expressed a love for liberty and piety, autonomy and community, weekly discipline and devout supplication on Sundays. Through their voluminous writings and practical enactments they crafted a liberal democratic order that claimed as universal the qualities that were emerging in the American middle class.

Since not all people chose change or were allowed to participate in the transformative processes at work in the United States, a cultural fault line slowly developed between the fortunate. beneficiaries of the American creed and those denied its liberating power. Luck is never even-handed and success far from uniform. For African Americans and white women, the promise of natural rights remained to be tested. Those who clung to older mores—whether poor farmers eking out a subsistence or the disdainful descendants of prominent colonial families—had less and less say in charting the country's direction. Those who repeatedly failed in their bids for an independent competence formed a wordless substratum in a society whose writers and speakers preferred to talk about success.

Emancipation had given men and women in the North a deceptive clarity about their political convictions while the cotton boom welded the South to its cruel, anachronistic labor system. Defending slavery placed the planter elite in opposition to the experimental thrust of Northern life. Slowly, but perceptibly, this central difference affected a myriad of institutional arrangements and social values that encouraged Northerners and Southerners to construe their differences as implicit challenges to one another. Many writers and orators focused upon the opportunities to move, to innovate, to express personal opinions as emblematic of what it was to be an American, but in making this restless, activist, ingenious, and accomplishment-centered person an American ideal, Northerners were characterizing the nation in a way that failed to account for the alternate ideals of the South. As the North used its impressive communications network to articulate and propagate its values, the white leaders of the South began to perceive themselves standing against the nation, straining at the bonds of union. By the end of their lives, the men and women of the first generation could only marvel that they had collectively created not one, but two countries. Neither immediate nor complete in its effects, this division marks one of the most portentous developments of the early nineteenth century.

This cohort of Americans also demonstrated a heightened awareness of "firstness"—of being the first to have rugs on their floors, to have steamboats and canals, national elections, public land sales, cheap newspapers, pianos wholly produced in the United States, and a president who wore shoe laces instead of buckles—the list goes on.[30] Had they met one another in old age, they could have reminisced about the same things: the fervor aroused by the French Revolution that split their leaders into antagonistic Federalist and Republican camps; General Anthony Wayne's victory over the confederated Indian tribes at Fallen Timbers that opened up the upper Ohio River valley for American settlers; the outpouring of grief at the death of George Washington; the Haitian revolt that created the first black republic; the Richmond theater fire of 1811 with its seventy-one fatalities; and Lafayette's triumphal tour through the states in 1825–1826. They could recollect the Hudson River voyage of the *Clermont*, the first successful steamboat; the Cane Ridge revival meeting that drew upwards of twenty thousand persons; or the solar eclipse in 1806 when the total darkness of a June morning sent birds flying back to their roosts.

Almost four hundred men and women in this cohort wrote autobiographies.[31] While the full sweep of social groupings are represented in this group, the preponderance came from white Northern clergymen. Methodists outnumbered every other denomination. A testament to the flowering of modern subjectivity, these autobiographies fail to adhere to a formula, even to suggest the cohesion of a genre.[32] Men and women wrote them at all ages, the greatest number coming from their pens at the end of life. That so many were published posthumously underscores the fact that they were usually written for an intimate circle of friends and family. From these summings up emerges a presentation of personal success—few failures wrote autobiographies—closely tied to a strong view of the country's own record of achievement.

⁂

LIFE-FASHIONING, like self-fashioning, captures the self-consciousness of those in the first generation who crystalized the social forms, political strategies, and economic possibilities that had been one potential of their parents' legacy. Through the memoirs of the first generation it is possible to see how America's revolutionary ideology got refracted through economic initiatives, social mores, and personal relations. Beginning my research with reminiscences, as I did, spotlighted the personal choices that in the aggregate formed trends and patterns. Their memoirs disclose otherwise elusive cultural themes. Novelties were simultaneously experienced and interpreted; ideas about what America should represent moved back and forth from spontaneous reactions to constructed narratives. These life stories also revealed the identities of a new group of leaders in the Northern states, leaders deeply committed to linking material and moral progress. Dispersed through hundreds of localities, they knew each other by the lines they spoke about America's emergent greatness.

The information that I gathered on the thousands of other active members of the first generation who had not written autobiographies provided some ballast for sailing through the early decades of the nineteenth century. Following their careers, I have been able to sort the unique from the relatively common. Because the champions of change were quick to identify progress with what it meant to be American, I have kept in mind those who declined to become pathbreakers or in fact were categorically excluded from the enterprise of defining America. This study does not deal directly with these men and women, but it does follow the process of nation-building mindful of the intellectual choices that led to their exclusion.

Some in my archive are far from typical, like Martin Van Buren, William Henry Harrison, and John Tyler who became presidents; or Daniel Webster, John C. Calhoun, Henry Clay, and Thomas Hart Benton who articulated the political goals of an entire region. Others like Ichabod Washburn,

Charles Goodyear, and Peter Cooper exploited the personal ingenuity that industrial development rewarded. Sarah Hale, James Fenimore Cooper, William Prescott, Lydia Sigourney, and William Austin formed a literary connection with the expanding world of readers. Charles Finney, Lorenzo Dow, and Alexander Campbell brought thousands of Americans into the evangelical fold. Alongside these famous figures are the far greater number of modest achievers who gathered the like-minded into a temperance society or set up a clock factory or started a frontier newspaper. They also succeeded in some small way in a society in which success became the knot tying together enterprise, expression, and reform. These men and women were not typical, but influential, the doers and interpreters of a charter generation. By the end of their lives, their vision of the meaning of America's experiment in self-government was gaining momentum, though still contested.

Europeans were astounded by the presence of social order in America in the absence of social solidarity. Their amazement emphasizes how unusual was the task of transforming colonial societies into the American nation, a process by and large undertaken by individuals. Although no period in the history of the United States has escaped intensive scholarly scrutiny, the lifespan of the first generation is rarely presented alone; normally it serves as a coda to the Revolutionary era or a preface to Jacksonian America. Nor has the public realm constituted in the decades after 1789 been sufficiently studied for its novel ordering mechanisms and its proliferating voluntary associations that linked private ambitions to public norms.

As they aged in the 1820s and 1830s, the first generation acquired an appreciation of how the isolation of their rural youth had given way to an enriched commercial society, thick with hooks into a larger world. It had been their task to sort out America's multi-layered European traditions while interpreting a New World mission complexly linked to the peoples of Africa and North America. Although they arrived on the American scene after the successful conclusion of the American War for Independence, the high drama of the event cast a long shadow over their lives. The Revolution had launched a new nation. Or rather, as one contemporary said in 1789, Americans now had a roof for a new United States; it remained for those coming of age to fill in the walls and furnish the rooms.[33]

2

RESPONDING TO A REVOLUTIONARY TRADITION

T HE FIRST-BORN CITIZENS in the United States began to exert their influence in public life just as Thomas Jefferson's presidential election ushered in an era of participatory politics, making way for a distinctive American political culture. In a very brief span of time, centuries-old ideas about officeholders and voters, law and social order, the government and the governed, came under novel scrutiny. What began as philosophical inquiry ended in democratic action. The fact that Jefferson belonged to the wealthiest group in the United States, the planter gentry of the South, has obscured the ideological significance of his election. Where many Southerners voted for Jefferson out of regional loyalty, in the North his supporters had waged all-out war against the Federalists' effort to criminalize as sedition what countless citizens considered free speech. The majority voted for the people's right to play an active role in politics—form clubs, monitor policies, and thrash out their opinions without fear of prosecution. Despite a strong Federalist showing at the polls, demands for a new era of liberty for ordinary white men created a momentum too strong for the staying hand of conservatives.

The rejection of the Federalists reflected more than a change of political personnel; it undermined a whole set of assumptions about who should exercise authority. The defenders of Washington's administration had spoken freely about the need for the steadying hand of the "rich, the able, and the well-born" while Jeffersonians championed free association and limited government.[1] Federalists retained the British belief that the people were the vigilant watchdogs of public liberty who should vote, but otherwise leave governing to the elected officials. In criticizing this passive role for a democratic citizenry, the Jeffersonians took quite literally the notion of governors as the servants of the people, answerable to them at all times. Struggling to awaken voters to the stakes involved in this controversy, the opposing sides succeeded in politicizing a new generation of Americans—the first to come to maturity after the Constitution.

Far more than Andrew Jackson, Jefferson and his supporters democratized American politics. They did so by addressing the anxieties that ordinary white men felt about the patronizing, elitist assumptions of the Federalists. They did so by bringing a host of newcomers into state and national office. They did so by implementing policies that enabled people to work out the terms of their lives with minimal interference from family, church, or state. Appealing more to middling Americans than to their social superiors, the new political spirit spread rapidly from city to countryside to frontier. John Ball, a mere lad of seven when Jefferson became president, remembered the old timers' rebuke of their minister for delivering political sermons. "Mr. Page," they told him, "we employ you to preach Jesus Christ and him crucified, but you preach Thomas Jefferson and him justified."[2] The inflamed political rhetoric of contested elections had spread all the way to the Congregational Church of Hebron, Vermont, whose members, Ball recalled, disapproved of the hubbub.

Political passions had become so superheated in the 1790s that men who had cooperated through the hazardous years of colonial resistance, revolution, war, and constitutional reform would cross the street rather than greet one another as colleagues.[3] Charges of blasphemy, heresy, and apostasy flew back and forth, indicating that the idea of an "issue"—a matter of policy upon which good men might honorably disagree—had not yet become part of their conceptual armature. If there were disputes, then only the moral failures of one's opponents could explain them. As an editorial in the Federalist *Massachusetts Mercury* put it, "Naturally there can but be two parties in a Country; the friends of order and its foes." Jefferson wrote a friend in a similar vein: "I hold it as immoral to pursue a middle line, as between parties of Honest men and Rogues, into which every country is divided."[4]

With Jefferson's victory, the once-tight braid of social, economic, and political authority came untwined, leaving the separate strands exposed and weakened. Those with social preeminence had to contend for political power; those with political power were not necessarily accorded social prestige. Those with wealth often failed to command social respect. Those newly admitted to citizenship challenged the authority of leaders who considered themselves born to govern. In the colonial era, officeholders in both church and state had exercised moral leadership. Voting to decide who among the recognized candidates would serve in which offices bore little resemblance to the open contests of the 1790s and 1800s. Their ideal had been "a *speaking* Aristocracy *in the face of a silent* Democracy," as Cotton Mather had expressed it.[5] Few expected the victorious "mushroom candidates" of the new era to take the place of the esteemed gentlemen who had run things for so long, nor had anyone reckoned with the void created by their absence. Natural rights philosophy assumed a community of interests among all who had rights to protect; it was silent on good governance.

Victory at the national level encouraged Jeffersonians to begin agitating at the state level for constitutional revisions to extend the suffrage. Maryland led the way in 1801 with a law abolishing property qualifications and requiring the secret ballot, but a constitutional amendment in 1810 took away its generous provisions from free blacks. In North Carolina, free African Americans exercised their citizenship rights until 1835.[6] Strict residency requirements continued, but the ambit of white citizenship widened and black suffrage grew with the augmentation of the free black population. While Virginia, Louisiana, Connecticut, and Rhode Island retained some form of property qualification until well into the 1840s, other states eliminated them. Entirely new groups, including adult sons living at home, apprentices, and wage-earners joined the ranks of voters.[7] Removing property qualifications from white men sometimes meant adding new burdens to other groups. Single, propertied women who had voted in New Jersey lost that privilege in 1807, and only sixteen African Americans met the property qualifications retained for blacks in the revised New York constitution of 1825, which had eliminated such qualifications for whites.[8] Even with these restrictions, a wider sampling of people could vote in the United States than had ever done so in any country.[9]

The dropping of property qualifications turned suffrage from a gentleman's privilege to a widely-shared activity of white men. Cities too replaced the colonial privileges of municipal freemanship for residential voting.[10] As politicians wooed voters, they invested them with the power to make decisive choices, nurturing a fascination with politics. Ordinary men, once excluded from politics, could now talk of public business in their taverns, parlors, commons, and streets. Jeffersonians effected these changes, suggesting that universal liberty meant freedom for all, or at least all white men. Only South Carolina's ruling oligarchy withstood the democratic pressure felt throughout the United States, succeeding with its constitutional reforms of 1808 to cement the power of the planter elite.[11]

First-generation publishers made the faces of American presidents familiar in broadsides and engravings like this one, entitled "American Star." Courtesy, American Antiquarian Society.

Elsewhere, voting became integral to concepts of manliness. Once it was no longer considered risky to express one's political opinions in public, politics became far more than a process for choosing officeholders, emerging as an arena for demonstrating knowledge about public policies and shrewdness in assessing candidates. As ordinary men reveled in their newly-acquired suffrage, those excluded from voting came to view it no longer as a class distinction but rather as a male prerogative that the avidity of public interest in politics only enhanced. The extension of the vote to most ordinary white men seemed a response to the nation's embrace of "natural rights," but the exclusion of women and many free blacks introduced new tensions even though nonvoters shared in the country's mania for partisan debate, if only by listening.[12]

The Republicans' success in winning the presidency for the first seven elections of the nineteenth century accurately measures the triumph of democratic politics, but Americans continued to battle over the scope and character of government power, sons and daughters succeeding parents as combatants at the turn of the century. The angry partisanship that erupted over the hotly contested presidential elections of 1796 and 1800 uncovered the unresolved questions facing Americans and their representatives—none more surprising than those clustered around the divide between free and slave states occasioned by the first emancipation campaign in the North. And there were ironies too, as Southern Jeffersonians pulled away from the spirit of free inquiry and Northern Jeffersonians found their public space filled by the very religious passions that had once seemed to them inimical to democratic practices.

Confronting a range of challenges, the first generation shaped the partisanship they inherited into two political cultures, one remarkable for its vibrancy and reach, the other retaining the old elite traditions pressed into new service defending slavery. Politics became a vortex pulling in private preferences along with public concerns. Parties took the lead in mobilizing voters for and against banks, tariffs, temperance, and the importance of honoring the sabbath. Controversies in churches and the professions also spilled over the walls of privacy into public print, turning publicity into democracy's most potent ally. Dueling, a European ritual largely confined to army officers, found a second life in the United States as the brutal mediator of partisan disputes among men struggling to find a civil way to disagree on matters of interest and principle. The vituperation of campaign polemics and the violence of political duels undermined the moral authority of party leaders, enabling preachers and reformers to pick up the fallen mantle of moral authority. With these developments, the liberal society that few had envisioned at the time of the Revolution took shape.

Far from being a closet philosopher, Jefferson acted vigorously once elected, dismantling the fiscal program that had enabled the Federalists to guide economic growth. He reduced taxes and cut the size of the civil service, despite the doubling of the country's territory. His policies more than fulfilled the Republican (and Federalist) expectations.[13] Casting an executive shadow that fell on a chain of successors, he popularized a strict constructionist view of the Constitution that minimized the range of national institutions and inhibited the use of federal power—the Louisiana Purchase and Embargo Act notwithstanding.

Jefferson's nationalism also differentiated him from the Federalists. Like many Southerners, he was an expansionist who believed that a strong union would facilitate westward growth, but he feared any concentration of power, worrying that it would always be exercised by the few over the many. On the other hand, if government oversight of the economy were strictly limited, men could make their own decisions, leading to a live-and-let-live society harmonized by cooperation. Leaving the market to determine the allocation of resources doomed a subsistence way of life and hastened the expulsion of the Indians from their native lands, but it also deployed power to ordinary white male bargainers and replaced the social influence of government with that of individuals, acting for their own well-being.[14]

Like the proverbial new broom, Jefferson swept out of the civil service all those with pronounced Federalist sympathies, including army officers down to the rank of captain.[15] Nothing could have expunged elite influence more thoroughly than this abrupt ending to the apprenticeship in power for the scions of Federalist families. Replacing them proved tricky. The Federalists had cultivated an officeholding cadre while rank and file Jeffersonians were new to politics. At the same time able candidates were turning away from politics—the president had to ask five men before he found a secretary of the navy. Pressed to fill the openings in his department, Secretary of the Treasury Albert Gallatin actually suggested that they might name women to the vacant posts, a notion that prompted Jefferson's brusque reply, "The appointment of a woman to office is an innovation for which the public is not prepared, nor am I." A decade later, Madison confronted a similar dearth of "officers and gentlemen" to lead an expanded army mobilized for the War of 1812.[16]

Jefferson failed to win a single elector in New Hampshire, Delaware,

Vermont, Massachusetts, New Jersey, Rhode Island, or Connecticut, a disparity that changed dramatically when he was re-elected in 1804. It was in the North where the democratic effect of the Republican victory had the most profound effect, though the greater hostility to blacks among Republicans limited the opening of participation to whites.[17] Within a decade the exuberant party press, frequent contested elections, and widespread recreational interest in partisan politics created a public sphere that ironically would soon be dominated by religious reformers with closer ties to the old Federalists than the new Republicans.

Jefferson had not been in office seven months before the *Connecticut Courant* called for his impeachment. The Massachusetts legislature put him on trial for hypocrisy in 1805. Virtue, the mainstay of republics, had never been more imperiled, according to New England leaders. Some Massachusetts Federalists had actually contemplated secession from the union, dismayed as they were by the Louisiana Purchase.[18] Yale's president Timothy Dwight announced that free governments would survive "only if revealed religion were allowed to create virtuous citizens who would elect virtuous rulers who in their turn would support institutions that created virtue."[19] Theodore Sedgwick, the last Federalist Speaker of the House, announced that "the aristocracy of virtue is destroyed; personal influence is at an end" while Senator Fisher Ames of Massachusetts more philosophically advised his fellow Federalists to entrench themselves in state governments and make them "a shelter of the wise, and good, and rich."[20] "I would never have abandoned the government personally," New York's Rufus King explained, "but from the most complete conviction that the people would make an experiment of democracy."[21] His son, a member of the first generation born after Independence, helped build Massachusetts's fledgling Democratic-Republican party, which carried the state in 1805; eleven years later the senior King became the last candidate the Federalists nominated for president.

Money, reputation, and social prominence would never be negligible factors in American electoral politics, but no political party would ever again gain the presidency by arguing that the families of established wealth and social prominence formed the nation's natural leaders. According to Samuel Goodrich, who grew up in the bosom of a prominent Connecticut family, the Federalists were finally overthrown because "the great body of the people had got possession of suffrage, and insisted, with increasing vehemence, upon the removal of every impediment to its universality." Democracy became "the watchword of popular liberty," Goodrich concluded, permitting "the radical or republican party" to attract "the great body of the European immigrants—little instructed in our history or institutions."[22] Democratic assertiveness, ignorance of traditional wisdom, newcomers to politics—these became the crude instruments that shattered the circle of virtue envisioned by Dwight.

In this, as in so many other ways, the values propounded by the old upper stratum of America ran athwart the geographic mobility and material abundance that had become manifest in the United States by 1800. Hindsight, however, writes a premature obituary for the Federalists, for they continued to vie for office for another three decades. Jefferson died in 1826 fearing their resurgence. In 1808 Federalists put up candidates for every single Congressional seat North of the Potomac River, and they continued to do well in some state elections through the 1820s, winning their last governorship in Delaware in 1823. Still, the deferential order the Federalists stood for had collapsed, and the Jeffersonians were able to hold onto the presidency through the next quarter-century, by which time democracy had found a new champion in Andrew Jackson.[23] In fact both Henry Clay and Andrew Jackson believed they were carrying on the traditions of Thomas Jefferson's party; only later did the "fact" of Jeffersonian and Jacksonian origins of the Democrats' party become fixed. The subsequent dominance of the Jeffersonian Republicans inspired repeated internal fissures as the succession of Bucktails, Barnburners, and Locofocos—the names given to New York splinter groups—confirms.

Defeat at the polls for many Federalists drained politics of all appeal. Deeply offended by the crass self-assertion of common folk, they turned their educated refinement into an end in itself, burnishing their links with the upper-class English they so admired. For these Federalists the outburst of political zeal from uneducated men proved the conservatives right: when the pot boils the scum rises. Their worst fears were realized after Jefferson shrank both the army's officer corps and the civil service. Other Federalists became the new administration's most articulate critics, keeping the political pot boiling through the first two decades of the nineteenth century. Hamilton, the lodestar of the Federalist party, helped William Coleman start the *New York Evening Post* when the Jeffersonian takeover of national government forced Federalists to found their own organs of dissent. Coleman's "political acrimony" ranked as "scarcely inferior to that of the *American Citizen*," its feisty Republican rival, according to John Francis, who said that a "continuous warfare was maintained between an enlarged democracy and the conservative doctrine of federalism."[24] Newspaper columns made political charges concrete, adding the printed insult to the personal injury that often provoked duels.

In Philadelphia, where radical democrats rallied around the leadership of William Duane, the fiery editor of *Aurora,* moderate Jeffersonians set up their own newspaper, the *Freeman's Journal,* in 1804. Duane made salient the tensions between economic and political freedom that would only become fully apparent with industrialization decades later. In the pages of the *Aurora* he inveighed against the hidden enemies of democracy: an independent judiciary, the common law bias against wage-earners, and a slumbering citizenry. The moderates, for their part, exploited fears that Americans might imitate the excesses of the French Revolution, calling their opponents within the Jeffersonian party Jacobins and Malcontents, which only brought down on themselves the dismissive name of Tertium Quids, roughly translatable as "third whats." The dispute spilled over into elections and lawsuits during the first decade of the century, energizing voters and setting forth at a fairly high level of political discourse the choices confronting democratic enthusiasts who also embraced the qualities of enterprise.[25]

Unlike the pamphleteering before the Revolution and the ratification debates, the polemics of the 1790s opened the arcana of government to outside inspection. The unchecked vituperation of public controversies changed the character of the American public realm. Anonymity and pseudonyms gave way to signed pieces. Vitriolic exchanges engaged the public in disputes that once would have been viewed as beyond their ken. In the course of the Jeffersonian attack on government, the idea of secrecy lost all contact with the supporting rationale that had long made a small group of officials and their gentlemanly friends privy to matters of state. Increasingly state secrets became a kind of public property. Had the Federalist elite secured its ascendancy, a public realm bounded by the gentry's sense of discretion might have emerged. Without that, publicity created a larger catch basin of readers and a dramatic augmentation in the kinds of conflicts deemed suitable for public airing.

Contemporaries disagreed about the value of this new public sphere. Samuel Knapp, a popular lecturer, acknowledged the evils of the prevailing political mores, but claimed that "these habitual disputes" were beneficial and perhaps "indispensable to the preservation of liberty." In Knapp's opinion public debate kindled ambition, and like hope animated "every thing it touches."[26] Similarly enthusiastic was Henry Marie Brackenridge, who looked back nostalgically to the Maryland evenings of 1817 and 1818 when men and women would gather for a "*barbecu*" and listen to political speeches delivered "from a stump or log of wood." Developing a talent for stump speaking himself, Brackenridge was elected to the Maryland legislature.[27]

A grimmer view of the first generation's politics came from Benjamin Silliman, a lawyer from a distinguished Connecticut family who later founded Yale's science departments. Reflecting on the behavior of his friends when talk turned to politics in his journal in 1795, Silliman described them as "ravenous wolves" despite their "most amiable and gentle disposition" in private life. Alexander Hamilton's son, James, believed that the bitter hostility in the 1812 era destroyed all social intercourse between the leaders of the different parties.[28] In a good many towns, one's friends were confined to the same party. Jeremiah Spofford, a Federalist physician who thought his hometown of Hampstead typical in its agitation over politics, had trouble building a practice. "It was difficult to acquire even the personal friendship of a political opponent," he noted.[29] Both William Henry Harrison and Joseph Story, as young Jeffersonians, lost sweethearts to the Federalist prejudices of their families.[30]

Commenting on the situation fifteen years later, DeWitt Clinton lamented that this "violent spirit has split society asunder, has poisoned the intercourse of private life, has spread gloom over our literature, has infected the national taste, and has palsied the general prosperity."[31] A German traveler in Pennsylvania concurred: "This mutual abuse, repeated until disgusting, shall if it goes unpunished become habitual, make the people indifferent to calumny and insult, and destroy all sense of honor; and then freedom of the press may have proved to be a Pandora's box."[32] As newspapers proliferated, they carried to the countryside the invective that had become the common feature of political life in the cities.

Conservatives like Dwight worried about an unpoliced public sphere, especially at a time when clergymen were forced to compete as community leaders with lawyers and politicians. The discretion that had marked behavior in colonial society along with the upper class preference for conducting conversations within a small circle of leaders collapsed before an onslaught of publicity. Identified opinions and published disputes transformed the conduct of political life. Being able to vote made propertyless men aware of themselves as political participants; even the young demanded their rights. When Harvard authorities ruled that there could be no allusions to party politics at the 1798 commencement day literary exercises, the undergraduates denounced the decision as an infringement of their free speech and refused to give any addresses until a compromise was worked out.[33]

The frothy political discourses, the marketing of printed material, and the enlarged circle of readers worked together to make publicity the shaping force in the public realm. The previous constraint on the range of discussible topics had served the ruling families. Now, not even the powerful Southern planters could prevent a free black like David Walker from publishing scathing attacks on their way of life. Northern anti-slavery writers intruded boldly into the once-private sphere of the patriarchal household.

With the widespread publicizing of conflicts came new tensions between "those in charge" and those who now felt empowered to inspect their officeholders' every move. What Francis had called "an enlarged democracy" in fact embraced many young men and women, white and black, who had been chafing under the restraint of their elders. Members of dissenting religious groups, free thinkers, and the newly prosperous all became participants in the disclosures and disputes that fleet-footed publicity carried to slave quarters, parlors, pioneer cabins, and urban tenements.

✦

THE RAUCOUS PARTISANSHIP of the new American style percolated through politics to other domains of public life, turning quasi-private power struggles into public property through the press. Confidentiality gave way to publicity in the most traditional and hierarchical areas of American society. Three well-advertised disputes in the U.S. Military Academy, the New York Episcopal Church, and the Cincinnati medical community reveal how publicity opened the once closed decision-making processes of conservative institutions to public scrutiny. The thirty-two-year-old acting superintendent at West Point, Captain Alden Partridge, resorted to a newspaper defense to fight court martial proceedings. Episcopalians squabbled over a school and a bequest while the doctors at the Ohio Medical College challenged one another to duels in the midst of arguments over the leadership of their fledgling school.

Just what role West Point was to play in the nation's life became a hotly contested question after its founding in 1802. When Congress debated appropriations for the military academy, South Carolina's young "war hawk" representative, John C. Calhoun, advocated several academies to ensure that the country would attract "genius and talent." Expressing a widely-held hypothesis about personal effort, he urged giving preference to the lower ranks of society, in an early example of affirmative action, not because "these classes actually contain a greater portion of talent, but that they have stronger stimulants to its exertion."[34] A year later, as secretary of war, Calhoun fell in with President Monroe's plan to turn West Point into a school for career officers along the French model, downplaying his earlier linkage of officer training to the defense of free government. Members of the West Point faculty wanted their students to get a purely scientific education, free of military discipline. Partridge opposed both Monroe's and the faculty's plans, preferring to emphasize military discipline in the shaping of an officer corps drawn, as he had been, from the great body of the people.[35]

The issue was joined when Partridge refused to yield his authority to Major Sylvanus Thayer who was sent to replace him as superintendent in the summer of 1817. Confronted with this challenge, Thayer, celebrated as the father of American technology, but evidently no fighter, retired to New York, leaving President Monroe, Secretary of War Calhoun, and Brigadier General Joseph Swift, the Point's first graduate, to figure out how to dislodge Partridge. Failing to persuade him to take another post, Swift instituted court martial proceedings. Though born a Vermont farm boy, Partridge knew enough of the world of publicity to respond vigorously in kind when an anonymous newspaper article criticizing him appeared. He fired off a defense of his actions to New York's *New Columbian* and gained for his efforts an additional court martial charge of having penned "an appeal in his name to the public, vindicating of himself in regard to the very matters for which he had been arrested."

Partridge's sympathizers characterized the 1817 trial as a pretext to confirm a political decision that had already been made while he pitched the conflict as one between laxity and strict military discipline. He further claimed that his adversaries encouraged immorality among the cadets by "openly extolling the writings of that prince of modern infidels, Voltaire."[36] In the end the court acquitted Partridge of fifteen specific charges, but found him guilty of reassuming command of what was no longer his post. In cashiering him, the presiding officer recommended clemency while criticizing the "frivolous and vexatious" nature of many of the charges, a rebuke that led Monroe's inspector general to publish a defense of the proceedings in the *Daily National Intelligencer.*[37]

Unbowed, Partridge tried repeatedly to make the trial transcript public, interpreting Calhoun's opposition as proof that Thayer had lied under oath. He left the Army and started his own private military academy in Vermont from whence he sallied forth from time to time for public occasions with a uniformed corps of volunteer cadets who gave proof of his enduring capacity to instill military discipline in young men.[38] When Andrew Jackson's victory in 1828 led to a new wave of criticism of the Military Academy, Partridge joined the fray with an anonymous charge that his beloved West Point had become an elite institution.[39] Congress never followed through with Calhoun's idea of establishing several military academies to tap talent throughout the country, but South Carolina and Virginia did, turning to Partridge for assistance in setting up the Citadel and the Virginia Military Institute.[40]

The widely publicized conflict in the New York diocese of the Episcopal Church also touched on education—in this case the preparation of Episcopal clergymen. Here the principals were John Henry Hobart, a similarly energetic and high-handed leader, and the faculty members of the General Theological Seminary, along with assorted Episcopal bishops and laymen. In the early decades of the nineteenth century, the Episcopalians were still recovering from the rupture with the Church of England and the aggressive local campaigns to disestablish the church, principally in Virginia. Having lost the fiscal support that went with establishment, the Episcopalians had to struggle to maintain the costly appurtenances of a churchly tradition.

At its triennial convention of laymen and clerics in 1817, the church—invigorated by a group of young bishops—voted to found a seminary to correct the deficiencies apparent in the prevailing system of individual tutoring for prospective clergymen.[41] The "general" in the title of the proposed General Theological Seminary was key, indicating that those who had urged the pooling of resources for a single seminary under the direction of the Episcopal Convention had triumphed over those who favored decentralized education with seminaries in each of the dioceses. Christopher Gadsden, a South Carolina clergyman and close friend of Calhoun, had pushed for the national seminary, convinced that Episcopalians needed to follow the path laid by the Presbyterians, who established a seminary at Princeton in 1812, and the Congregationalists, who had started Andover Seminary in 1808 after the Unitarians took over Harvard.

Bishop Hobart, well known to New Yorkers for his voluminous writings, favored a national seminary as long as it was in his diocese under his direction. He got half a loaf. A consensus formed on the New York site with the Convention exercising oversight. Not impressed with this arrangement, Hobart turned his back on the fledgling school with its two young professors and six divinity students. His neglect created an opportunity for Connecticut's bishop to lure the seminary to New Haven in 1820. Undaunted, Hobart began raising funds for his own diocesan seminary. Here things might have remained had not a recently-deceased New York merchant made a sizeable bequest for a general theological seminary. But which seminary—the already functioning General Theological Seminary in New Haven or the New York one of Hobart's design?

The issue with all its attendant friction over doctrine, local control, and curriculum prompted a rash of publications. The neglected faculty began the pamphlet war by justifying their ways to Hobart, which he answered with a brief history of the movable seminary in his *Pastoral Letter*.[42] Next Bishop Brownell and the Board of Trustees published a rather innocuous set of regulations describing the organization of the New Haven school, which elicited a highly vitriolic pamphlet, *An Address to the Episcopalians of the United States*, attacking the seminary for requiring scholarship students to do missionary work. *An Address* prompted so many rebuttals that *The Christian Herald* came to the aid of the weary readers with "A Review of Pamphlets on the Theological Seminary."[43] In the end the ambiguity over the $60,000 bequest led all parties to compromise, and the seminary returned to New York under the direction of the Convention, but not before the disputants had publicly canvassed the relative evils of New York's corrupting influence and the competitive advantages of an incorruptible Yale.[44]

Yet another imbroglio in the early republic was exposed through a pamphlet war, this one triggered by Daniel Drake, founder of the Medical College of Ohio. Cincinnati's first trained physician, Drake inspired a number of institutions, but his major interest lay in medical education, which he furthered by securing from the state legislature articles of incorporation for the Medical College of Ohio and the Commercial Hospital and Lunatic Asylum, said at its founding to be the only hospital in the nation devoted exclusively to teaching.[45] By the end of 1820 the Medical College of Ohio was ready to open with President Drake, two associate professors, and twenty-four medical students. Very quickly, Drake became embroiled in a nasty fight with one of his professors, which led to a dueling challenge and the subsequent dismissal of the professor.[46] By the close of the next session animosity among the faculty of the Medical College had prompted two of the five members to resign whereupon the remaining two voted to dismiss Drake as president.[47] An outraged public got Drake reinstated, but having received another offer from Transylvania, he left his beloved Cincinnati for Kentucky, a roundtrip he was to make two more times in his well-peppered career.[48]

Never one to avoid the pen, Drake detailed the events of this raging conflict in a forty-two-page pamphlet, *A Narrative of the Rise and Fall of the Medical College of Ohio* in 1822. The Medical College did not fall, however. When Drake returned to Cincinnati ten years later to organize a medical department at Miami University, the college's trustees threatened suit, leading to a merger of the faculties and a rejuvenated Medical College of Ohio. Once again dissension followed Drake. His departure from the Medical College precipitated a flurry of publicity, including publication of Drake's letter of resignation.[49] Explaining in one of his many pamphlets why doctors endured more rivalry than others, Drake cited the establishment of medical schools as one of the causes of professional quarrels![50]

People welcoming new values rarely reckon with the cultural upheaval involved in adopting them. The publicizers of these power struggles did not think that they were redefining social norms in America, yet they found acceptable a degree of public exposure that would have disturbed their parents. Publicity required an expanded reading public and the aggressive practices of publishers.[51] Important too was the absence of endowments and foundations or the patronage of an established upper class to sponsor schools and churches. Without them, almost all institutions in America had to raise funds from a larger public; standing on ceremony and protecting privacy would probably have turned off likely donors. Nor did dependence upon government, as in the case of the Medical College of Ohio or West Point, alter very substantially the need to mobilize favorable public opinion. Despite indignation at this pervasive publicity, the most cloistered disputants took their causes to the public, usually through the press, allowing ordinary readers to become knowledgeable about what had once been confidential proceedings.

DEMOCRATIZATION FOR Americans in the early nineteenth century involved as much as anything finding a comfort level with the new no-holds-barred conflicts in the larger realm of civil society. The printed reports of power struggles created interpretive communities in which people took sides and enjoyed the conviviality of standing together in publicized, if not always public, quarrels. Published accounts of various disputes carried politics into the parlor, where women joined in the general discussions of popular issues. The intense politicization of public life from political and institutional controversies accustomed Americans to public disclosure. Publicity in the ensuing years transformed the relations between the powerful and authorized and the subordinate and instructed; it also moved policy debates from the closed and obscure to the open and transparent. The boundaries between private and public came to rest upon what was and was not known. The arcana of government no longer formed a protective seal around the public figure.

The astounding frequency of dueling gives one measure of the tensions the new political style generated. The *code duello* was a creation of aristocratic societies in which leisured men—particularly army officers—protected their honor with the avidity of trained marksmen. Introduced into the United States by the Europeans who came to fight in the Continental Army, dueling acquired a peculiar, American twist—the predominance of politics as the trigger of a challenge.[52] In Europe, fights over women and gambling provoked most of the duels; in the United States dueling throve on partisan warfare, an incongruous companion to democratic politics and popular newspaper–reading. Vice President Aaron Burr's slaying of Alexander Hamilton on the dueling grounds of Weehawken, New Jersey, was but the most spectacular of political duels. Contemporaries estimated that over one hundred men had lost their lives in the first twenty years of the century, with many more wounded.[53]

Hamilton himself had had ten previous brushes with challenges, one of them with James Monroe. He had already lost a son, Philip, who precipitated his fatal duel by loudly mocking a Jeffersonian speaker.[54] Michael Taney, father of the chief justice and a Maryland political figure, killed a neighbor in a duel. A heated congressional campaign prompted the duel that killed Richard D. Spaight, a prominent Virginia politician.[55] Andrew Jackson, who enjoyed his reputation as a duelist, slew a young political opponent in cold blood. The man, having grazed Jackson in a first shot, had to stand at the mark while Jackson recocked his gun.[56] An election day quarrel led to a duel between first cousins raised on adjoining Virginia plantations. One of them suggested three ordeals of leaping together from the dome of the Capitol, fighting on a barrel of powder, or meeting hand to hand with knives, but Armstead Mason and John McCarthy eventually accepted muskets at six paces, an encounter that left Mason dead and Congressman McCarthy seriously wounded.[57] In 1820, the public mourned the death of Stephen Decatur, a hero of the War of 1812, who was felled in a duel.

Americans' fondness for publicity led to their only innovation to the morbid tradition. When General James Wilkinson challenged Congressman John Randolph of Virginia to a duel in 1804. Randolph declined the invitation. Wilkinson waited until Congress had reconvened and posted insulting notices at taverns and street corners all over the Capital. The practice caught on and soon newspapers became the conduit for "postings." Unable either to rein in their rhetoric when debating issues or to tolerate the "slash and burn" style of party politics, Congress became the spawning ground for many a duel, popular usage designating a field in nearby Bladensburg, Maryland, the "Congressional dueling ground."

A floor battle over Jefferson's embargo led to the first duel between two congressmen. Republican Representative G. W. Campbell of Tennessee condemned "petty scribblers in the party newspapers" for circulating reports of a French influence behind the president's policy. New York's Barent Gardenier rose to the bait with a long harangue about a nefarious influence surrounded by "darkness, secrecy, and impenetrable mystery" to which Campbell retorted with accusations that Gardenier himself must be "the screen to convey these groundless slanders to the public—the common trumpeter who gives no importance to what he makes public." When Gardenier demanded a retraction, Campbell refused, and seriously wounded Gardenier in the subsequent duel.[58]

A duel between John Randolph and Jefferson's son-in-law Thomas Mann Randolph—triggered by a trivial debate over a salt tax—was barely averted in 1806 after Mann had virtually issued a challenge to Randolph on the floor of Congress. Eliza Quincy wrote a friend from Washington in 1809 that the talk of the town concerned a duel between Mr. Pearson, a Federalist from North Carolina, and Jurist John George Jackson, who was President James Madison's brother-in-law. Another duel a few days earlier, she reported, had taken the life of a young man of seventeen, and people feared that yet one more dispute between the president's secretary and a member of Congress might end in the same way. "What a state of manners and morals," she exclaimed.[59]

Newspaper editors were particularly exposed to challenges and fought many a duel. Colonel Eleazar Oswald, editor of the *New York Advertiser,* wounded Matthew Carey, the prominent Philadelphia publisher; another between Boston editors, Benjamin Austin, Jr., of the *Independent Chronicle* and Benjamin Russell of the *Columbian Centinel,* ultimately led to the murder of Austin's son and a spectacular trial.[60] Newspaper wars in Boston did not lead to the same number of duels as those in New York, where John Daly Burke, an outspoken Irish editor, was killed dueling in 1808; only the timely intervention of Brockholst Livingston prevented the city's two most contentious editors, James Cheetham and William Coleman, from meeting on the dueling grounds.[61]

The pervasiveness of political duels points to the peculiar tensions generated by democratic partisanship in a country whose institutions had run ahead of its mores.[62] The invective generated by competitive elections had caught the participants by surprise. The widespread publicizing of disputes, given peculiar force when printed, had invigorated notions about a man's need to defend his honor, with violence if need be. A South Carolina pamphleteer maintained "that three-fourths of the duels which have been fought in the United States were produced by political disputes," but he saw no relief when "party violence is carried to an abominable excess" and American society "continually agitated by political heats and animosities."[63] Alfred Lorrain discovered that in New Orleans after the War of 1812, public opinion held that no man "unless he was a member of some Church, could refuse a challenge," adding that "hardly an official or political man there had escaped being called into the field."[64] With riots infrequent in the early republic, duels were the most public and publicized form of violence within the country.

Editors editorialized, preachers preached, and college presidents inveighed, but the personal nature of partisan attacks kept dueling alive.[65] As late as 1817 an attack on dueling in the popular journal, *Portico,* elicited a spirited defense that claimed the right to protect one's reputation as one of those "certain natural rights unalienable" above the law.[66] And indeed the law did very little. Warrants went out for Burr's arrest in both New Jersey and New York, but he escaped indictment by fleeing and was never brought to trial. Similarly, when a duel between two New Yorkers arguing over the voting of tenants led to a death, an indictment of the successful duelist went nowhere.[67] Tennessee legislators discovered that lawyers fought almost 90 percent of all duels, so they required a disavowal of dueling for admission to the bar. Most states had laws disqualifying duelers from holding political office, but dueling remained a feature of American political life, North and South, through the 1830s.[68]

Few had the courage or the audacity to decline invitations. Martin Van

Buren had made public his opposition to dueling, but when he got a summons he felt that his standing in "public opinion" required a response.[69] Drake was unusual—a doctor rather than a politician—in refusing the challenge from his opponent in the Ohio Medical College squabble.[70] A friend of James Hamilton, another son of Alexander's, actually issued a challenge for James after hearing a speech disparaging the politics of both father and son. The offending speaker refused to accept the challenge, and Hamilton noted grimly in his memoirs, "his refusal resulted, as was usual at that time, in his being posted in the newspapers as a coward."[71] However, when a prominent Republican, John Mercer, fled to his estate rather than accept a challenge from Robert Goodloe Harper, he was able to get back into politics after friends arranged an apology.[72]

Out of fear of these murderous acts of revenge, Jefferson cautioned his grandson not to worry about defending his reputation, because, as he explained, it lies "in the hands of my fellow citizens at large, and will be consigned to honor or infamy by the verdict of the republican mass of our country, according to what themselves will have seen, not what their enemies and mine shall have said."[73] Likewise when the hot-headed Randolph assailed President John Quincy Adams and Secretary of State Henry Clay for their Panama policy, Adams contented himself with grumbling in his diary while Clay, a Southerner, felt his honor had been sullied and issued a challenge to Randolph.

John Neal, a puckish New England editor, alone in his generation seemed to have been sufficiently detached from the ethic of the *code duello* to mock its pretension. Tossing off novels annually to pay for his law studies in Maryland, Neal included eight pages of caustic commentary on the politics of Baltimore's most prominent lawyer, William Pinckney, who unhappily died while *Randolph* was in press. Outraged by this printed disparagement of his father, Pinckney's son challenged Neal to a duel. Unfazed by this act, Neal not only declined the invitation, but published young Pinckney's letter with comic notation in his next novel, *Errata*.[74] Not content with this wicked attack, Neal produced still another novel, *Keep Cool*, which, according to him, was written chiefly for the discouragement of dueling about which "I was eternally in hot water." Entertaining what he called "very tender, seasonable, talkative scruples of conscience" about dueling, Neal created a story in which his hero is insulted, fights what anybody would call a justified duel, kills his insulter, and never enjoys a happy hour afterwards.[75]

As early as 1802, a Virginia congressman had proposed appointing a committee to inquire whether it would be expedient to disqualify any duelers "from holding office under the government of the United States," but the House refused to consider his motion. Four years later Congress did pass a regulation prohibiting army officers from sending challenges to other officers. Amos Kendall remembered that would-be duelers at Dartmouth College had been suspended, and as late as 1818, the University of Pennsylvania's president thought the issue serious enough to publish a powerful anti-dueling lecture for the student body.[76] Finally in 1838 a duel between Representatives Jonathan Cilley of Maine and William Graves of Kentucky, attended by several other congressmen, produced sufficient outrage that Congress passed an anti-dueling law evoking "the highest constitutional privileges of the House" that "no member be questioned in a hostile way." It condemned challengers to five years in prison, though no one was ever charged under it.[77]

PROMPTED BY THE flagrant contradiction between slavery and the principle of equality, some Americans—North and South, black and white—formed anti-slavery societies in the 1780s. Because they took natural rights literally, they began working for the repeal of those state laws that had created property in human beings. From the simple preamble to the Massachusetts state constitution to the intricate legislation providing for gradual emancipation in New York, Connecticut, and Pennsylvania, Northern states found ways to end slavery, starting with Pennsylvania in 1780 and ending with New Jersey in 1804.[78] The New York Council actually vetoed the legislature's abolition act of 1785 because it had denied freed slaves the vote, a measure the councilors found "repugnant to the principle on which the United States justify their separation from Great Britain."[79] More often supported by Federalists than Jeffersonians, these first emancipation successes led to a peaceful abolition that gradually cleansed the North of slavery as it simultaneously divided North and South into separate societies. The old surveyors' boundary between Maryland and Pennsylvania—the Mason-Dixon line—became the symbolic divide between the domain of natural rights and the territory of slavery.

Signaling a sudden awakening from the slumber of thoughtless toleration, the outpouring of antislavery zeal in the North was itself an ominous development at a time when so few other sentimental ties existed to bind Americans into a national union. A system of coerced labor that had been introduced into the British colonies with scarcely a murmur of opposition suddenly appeared like a stain on the escutcheon of republican honor that the newly-independent states were crafting. The burgeoning free black populations of the cities also gave thousands of self-liberating slaves a destination in their flight and vastly complicated the relations among the states and the federal government. African Americans during the War for Independence had publicly given the lie to the assertion that they had acquiesced in their status. Promised freedom by British field commanders, they fled in great numbers to the British lines, where they enlisted in the King's service when the war zone reached their neighborhoods. In 1813 they made for enemy's lines again, demonstrating anew slavery's inherent fragility.

In states like New York where one quarter of the laborers of Manhattan had been enslaved, abolition represented the most peaceful intrusion upon private property in the annals of government, advertising the power of legislative majorities to deliberate and act in novel areas. Effecting a general emancipation, even if gradual, tested the legislative and law-enforcement skills of the states' officials. In Pennsylvania and Delaware some owners covertly sent their slaves South to avoid their liberation, prompting Quaker activists to patrol the borders. After the 1799 gradual emancipation act, New York passed an intricate set of statutes to thwart stratagems to evade the laws, among them one guaranteeing slaves freedom if their master had promised it to them.

New York courts interpreted the hiring out of a slave as a fraudulent evasion of the abolition law, a decision that enabled Austin Steward to gain his freedom in 1815 at twenty-two, instead of in 1827, the date for the complete abolition of slavery in the state.[80] Isabella Van Wagenen, who became famous as the passionate antislavery speaker Sojourner Truth, successfully called on a New York grand jury to get her five-year-old son returned from Alabama after he had been sold by their former owner.[81] In Connecticut a 1788 act freed enslaved persons born after 1792 and others when they reached the age of twenty-five. Closing his memoir with his liberation in 1815, James Mars exuded confidence that "the time is not far distant when the colored man will have his rights in Connecticut."[82] The doors that eventually closed on African-American hopes for full citizenship in the United States had not yet swung shut.

Nationally the free black population in the United States tripled while that of enslaved persons doubled. The free African-American population in fact grew faster than any other group, from under 10,000 at the time of the Revolution to 197,000 by 1810. Baltimore alone registered an increase from 300 to 5,600.[83] Massachusetts reported no slaves in the first census of 1790; it shared with New Hampshire and Vermont the honor of being the only states in the antebellum period with "color-blind" constitutions.[84] New York gave propertied blacks the vote, but most states—even those carved out of the Northwest Territory where slavery had always been forbidden—denied suffrage to African Americans. Congress passed a number of measures hostile to blacks: candidates for naturalization had to be white, militia enrollment was restricted to white male citizens; and African Americans could not carry the U.S. mails. Nothing if not inconsistent, Congress left enlistment in the Army and Navy open to blacks, though barring their entrance into the Marine Corps.[85]

For Southerners the effect of Northern emancipation was complex and elusive. It came fast upon the heels of the Revolutionary War, when slave-owners had watched much of their human property flee to the British lines. Afterwards bands of self-liberated blacks had harassed the coastlines of Georgia and South Carolina, and records in Virginia reveal a marked increase in the number of deadly assaults by blacks on whites. Gangs of runaways from North Carolina and Virginia set up their own communities deep inside the Dismal Swamp, a marshy tract of land lying between the Chesapeake and Albemarle Sound.[86] Northern legislation added to the fragility of the Southerners' slave system. Worse, it institutionalized a division among men of property at the very moment that the states had agreed to form a more perfect union by ratifying the Constitution. It also compromised the Jeffersonians' principles, for Federalists, and later, Whigs, proved much stouter friends of racial justice than the Republican party, which only grew more hostile to the nation's free blacks.[87]

Since the revolutionary rhetoric about natural rights and innate equality had been invoked in several of the Northern emancipation statutes, it seemed possible that principle might trump skin color as the basis of American nationality. Northern abolition also gave a literal meaning to the natural rights doctrine. Most of the Northern abolition laws fixed July 4th as the day when enslaved persons reached the statutory age of liberation. Calling attention to the acute contradiction between that liberty ordinary Northerners wanted to expand and the slavery that planters intended to protect aggravated relations between the sections. The Declaration of Independence after all had been the founding document for all the states. Slavery brought out the tension between liberalism and democracy, as Southerners spoke more and more fervently in favor of individual rights and limited government, and Northern reformers sought to strengthen government in the name of popular causes.

Northern antislavery agitation brought the subject out of the study and into daily life. The swiftness of Northern rejection of slavery after Independence threw Southerners on the defensive in the union that they—particularly Virginians—had expected to dominate.[88] The area north of the Mason-Dixon line became a refuge for self-liberating slaves, despite the Constitutional provision for retrieving runaways. Intrusive Northern statutes dictated terms to Southerners traveling in the free states with their bondservants, compromising the domestic privacy of slave-holders. These laws concretized an anti-slavery position that had previously been confined to the realm of high-minded talk.

When African slaves in the French colony of Saint Domingue revolted in 1791, slaveholders confronted a new threat: the possibility of domestic insurrections. Indeed, when success crowned the Haitian revolution, Southerners tried to halt the spread of the news.[89] Confronted with a black independence movement, Jefferson recoiled and denied Toussaint-Louverture the recognition that he had been accorded by his predecessor, John Adams. Free blacks, blamed for fomenting discontent among those enslaved, became the targets of aggressive legislation. The North Carolina General Assembly called for the suppression of any gathering of free Negroes and passed a law forcing all of them to "wear a badge of cloth" designating their free status.[90] Playing cards with a slave could earn a free black up to "thirty-nine lashes on his bare back" under the North Carolina code that also called for auctioning off those free blacks who could not pay their fines.[91] Virginia required any Negro who had become free after 1806 to leave the state within twelve months. In the ensuing years, the states kept adding to the burden of being black.

Southern representatives to Congress in the 1790s faced an avalanche of anti-slavery petitions at the outset of each session. Nothing exacerbated the tensions between slave and free states more. On the one hand citizens petitioning their government demonstrated the vigor of representative government; on the other they occasioned acute embarrassment to Southern representatives who deeply resented being lectured by strangers in public. South Carolinians and Georgians gave their critics no quarter and insisted that slavery was strictly a state issue, whereas representatives from Virginia and Maryland favored accepting the petitions on formal grounds. Confronted with threats from Deep South representatives to break up the union, congressmen formed a consensus that slavery lay outside the legitimate concerns of the national government, despite continued public discussions on the subject.[92]

Even George Washington, who freed his slaves upon his death in 1799, had argued the need for Southern vigilance against the power of the federal government. From the perspective of the South Carolinian white gentry, the reception of antislavery petitions in Congress was proof that the Jeffersonians were insufficiently alert. In response to this fear, a group of Carolinians, including both Federalists and Jeffersonians, founded the College of South Carolina in 1805 to train the scions of their prominent families to lead the South's aggressive defense of slavery.[93]

America's congressmen got a sharp reminder of their dependence upon voters when they decided to give themselves a raise. Anticipating some criticism, the representatives asked Richard Johnson, a popular Kentucky war hero credited with killing Tecumseh, to introduce the Compensation Act of 1816. The bill nearly doubled congressional salaries, and the public—still reeling from the economic dislocations of the war—used every public occasion and variety of print media to register their collective outrage. A surprised Johnson claimed that the act had "excited more discontent than the alien or sedition laws, the *quasi* war with France, the internal taxes of 1798, the embargo, the late war with Great Britain . . . or any one measure of the Government, from its existence."[94] Joseph Gales of the *National Intelligencer* supported the bill with the argument that higher salaries would lure poor men into office, but his sampling of several hundred newspapers revealed the furor that the Compensation Act had created abroad in the land. Who could have imagined, an astonished John Randolph asked fellow congressmen, that after all the burdens of the War of 1812 the American people, "the great Leviathan, which slept under all these grievances, should be roused into action by the Fifteen Hundred Dollar Law?"[95]

The pillorying of congressmen suggests that more than money was at stake. Since the tumultuous electoral politics of the 1790s, the leaders of the Federalist and Republican parties had taken upon themselves the power of nominating presidential candidates in caucuses.[96] Quite possibly the public resented the appropriation of this public solemn duty by politicians. The Compensation Act also awakened citizens to their joint identity as voters and taxpayers. When given the opportunity in the next election, they voted incumbents out of office in record numbers. Nearly 70 percent of the Fourteenth Congress did not come back to the Fifteenth, a figure 20 percent higher than normal. Such luminaries as Daniel Webster and Timothy Pickering declined renomination, a wise move considering the retribution visited upon their colleagues. In Kentucky, the enormously popular Henry Clay barely survived the purge, and most of those who were returned had been forced to pledge themselves to repeal the act, which in fact they did when Congress convened.

For their part, congressmen were inclined to place all the blame for the people's wrath upon "the malevolence of the press" or, as one coyly put it, "the false clamors in circulation by the typographical gentry." Since many states had officially instructed their congressmen how to vote, the repeal movement provoked discussion about how much instruction to representatives the constitutional order of the United States could tolerate. "Have the people of this country snatched the power of deliberation from this body?" an alarmed Calhoun demanded. John Tyler, the future president then newly elected to the House from Virginia, responded that a representative who set his opinion at variance with the people was representing only himself; General William Henry Harrison, also serving a first term, concurred, saying that representatives were agents of their constituents, bound by a "moral obligation to execute their will."[97]

⁂

THE SWIFT RESPONSE of voters in 1816 had accurately conveyed the vitality of American democracy and the role of ordinary voters in it, but political participation represented but one part of the lived liberty of white men. Propertyless men acquired the vote and adolescent sons and daughters wrested the freedom to leave home at a young age, but when they took jobs they were thrown back into a centuries-old regime of control, regardless how autonomous they might be in public matters. The nation's householders and employers enjoyed a venerable form of private power, elaborated by the English common law, over their dependents among whom were counted employees. Although attacked for its English provenance and old-fashioned procedures, the common law easily withstood the radical threats to replace it with codified legislation.[98] More resilient than the tradition of deferential politics, it survived its critics to become the most important influence upon the adjudication of contracts, wills, and altercations between employers and their employees. The distance between voter and officeholder shrank dramatically in the years after 1789, even as American courts shored up the rights and privileges of masters over their servants, but political and economic developments worked at crossed purposes during the first decades of the nineteenth century.

The dropping of property qualifications turned more and more men—especially young ones—into voters while the growth of industry increased the number of wage-earners, which meant enlarging the domain of common law's master-servant strictures.[99] The common law assured that submission in the private realm of work would continue even as the ambit of freedom for ordinary white men increased in the public sphere. While by no means totally resistant to change, the common law offered a structure for Americans, a litigious people, to think about property, their rights, and the rules of social life. Its provisions kept intact the authority of the white household head whose powers were significantly augmented if he employed others on his farm or in his shop.[100] Protected by law and enhanced by custom, the role of the householder was also shaped by the social prejudices that British settlers had brought with them. No longer a patriarch to his adult children, the father-householder still remained a powerful figure who was expected to maintain control of his dependents. A distinct minority, household heads represented less than 15 percent of the population, all living in varying degrees of harmony or conflict with their dependent children, servants, and wives in a country publicly dedicated to liberty and equality.

Conservative worries about maintaining order resurfaced. "After finding power to originate in the free and independent man," a jaundiced observer of the transformation of American society asked querulously, "we have yet to inquire, whether this free and independent man will voluntarily submit to the restraints which the good of the community requires of him."[101] For those who remained in the older towns of their birth, local self-governing traditions provided cohesion in a social world elsewhere in flux. Churches also disciplined their members, including household heads, but only if the man and woman chose to remain within the censoring congregation. Few Americans escaped the prevailing Protestant contempt of idleness, indulgence, and incivility, a set of values that community-builders struggled mightily to instill on the frontier. Everywhere towns exercised their greatest control over those who sought charity. Overseers of the poor in Vermont were still auctioning off their indigent in the 1820s, paying the lowest bidder for their upkeep.[102] Wherever common sentiments prevailed, social pressures did the work of parents and police.

A convergence of events between 1819 and 1822 brought enough bad times to dampen the ebullient spirit of democratic politics. The War of 1812 had created a cluster of national heroes, giving the first generation a chance to demonstrate a fresh enthusiasm for their union, but it also wreaked havoc with lives and enterprises and strained the nation's finances. The constriction of credit nationwide precipitated bank closures and bankruptcies, bringing a long period of prosperity to an abrupt close. During the punishing years of 1819 to 1821, families struggled to hold on to the farms and businesses that they had used as collateral for loans. Foreclosures stirred old fears that privilege was reappearing in new guises in America's turbulent, credit-driven economy. Success became more selective, as one decade's frontier became the next decade's settled area. America's vibrant political culture endured, but above this base line of democratic change, economic failure and sectional dissension pushed the melody of many individual lives into a minor key.

Missouri, the first state newly carved out of the Louisiana Purchase, sought admission to the union in 1820 with a constitution acknowledging slavery. Political passions, always volatile on this issue, erupted well beyond the confines of Congress. Two years later, Denmark Vesey's aborted plans to lead a slave uprising in Charleston, South Carolina, complicated and intensified concerns about American slavery, raising the stakes for Northern antislavery advocates and deepening Southerners' sense that only fellow slaveholders could fully understand their situation. As dashed hopes multiplied faster than success stories in these years, the disappointed participants in America's free society found it increasingly difficult to understand what had happened to their sanguine anticipation of prosperity. Soon their sense of grievance would find voluble expression in the presidential campaign for Andrew Jackson while a new party would emerge to sustain those who shared the nation-building enthusiasms of the first generation.

TWELVE YEARS after the ratification of the Constitution, a national elite, established with such high hopes for forming a stabilizing center, had been ousted and with it went that union of social and political power essential to a ruling class. The Jeffersonians had challenged a fundamental feature of traditional hierarchies—the belief that nature had produced the few and the many. People of wealth continued to enjoy a disproportionate share of political power, but elite mores no longer predominated in the public sphere: understandings were no longer tacit, nor were policy discussions private. Rambunctious partisans cleared a space for contentious voices in the 1790s when Jefferson's followers claimed the right to discuss Federalist policies. Despite guilt by association with the French Jacobins, these activists with their political clubs and party newspapers succeeded in legitimating political gatherings at a time when state legislatures still deliberated in secret. With great gusto, they rejected conservative notions that citizen action should be confined to voting. Intense, widespread political participation became a sustained feature of American public life.

The prosperity of ordinary farming folk, the inventions of unknown geniuses, the marketing innovations of village entrepreneurs—all confirmed the truth of popular values. The spirit of Prometheus unbound continued to animate the successful in the United States. Westward migrating families viewed their taking up of land in the national domain as a movement to spread democratic institutions across the continent. Such a wholesome demonstration of the moral worth of ordinary white men and women created images and myths that could resonate among Americans without evoking the curse of slavery, nor troubling the national conscience about violently displacing the indigenous peoples. As an English traveler commented, "A good citizen is the common designation of respect" in America, for when someone wishes to call his neighbor a virtuous man, he says "he is a very good citizen."[103]

Working out the terms of democracy and nationhood became a self-imposed task for the first generation because the United States had been formally united with nothing but abstract notions about either. It fell to those born after the Revolution to mold national sentiments around their own unique experiences of opinion-forming and consensus-building, but these were not uniform. The success of the first emancipation movement removed the incubus of slavery from the North, but left Southern states with a "peculiar institution" to explain. It also cut across colonial class lines, eliciting the support of the Revolutionary gentry of New York and eminent Quakers in Pennsylvania while Jeffersonians, a mixed group of Southern planters, aspiring Northerners, and native-born and immigrant workers, pulled further and further away from the Revolutionary commitment to universal natural rights.

Abolition legislation freed Northerners from the blatant hypocrisy of celebrating American liberty while holding "human chattel." Its success encouraged other Northern campaigns for moral reform and social betterment while making Southerners deeply suspicious of Northern intentions. Running along a different ideological axis, many New Englanders and most of the urban elite deplored the eruption of popular politics in the 1790s, some Federalists actually withdrawing from civic life. Ordinary white men, North and South, responded enthusiastically to their inclusion in the body politic. Issues of class were added to those of regional differences to be worked out by an inexperienced citizenry. Only the status of women—somewhat unsettled in Revolutionary times—remained secure, awaiting later events to challenge the reigning patriarchal definition.

As economic initiatives burgeoned, unencumbered by the direction of the state or a moneyed elite, many white men in the middling ranks of society acquired the confidence to make their sentiments those of the nation. American voters came to think of themselves as possessing political convictions that they should be prepared to defend, if necessary. Although political parties would impose some discipline upon the electoral process, they never succeeded fully in channeling to their own ends the popular images and discursive habits formed in these early decades of the nineteenth century. Convictions about personal worth, opportunities to join an expanding commercial world, and changes in voter requirements converged to enhance the prestige of the plain-spoken white male whose homely virtues writers rarely tired of extolling.

Those Northerners who were inclined to see slavery as an unmitigated evil gave vent to their indignation in the popular press. Subtly, the activities of reading and publishing became linked in the minds of slaveholders with noxious, antislavery agitation. And most portentously, Southerners began to see in every political initiative coming out of the North a prelude to a full-scale attack on slavery. The range of tolerated public expression diverged strikingly across the land. The North supported a flourishing publishing industry and a robust civic scene while, after a flurry of democratic initiatives in the South, the planter elite succeeded in confining important political discussions to the privacy of their gatherings. The more Northerners began talking about the nation and identifying their opinions as those of the nation, the more Southerners saw themselves standing outside the web of sentiments being spun up North, making all the more ironic the leadership that Virginia exerted through the Revolutionary era.

Northern abolition shocked Southerners. When the Haitian revolt was followed by two narrowly-averted slave rebellions in Virginia and South Carolina, Southern equivocation on slavery ended: slavery should be considered permanent in the United States, the rights of slave owners honored as those of any other man of property.[104] The status of the slave as both a capital investment and a recognized piece of property stirred mixed feelings among Northerners. Reformers had to contend with a strong tide running for the personal autonomy of the householder and an entrenched sense of white superiority. As in the case of the power conferred upon employers by the common law, race prejudice compromised American democracy from the very beginning. Despite a rhetoric filled with tropes about empty canvases and virgin continents, the natural rights philosophy of the Declaration of Independence had in fact entered a crowded field of authorities, taking its place alongside a patriarchal legal system and a strong biblical tradition.

The democratization of American society supplied the passion, the issues, and the discourses necessary for detaching the country from its monarchical roots. The surviving common law, however, unobtrusively sustained the domination of the master in the home and workplace. The Constitution committed "we, the people" to establish justice and insure domestic tranquility, even as it recognized slavery and the rights of the slave-owner to federal protection. Ordinary white men spoke of their new social order as universal and natural with little thought about the structured exclusion of Indians, people of color, and women. Still, the presence of high moral principles at the country's founding turned perfectly normal patterns of domination into vexed issues. Whether inspired by democratic principles, Christian zeal for perfection, or an enlightened sense of progress, American reformers would not leave the public conscience at peace. Participatory politics ushered in an era of conflict that competition in the marketplace and denominational pluralism only exacerbated. Prosperity did not lessen these tensions; rather it heightened them, cultivating among Americans a concrete sense of their self-interest and an awareness of how public policies and social movements might affect it. The hopes for liberty with equality, justice, and the unimpeded pursuit of happiness were extravagant, yet believable enough to excite the imagination.

3

ENTERPRISE

THE ELABORATION OF A COMMERCIAL society took place in the United States under circumstances that forged a powerful link between political and economic freedom. Nations have been described as "imagined communities," but the United States became more of an imagined enterprise.[1] In 1789, a long period of warfare, uncertainty, and depression came to an end. Americans had paid dearly for their Revolution, but at last the crushing burden of debt had been lifted and prosperity returned. In the ruminations of those born after Independence we get glimpses of the bedrock under America's culture of capitalism: national goals cemented for personal ambitions to an imagined national enterprise that vindicated democracy in a world of monarchies.

The establishment of the new government under the Constitution coincided with an economic pick-up: the funding of the Revolutionary debt executed by Alexander Hamilton created a new pool of capital. Once elected president, Jefferson worked swiftly to democratize Hamilton's ac-complishment, dismantling the Federalist fiscal program, reducing taxes, and cutting the size of the civil service. Letting the charter of Hamilton's Bank of the United States lapse freed money and credit from national control, leaving individual states and private corporations to supply the country with competing banks.[2] For the next half-century the states took the lead in promoting economic developments; building an infrastructure of banks, roads, and canals; and offering bounties, licenses, and charters for promising and unpromising economic ventures alike. Unlike the Federal-ists, who still fondly hoped for the supervision of the wise at the center, the state's economic initiatives formed a vortex for popular politics.[3]

Had the Federalists passed on their power to like-minded men in 1800, the course of economic development in the United States would have been guided by government officials attentive to the nation's major investors. The intertwined social and economic prescriptions of a national elite would have informed policies for the country as a whole. Bankers and lenders would have controlled the flow of credit. The pace of settlement would have been slower as land passed first to large speculators, as it did in the Federalist era, and then to the farming family. Instead, a new political movement explicitly hostile to the exercise of government authority tri-umphed, and the fiscal stability achieved in Washington's administration redounded to the benefit of the very people intent upon liberating them-selves from the restraint of their social superiors. Women, blacks, servants, and the indigent continued to be constrained by law, but no elite group in America would emerge with the power to close off the access of ordinary white men to economic resources.

If the Constitution provided the foundation of America's liberal soci-ety, the free enterprise economy raised its scaffolding. After Independence a new economic order took shape, the old one all but disappearing after the break with Great Britain. Without imperial control over land and credit thousands of bootstrap operators could act on their plans with little but high hopes for their financing. Jefferson's commitment to decentralizing governmental power dispersed opportunity to rural areas—areas where the water power of brooks and streams was cheap and plentiful. The gradual emancipation of slaves in the Northern states redirected capital from long-term investments in labor. International trade throve because of the fa-vored role of the United States as a neutral carrier for France and England, again at war.

The national domain, acquired at the end of the Revolutionary War, acted as a constant stimulus to economic development: prodding states to improve access, luring skilled farmers onto fertile land, and adding thousands of professional opportunities in the western communities that sprouted across the frontier. The Constitution added governmental muscle to the thrust of American families against the indigenous populations in the trans-Appalachian West. Native American tribes fought fiercely to preserve their ancestral lands, but they now faced a united government with a peacetime army to put in the field against them. It would not be amiss to conclude that the yearning for economic independence among ordinary white Americans sealed the fate of dependency for Native Americans.

The commercialization and democratization of the United States worked interactively to spread revolutionary changes, bolstered by a prosperity that promoted the construction of roads, the extension of postal services, and the founding of newspapers in country towns. The United States became a safe place for European investors just when the wars of the French Revolution put a premium on American foodstuffs and neutral shippers. British demand for cotton for its textile mills coincided with the invention of the cotton gin, revitalizing Southern agriculture, which had been particularly hard hit by the Revolutionary War. Within a decade, merchants, freed from British restrictions, sent ships up the California coast, across the Pacific, and into the Indian Ocean. The lifting of colonial restrictions on manufacturing unloosed Yankee ingenuity. Workers sought out the hundreds of little factories that sprang up along the waterways being tapped for power in the East. Steam engines and water power topped up this heady mixture of novel enterprises, accelerating the pace of economic development and adding manufacturing to the nation's expanding agricultural base.

Hundreds of people—many of them ingenious youths—responded to the incentives to produce something for the market. Farmers were as eager for innovations as city dwellers, a taste that astounded Europeans, accustomed to the backward ways of rural folk.[4] While lots of aspiring entrepreneurs failed to rise above the poverty of their farming families, enough succeeded to attract the startled attention of those expecting resistance to change from country men and women. With few exceptions, entrepreneurs came from those outside the circle of old wealth. This meant that manufacturing profits accrued to a new middle class distinguished by its ingenuity and work ethic. When these unknown innovators succeeded, their success lent credibility to claims that political freedom would inspire economic progress. So strong was the imaginative linking of political and economic liberty into a single cause of prosperity that every economic downturn jeopardized the reputation of democratic governance. "Panics" and "busts," when they came, turned quickly into political crises because of the association of the two freedoms, raising in new guises old questions about distributive justice.

With the invention of the cotton gin in 1793, the short-staple cotton grown all over the South became commercially profitable, triggering a Southern expansion that more than matched the grain frontier of the North. Simple to imitate—to Eli Whitney's great chagrin—cotton gins popped up all over the South; land that had been marginal assumed new value as soil for producing the fiber that was transforming textile-making. More profitable than any other undertaking in the United States, slave-worked cotton plantations reaped the benefits of an industrial revolution in Great Britain. The ease of marketing this valuable crop in turn promoted diverging concepts of work and wealth-getting between Northern and Southern states.

The planters who benefited from their advantageous situation in a world market created a way of life strikingly different from that of their slaves and the slaveless white majority in their midst. They became the great consumers of the American economy, using spare slave labor to build handsome plantation houses, where a gracious style of hospitality set the South's elite off from the penurious Southern whites and blacks as well as the vast majority of Northerners. Their economic success promoted specialization as Southern demand for foodstuffs, lumber products, and manufactured goods stimulated economic development elsewhere in the United States.

Six technical and organizational changes influenced the early nineteenth-century American economy: the rapid integration of surpluses from new farms into the market, the applications of steam power, the expansion of retailing, the perfection of machine tools, the use of corporations, and the proliferation of banks. Looked at through the working lives of the first generation, what is personal in this economic transformation becomes conspicuous. Ordinary men got access to cheap land, cheap credit, and ready markets at home and abroad for their crops, their products, and their services. The adventures of John Ball and his sister, Deborah, tell a lot about how young people responded. The Balls' father had been a part of the exodus of New Englanders from the overpopulated flatlands of New England into the hill country of Vermont during the last years of the Revolution. Once a year the senior Ball went to Boston to exchange his butter and cheese for manufactured items; otherwise the family was pretty much self-sufficient.

The tenth of ten children, John Ball determined to leave home when he was a teenager, though accepting without challenge his father's claim to his labor until he was twenty-one. He struggled to gain more schooling over the objections of his father, whose own education had been limited to reading, writing, and ciphering. Finally Ball got to study with a nearby clergyman, who made the crucial decision to teach this frontier lad Latin, an intellectual attainment that opened the doors of Dartmouth to him. The books Ball had access to at home included the Bible, Watts's *Hymns*, Webster's *American Spelling Book*, Morse's *Geography*, and Adams's *Arithmetic*—not much as a library—but a telling testimony to the reach of New England literacy. Mindful of the obligations he was born into, Ball struck a deal with an older brother, to the effect that "if he would stay and provide well" for their parents, he would relinquish his claim to the family property.[5]

Even more remarkable for the era, Ball's sister also formed a plan for escaping her isolated Vermont home. Her brother described Deborah as possessing "a vigorous body and mind" and being quite self-reliant. Having learned the tailoring trade, she moved to New York after marrying William Powers, who started one of the country's first "floor oil cloth" manufacturing establishments. Crowned with quick success, Powers built a five-story brick factory, only to perish the next year in a fire that destroyed it all. Saddled with an eight-thousand-dollar debt, Deborah Ball Powers offered her creditors the remains of the factory if they would extinguish the debt. They refused, so she hired a housekeeper and took over the operation, learning to do all the designing and ornamenting herself. Ball helped his sister run the business, traveling a circuit from Troy to Baltimore taking orders from linoleum samples. Reflecting on her surprising competence, Ball noted how "at first she seemed much to rely on me in all matters of business, but after a time she showed a readiness in taking a part in all the concerns of the establishment."[6] Relieved of this responsibility, he was free to move on.

Although Ball had been admitted to the New York bar after studying law, he played the rolling stone for years, going South to Georgia to run a school and then back to New York to help his sister. His youthful encounters demonstrate that the early republic was a "small world," his Dartmouth days coinciding with the battle over the college charter that ended in a famous Supreme Court case. The infamous Aaron Burr, still litigating at eighty, put in a court appearance at Utica the day Ball was admitted to the New York bar. Later, when visiting Washington, D.C., he called on Andrew Jackson at the White House, who received him "kindly" even though he had no introduction.[7] Enterprising men knocked against enterprising men like so many billiard balls. In early 1832 Nathaniel Wyeth, who had proved his mettle exporting ice from Walden Pond, organized an expedition to Oregon that attracted Ball's attention. Wyeth in turn had been inspired by the Pacific dreams of Hall Jackson Kelley, a New Hampshire schoolteacher and surveyor who became obsessed with the idea of colonizing the far Northwest even though—or perhaps because—the pristine area between the Mississippi and the Pacific had changed little since Columbus's landfall in the New World.

Joining the Wyeth party in Baltimore in 1832, Ball rode on the longest stretch of railroad in the United States, the Baltimore and Ohio Railroad. Next the party followed the National Road on foot to Pittsburgh from whence they took a boat to Cincinnati. Ever the fortunate traveler, Ball found himself in the company of Lyman Beecher, the most famous minister in the United States, then on his way to a rendezvous in the West as president of Lane Theological Seminary. Beecher was an object of awe and interest to the others, Ball recalled, though one irreverent passenger, noting the care with which Beecher walked the unbulwarked deck, queried, "Mr. Beecher is so much more cautious than we sinners?"[8] From Cincinnati the Wyeth expedition passed on to a settlement of Mormons before plunging into the uncharted wilderness along the Oregon Trail. The last fellow Americans they glimpsed were soldiers on a steamboat going up the Mississippi to fight in the Black Hawk War.

Two years later Ball was back in New York, where his friends urged him to make a book of his travels. Even adventures had become commodities.[9] Ball's great financial opportunity came in 1836 when two Troy physicians and his sister's partners pooled their money to invest in Michigan land and proposed that Ball, the intrepid wilderness traveler, go to the new territory and make their land selections for them. "It was the great year of speculation," Ball remembered, "and I have always thought it strange that so sober men as those would have yielded to the mania that so pervaded the country."[10] He, nonetheless, took them up on their proposition, remaining in the territory to become a prosperous pioneer of Grand Rapids, a state legislator, and the architect of Michigan's public school system. At age fifty-six he married and had a family of five children.

John and Deborah Ball's early departures from home give us a glimpse of a drama repeated over and over within traditional New England homes.[11] Despite their self-sufficient ways and close-knit families, patriarchs found their authority crumbling as economic growth brought new opportunities to the young. Eventually four of the surviving nine Ball children left home, never to return; five remained to replicate their parents' lives on nearby farms. Like his sister, when John Ball left Vermont, he also left rural America to join the growing amorphous urban middle class of white-collar workers, storekeepers, manufacturers, and professional men.

Times were good when Ball moved from practicing law to running a private school in Georgia, to partaking in America's colonizing forays into the Pacific, and back to the States for successful land speculation in Michigan. Those coming of age in the 1790s were entering a long period of prosperity, interrupted only by abrupt downturns with the Embargo of 1807–1808, the War of 1812, and the Panic of 1819. For the thirty-five years after 1790, European demand for American foodstuffs remained high. A printed solicitation for business sent from a Barcelona firm said that American wheat and flour were constantly in demand in this place "which, in years of abundance never produces more than for four Months provisions." Even in England food production did not catch up with population until the 1820s, shortfalls leading to large American imports.[12] The profits from grain and cotton crops spread rapidly through the American states, filling thousands of pockets with enough money to finance new ventures, whether they involved moving to a teaching post, starting a store, working on an invention, buying supplies for a frontier stake, venturing a cargo to the West Indies, buying a slave, or making a strike for one's own freedom from enslavement. From an accountant's point of view, young Americans were poor, reckless, and debt-prone, but a risk-taking genie had been let out of the bottle of tradition, and not all the prudence of the ages could stuff it back in.

⁂

IN SPITE OF ALL this activity, the country was economically primitive by any present-day standard. Until the end of the 1820s, only those living on the nation's rivers could be sure of long-distance transportation, and then only in one direction. Roads did not go very far inland and were impassable in rainy months. In 1790, close to 90 percent of the population was engaged in farming, much of it of the most basic kind. Most people lived in very simple houses, often of their own making. Enslaved families were crowded into barracks-like cabins. Olive Cleaveland Clarke, who grew up in western Massachusetts, remembered seeing her first carpets when she was seventeen, and she had to visit Northampton to make her acquaintance with a piano.[13]

Life expectancy was not high: age forty-five for both white women and men who lived to be twenty. For African Americans the picture was much bleaker. Life expectancy dropped as low as thirty-five, with black infant mortality twice that of white babies.[14] The remarkably low mortality rates of the eighteenth century had taken a turn for the worse in the 1790s, and continued high for the next hundred years as the new killers—tuberculosis, yellow fever, and cholera—took their terrible toll.[15] White women in 1800 bore an average of seven children; enslaved black women nine, with each delivery a threat to their health.[16] Such high fertility made for a youthful nation; 58 percent of America's population was under twenty in 1820 as compared to 44 percent in 1899 and 18 percent in 1940![17]

How long people worked also made life hard by today's standards. Ten hours a day, six days a week was the norm. Wages, good by European standards, were far from generous when the cost of living was factored in—food, clothing and shelter took 80 percent or more of a worker's wages.[18] Average unskilled laborers got seventy-five cents a day in the early part of the century, and frontier farmers paid workers even less for the back-breaking work of clearing the land. Slaves hired out got comparable wages. Laborers in Pittsburgh could earn two dollars a day, although in New York City not even 1 percent of the population earned the equivalent of $7,000 in 1980 dollars.[19]

But people take their bearings from what has gone before them, not future, unimaginable attainments. And what Americans in the early republic experienced was the steady reworking of the material environment—acres brought under the plow, steam engines applied in unfamiliar ways, rivers and streams dammed and sluiced to power mills, canals, and roads cut through the wilderness. The market's opportunities came in new guises to new participants. The digest of patents that the first commissioner put together reveals the full sweep of commercial imagination. Scores of inventors patented devices in metallurgy, chemical processes, hydraulic implements, machine tools, and household conveniences.[20] And every idea that found material expression in novel artifacts proved just how wrong were the old-timers who invoked the past to predict the future. Reflecting on this, Chauncey Jerome said he could not "now believe that there will ever be in the same space of future time so many improvements and inventions as those of the past half century—one of the most important in the history of the world."[21] Novelty, always experienced as a break with the expectation of how things were going to be, became the most constant feature in the lives of Jerome's generation.

Not everyone favored these changes. The manufacturers' use of water power in rural areas provoked contention over fishing rights along the rivers. Manufacturing and farming families disputed the justice of paying taxes for schools.[22] Religious groups like the Hicksite Quakers viewed banks, agricultural societies, missions, chemistry, and the Erie Canal as signs of an unwholesome desertion of true piety.[23] Pockets of opposition to commercial intrusion into traditional ways of work and life like these remained throughout the country, but most conflicts broke out among economic competitors when new development made salient how diverse interests would be affected by specific changes.

After Jefferson's election, the westward movement of families away from eastern centers of authority and refinement, a development that Federalists had dreaded, accelerated. When land offices opened on the frontier, land sales soared. In 1800 some 67,000 acres passed into private hands; 497,939 acres did so in 1801. By 1815 annual sales hit one and half million dollars, more than doubling four years later.[24] American geographic mobility astounded foreign visitors, who wrote home about the forests of masts in American harbors and the undulating train of wagons snaking their way to Pittsburgh, from whence they could raft down the Ohio. To these visitors, American society offered an ever-changing visual landscape as people moved, roads were graded, land was cleared, and buildings were raised in a reconfiguration of the material environment that went on without rest.

Eager for farms of their own, poor white Americans pushed west in a never-ending stream, with confidence in their right to the land. Skirmishes and set battles continued throughout the settlement of the Ohio and Mississippi Valleys, for land acquisitions on the other side of the mountains had to be bought, negotiated for, or wrested from the Indian tribes. The adjective "hostile" became permanently linked to the word "Indians," as newspapers reported their tenacious fight to save their ancestral hunting grounds. John Jay Smith reported that migrants from Pennsylvania pushed west to Ohio even though there were vast tracts of land remaining in the center of their state, still dotted with Indian occupants. Two-thirds of the landless white men of Virginia moved West in the 1790s.[25] Americans learned early to move towards opportunity, laying the basis for an enduring national trait. Between 1800 and 1820, the trans-Appalachian population grew from a third of a million to more than two million. Never again would so large a portion of the nation live in new settlements.

There must have been something wondrous about growing up when the pinebreaks and forests, teeming with game, yielded to the plough, the ax, and the managed fires of frontier farmers. Stands of hardwood trees, covering the land, opened up farther west to prairies ablaze in spring flowers. Allen Trimble's family passed through the Cumberland Gap with a party of five hundred moving west in military formation under the tight discipline of a former Continental Army officer. The Trimbles rather quickly carved out a farm in Kentucky, clearing twenty acres the first year with the help

Fascinating foreigners and Americans alike, families moving west formed a human chain, as this illustration from *The Farmer's and Mechanics Almanac* indicates. Courtesy, American Antiquarian Society.

of several slaves they had brought with them. Once the cane break had yielded to cultivation, one acre would produce an astounding 150 bushels of corn. Listening to a Revolutionary veteran regale a group with stories of herding hogs for the army, Trimble persuaded his father to finance a drive to Virginia, where he could collect on the difference between that state's ten dollars per hundred price for pork that brought less than two dollars in Kentucky. Fitted out with a compass, the twenty-year-old Trimble drove six hundred pigs through both trackless wilderness and settled land lying between Kentucky and the Chesapeake, negotiating a sale near Washington that was so handsome that Trimble repeated the trip twice.[26]

As long as western farmers were dependent upon rivers and wagons for transportation, there wasn't a single crop that could pay for its freight back east and very few that could make returns on the river trip south to New Orleans. This left the frontier with persistent gluts. When farmers had too much corn, they fed it to their hogs and produced a hog glut. Distilling their grain into whisky became so attractive that soon they had a whiskey glut.[27] But the steamboat came to their rescue. Robert Fulton's *Clermont* crossed the Hudson in 1807, the same year John Stevens took his steamboat on a successful sea voyage, but it was Nicholas Roosevelt who caused a sensation with the first steamboat on the Mississippi in 1812, in part because Mrs. Roosevelt gave birth before they reached New Orleans.[28] After the steamboats demonstrated that they could stem the rough currents of the western rivers, they found their natural medium. By 1818 there were twenty of them plying the waters of the Ohio and Mississippi, and by 1829, two hundred. With adequate transport, whiskey, rum, and other distilled spirits became the third most important domestic product, representing 10 percent of the nation's entire industrial output.[29]

After the War of 1812, Congress gave its veterans 160-acre bounties in land lying between the Illinois and Mississippi rivers. Most veterans sold their patents to land speculators in eastern cities, but the traffic created new opportunities because the land title had to be recorded in Illinois. Christiana Tillson's husband went west to survey one of these bounties for a Massachusetts investor, so impressing the land recorder that he took him on as a clerk to help clear the backlog. From this vantage point, Tillson found good land for himself, becoming a founder of Montgomery County. He brought his wife west in a specially-built carriage that covered a hundred miles in three days, but most families plodded along with their wagons, some as long as sixty feet and many gaily decorated with ribbons.[30] Morris Birkbeck, an English immigrant who settled in Illinois, remarked that New Englanders were "known by the cheerful air of the women advancing in front of the vehicle; the Jersey people by their being fixed and steadily within it; whilst the Pennsylvanians creep lingering behind, as though regretting the homes they have left."[31]

Birkbeck, an astute observer, marveled at the skill of private town planners. Proprietors start new towns, he explained to his English readers, and attract a doctor, a lawyer, and a schoolteacher who might also serve as a religious leader. "Hundreds of these speculations may have failed," he conceded, "but hundreds prosper; and then trade begins and thrives, as population grows around these lucky spots." "One year ago," he explained, "the neighborhood of this very town was clad in 'buckskin;' now the men appear at church in good blue cloth, and the women in fine calicoes and straw bonnets."[32]

It was just this kind of rhapsodic report that stirred the ire of Birkbeck's fellow Englishman William Cobbett, who traversed the same terrain wondering why English farmers, used to "a snug homestead, eating regular meals, and sleeping in warm rooms," should move to Illinois in order to compete with an American farmer "who has half a dozen sons, all brought up to use the axe, the saw, the chisel and the hammer from their infancy, and every one of whom is a ploughman, carpenter, wheelwright, and butcher, and can work from sun-rise to sun-set, and sleep, if need be, upon the bare boards?" Cobbett met a farmer from Connecticut who was migrating to Little York, Pennsylvania, because he hadn't the means to buy farms for his five sons. For such a man, "born with an axe in one hand and a gun in the other," Cobbett explained, "the western counties are ideal, for his sons will help him clear cheap land in Pennsylvania and each will then have a farm of his own."[33]

Access to land meant maximizing family labor. One Ohio pioneer, finding that his hundred-acre farm did not offer "full employment" for his sons, plunged all of his savings into buying enough land to absorb their full working capacity, showing us that farmers not only thought in terms of capitalizing their labor, but considered their sons' labor in those terms as well.[34] Stephen Cooper, who moved with his family from Virginia to Boonslick, Missouri, a hundred miles from any other settlement, remembered living "very plain," raising hemp, flax, and cotton, which the women manufactured for such clothing as they all wore, but, he added, "we had great abundance of horses, cattle, hogs, and sheep."[35] Although much of the land in Ohio was poorly drained, most chroniclers of the frontier remarked on the astounding yields from the new lands when compared to the exhausted acreage of Virginia or the rock-strewn fields of New England from whence most settlers came.

The remarkable crop-yield differentials between the Ohio country and New England caused problems at both ends. The ease of growing crops on western lands undercut the marketing prospects for farmers in the East, which had begun to brighten. The turnpike mania of the 1790s had integrated the villages of New England into the commerce of the sea coast towns, and farmers began to sell their livestock and dairy products to the cities, which were doubling in size with every passing decade.[36] Those established on the best lands or those near cities could get by, but others who had pushed onto marginal lands in the preceding generation were hard-pressed to compete. Raising merino sheep and Morgan horses gave northern New Englanders a brief respite, but soon Ohio graziers were wintering over sheep for a dollar when it cost two in Vermont. In the end New England's best export was its farming families, the intrepid Yankees who pushed into the West on sleighs, on foot, and in wagons, carrying with them their farming lore, their work habits, and their religious preferences.[37]

Specialization offered another commercial opportunity. Wethersfield, Connecticut, for instance, sent to market one and a half million onions annually.[38] Levi Dickinson invented a broom made from corn stalks in 1797. One man working four months could harvest enough broom corn to make six hundred of them. By 1833 the townspeople of Hadley, Massachusetts, produced half a million brooms a year.[39] Lucy Kellogg's memoirs give a sense of how a Massachusetts farm family responded to market cues. She and her sister learned how to braid straw and earned enough to buy their own clothes until the straw business failed during the War of 1812. Next, they set up a couple of looms and took cotton yarn from the factories that were beginning to spread through the state. Because the States were cut off from English goods, they were able to sell fine shirtings, gingham dresses, and bed tickings that were "good enough in time of war." Explaining that her father had inherited a small farm, Kellogg reported bemusedly that "in accordance with the instincts of New England people, they must sell their farm and move to New Hampshire or some other new place," but after a stint in merchandizing in New Hampshire, her family returned to farm in Worcester.[40]

SOUTHERN PLANTERS would have grown wealthy in the early national period whether the North had expanded or contracted, remained rural or become urban, developed a worldwide commerce or continued to ply the waters of the Atlantic. Events elsewhere shaped their economic destiny. Great Britain's revolutionary technology for manufacturing fabric triggered an unprecedented demand for raw cotton. Rarely in history has one spot on the globe become favored above all others, but such was the case of the American South in the first half of the nineteenth century, as it had been earlier for the sugar cane–growing islands of the Caribbean and would become later for countries rich in oil deposits. Subject to booms and bust, particularly during the rapacious scramble for land when each territory opened up, the cotton economy brought great wealth to the nation as a whole, its marketing and shipping adding measurably to the prosperity of the North Atlantic states. Against the measurable wealth that slave labor created must be placed the immeasurable loss to the South of cultural capital in skills not learned and lessons in adaptability postponed. Even less tangible was the enormous drain of the region's moral resources spent defending a social system that others found increasingly indefensible.

William Grayson painted a graphic picture of the impact of the cotton boom in his hometown of Beaufort, South Carolina. Recalling the beautiful orchards of a neighbor, he detailed their bounty "in all good things." "Oranges were plentiful, figs without number, peaches and pomegranates in profusion," he chronicled with evident nostalgia, warming to the climax of his story:

> The cultivation of a great staple like cotton or tobacco starves everything else. The farmer curtails and neglects all crops. He buys from distant places not only the simplest manufactured article like his brooms and buckets, but farm productions, grain, meat, hay, butter, all of which he could make at home . . . Under this system the country that might be the most abundant in the world is the least plentiful. The beef is lean, the poultry poor, the hogs a peculiar breed with long snouts and gaunt bodies . . .[41]

Speculation in cotton futures became almost as popular as gambling. Money chased after the acres and field hands that would bring high returns. E. S. Thomas, the nephew of the famous printer and bibliophile Isaiah Thomas, like many another Yankee, went South to find his fortune. Opening a book store in Charleston, Thomas made several trips to England, returning from his fourth voyage in 1803 with a printed catalogue of 50,000 volumes in every branch of literature, arts, and sciences. His venture coincided with South Carolina's provocative resumption of the foreign slave trade, which had lapsed during the Revolution. "The news had not been five hours in the city," Thomas recalled, "before two large *British Guineamen* that had been laying off . . . port for several days, expecting it, came up to town; and from that day my business began to decline."[42]

Cotton expansion absorbed almost all the investment capital and entrepreneurial initiative of Southerners who, like their Northern counterparts, built canals and turnpikes and speculated in bank stock. Yet the nexus of issues clustering around the use of slave labor blunted the stimulus of high profits, for slaves produced more than labor; they also stored and reproduced wealth. In New England, when teenage children started to strike out on their own, parents began to save for their old age. While Northern savings went up, aging Southerners looked to the seemingly inexorable rise in the value of their slaves to provide for their old age. Small farmers throughout the South welcomed internal improvements and celebrated progress, but the rigidities in the slave economy repeatedly frustrated their efforts while its benefits forestalled the day when Southerners would have to respond to changing markets and new technologies.[43]

The biggest losers in this new era of Southern expansion were African Americans, whose opportunities for manumission practically disappeared once the profits from cotton raised the value of their labor. The price of slaves more than doubled within a decade, tempting the planters of Virginia and Maryland, where agriculture was declining, to sell their stock in human beings. Having preened themselves on the price of their slaves, plantation masters had to take but a small step psychologically to realize that sum in a sale. The domestic slave trade represented the one entrepreneurial activity in the South. Enslaved families lived with the constant threat of being sold down the river, often separately. Hundreds of thousands of African Americans were wrenched from kith and kin and force-marched to Georgia, Mississippi, and Alabama, carrying the institution of slavery deeper into the continent. By 1820 over a million African Americans had moved beyond the boundaries of the original slave states to Alabama, Mississippi, and Louisiana.[44]

Slave sales could be very impromptu affairs. Birkbeck described such a one in Virginia: "I saw two female slaves and their children sold by auction in the street—an incidence of common occurrence here, though horrifying to myself and many other strangers." "I could hardly bear to see them handled and examined like cattle," he wrote in his journal, "and when I heard their sobs . . . at the thought of being separated, I could not refrain from weeping with them."[45] So novel was the scale of the domestic slave trade that Warner Mifflin, a Delaware Quaker, wrote President John Adams to alert him to "this atrocious and abominable Crime."[46] Always subject to the abuse of masters, enslaved African Americans were also pawns of a judicial system that defined them as property. Where slave law reigned, they were regularly seized for debts or appraised and condemned by the courts in litigation over contracts and inheritance. They could be adjudged defective merchandise or used to compensate litigants. When slave-owners died it required no hard-hearted master to break up a family; court-ordered sales would do the job. Rising cotton prices after 1819 pushed up the value of slaves, enhancing the property of every slaveholder, cotton planter or not. They acted as a mighty bulwark against conscience when slavery represented 44 percent of all wealth in the five major cotton-producing states.[47]

The prosperity that pumped new life into the institution of slavery also provided opportunities for a very few African Americans to escape it and join the growing population of free people of color. The largest planters could afford to have their slaves accompany them on hunting trips, but poorer men felt hard-pressed to get a regular return on their investment. Hiring out their slaves during slack times yielded extra income and offered slaves themselves a bargaining chip. Sometimes the slaves moved from rural areas to the towns, where work was more plentiful. This practice became common throughout the South, sometimes offering a stepping stone to freedom for slaves, either through manumission or self-purchase.

For Colin Teage and Lott Cary, being able to sell their own labor offered the key that unlocked the shackles of slavery. Teage was born a plantation slave, but falling tobacco prices prompted his master to sell him to the Richmond owners of a harness and saddle factory. Flourishing in his trade as a saddler, Teage learned to read in the city and became a charter member of the interracial Providence Baptist Church. Hiring out also expanded the horizons of Lott Cary, who moved from skilled labor at a nearby plantation to a tobacco factory in Richmond. His co-workers at the tobacco warehouse taught him to read, and with literacy he became the head of the factory. Cary's employer rewarded his excellent service with five-dollar bonuses and allowed him to sell small packets of waste tobacco on his own.

Soon Cary became supervisor of Richmond's largest tobacco factory. After the death of his wife, he purchased himself and his two children for $850, a sum raised in part through a subscription to which his employer contributed. Meanwhile Teage had become head of the saddlery, and within ten years had saved the $1,300 necessary to buy his freedom and that of his family. Like Teage, Cary joined the Baptist Church, which soon licensed them both to preach to the blacks in Richmond and surrounding plantations. When the opportunity to go to Liberia presented itself in 1821, Teage and Cary left with their families.[48]

Since these hiring-out practices brought slaves into the money economy, they were often proscribed by law, but to little effect. Left the property of his master's unborn child, William Hayden was hired out annually until he had saved the sum to buy his freedom.[49] Moses Grandy earned enough money cutting canals on hire to purchase both his and his family's freedom.[50] Even more enterprising was Free Frank McWorter whose master took him from South Carolina to Kentucky, where he hired him out as a farm worker and jack-of-all trades. From being hired out to hiring out oneself and contracting on one's own for a fixed share of earnings was but a small step conceptually, but a large one in practice. In Free Frank's case it led to independence and a frontier career as a saltpeter miner, stock raiser, land speculator, and founder of New Philadelphia, Illinois.[51] Austin Steward, taken from Virginia to New York, won his freedom twelve years earlier than the law allowed because his owner hired him out in defiance of the New York judicial decision that interpreted the hiring out of slaves as a fraudulent evasion of New York's emancipation law.[52] Still more slaves got their freedom when their masters, like Virginians John Rankin, Edward Coles, Thomas Worthington, and dozens of North Carolina Quakers, moved to the Northwest Territory, sometimes to liberate their slaves.

Actual and threatened sales punctuated the life story of Charles Ball, which began in Maryland when his master's death led to the sale of his mother. Eventually Ball was sent to the cotton fields of Georgia and South Carolina and thereafter sold repeatedly, almost always because of the death of an owner. His entrepreneurial skills manifested themselves when one of his masters asked Ball, who had grown up fishing the Potomac, to erect a seine fishery on his river plantation. With skill and duplicity, Ball was able to bring in enough fish to enter into trade with the provision boats plying the river. Southern law criminalized such activities, but he had no difficulty making a deal with the shipmaster. Ball acquired a knowledge of commercial life from this venture that later helped him survive as a free man after he effected his escape.[53]

The boom periods that came with each opening of western lands quickly sorted out the winners and the losers in the South. After the riches in land and slaves became concentrated in the hands of a few successful competitors, the losers often moved onto the next frontier or went into the many mountainous regions of the Appalachians. There poor white families formed a distinct way of life. In the back country of the South—among the hills of North Carolina, Virginia, and Alabama—existed the nation's largest group of subsistence farmers. Blessed with a mild climate and plenty of forage, families lived off their livestock, cut off from the buzz of commercial development. Left alone these Southerner graziers—many of them descendents of the Scots-Irish—existed seemingly out of time. In the nation, though not in the market, they sustained their independent way of life until the Civil War, when the Confederacy's need for soldiers and food supplies spelled an end to their isolation.[54]

The panic of 1819 hit South Carolina particularly hard. Prices fell sharply for Sea Island cotton, and New Orleans overtook Charleston as the leading exporter of short-staple cotton. Merchants, cotton factors, and lawyers began to promote agricultural improvement. John A. Legaré founded the first journal south of Baltimore devoted to farming. *The Southern Agriculturist* lasted eighteen years, during which time Legaré toured plantations to drum up support for crop diversification and agricultural experimentation. In his travels, he discovered plantations where slaves carried corn in their arms from fields while horses and wagons stood idle. He talked to planters who opened more land than they could ever cultivate and heard them swear that Negroes could not be taught to work a plow.[55] He saw slaves breaking land with hoes instead of plows, and he came to see that masters took great pleasure in having extra slaves on hand for fishing and hunting excursions. The hold of habit and the near-universal ignorance of elementary science among planters astonished Legaré, but little came of his efforts, because demand for cotton returned with its reassuring promise of profits, despite inefficient labor practices.

***

AMERICA'S FIRST millionaires came from the trailblazers of new trades, like the voyages to India that made the fortunes of Eli Derby and John Norris.

A few years after the *Columbia* docked in Boston harbor following its completion of an around-the-world voyage, the schooner *Rajah* returned with the first cargo of pepper brought directly to the United States. Garnering a 700 percent return, the *Rajah's* voyage increased considerably the numbers in the Sumatra trade.[56] Soon merchant capital and merchant expertise moved aggressively into the high-risk, lucrative business of being the neutral carriers for European belligerents during the intermittent warfare that ended with Napoleon's defeat in 1815.

Equally enterprising were the Yankee shipmasters who scorned the laws of Spain to trade with the Alta Californios who grew grain and grazed cattle in the coastal valleys of the golden state. Isolated from Mexico (it took seven months for them to receive news of Spain's overthrow in 1821), the Californios welcomed the ships that brought them cloth, shoes, tools,

Salem, Massachusetts was a major shipbuilding center and site for the first American trade forays into the Orient. This certificate of the Salem Marine Society reflects that city's pride in their shipping prowess. Courtesy, American Antiquarian Society.

and spices in return for the otter pelts in high demand in China. The Bostonos who first appeared in 1796 quickly routinized their stopovers in California on their voyages to Asia, bringing back porcelain and silks for the ranching families. Soon they organized their own otter-hunting parties along the coast in sea-rigged canoes and developed a secondary trade in California hides for New England shoemakers. Although impressed by the beauty and fertility of California, one New England sea captain, William Shaler, reported the absence of either a physician or a flour mill, noting that "California wants nothing but a good government to rise to wealth and importance."[57]

The principal citizens of American cities were merchants or lawyers—the former to make the money, the latter to adjudicate the suits that money provoked. Unlike colonial seaports, which had depended upon the Atlantic either as a source of fish or as an avenue to the Caribbean and Europe, cities of the new United States would grow wealthy in the nineteenth century by capturing the trade of an expanding hinterland. Philadelphia, New York, and the upstart city of Baltimore all drew on the ever-expanding production of their own catch basin of farmlands to sustain their growth. In 1790 only 202,000 people out of a population close to 4 million lived in towns of more than 2,500; by 1825 that number had risen to 1 million in a population of 11,252,000.[58] With growth rates of over 50 percent per decade, America's cities sparkled with new building, making investments in real estate extremely appealing.[59] New York's population soon outstripped all other cities, with Philadelphia, Boston, Charleston, Baltimore, and New Orleans among the top six. The parallel growth of America's rural areas meant that not until 1840 did the proportion of those living in towns over 2,500 exceed the level in 1690!

While much of the wealth of the seaport merchants went into urban real estate, by the 1820s even America's most conservative investors recognized the attractiveness of western lands and internal improvements.[60] Many other holders of urban wealth needed the help of an expert to make their choices. The time was ripe for the development of investment trusts to sweep up the savings of the wealthy, not to mention the urban middle class of clerks and professional men. Nathaniel Bowditch, Boston's polymath scientist, merchant, and mathematician, initiated the first extensive trust business at the Massachusetts Hospital Life Insurance Co. By 1830 there were a variety of companies dealing in fire insurance and annuities as well as simple savings in Philadelphia and New York as well as Boston.[61] In this as in so much else a new age was dawning, for earlier neither the statistical nor the moral underpinnings for such enterprises existed. Where calculating the likelihood of accidents once abraded the sensibilities of those who stoically accepted the hand of God in human affairs, insuring against possible loss increasingly appeared to make good common business sense, insinuating market rationality into popular thinking.

The wealthy of the old colonial seaports tended to be unimaginative investors, but Moses Brown of Providence and the Lowells and Lawrences of Boston proved to be stellar exceptions. One of four brothers of a prominent colonial merchant family, Brown brought the secrets of the famous English cotton manufacturing system to America in the person of Samuel Slater who reproduced Arkwright's cotton-spinning machinery for him. After visiting an English factory, enthusiasm for textiles also spurred on Francis Cabot Lowell, a member of the new generation. Returning to Boston he got some fifty families to join him in forming the Boston Manufacturing Company. Capitalized at $400,000, Lowell's group built the world's first integrated textile factory at Waltham, Massachusetts in 1814.[62]

The Boston Associates went on to establish entirely new towns at Lawrence and Lowell and another factory at Manchester, New Hampshire. While most American textile mills as late as the 1830s hired fewer than twenty hands, the Associates' employee rolls ballooned to four hundred, six hundred, and eight hundred, the lion's share of jobs going to women and children. Advertising throughout the agricultural communities of Northern New England, Boston's pioneering industrialists drew young, unmarried women from their family farms in Vermont and New Hampshire to planned communities of dormitory living, strict discipline, and female conviviality.[63] Their employment policies form a major chapter in the history of women in the United States, for they were the first manufacturers to turn to female labor in the early years of industrialization, taking advantage of women's dexterity in operating the new machinery and the cheapness of their labor. In the traditional rural economy of this region, the wages of children and women had been low—about a quarter of what men were paid, rising to half for factory jobs. Along with textiles, Northerners began manufacturing boots, shoes, hats, paper, and woolens, all industries using female labor.[64] Like cheap water power, low wages underwrote hundreds of new ventures, many of them failures.

The success of the Lowell Associates helped turn Massachusetts into the most thoroughly industrialized section of the United States, second only to Great Britain in the world. Manufacturers in Springfield, Philadelphia, and Providence proved to be equally assiduous in exploiting the domestic market for textiles.[65] Within the first twelve years, the Bostonians' dividends began to exceed the amount of their original pooled investment. Flush with profits, the partners put money into mining, canal companies, and railroads. The first railroad in Massachusetts, built in 1825, ran between Lowell and Boston.[66] Despite the boldness of their production system and their social engineering, these Boston entrepreneurs followed the conservative financial strategies of an elite. They did not maximize profits so much as they secured the growth of their wealth. Achieving their goal of establishing fortunes, individual family members were free to pursue careers in philanthropy, education, and reform.

The truly unexpected development of the early nineteenth century came from the boot-strap manufacturing ventures that proliferated in the rural North, independent of the investment plans of the nation's wealthy.[67] Textile factories and railroads—even cargoes for Atlantic voyages—took a considerable amount of capital to finance, but artisans-turned-manufacturers scraped by with very little start-up capital. Merchants of the seaport cities, many of them members of prominent colonial families, sought safe investments in real estate, but mechanics, tradesmen, and farmers with little or no capital turned their brains and hands to making something new.

In Newark, Moses Combs, a master shoemaker and tanner, got local farmers to make shoes during their winter fallow seasons. A natural merchandiser, Combs introduced Newark shoes to both the New York City and Southern markets in the 1790s. Thirty years later, one-seventh of the Newark labor force devoted itself to shoemaking at a time when applications of steam-driven machinery were still two decades away. The substantial productivity growth of the early nineteenth century came largely, experts say, from changes "in organizations, methods, and designs which did not require much in the way of capital deepening or dramatically new capital equipment."[68]

Shoemaking was an interesting example of an ancient craft transformed under the expansion of national marketing. The memoirs of Arial Bragg encompass the changes in the industry from 1790 to 1820. Struggling to buy out an onerous apprenticeship in rural Massachusetts, Bragg learned that a shoemaker in Brookline was looking for help. He succeeded in getting hired to make boots, though he confided in his memoirs that he had never before heard of the novel practice of one shoemaker hiring another, adding that there was not "a Shoe Store in the town of Boston at that time." With unremitting application, Bragg tells his readers, he cleared seven dollars a month and paid off his indenture. At that juncture, he considered continuing as a journeyman, but decided that working "for the market [was] far better than journey work."

Falling in with "a speculator in leather," Bragg decided to make calf shoes for the Providence market, taking ten dollars in savings to buy $2.50 worth of tools and getting forty pounds of sole leather on credit. When this venture returned him eighty dollars, he spent forty dollars for new clothes and the remainder for "a first rate silver watch." To "work for the market" meant that Bragg had to peddle his own stock, a difficulty that made very attractive orders from the South to make "negro shoes." As he recounted it, he "went to work for the slaves of the South; little regard being paid to the quality either of stock, or work." Hiring accomplished shoemakers for eighty to ninety dollars a year, Bragg leased a house and hired his mother to cook for his employees.

Only in the first decade of the century did shoe stores appear, cutting the link between shoemaker and shoe-wearer. Shoemaking itself advanced when right and left shoes were introduced for the first time. In the ensuing years, Bragg worked for others, hired cordwainers, went into retailing, bought land parcels, and then settled down to making shoes again, adding one employee a year until 1809. Bragg's autobiography also reveals the underside of enterprise, recounting dead times, bankrupt customers, family deaths, and exhausted resources. Whatever battering he took, there was no place for Bragg to turn except the market, with its episodic reward for effort.[69]

Two factors democratized opportunity in manufacturing in the first decades of the nineteenth century. The men with the most money in America—those who might have been able to monopolize winning projects—moved slowly into industrial ventures. Second, the energy for much manufacturing came from creeks and streams, tying production to rural millsites that were readily accessible to farmers and their sons. Zachariah Allen, a well-connected Providence inventor, fashioned a little homily from the location of American mills: steam aggregates workers and promotes vice while water power disperses them with benefit to their morals.[70] The sudden appearance of factories even found expression in jest. Olive Cleaveland Clarke remembered that a tour of a new theological seminary prompted her brother to remark that here they "would manufacture ministers."[71]

Independence brought the industrial competition that the British had long feared. Scottish merchant John Melish concluded after several tours of the country that Britain would no longer be the manufacturer for America, because "the seeds of manufacture, are sown throughout the country, never to be rooted out, and, so far from the *interior* being dependent upon the *cities* as heretofor, the cities will, in all probability, become dependent on it."[72] American inventiveness ran through a gamut of goods. William Austin Burt, a Massachusetts farm boy and self-taught mathematician, invented the typewriter and a solar compass. Benjamin Thompson published plans for a drip coffeemaker. Abel Porter brought prosperity to his hometown of Waterbury, Connecticut when he set up a rolling mill to produce millions of buttons from gilt and brass to bone, ivory, and prunella buttons for women's clothes and lawyers' gowns.[73] The kaleidoscope, invented by an Englishman, was fabricated in such rude style and great quantities in the United States that it became a plaything for children.[74]

Peter Cooper was a veritable invention machine. Apprenticed to a coachmaker in Manhattan in 1807, his grandmother gave him the use of an outbuilding for his tinkering so he'd stay at home at night. There in her garage he invented a machine for mortising the hubs of carriages. After going to work for a shearer, he redesigned the shears, selling them as fast as he could produce them. He went on to manufacture glue, glass, and chalk and design locomotives. In his autobiography, Cooper described how his stint as a young father, taking care of their baby while his wife fixed dinner, led to his inventing a mechanism to rock the cradle, keep off the flies, and make music. As his editor astutely commented, "Mr. Cooper's mind is not one of great invention, but a mind of great contrivance." Americans liked contrivances, as the brisk sale of Cooper's patents and licenses confirmed.

Amasa Goodyear worked with his father making military buttons, spoons, and scythes along with the spring steel manure forks of his father's invention, "universally considered . . . one of the greatest improvements ever made in farming implements," according to Goodyear. Although he and his father successfully competed with English hardware imports, Goodyear's attention was riveted to the challenge of hardening gum-elastic, a quest that took him through a decade of failed experiments, bankruptcies, and imprisonment for debt before he perfected the vulcanization of rubber.[75]

Conditions in the United States were more favorable to artisan-capitalists like Cooper and Goodyear than in either England or France. Where Britain more carefully divided labor tasks to improve productivity, Americans looked to machines. Since many industrial ventures required little capital, young men like Cooper could easily act on their production schemes. As Ariel Bragg's story demonstrated, a man could secure start-up funds with a bit of pluck, a skill like shoemaking, and an honest face. With the increased mobility of men and women and the enhanced circulation of printed material, what economists call "information costs" fell precipitously, and the remarkable lack of secrecy in the United States led to continuous improvements in tools, materials, and processes.[76] Rarely was there a division between ownership and control, and individual proprietors and small partnerships ran most workshops, despite the availability of the corporate structure.[77]

The transformation of artisanal masters into managerial employers did not check the resentment from those left to do the manual labor. Cordwainers were among the first American workers to organize. In 1805–1806 the national cordwainer strike led to indictment for criminal conspiracy, and employers in Lynn, Massachusetts, the center of shoemaking in New England, came out stronger. Cordwainers brought under the benign control of Moses Combs in Newark formed a union in 1830 that kept wages high. With higher production costs, Newark lost the southern market to the more competitive Lynn. The size of Newark's industry was confined thereafter, but Newark cordwainers continued to flourish because their fine craft work met the demands of the luxury market across the Hudson.[78]

Holmes Hinkley, another poor New England boy who made good, this time as a producer of steam locomotives, left one of the few accounts of a labor dispute. In his autobiography Hinkley described how he had yielded to his workers' demands for higher wages while filling a rush order, only to fire the "ring-leaders" after the job had been completed, a reminder of the power of the common law tradition of "at will" employment.[79] Josiah Warren, who founded philosophical anarchism in the United States, opened an "equity" store in Cincinnati to prove his theory of exchanging labor for labor. Selling goods at cost, it closed in two years.

Contemporaries looked on factory work as benign when compared to the farming life. Chauncey Jerome, one of the trailblazers of the clock industry, painted a particularly grim picture of what life held for him after his blacksmith father died in 1804: "There being no manufacturing of any account in the country, the poor boys were obliged to let themselves to the farmers, and it was extremely difficult to find a place to live where they would treat a poor boy like a human being." John Thompson echoed Jerome's lament when he explained that he "did not want to work for the farmers thereabouts, for they worked late and early and their work was too hard for me." James Riley recalled that the farmers he worked for were loath to release him for schooling despite his apprenticeship agreement.

Part of Eli Terry's revolution in clockmaking, Jerome chronicled the redesigning, downsizing, and introduction of brass parts that turned Connecticut's Litchfield County into the clockmaking center of the world.[80] Landing a job making dials for clocks, Jerome discovered a vocational passion, unabated by his guardian's caution that "there was so many clocks then making, that the country would soon be filled with them." By 1816, he had his own shop and was shipping clocks to South Carolina.[81] When others of Terry's former workers set themselves up in business nearby, they provided the inventive stimulus and competition to drive the price of clocks down to five dollars, creating at the same time the problem of marketing this great volume of clocks. Jerome got the idea of selling his clocks in Great Britain at a time when British customs officials were enjoined to confiscate any imports suspected of being priced under their cost of production. The world's great dumpers, the British were not going to allow anyone else to dump on them. It took three shipments before Jerome convinced British officials that his prices actually reflected his production costs.

Living in an era when jacks-of-all-trades flourished, these early entrepreneurs showed a surprising willingness to venture outside the realm of their experience. Leaving behind the hallowed work patterns of farming, a surprising number of them shifted from trading or retailing to manufacturing, only to be forced back to commerce by business failures in the highly volatile second decade of the century. The steam engine designer-producer Holmes Hinkley plied his carpentry trade for years before going to work in a machine shop. When that shop failed and he was forced to accept back wages in tools, he set himself up as a machinist. His partner, however, "got sick of life, and hanged himself."[82] Bad luck had its own discouraging pattern, for profitable trades drew competitors like flies to honey, and good times were inevitably punctuated by bad ones.

The statistics that measured the dynamic pace of change in the American economy veil the human disappointments. Mechanics' memoirs are filled with stories of bankruptcies, fires, defaulting partners, and currency crises.[83] Failure in many cases was only temporary, however, and the low entry cost of both retailing and manufacturing enabled many of those who went bankrupt to rebound. Working alongside those responsive to the imperatives of the market were men and women averse to taking risks and critical of an economic environment that seemed only to reward those lured by dreams of riches to risk family security.

The ebullience of the economy owed much to the overwhelming novelty of so many consumer goods. Comparisons of the inventories of estates in rural Kent County, Delaware between 1772 and 1840 reveal the tremendous range of domestic amenities that had been added to the humblest households. Under the rubric of ceramics, an inventory for a median household listed "vegetable dishes, a cream pourer, sugar dish, cups and saucers, pitchers, glass tumblers, wineglasses, decanters, a punch bowl, pickle dishes, mugs and dining plates," almost all of them made within a fifty-mile radius.[84] With unabashed patriotism, Charles Ingersoll, a gentlemanly man of letters, exulted that where "American ingenuity has been put to trial it has never failed."[85] Ingersoll captured the essence of American invention when he linked it to American consumers: "In all the useful arts, and in the philosophy of comfort,— that word, which cannot be translated into any other language, and which, though of English origins, was reserved for maturity in America, we have no superiors." Going on to explain that liberty and the American disposition to learn led to the "superior aptitude, versatility and quickness" of the country's mechanics, artisans, and laborers, Ingersoll contrasted mechanics in Europe, who were "apt to consider it almost irreverent, and altogether vain to suppose that any thing can be done better than as he was taught to do it by his father or master," with American mechanics, who were sure that anything could be improved upon.[86]

Nowhere were changes more needed than in retailing, which developed swiftly after 1815. Despite his innovations that revolutionized the manufacturing of clocks, Eli Terry would regularly lash two or three tall grandfather clocks to his horse and set out for nearby villages, looking for customers. The principal retailers of the 1790s were peddlers. Some, like Ariel Bragg with his shoes and Terry with his clocks, peddled the goods they had made. More common were the Yankee peddlers who circled through the mid-Atlantic and Southern states carrying an assortment of items to sell. Bronson Alcott noted that the peddlers generally constituted most of the passengers on the many coastal vessels plying the waters between New Haven and Norfolk.[87] Nor did their influence end with sales. From regular sweeps of the country by individual traders sprang up new industries like the brassworks of Rhode Island, which depended on peddlers to bring back the scrap copper used for brass buttons.

More aggressively entrepreneurial in his peddling, Thomas Douglas worked New England states and New York in the summer and New Jersey, Pennsylvania, and Virginia in winters. His first stock of $500 yielded $1,200 in sales, from which he bought $1,000 worth of goods to carry out West. In Cincinnati in 1813 he found a city "peopled by a liberal, industrious, enterprising population, who, instead of adhering to the ignoble practice—for I can not call it policy—of 'Dog *eat* dog,' seemed to take pleasure in assisting and pushing forward every enterprising, industrious young man who came amongst them."[88] Asa Sheldon, freed from his indenture by the death of his father when he was fifteen, regularly carried hops, shoes, wheat, and flour to southern markets with returns in cotton to Baltimore, Philadelphia, New York, and Boston, after gaining a financial toehold in a part interest in a mill. This trade flourished during the War of 1812, but peace destroyed the protected market peddlers had enjoyed.[89] Northern and Southern itinerant traders formed a vital link between a decentralized production system and consuming households in a still rural America. Novelties themselves—people in their twenties escaping the farm life—peddlers provided the retailing innovations necessary to distribute the proliferating goods coming from artisan-entrepreneurs and emerging factories.[90]

The pioneer retailers of Philadelphia, almost all born on farms, were immortalized in *Biographies of Successful Philadelphia Merchants,* which reads like a history of the retailing business: John Grigg first opened a store for medical and educational books, greatly aided by the "rapid extension of the public school system"; David Jayne stopped practicing medicine to open Philadelphia's first drugstore; Thomas Sparks began life as a plumber—i.e., one who worked in lead—and exploited the possibilities in retailing "plates, waiters, mugs, flagons."[91] What these lives chronicle is the swiftness with which manufacturing passed from an artisanal phase to a commercial one. By the first decade of the century there were enough stores to cut the direct link between producer and consumer, leaving the producers as wholesalers. That many a large order came to artisans from the South only indicates how the concentration of resources in the cotton fields promoted specialization elsewhere.

During the first three decades of the nineteenth century, merchants and shopkeepers scoured the urban hinterlands for food, fibers, and skins that could be sold to manufacturers for processing, then turned around, and offered for sale the textiles, tools, printed works, and household goods that issued from the new factories. In the city directory of Utica, New York in

1817, for instance, 17 percent of the people listed claimed the occupation of merchant.[92] The thousands of linkages that made up America's internal market—the largest in the world—were put together by these individual traders, carrying goods on their backs like the Yankee peddlers or driving teams of horses down South, as Sheldon had done, loaded "with hops, shoes, wheat, dried beef, and flour."

In the city, retailers were moving towards special lines of goods like drugs or medical books, but frontier merchants developed general stores that provided a variety of critical functions to pioneer families. They took country produce in payment of store purchases, acted as bankers, extended credit, made loans, and served as brokers in financial transactions. At the same time they took on the processing of farm produce, turning hogs into pork, cattle into beef, and wheat into flour.[93] Americans spent just about the same amount for food in 1825 as they had in 1775, but they succeeded in registering their demand for greater variety and purchases in small amounts at their country stores.[94]

IN THE OPENING decades of the nineteenth century the country was awash with individual ventures like Deborah Power Ball's linoleum factory and Arial Bragg's shoemaking shop. Indeed, the United States had far more plans for personal enterprise than savings to finance them. Families eager for a farm on the frontier lacked the down payment; artisans with the know-how to go out on their own needed start-up funds. Communities had blueprints for draining swamps, improving roads, and cutting canals, but no capital to put their plans into operation. America's wealthy tended to sink their money into overseas trade and real estate; foreign investors preferred government bonds; modest savers most likely lent to relatives. Almost everyone wanted credit, from the humblest householder trenching on the grocer's faith to the many associations of land speculators staking out future metropolises.

State legislators, open to voter pressure and eager to give their constituents competitive advantages, fell in line with the demands for more credit and approved new bank charters with amazing swiftness. There were three banks in the United States in 1790, twenty-eight in 1800, 102 in 1810, and 327 in 1820. In Rhode Island the number of banks increased from one for every 3,357 people in 1810 to one for every 1,681 a decade later. Each city's second group of bank organizers represented younger lawyers, aspiring clerks, small manufacturers, and lesser merchants who formed banks to create capital rather than conserve it. Control of banks enabled them to tap into the savings of the community.[95] When Thomas, the New England bookseller in Charleston, was denied full credit from a local bank, he succeeded in getting a charter for the Planters and Mechanics Bank, gloating many years later about his capacity to get even.[96] A group of Philadelphia merchants who felt that they had been treated unfairly by existing banks started a new institution specifically directed to men of smaller means, pricing their shares at one hundred dollars, considerably below the norm of four hundred dollars. Sometimes only half of the cost of shares was demanded. In New Hampshire, opening up the Federalists' banking preserve became the Jeffersonians' principal campaign issue. With the uniting of small pools of capital in new banks, the Jeffersonians argued, "the industrious citizens might share with the more wealthy in the benefits" of banking.[97]

Far from being the rich man's preserve, banking offered hundreds of local savers an investment possibility. Stalwarts of the old order like Boston's Nathan Appleton and New York's Isaac Bronson decried the leveling tendency in easy money policies, but ordinary people resoundingly approved.[98] Soon legislators were yielding to popular pressure for corporations for surfacing roads, building canals, and starting insurance companies. Some states passed general incorporation acts. Even in those states that did not, entry into the banking business got easier and easier in the years before 1819. Bitterly opposed initially, the already-established discovered, to their chagrin, that no amount of banking wisdom could stay the hand of the legislators, who had the power to grant new charters. New Hampshire, a small state undistinguished for wealth in any category, had ten banks in six different towns by 1813, four of them in Portsmouth, a town of less than six thousand.[99] Competition, although only grudgingly accepted by bankers themselves, greatly facilitated the expansion of business in the first decades of the nineteenth century. New banks also had the means of compelling cooperation. If a bank refused to receive their notes, they could call for specie payment for the other bank's notes that passed through normal business transactions into their possession.[100]

During buoyant periods when bank notes gave market participants the wherewithal to put in effect their plans, the extra notes were a kind of borrowing against the future, the deployment of faith in lieu of savings. As long as people had high hopes, they accepted bank notes gladly, but any contraction of credit exposed the fragility of the system. Cautious creditors could call in their debts or demand specie payment for the notes they held. American banking practices encouraged inflation, and inflation primed the pump of economic activity, arousing conservatives' fears on both counts. In personal reminiscences banks figure as the principal source for currency—welcome, unregulated, and amazingly good at flooding the nation with notes.

Since bank notes were often presented for payment far from the point of issuance, shopkeepers had no way to determine their value. Eager to make a sale, they usually erred on the side of liberality. The slightest hint of value sufficed for circulation. Ichabod Washburn described the trepidation he felt passing his master's "uncurrent five dollar Ohio Bank Bill" during a trip home through central Massachusetts. Washburn was astonished when a tavern keeper accepted the bill and gave him $4.50 change. He carefully avoided the man on the return trip.[101] John Neal, reminiscing from the safe shores of old age about his work in a haberdashery shop, described learning how to "lie-cheat-swear-and pass counterfeit money-if occasionally required." Indeed, he recalled that he and his fellow merchants would never turn down a sale because payment was offered in counterfeit bills. Estimating that 10 percent of the bills circulating during his business career in the first decade of the nineteenth century were worthless, Neal conveyed to a more law-abiding age the merchant's settled maxim: "if you buy the devil, the sooner you sell him, the better."[102]

In an 1824 piece Neal ironically characterized the United States as a country "where that, which was counterfeit, and that, which was not, were exceedingly alike, not only in appearance, but in value."[103] William Stuart, whose autobiography claims him as "the first and most celebrated counterfeiter of Connecticut," revealed a different form of Yankee ingenuity when he described how he fobbed off ten-dollar bills drawn on Philadelphia and Albany banks counterfeited in Canada.[104] The trick was to cash the bills for a small item and then use the change as an alternative payment should anyone protest a counterfeit bill. It is hard not to conclude that the voracious appetite for money to buy and to sell meant that bad notes augmented the nation's wealth.

Despite the abandonment of sound banking principles, bank issues were stable from 1790 to 1810, not becoming seriously deranged until the War of 1812, when the government, without its own bank, had to scramble for funds and paid exorbitant interest rates.[105] This experience prompted President Madison to seek a charter for a second Bank of the United States in 1816, but the era of state banks and private banking corporations had already fully established itself, and the second B.U.S. ended as ingloriously as the first had twenty years earlier.[106]

No one understood these processes very well, so it was easy to make banking a scapegoat, which indeed is what happened in the panic of 1819 when banks in Pennsylvania, Virginia, and South Carolina suspended specie payments altogether. John Bailhache described a classic case of retrenchment. He was a principal stockholder of a new bank in Chillicothe when the Second Bank of the United States called in their bank's notes. "We made urgent calls upon our debtors to help us," he explained, but, "as every thing went down in a crash, our calls were generally disregarded." One failure followed another until his various endorsements far exceeded his available resources. "I did not," he recalled, "like many others thus circumstanced, try to cover up my property; but stood at my post, determined to fall honorably, and labored night and day to extricate myself, in which I was nobly aided by my wife," adding poignantly that it took "ten or twelve of the best years of my life to retrieve this false step."[107]

Most businessmen operated with small savings sweated from their own labor and larger borrowings, usually from friends or relatives. A punishing process of adaptation lay behind the dynamic economic development of this period. Commercial growth was rapid, unregulated, and marked by sudden reversals of good times and bad. Neither farmers, clerks, professional men, nor manufacturers escaped these unexpected downturns. Debt acted as a mighty leveler in this ebullient society, and it figured in almost every autobiography. Anson Jones had to declare bankruptcy when he was sued for his board as a medical student.[108] Samuel Foot went to prison for his brother's gambling debts.[109] Workers lost back wages when their employers went broke. James Finley lost his frontier farm "by going security, or appearance-bail" for one of his neighbors. Because the court was forty miles away in Chillicothe, he did not go to lift his bonds, so when his neighbor decamped after a judgment went against him, Finley had to pay the debt.

Enjoying a measure of prosperity as a lawyer, John Chambers invested in the hemp business, which failed and plunged him into debt. His remembrance of the event conveys well the stoicism expressed about such reverses. "I kept my business to myself," he wrote, "and maintained my credit until I struggled pretty well through my indebtedness living economically and wasting nothing."[110] Most entrepreneurs failed at least once in their careers, and all were exposed to the consequences of the bankruptcy of their bosses or associates. Lucy Reynolds, a schoolteacher from Oneida, New York lost over one hundred dollars in the Farmer's Cotton and Woollen Factory. She reported being astounded that it could just go broke, "but after a little reflection, I was enabled to look on 'the bright side of things.'"[111]

The capacity of industrial capitalism to concentrate economic power and forge a new elite could not be foreseen. Americans, especially in the North, viewed commercial expansion as the moral and material handmaiden to their liberal society. For many years after the Revolution, whatever class antagonisms existed pointed back to the residual traces of conflicts about privilege. Conservatives then were not proto-industrialists, but defenders of obsolete cultural traditions. Competition, far from being associated with grinding the face of the poor, stirred up hopes of advancement in ordinary men and women, who vigorously rejected the aristocratic notion of natural inequality.[112] Such a conviction was reinforced by men like John Jacob Astor, who introduced profit-sharing to his men, relying in his struggle with the French for control of Hudson's Bay trade upon the entrepreneurial initiatives of his employees.

With economic pursuits that had previously been regulated now open to all comers, the economy could be construed as voluntary, free, even natural. The facts seemed to confirm the most potent ideological legacy of this era: the idea of a natural harmony of interests mediated by natural economic laws. Of course the national market required a legal framework, but memories of the contribution of the Constitution and John Marshall's decisions receded quickly from public consciousness in ensuing decades, making it easy to think of economic activities as operating without government help. The less heard from conservatives about public order and preserving continuity, the less conspicuous became society's role in facilitating economic development, even though the federal government continued to sell land at administered prices and to protect interstate commerce while states conferred licenses, franchises, and bounties on speculative development, sometimes with democratic abandon. In both cases, public authority appeared merely the handmaiden of private enterprise, helping along a natural process.

Retrospectively we can see that capitalist growth led to the creative destruction, to use Joseph Schumpeter's term, of stable ways of life. The elaboration of a national market depended upon many, many young men leaving the place of their birth and trying their hands at new careers. The range and sweep of their entrepreneurial talents, defined best as the ability to take on novel economic undertakings as personal ventures, suggests the widespread willingness to be uprooted, to embark on an uncharted course of action, to take risks with one's resources—above all the resource of one's youth. Those who did so turned themselves into agents of change. Both in personal terms for the young men seeking early adult independence and in the political terms of the Jeffersonian-Federalist debate, the freedom to innovate, to aspire, to seek a range of individual satisfactions in the market acquired a good reputation. To fail to mark this feature of the early republic is to obscure a very important element in American history: the creation of a popular, entrepreneurial culture that permeated all aspects of American society. Commerce appeared not as a divisive force to ordinary Americans in the early decades of the nineteenth century, but rather as the carrier of progress for an energetic, disciplined, self-reliant people.

As John Adams observed to Josiah Quincy, "there is no people on earth so ambitious as the people of America. The reason is," he went on to explain, "because the lowest can aspire as freely as the highest."[113] No quality has so marked the character of American social life as individual aspiration, turning the United States into a magnet for immigrants and a wellspring of hope for the adventurous. If working for others alienates men and women from their handicraft and talents, imagining one's own future path—what came to be called careers in the early nineteenth century—grounded men and women in their own fantasies. Personal planning weakened the ties to community, but opened up the possibility of affinities based on moral and intellectual commitments. An ideology that linked economic and political freedom also fused the goals of the nation and its citizens. The less Southerners could identify with these convictions the less they shared in the emerging national spirit, which interpreted prosperity as a vindication of American independence.

4

CAREERS

Mores and institutions had worked in tandem to limit young people's choices in the colonial era. Ministers could not preach without a license; only the largest cities had newspapers. There were no bankers as such; credit flowed from foreign to American merchants, or might be secured from relatives. Parents, magistrates, and the crown controlled access to land, which meant that they held the keys to the most critical resource for work and independence in an agrarian society. Occupations other than farming had been few. Storekeepers appeared in good-sized towns along with a physician, one or two lawyers, a few schoolteachers, and a cluster of artisans making shoes and barrels, working up silver, or turning out furniture. Millers, brewers, and wrights of various sorts served rural communities; surveyors flourished, but usually as a part-time calling engaged in by the likes of George Washington. No one made a living as a politician or a writer; few as artists; engineers hardly existed; teachers were scarce; seafaring was confined to the Atlantic; and manufacturing, often proscribed by imperial regulations, barely figured in the colonial economy.

All this changed rapidly after the Constitution created "a more perfect union." The proliferation of new towns formed after 1789 involved a simultaneous replication of community services—stores, post offices, printing establishments, newspapers, lawyers, doctors, and local office-holders. At the same time, the enlargement of trade promoted jobs in clerking that required minimal literacy. Filled with a zeal for uniting disparate regions into one country, Congressional nation-builders created a first-class postal system, giving subsidies to newspaper publishers to mail their printed products throughout the states.[1] While the population doubled between 1800 and 1820, the number of miles of post roads grew twenty-one-fold from 1,875 to 44,000, with post offices increasing thirtyfold from 75 to 2,300. The sharing of newspapers from town to town stimulated the public's taste for the latest news and simultaneously created a new information network coterminous with the nation itself.

News did more than satisfy curiosity; it delivered food for thought and items for conversation. It provided the stuff of an urban sociability for a people who still lived in the country. Even on the frontier, most farmers were eager to produce for the market and demanded the public roads and canals that would connect them to it. They also supported the ancillary trades of wholesaling, processing, and retailing that made their crops profitable. The opening of fertile land in Kentucky, Tennessee, Ohio, Alabama, and the western parts of the old states guaranteed that the number of farmers would grow, but their predominance slowly declined, as more and more people sought urban occupations.

The same public goals that moved congressmen to favor the post office were at play in promoting literacy. Citizens needed to be informed; commerce conducted over long distances required proficient readers, writers, and calculators. Where earlier literacy had been advanced for religious and commercial reasons, reading now was thought to bring immediate fulfillment and prospective benefits.[2] In a mutually stimulating fashion, patriotism, religion, recreation, and trade promoted the popularity of newspapers, printed sermons, organizational tracts, and specialized journals that entertained and edified. These publishing ventures created jobs that had never existed in great numbers before. New avenues of employment multiplied in writing, publishing, journalism, schoolteaching, law, politics, medicine, civil engineering, painting, and preaching. Following the careers of those in the first generation is to watch the sprawling American middle class materialize, summoned into existence by political independence, thickening trade connections, and religious revivals, all tied together by print. With these men and women, America's liberal society found its architects and champions, their careers giving substance to the hope that free choice, free trade, and free speech could flourish within a self-regulating social order.

Publishing in the United States was booming, stimulated in part by the responsiveness of enterprising booksellers who were laying trading networks across the countryside.[3] Their initiatives amplified the imaginative reach of ordinary consumers, who were acting without reference to authority or majority vote. Becoming more elaborate and dense, the market enhanced the range of choice in the same decades that choice itself became a signifier of American distinctiveness. John Griscom's library club in Burlington, New Jersey, for instance, sought out the "current literature, and progressive science of the day and age," subscribing to half a dozen of the best British periodicals. As Griscom rather pompously put it, "Promiscuous reading (restrained within the bounds of sound morality) although somewhat unfavorable to the acquisition of thorough or profound knowledge, has the advantage of diversifying the talent, improving the taste, and preparing the individual for more enlarged usefulness and influence in society." Reading had become a necessity of life; it had also become the principal activity of nation-building.[4]

James Fenimore Cooper might have been the first novelist to make a living from his pen, but among his contemporaries were dozens of others who ministered to the reading appetites of their generation by translating, editing, copying, or dashing off pieces for newspapers, journals, compendiums of useful knowledge, and volumes devoted to "eminent" poets, statesmen, and scientists. Most of these writers came from New England, and their work subtly deepened and broadened the influence of the old Puritan mindset.

Timothy Flint is a case in point. Constantly embroiled in controversies with his congregation in Lunenburg, Massachusetts, Flint held Federalist views that grated on their Jeffersonian sympathies (it was a back-country town). His chemical experiments opened him to charges of counterfeiting, so Flint went west for the Presbyterian Missionary Society of Connecticut. After a couple of years he broke with the Society, becoming a solitary missionary, reliant on a wealthy kinsman to keep the wolf from the door. Defending the West against the fulminations of Yale University President Timothy Dwight, Flint created enough of a stir—and a readership—with his *Recollections of Last Ten Years,* that he was soon editing the *Western Monthly*

Review, a very ambitious journal of opinion. Simultaneously, he published four novels, two works on western history, a descriptive geography, a biography of Daniel Boone, and his *Lectures upon Natural History, Geology, Chemistry, the Application of Steam, and Interesting Discoveries in the Arts.* Mrs. Trollope, the formidable English travel writer, found Flint her most agreeable acquaintance in Cincinnati. "One of the most talented men I ever met," she wrote, adding that "he is the only person I remember to have known with first-rate powers of satire, and even sarcasm, whose kindness of nature and of manner remained perfectly uninjured."[5]

The lure of making money from writing formed the plot for Flint's novel, *Arthur Clenning,* which revolved around a literary entrepreneur's search for Captain James Riley in order to do a sequel to his *Authentic Narrative of the Loss of the American Brig Commerce.*[6] Riley's *Authentic Narrative* had been a publishing phenomenon, selling close to a million copies in six editions. Forced into slavery by North Africa merchants who bought him and his mates after their shipwreck, Riley, an authentic hero, learned Arabic so he could negotiate with his captors. The story of his fifteen-month ordeal mirrored for the first generation the courage and savviness they longed to see in themselves, just as his success in getting his memoirs into print reflected their material ambitions.[7]

A New Englander like Flint, John Neal also turned a talent for writing into cash. Supported through an impecunious childhood by his widowed mother, Neal failed as both a wholesale dry goods dealer and a storekeeper in Boston and Baltimore before he took up law, paying for his education with the profits from the five novels he dashed off in three years. Dubbed O'Cataract for his prodigious output, Neal simultaneously helped in the editing of the *Baltimore Telegraph* and *Portico* while preparing an index for Hezekiah Niles' *Weekly Register.*[8]

Like many a fledgling writer in this period, Neal smarted from the querulous question, "Who reads an American Book?" posed by the sardonic Englishman, Sydney Smith.[9] More resolute in defending the literary honor of the United States than most, Neal traveled to England and convinced the editor of *Blackwood's* to publish a series of articles on American arts and letters in which Neal posed as an English critic. Covering over one hundred Americans in alphabetical order, he discoursed wittily about the literary style of the country's founding fathers, providing acerbic commentary on contemporary newspaper editors, clergymen, scientists, painters, historians, "Mrs. President Madison," and himself.[10] Returning to his home in Portsmouth, Neal continued to practice law, fulminate against dueling and intemperance, and publish a steady stream of pamphlets, speeches, and newspapers, including *The Yankee,* which he edited from 1828 to 1829.[11] Considered by many to be America's first aesthetic critic, he irritated a young James Russell Lowell, who penned the lines: "There swaggers John Neal who has wasted in Maine,/ the Sinews and cords of his pugilist brain." But Lowell's sarcasm didn't prevent two Bowdoin students, Nathaniel Hawthorne and Henry Wadsworth Longfellow, from finding much to admire in Neal.[12]

Baltimore acted like a magnet for the talent of the first generation, with a commercial infrastructure for printers, publishers, and booksellers, all of whom doubled in number in the first decade of the nineteenth century.[13] Its best-known citizen was Hezekiah Niles, a self-made publisher and self-taught economist whose *Weekly Register,* known familiarly as *Niles' Register,* was chock full of statistics, opinions, history, biography, and news. Starting with 1,500 subscribers in 1811, *Niles' Register* soon was being sent to 4,000 households all over America, adding a thousand more subscribers each year. Turned into a nationalist by the beating American shippers took at the hands of European belligerents during the protracted warfare of the Napoleonic era, Niles ardently supported protective tariffs for American manufacturers, a position that cost him Southern readers in the 1820s. His career was a testament to his faith in information. He regularly sent out free informational supplements to his subscribers and responded to the more than 4,000 letters subscribers sent him annually. Niles managed to stave off bankruptcy in the difficult years after the War of 1812 by selling ten-dollar lottery tickets for sets of the *Register.* No ordinary journalist, he was honored by having both Michigan and Ohio name towns after him.[14]

Paul Allen, a transplanted New Englander like Neal, carved out an enviable career in Baltimore as newspaperman, poet, author, and co-editor of the Lewis and Clark journals. Thomas Jefferson called Allen "one of the two best writers of America," but Allen had to vie for that honor with Robert Walsh, who distinguished himself as a literary critic and political analyst while launching an impressive stream of journals and newspapers. Also contributing to the literary scene in Baltimore was Henry Marie Brackenridge, who deserves recognition for producing America's first commissioned potboiler, a history of the War of 1812 written in six weeks for an advance of three hundred dollars. Returning to the valleys of the Ohio and Mississippi Rivers that he had visited as a child, Brackenridge wrote a series of newspaper articles that Jefferson urged him to republish. Appearing as *Views of Louisiana,* the book established Brackenridge's reputation as an expert on the West and led to the contract for his *History of the Late War.* "My task was thirty pages of foolscap," he recalled, "which I had ready in the morning with the corrected sheets (sixteen pages octavo) when the printer's devil paid me his visit." The book sold two thousand copies in seven months and garnered Brackenridge a seat in the Maryland legislature, its popularity attributable in part to the hostility he expressed towards the Indian tribes whose cause Brackenridge later warmly endorsed.[15]

While Neal, Niles, Allen, Walsh, and Brackenridge shone as the cynosures of America's writing profession, their careers were typical of the opportunistic mix of occupations—practicing law, teaching, editing, translating—pursued by the several hundred writers flourishing in this period. Robert Sands, abandoning a law career for literature, edited the *Atlantic Magazine,* the *New-York Review* and *New-York Commercial Advertiser* while turning out poems and essays.[16] Richard Dabney, one of a few Southerners to earn his living as a writer, moved to Philadelphia to find work editing and translating. Dabney also laid the foundation for the serious study of Italian literature in the United States, just as the young Unitarian minister Joseph Stevens Buckminster brought German biblical scholarship to America when he spent an inheritance amassing the great texts in that tradition.[17] In addition to those who devoted themselves entirely to literary or journalistic careers were authors like Willard Phillips, who practiced law and dealt in insurance while editing the *New England Galaxy.*

Publishers emerged as important figures in these decades, assuming for the first time the role of intellectual merchandisers. They reprinted popular European titles and sponsored American journals, annals, travel guides, memoirs, gazetteers, histories, and compendiums of various sorts while overseeing the development of extensive bookselling routes.[18] Joseph Delaplaine and Eliakim Littel, following the lead of trailblazing Matthew Carey, extended the range of American publications, connecting the centers of writing, editing, translating, and importing in Baltimore, Philadelphia, New York, and Boston to readers along the Atlantic seaboard, on the frontier, and in the rural South, where publishers were relatively few.[19] Charles Jared Ingersoll estimated that in 1822 there were more than two hundred wagons traveling throughout the country, "loaded with books for sale."[20] It was this enterprise that collapsed the differences between rural and city folk that so amazed foreign travelers.

Relying upon clergymen for religious works and scholars for scientific titles, America's publishers stimulated a lively commerce in intellectual property. Their patrons were members of a reading public with a voracious appetite for information and knowledge who also needed guidance through the labyrinthine world of the word. Samuel Miller, a leader in the Presbyterian stronghold of Princeton, complained that the booksellers had replaced the aristocrats as "the great patrons of literature." "The spirit of trade," he went on to explain in 1803, "leads men to write in accommodation to the public taste, however depraved." Less censoriously, Jefferson summed up the symbiotic relationship of newspapers and their readers when he quipped that "editors are but cooks who must consult the palates of their customers."[21]

The simultaneous growth of female literacy and the publishing business opened up a broad spectrum of writing opportunities to women. Few writers—male or female—could match the success of Sarah Buell Hale. Born on a New Hampshire farm to a reasonably prosperous family, eighteen-year-old Sarah Buell started a school that she ran for seven years. In quick succession her mother and sister died, followed by a brother who perished at sea. After what she characterized as "this torrent of death, disappearance, and debacle," she married David Hale, a young and promising lawyer. Five children arrived in seven years, but David barely survived the birth of the last one. Left a widow at thirty-four, Hale and her sister-in-law opened a millinery shop—"one of the few occupations that genteel but needy women might enter." By the time this venture failed, Hale had already entered poetry contests, contributed to periodicals, and published a novel and book of poems. John Lauris Blake, an Episcopal clergyman deeply engaged in publishing, invited her to Boston to edit *The Ladies Magazine,* an ambitious enterprise that met with immediate success. After nine years, Hale succumbed to the blandishments of Louis Godey, a publishing innovator, and moved to Philadelphia to edit *Godey's Lady's Book,* which engaged her talents for the next forty years![22] By 1837 the magazine had 10,000 subscribers, in 1849, 40,000, and by 1860, a record-breaking 160,000—equivalent to a million in today's population.

Samuel Goodrich, who made a fortune writing the "Peter Parley" children's books, published the stories, verse, and essays of Lydia Maria Francis Child, Lydia Howard Huntley Sigourney, and Catharine Maria Sedgwick.[23] Like most publishers, Goodrich started a number of journals, most of them ephemeral, but even short-lived periodicals provided outlets for the fiction, poetry, and criticism of scores of amateur writers. Abandoning anonymity against her husband's wishes, Sigourney redoubled her writing efforts when his business declined, establishing a personal and highly profitable reputation.[24] Moving to Charleston with her clergyman husband, Caroline Gilman achieved widespread recognition for her poetry, memoirs, and editor-ship of *The Southern Rose*.[25] Almira Hart Lincoln Phelps popularized science with her textbooks on botany and chemistry while teaching at the famous Troy Institute run by her sister, Emma Hart Willard, who herself produced the country's most innovative geography texts. Phoebe Hinsdale Brown composed hymns; Louisa Caroline Tuthill wrote fiction and children's literature while editing *The Mirror of Life*. Margaret Bayard Smith drew on her experiences in Washington, where her husband, Samuel, published the *National Intelligencer,* for both her fiction and nonfiction.[26] Catharine Beecher pioneered publications on the domestic arts as did Lydia Maria Child with her eminently practical *The Frugal Housewife*. Mary Hunt Palmer Tyler drew upon her experience rearing seven children to produce a popu-lar guide to children's health, *The Maternal Physician*. "At no period, since the revival of learning in Europe," the editor of *Memoirs of Eminent Females* announced, "has the female sex written so much and so well as in the last half century."[27]

The subject of women clearly fascinated writers, particularly the ideal-ized woman, who figured in ruminations about faith, family, and fashion. Hale thrashed endlessly in the thicket of rationalizations about her bounded world, offering the latest bulletins on female comportment from the editorial office at *Godey's* while she herself demonstrated how to suc-ceed in a man's world. Despite her seeming accommodation to a restricted ambit of action, Hale's pronouncements could be perversely provocative, as when, after conceding that "women of all stations and temperaments" were converging on the common goal of marriage, she commented on the absurdity of expecting women to exhibit "that variety of talent, or those prominent and peculiar qualities of mind, that distinguish men of different professions and dissimilar occupations."[28]

Like Hale, Sigourney acquired influence through a writing career, join-ing Hartford's thriving group of authors and publishers in 1814. She also maintained the same tension between the ideal of womanhood and the allure of a larger canvas for women to paint their lives upon. In her essay "On Self Knowledge"—much indebted to Adam Smith's *Theory of Moral Sentiments*—she argued for the cultivation of introspection, pointing out the power of formal intellectual effort for women, especially "the art of writing accurately the thoughts that arise in our minds." "This exercise can scarcely be commenced too early," she advised, "or practised too much, for it continually excites new ideas, and aids the mind in the progress of knowl-edge."[29]

Applauding "a modern system of female education" that included science, Sigourney rejected the notion that knowledge made a woman unfit for domestic responsibilities. Instead she urged all women to succeed in some attainment, recalling the advice that Revolutionary leader Henry Laurens, when incarcerated in the Tower of London, had written to his daughters: "prepare for the trial of earning our daily bread by your daily labor. Fear not servitude: encounter it, if it shall be necessary, with the spirit becoming a woman of an honest and pious heart."[30] When Jefferson's granddaughters faced the prospect of poverty, they chafed at the fact that they could not work. Cornelia Randolph wrote with some bitterness that not until they sank entirely would it "do for the granddaughters of Thomas Jefferson to take in work or keep a school," to which Ellen Coolidge penned an echoing note: "My sisters are losing heart . . . My sisters wish to *work* for their own support, but [they are] the granddaughters of Thomas Jefferson."[31]

With death striking down parents and husbands with fair regularity, the need to be prepared was real enough, as some women saw clearly. Two bold thinkers, Sarah Grimke, the South Carolinian turned abolitionist, and Frances Wright, an English heiress who became a reform lecturer in the United States, took on the issue of women's place with a frankness that must have had something to do with their status as propertied single women. Grimke penned *Letters on the Equality of the Sexes and the Condition of Woman*, "venturing," as she expressed it, "on nearly untrodden ground."[32] She bitterly charged that men, having distorted women's nature by subjecting them to men's will, dared to label the product of their "ruin" inferior. Frances Wright spoke just as frankly about the need to reform woman's estate and the institution of marriage. Settling finally in New York, she shocked Americans by going on the lecture circuit to air her views on slavery [she had set up an experimental plantation for free blacks in Tennessee], economic justice, birth control, and women's rights.

Publicity, broadly defined as the articulation of fantasy, fact, advice, news, and arguments in printed products, influenced women's careers in surprising ways, especially since it gave rise to an outpouring of literature that idealized marriage and mothering with an ardor that turned customary arrangements into a cult of domesticity.[33] Much of this writing was done by women making room for their ambitions in the expanding world of publishing. The more women's sphere became conceptually distinct from that of men, the more women's special qualities attracted attention, throwing into the currency of public conversations ideas about the nexus between biology and society, nature and education, endowments and environment. While hardly more confining than women's traditional position, descriptions of women's remarkable beneficence and nurturing capacity fostered as many novel readings as conventional ones. Teaching in schools, organizing philanthropy, augmenting the services of the nation's proliferating churches, women revealed for the first time their imaginative capacity to rework social prescriptions.

Imports of English fiction poured into the United States after Independence, but Americans soon started producing their own print entertainment to slake their insatiable appetite for amusement. Beginning with a trickle of novels in 1785, the list grew to a total of 172 over the ensuing forty years. By 1824 twenty American titles were published each year, many of them written by women of the first generation.[34] Commercial expansion and democratic politics promoted both literacy and literature, which in turn did more to facilitate women's access to a larger world than any other development in the early nineteenth century. Unlike the campaign to be recognized as citizens in the 1840s, the effects of publishing and writing did not appear to intrude upon male prerogatives. Indeed men were among the most ardent defenders of women's education. The subtle consequences of participating in the public realm through print proved hard to trace and even more difficult to condemn.

Boasting of America's vibrant publishing industry, Ingersoll reminded a Philadelphia audience that American authors had written over 150 books covering "romance, travels, moral philosophy, mineralogy, political and natural geography, poetry, biography, history, . . . botany, philology, oratory, chemistry applied to the arts, statistics, agricultural and horticultural treatises, strategy, mechanics and many other subjects." By 1816 Americans had begun manufacturing printing equipment, which enabled them to produce books so cheaply that almost all editions of European writings were printed in the United States, instancing a Senate inquiry in 1822 that showed that the American book trade grossed between 2 and 3 million dollars annually. Candor forced Ingersoll to report that American presses had issued half a million volumes of Walter Scott's *Waverly* novels in the last nine years, after boasting that four thousand copies of a recent American novel had been sold immediately.[35]

The number of newspapers produced in the United States took quantum leaps too. The 92 weeklies and bi-weeklies of 1790 grew by 1810 to 371 papers, many of them dailies. In that year Americans bought 24 million copies of newspapers annually, the largest aggregate circulation of any country of the world, regardless of size. The early part of the century also measured the largest increase of newspaper copies per capita, from 3.4 in 1810 to 5.1 in 1820.[36] This was a remarkable figure considering that of the 8 million Americans, half were under the age of sixteen and a fifth enslaved and forbidden to read. In New York, for instance, the three newspapers published at the end of the Revolution had grown to 66 by 1810, then to 161 eighteen years later, among them Samuel Cornish's *Freedom's Journal,* America's first newspaper published by an African American.[37] Not even New York's exploding population could match that increase in newspapers; by 1830 121 towns in the state had had a newspaper at one time. Many of them, like the *Weedsport Advertiser,* sprung to life with the completion of the Erie Canal.[38]

Behind this phenomenon was the legion of editors who followed the settlers west, hardly waiting for the dust from the wagons to settle before transporting a printing press to a new community. Eber Howe's newspaper career forms a template for the western journalist. Born on the New York frontier, Howe carried from his childhood the memory of the excitement stirred by the post rider blowing his horn at each house of a *Geneva Expositor* subscriber. "With what avidity the family circle would gather round to hear my father read the wonderful doings of that great human butcher [Napoleon Bonaparte]," he wrote in his memoirs. He remembered too that after moving to Canada, they suffered without a paper until a man appeared as if by magic one day, walking through snow with the *Buffalo Gazette,* having fashioned a living for himself with a newspaper delivery route.[39]

Moving to Buffalo as a teenager, Howe responded to an ad for a position in a printing office, feeling very much like Benjamin Franklin, whose autobiography had enthralled him as a boy. Five years later at age twenty, he set out for Cleveland with a horse, saddle, bridle, valise, and twenty-five dollars in cash. Without subscribers, he started the *Cleveland Herald,* which he distributed himself on horseback to three hundred householders, many of them paying him in corn, not infrequently in the form of whiskey. Receiving mail once a week from Buffalo, Pittsburgh, Columbus, and Sandusky, Howe brought the scattered farmers of the Western Reserve the latest news—forty days old from Europe, ten from New York.[40] Like most of his colleagues, he formed and dissolved partnerships, sometimes with former rivals, as he moved about the state in search of larger pools of subscribers. When he started the *Painesville Telegraph* in 1822, the town had a population of two hundred people with five lawyers and three doctors and several

The front page of *The Ohio Repository* for Friday, October 8, 1819, contains a medley of poetry, homilies, and advertisements typical of the country's proliferating newspapers. Courtesy, American Antiquarian Society.

distilleries turning rye and corn into "blue ruin."[41] By 1830 the population was 1,499. Selling the *Telegraph* to a younger brother, Howe started up two more papers in Ohio, living long enough to be eulogized as "a pioneer printer."

The social implications of a commercially-articulated reading universe did not escape notice. Ingersoll saw newspapers as "the daily fare of nearly every meal in almost every family; so cheap and common, that, like air and water, its uses are undervalued." Calling a free press "the great distinction of this age and country," he reaffirmed the convictions of the founding fathers, who had passed the laws underwriting both postroads and newspaper mailings. The newspaper-reading habits of average Americans astounded the French *philosophe*, Pierre Samuel Dupont.[42] Teachers used newspapers for lessons about the world, organizing "news classes" in which pupils read and discussed the "great events in Europe, Asia and Africa."[43] This focus on information exercised an unexpected impact on slavery. Earlier Southern slaveholders had benefited from the South's discursive isolation, but Northern readers' intense interest in slavery promoted a steady stream of published, often critical commentary on Southern institutions written by outsiders.

Ludwig Gall, a German visitor, extolled newspapers as a window on America. The nation's "morals and habits of thought, its ruling passions and tastes, are more reliably read from newspapers than reports by the most observant and intelligent travelers who have written about this country," Gall thought. He marveled at the amount of news packed into them. "Which is more astonishing," Gall asked, "the great speed at which these newspapers are produced, or the excited curiosity with which the otherwise phlegmatic Americans storm the newspapers' offices before the appointed hour and gobble up the produce of the presses the minute it sees the light of day?" Calling them "news factories," Gall noted the catholic range of their readers:

> From the businessman engaged in worldwide trade, to the junk-dealer who sells used clothes to Negroes, everyone is seen with newspapers in hand. The little mulatto bootblack gives one to his customer, for entertainment, while his boots are being shined, and reads it himself when he has no customers. The fruit vendor saying to a passer-by examining her peaches, "Would you like to see this?" is not offering fruit but a newspaper she has been reading . . . You meet newspaper readers everywhere; and in the

evening the whole city knows what lay twenty-four hours ago on newswriters' desks . . . The few who cannot read can hear news discussed or read aloud in ale- and oyster-houses.[44]

The commercial underpinning of the American press did not escape Gall's notice. He calculated that Philadelphia's eight newspapers printed 700,000 octavo sheets of news a week—none able to bear the cost without half of each issue being devoted to the advertisements.[45]

Careers in writing, journalism, and publishing flourished because of the heightened awareness of the importance of communication in the United States, a realization that pushed education to the forefront of attention. Viewed as the sinews of national growth, communication relied upon literacy and literacy upon the schooling of America's burgeoning population of children. Joseph Caldwell, a North Carolina advocate of education, nicely captured the connection: "to him who can read, the press is a watch-tower from whose summit he can extend his view over the whole earth . . . unexampled in the past ages of the world." "To what but the press does the present generation owe its superior light," he asked rhetorically.[46] A transplanted Northerner, Caldwell undoubtedly was aware that the newspapers phenomenon was largely a Northern one. Before any state had been formed, the Northwest Territory had thirteen newspapers while North Carolina, a hundred and fifty years old with a population close to half a million, had only four. Twenty years after statehood, Ohio had forty-six papers in thirty-six locations while Georgia could claim only ten newspaper towns. Both cause and effect, literacy in Southern states lagged behind that in the North, as did the number of villages and towns.[47] Plantations—sometimes as large and productive as Northern hamlets—failed to stimulate the same avid interest in news or the literacy to read news firsthand.

With the production of newspapers, journals, and incidental writings running ahead of all other manufacturing ventures in the United States, teaching was the key to opportunity for those of the first generation coming of age. District schools and private academies hired thousands of teachers on yearly contracts. Preferring men over women, they frequently got "men" who were but seventeen- and eighteen-year-olds. The pay varied with the district, but was uniformly low, and many teachers had to move from pillar to post during the year as district families rotated the provision of the schoolteacher's board. Young men and women turned to teaching to support a bid for independence, churning annually through primary schools, where farmers' children went for a few months for four or five years to learn the fundamentals of reading, writing, and "summing."

Perhaps one of the least explored differences between the Northern and Southern states stems from the ease with which Northern boys escaped the heavy hand of parental control during the same years that Southern fathers succeeded in holding on to their sons. The difference in public support of education had the unintended consequence of severely limiting the opportunities for ordinary young Southerners to move out into a larger world. Only in the frontier area of Georgia, Alabama, Mississippi, and Louisiana did they find openings comparable to those in the North, and only then during the few years of fierce competition for choice land. The highly capitalized Southern agriculture left the scions of elite families waiting for an inheritance of slaves and land. In fact rich and poor fathers had more success in stopping sons and sons-in-law from leaving home, almost always with the backing of Southern white women, who deplored moves that broke the intricate ties of family.[48] Poorer Southern sons lacked the education to follow the road of literacy to new occupations.

The command of the three Rs that enabled farm lads to get teaching positions represented exactly the skills demanded in stores, law offices, and newspaper plants. Clearly a stepping stone rather than a career, teaching jobs offered young people a way out of the rural isolation in which most of them had grown up, but, as one educator noted, "so many opportunities are open for industrious enterprise, that it has always been difficult to induce men to become permanent teachers."[49] Rather a brain dispersal than a brain drain, teaching jobs created an occupational loop. Farmers ponied up the tax monies so their children could function in a modernizing world, providing, as they did so, the start-up funds for hundreds of careers in commerce that in turn contributed to the demand for literacy to which the school districts were responding in the first place. Fathers might have wanted to keep their children at home, but having taught them personal discipline, inured them to hard work, inspired them with a love of independence, and sent them to the district school, they had unwittingly prepared their offspring to take advantage of the myriad ways for getting ahead by getting away.

The principal appeal of teaching came from the independence a cash wage conferred on restless young men or women, though it would be a mistake to think that all teachers fit this mold. Teaching enabled John Ball to work his way through Dartmouth; John Chambers, Humphrey Howe Levitt, John Belton O'Neall, and Amos Kendall eased their entrance into law careers by a little teaching. Anson Jones left the poor Berkshire farm of his father because he could support himself teaching in country schools while studying medicine. Christiana Tillson taught young women on the Illinois frontier in exchange for housework.[50]

Teaching was also an occupation tailor-made for avid learners whose very intellectual predispositions drove a wedge between them and their rural companions. Bronson Alcott, animated by "a curiosity to see beyond the limits of my paternal home and become acquainted with the great world" poignantly described his childhood situation: "thrown into the society of ignorance and selfishness, and removed from the means of moral and intellectual improvement. A mind ardent in the pursuit of knowledge and a heart seeking for happiness in the sterile soil of my native town . . . without books, without friends to which I could apply for instruction and happiness . . ."[51]

An amazing number of women took advantage of the quickening of interest in girls' education to establish their own schools, and many more were hired to teach, mastering math, the classics, and the natural sciences in order to earn positions in the private academies that sprang up everywhere, North and South.[52] Julia Hieronymus Tevis acquired very advanced views of women's need for education through her German-born father.[53] After moving back from Kentucky for their children's education, the Hieronymuses settled in Washington, D.C., where her father had enough money to build a commodious house and to send Julia to a private academy. She led a rather glamorous life in Washington, attending the balls and receptions that enlivened the city when Congress was in session. In her memoirs, she described the great "illumination" in celebration of General William Henry Harrison's victory over the Indian confederation led by Tecumseh, and she barely escaped the city in 1814 when the British troops reduced the Capital's public buildings to ashes.[54]

All this changed when Julia's father lost his money, pulled down by a bankrupt friend whose note he had cosigned. The family's house and goods were sold at auction and Julia left home to take up a teaching job in Virginia, learning soon thereafter of her father's death. She then became the virtual head of her family, bringing her mother and younger sister to the small town in Virginia where she was flourishing as a schoolteacher and after-hours art instructor, but not without cost. As she recalled: "I soon learned that the life of a faithful teacher must be one of toil and unremitting care. All my fair visions of romance faded into stern reality as my responsibility for others increased."[55] A further break with her social past took place when she became a Methodist, a religious conversion that brought her into contact with John Tevis, a young circuit rider, whom she married after a short courtship.

A young bride, Tevis revealed a determination that quite astounds. On the couple's honeymoon trip to Kentucky, she talked her husband into converting a house, presented as a wedding gift from his father, into a boarding school. Forthwith Julia Hieronymus Tevis designed and founded the Science Hill Academy in Shelbyville, Kentucky, choosing a name that would announce her goal of offering a serious education to young women. Giving birth to her first child just a few months before opening her school, Tevis turned Science Hill into a self-supporting academy while bringing up seven children.[56] With 230 students, most of them boarders, the school became a life-work for Tevis, who presided over its fortunes for the next fifty years.

To a remarkable degree women were able to capitalize on the general enthusiasm for educating future mothers, now construed patriotically as providing the critical bridge between childhood and republican citizenship. North and South they stepped forward to claim the teaching jobs that materialized quickly during the early decades of the nineteenth century. Emma Hart Willard opened her Troy Female Seminary in 1821, her fame having spread across the country after she petitioned the New York legislature to give state aid to girls' schools.[57] The sixteenth of her father's seventeen children, Willard, like Tevis, had flowered under paternal nurturing, this time from a Jeffersonian admirer of Locke who had been cast among the Federalist farmers of Berlin, Connecticut. By the time she was fifteen, Willard had started teaching, conducting classes in her father's house while she continued school herself. At twenty-two, she married a fifty-year-old widower in Middlebury, Vermont, where access to the texts and examinations of Middlebury College opened up a larger scholarly world to her. When the Troy Common Council voted to raise four thousand dollars for a female academy, Willard saw the promise of a small factory town on the Erie Canal and seized the opportunity to put her ideas into action.[58]

Access to academy education became critical to these pioneers in women's education, but equally important was the support they gave each other, hiring one another in their schools while they raised money and circulated plans for new schools and seminaries for women. Starting a school was the youthful passion of Lydia Sigourney, who opened one for "young ladies" with a friend when she was twenty.[59] Caroline Lee Whiting Hentz ran several schools with her husband, as did Lavinia Stoddard.

Willard hired her younger sister, Almira. Mary Lyon taught in and started schools with Amanda White and Zilpah Grant from one end of Massachusetts to the other, all the time gathering supporters for her grand ambition, realized in the founding of Mount Holyoke, America's first women's college. A summer-school teacher by the age of seventeen, Lyon took a thirty-seven-dollar inheritance from her father and spent it on tuition, alternating between teaching and being taught for the next eight years. Like Willard, her exposure to lectures at Amherst College and Rensselaer School fired her with the desire to bring higher education to women, reflecting in part the excitement generated by the fifty-six new private colleges and eighteen public ones opened for men in the fifty years after Independence. Catharine Beecher also saw the importance of training teachers, writing, and speaking on behalf of women as natural leaders in education.[60]

For many men and women the ability to teach became a kind of insurance policy. John Neal's mother was widowed with one-month-old twins, so she opened a private school to attract the students her husband had taught in the district school, an endeavor she maintained for thirty-five years, the last fifteen with help from her daughter.[61] In a tale told over and over, Lucy Audubon, the wife of ornithologist John Audubon, went back into the classroom to support the family when the economic downturn of 1819 wrecked their family finances.[62] The unequal pay in teaching inspired a young Lucretia Coffin Mott to seek equality for women.[63] Mary Nelson learned Latin in order to teach her younger brother because her father could not afford formal schooling for him. Mary Tyler, desperate for money after the death of her husband, helped her daughter, Amelia, set up a school in their home for the benefit of her younger siblings and for the income it would bring in. Such schools were often preferable to the district ones, and parents, unable to rely on comprehensive state programs for education, gladly took advantage of their neighbors' skills.[64]

Adversity pushed Harriet Cooke into the career of school proprietor. "I never was a child," Cooke announced on the first page of her autobiography, an impression no doubt fortified when the death of her father thrust new responsibilities upon her as the oldest of four children. At sixteen she became a schoolteacher and taught for five years before she got married and began a family. During the War of 1812, Cooke's husband went into the mercantile business with her brother, incurring debts from a bad army contract that landed him in debtor's prison. For the next six years, she went back to teaching while he sought work in Georgia. When yellow fever carried off her husband, Cooke borrowed money to run a boarding house for Northern traders in Augusta. She only ran up more debts in that business, so she returned to Vermont to begin a school in Vergennes. Successful at this venture, Cooke at age fifty was able to contemplate a range of career choices, including the editorship of a magazine "designed expressly for the improvement of young ladies" and a teaching job in an Illinois mission. Instead she accepted an invitation to begin a seminary in Bloomfield, New Jersey, an undertaking she shared with her eldest son.[65]

Adults too demanded instruction in the changing world after the Revolution. Itinerant teachers of calligraphy went from town to town, offering courses in cursive writing, while scientists and instrument-makers in the larger cities set up classes for all ages and both sexes in chemistry, geology, and natural philosophy. The young Bronson Alcott ran a writing school in Warrenton, Virginia, while peddling through the South. Benjamin Owen Tyler, a country boy from western Massachusetts, offered three-week courses in penmanship from Bennington, Vermont; New York City; and Washington, D.C.–all the time perfecting a kind of speed system that gave students a fine hand within forty-eight hours.[66]

John Griscom turned himself into a science lecturer after someone presented him with a copy of Lavoisier's *Chemistry*. Soon, according to his son, he was lecturing to enthusiastic groups of "merchants, mechanics, apprentices, professional men, [and] females" on chemistry, natural philosophy, and mineralogy.[67] Others discovered new frontiers in quackery, as testified in trochaic verse by Andrew Comstock, a Hartford physician:

> "And besides, –I'm in the market!"
> Studied Elocution and music
> I discoverd how to cure, sir,
> stamm'ring, and defective utt'rance,
> and to change felsetto voices
> from the high and squaking treble
> to sonorous *baritone*.[68]

The passage from amateur to professional was hardly more difficult for men who wished to become lawyers than it was for those who became teachers. Indeed for many a young man, a year or two of teaching was the natural warm-up to the clerking in law offices that opened up careers. While several colleges established professorships of law, these lecturers offered little help with the technicalities of the law, that being left to the practicing attorneys who offered their clerks such training in return for doing the drudgery of the office. Such in fact was the origin of America's first law school, the one Tapping Reeves established in Litchfield, Connecticut in 1778.[69] Litchfield attracted New England scions and prodigies like the young John Calhoun of South Carolina, but most aspirants sought to master little more than pleadings and writs. Martin Van Buren, who entered a lawyer's office after leaving the local academy at fifteen, claimed that he never engaged in serious study. In fact, the early practice of law left him "adverse to reading."[70] With preparation so minimal, lawyers were abundant. Of those who entered the profession, usually like Van Buren at the age of twenty, at least half of them left it to pursue other callings. It was not uncommon for men to have done a little teaching, clerking, lawyering, newspapering, and officeholding over their lifetimes.

As with teachers, most lawyers grew up on farms, the chance of a law career coming as a kind of deliverance. Samuel Foot's family claimed descent from seventeenth-century founders of Wethersfield, Connecticut, but soil exhaustion colored his youth with the dark shades of poverty. His parents eked out a meager existence on a Watertown farm "greatly exhausted by continued cropping," and Foot barely escaped becoming the sixth generation farmer of an exhausted family plot, destined for the repeated rounds of ploughing, hoeing, cradling, reaping, mowing, and making fences. When the health of Samuel Foot's father gave out, he trained his youngest son, the twelve-year-old Samuel, to take over management of the place. His parents had nothing but the farm and had been obliged to sell some fifteen acres of that to clear themselves of debt. "There seemed to be nothing before me but a life of hard work on the old farm," Foot recalled, "no hope or prospect of an education for me." His eldest brother rescued him from this fate with a proposal to take fifteen-year-old Samuel on as a law clerk, and then arranged for his entrance into Union College from whence—after a long apprenticeship in what Foot remembered as "disciplined and self-denying labors"—he became a lawyer and a judge of the New York Court of Appeals.[71] John Chambers recalled that at age fourteen he could barely "read or write intelligibly" before an uncle offered him a legal education in exchange for clerking in his office. He seized the chance. Swept up in the fervor of the war with Britain in 1812, he ended up an aide to William Henry Harrison, who became a lifelong patron, later appointing him territorial governor of Iowa.[72]

Practicing law was the career most compatible with office-holding, which increased markedly in the nineteenth century, despite Jefferson's downsizing of the government. Population growth, recording land titles, and staffing the country's dual judicial system led to many positions to be filled, including commissioners to deal with bankruptcies, estate auctions, and the laying out of roads. The twenty-five state legislatures of 1820 regularly chose three thousand members. Each ten-year census multiplied the number of seats in the House of Representatives, the five reapportionments after 1790 increasing the size of the House from 105 to 240. With a population of 33,000 mandated for each district, Northern representatives came from a pool of approximately 6,600 white adult men; Southern representatives, closer to 4,000.[73] Representative strength also shifted to the West, following population growth. Only New York among the original states continued to increase its proportion of representation after the 1810 census. By 1820, new states enjoyed over 25 percent of congressional representation, a development particularly favorable to frontier lawyers.

The predominance of politics in American life gave lawyers a scope of influence that previously had been enjoyed by religious leaders. The Presbyterian Lyman Beecher complained that lawyers had displaced clergymen as the interpreters of public events. Ambitious lawyers acknowledged the importance of honing their speaking skills. John Belton O'Neall, who became an important South Carolina legislator, remembered practicing his own extemporaneous speaking every night when he was studying for the bar. Young lawyers erred, he maintained, when they turned down those speaking invitations without fees, for they could never get enough practice speaking.[74] Legal tyros noted that Baltimore's most distinguished lawyer, William Pinckney, took his turn on the "stump" in the woods where lawyers and debaters gathered for evenings of political oratory and drinking. John Quincy Adams marveled that "the principal leaders of the political parties are travelling about the country from state to state, and holding forth, like Methodist preachers, hour after hour to assembled multitudes, under the broad canopy of heaven."[75]

Like lawyers, physicians received their training working with a practitioner, sometimes supplemented by a lecture series at one of the country's new medical schools. Daniel Drake, though far from typical with his successful career as author, educator, and civic leader, started out the way most aspiring doctors did. He left his home on the Kentucky frontier at the age of fifteen to move to Cincinnati—in 1800 a frontier outpost with four hundred inhabitants—where he studied medicine with a doctor for three and a half years before entering into a partnership with his mentor. By 1804 they billed three to four dollars a day with hopes of collecting a quarter of it. The next year Drake was able to go to the University of Pennsylvania for a year of lectures, returning to marry the love of his life at age twenty-two.[76]

While most men practiced medicine without institutional instruction, nine schools granted degrees to 225 graduates in 1817. Students normally spent three years in medical school in sessions of eight months. They paid their teachers through admission tickets, and, like Drake, usually did not possess bachelors' degrees. However much contemporaries bemoaned the dilution of medical education that had taken place soon after the Revolution, students' eagerness for an education "with the least expenditure of time and money" inhibited reform. Nor were medical school professors, who could earn eight times the average doctor's income, interested in raising standards or discouraging students by establishing entrance requirements.[77]

With his penchant for statistics, Ingersoll estimated in 1823 that there were about ten thousand physicians in the United States. Assiduously comparing the United States with Europe, he asserted that many "medical errors and prejudices, now abandoned in Europe, were first refuted here." He also noted that America's energetic treatments had been dubbed "heroic medicine," construing as optimal all of the accommodations American doctors had been forced to make to their situation:

> The pernicious and degrading system which subdivides labour infinitesimally—a system useful perhaps for pin-makers, but most injurious in all the thinking occupations—has no countenance in America. The American physician practices pharmacy, surgery, midwifery; and is cast on his own resources for success in all he does: The consequence of which is, that he is forced to think more for himself, and of course to excel . . . Every hamlet, every region abounds with educated physicians . . .[78]

If lawyers benefited from the expansion of elected and appointed officeholders in the early republic, doctors found their talents and prestige enhanced by the awakening interest in natural phenomena of all sorts. Here again the popularity of journals played a role with a succession of new ones, like Drake's *Western Medical and Physical Journal,* appearing in the early decades of the nineteenth century. Edited by doctors, the *Philadelphia Medical Museum, Medical and Philosophical Register,* and New York's *Medical Repository* drew articles from correspondents all over the country, running as many as fifty letters in each issue. Practitioners reported on difficult deliveries, diseases afflicting animals, uses of mercury, symptoms of mysterious epidemics, and the yellow fever outbreaks that visited American cities with relentless fury. While the journals addressed with some consistency the need to protect the profession from "hackbones," they also displayed great confidence in the progress of medicine. The *Medical Repository* took particular care to celebrate American advances and European notice of them. In 1807 the editors credited new medical knowledge with liberating commerce from previous restrictions based on mistaken views about the "transportation of pestilential diseases from one country to another." They also hailed the expansion of medical education as "incessantly widening the boundaries of learning, and conveying its beneficial influence to the most distant and benighted" places in the country and later claimed that medicine was cherished more in the United States "than in any part of the world."[79]

Some practitioners in this cohort did have distinguished careers. George McClellan pioneered new techniques in the amputation of whole limbs and introduced clinical methods of teaching.[80] Samuel George Morton ranged well beyond the study of medicine into geology, paleontology, and zoology, his work on the Lewis and Clark Expedition virtually initiating the systematic study of American fossils. Both William Darlington and Jacob Bigelow published works on botany, and Oliver Wendell Holmes pronounced Biegelow's 1835 work, *Discourse on Self-Limited Diseases,* to have had a greater impact on medical practice than any other published in the United States. Walter Channing initiated the use of ether during childbirth, while Franklin Bache, the great grandson of Benjamin Franklin, became an important theorist in chemistry. The most remarkable career was that of William Beaumont, a relatively untrained army surgeon on duty at Fort Mackinac who encountered a Canadian laborer with a gunshot wound in the abdomen that had left a hole the size of a man's fist through which he could observe the stomach. Beaumont had the good sense to "seize, for a time, a remarkable opportunity for fame" and took Alexis St. Martin into his home, where he studied the processes of digestion. His publication of the findings from his 238 experiments opened a new era in the study of the stomach's functions.[81]

Just as scientific curiosity gave doctors a chance to participate in a broader intellectual community, so military service in the early republic opened up the novel careers of civil engineering and western explorations. The U.S. Military Academy founded at West Point in 1802 attracted in its first thirty years almost as many cadets from tiny Vermont as mighty Virginia, appealing as it did to the poor boys of the surrounding states.[82] The build-up of the Army after 1808 increased the number of army officer commissions available to the men of the first generation. With tensions between the United States and Great Britain mounting, Congress authorized more army units and set about finding men with ties to the Jeffersonian party to become officers.

Between 1808 and 1814 the size of the officer corps went from 191 to 3,495, the combined strength of men and officers reaching 62,674 during the last year of the war. Over a hundred young company commanders, virtually all of them having left peacetime occupations in farming, trade, and the law, earned the rank of general on the battlefield. At the end of the war Congress voted to reduce the army to 12,383 soldiers commanded by 674 officers, more than three times the number six years earlier. Winnowing out incompetents, the government created a professional fighting force to use against the Creeks, Seminoles, Sauk and Fox who were defending their ancestral lands from a new wave of American migration, swollen in part by the land bounties given the discharged soldiery.[83]

The training necessary to fortify harbors and situate forts involved exactly the same skills needed for the country's many transportation ventures. West Point provided the best education in civil engineering and its graduates, often lent by the U.S. Army as a kind of public subsidy, became the principal designers of the nation's first railroads. The career of Stephen Long exemplifies the range of opportunities available to army officers. Joining the army during the War of 1812, he later led a well-funded expedition to explore the area between the Mississippi River and the Rocky Mountains in 1820. Taking with him a covey of naturalists, Long became a national hero when he discovered Yellowstone, returning to the West in 1823 to explore the sources of the Minnesota River.[84] In 1828 the Army assigned Long with Captains William Gibbs McNeill and George Washington Whistler (the painter's father) to help those "few enterprising and influential citizens of Baltimore" who had raised $3 million to build a railroad connecting Baltimore to the Ohio River. In fact 22,000 people had subscribed to 41,788 shares of the B&O stock within three days, inspired in part by their fear that New York would gain dominance of the inland empire through the Erie Canal.[85] In a far from smooth operation, the Army's civil engineers were soon entangled with the high-handed civilian superintendent of construction, prompting Long to leave the B&O to produce locomotives that used anthracite coal as fuel while McNeill and Whistler hitched their wagons to the railroad star and sited most of the antebellum Eastern lines.

Daniel Tyler, Jonathan Edwards's great-grandson, elected to go to West Point rather than follow the footsteps of his three older brothers to Yale.[86]

Draon by J. Neilson.   Eng. by A.B. Durand.

Asher Brown Durand engraved this illustration for James Wallis Eastburn's *Yamoyden, a Tale of the Wars of King Philip,* published in 1820. The man sketching in the foreground suggests the favorite themes of the Hudson River Valley school of American painters. Courtesy, American Antiquarian Society.

Able to stay in the Army after the 1821 reduction, Tyler became involved in artillery education, which led to a year's leave to translate a French work on the subject. When he discovered that this system was already obsolete, Tyler spent a year in Metz angling for drawings of the new artillery, something he secured with the help of America's old friend, the Marquis de Lafayette. Returning to the United States, Tyler was assigned to the Springfield Armory, where he conducted an efficiency study, "watch in hand." Although he left the army when he was passed over for promotion, his engineering training led him into a successful career in canal and railroad building.[87]

Art represented a far more rarified career choice at the time. Chester Harding, who became a distinguished portrait painter, remembered the thrill he felt in 1818 watching a man in Pittsburgh drawing a likeness. He had never before seen such a representation. His experience was similar to that of John Neal, who claimed he had never seen a decent drawing during his childhood in Portland, Maine. In the United States in 1800, extant paintings would have numbered in the hundreds. By contrast, it has been estimated that by 1650 there were two and a half million pieces of art in the Netherlands.[88] This aesthetic deprivation of the cohort born after Independence soon ended as Americans developed an avidity for portraits, miniatures, landscapes, furniture stencilling, and barn painting. Every blank surface demanded embellishment. Within three years Harding himself, having badgered his acquaintance into teaching him how to draw, was traveling throughout the United States painting "heads" for twenty-five dollars apiece.[89]

Harding was born into poverty, his father being an improvident Massachusetts inventor working on a perpetual motion machine. On the New York frontier Harding became familiar with "that great civilizer," the ax. Musically talented, he served as a drummer in the War of 1812, an experience that left him with a fund of wry stories. Falling behind the troops one day, he asked a farm wife which way they had gone. "Oh," replied the woman, "you have only to follow the feathers." Apt to weave his memories around music, Harding recalled that when sickness began to thin the soldiers' ranks, the song that signaled the return from a burial, "Away goes the merryman home to his grave," became their constant companion.[90]

After the war, Harding went into cabinetmaking with his brother, ran up debts, tried his hand at tavern-keeping, got married, and finally fled to Pittsburgh to avoid imprisonment for debt. In Pittsburgh, having set himself up as a sign painter, he heard from his brother that good portrait painters in Lexington got fifty dollars a head. Harding, by now a father, borrowed enough money to buy a large skiff with a barber friend, and the two embarked with their families down the Ohio, sometimes just floating on the river while the men—both clarinet players—gave themselves over to music. In Kentucky, Harding launched himself as a portrait painter, doing one hundred portraits at twenty-five dollars a head in six months, among them those of an Osage chief, the eighty-six-year-old Daniel Boone at his Missouri home, and Territorial Governor and Revolutionary hero William Clark. Lacking technical skill, Harding succeeded with a natural talent for capturing "likenesses," moving from Cincinnati to St. Louis, Boston, and Washington, where President John Adams and all the judges of the Supreme Court sat for him. After doing a full-length portrait of Supreme Court Chief Justice John Marshall, he remarked that he took "great pleasure in painting the whole of such a man."[91]

Eager to clear his name, Harding paid off the debts he had fled from earlier and moved on to bigger things. Within a dozen years he had a studio in London and was painting members of the royal family, including the Prince of Wales. Indeed so phenomenal was his success in Boston that the great painter, Gilbert Stuart, had been wont to ask friends, "How wages the Harding fever?" Harding himself attributed his triumph in London "to the circumstance of my being a backwoodsman, newly caught."[92] Soon he took in the unhappy fact that his family, left behind in America, would not be accepted in the social circles he frequented as a single artist, so Harding returned to the United States and settled down in Springfield, Massachusetts.[93] Recounting his life in a picaresque manner that offered a witty contrast to the more pious accounts left by his contemporaries, he called his memoir *My Egotistigraphy.*

Harding's success was closely tied to the urban tastes emerging in the United States in the first decades of the nineteenth century, but old-timers found the craze for having one's portrait painted alarming. When he tried to impress his grandfather with the earnings he brought back home, the old man told him witheringly that it was "very little better than swindling to charge forty dollars for one of those effigies."[94] Less gifted artists than Harding were traveling the back roads with their palettes and stock figures doing family portraits for more modest sums. The same families that wished to capture themselves on canvas were also likely to want to embellish their homes and brighten their barns. Possession of disposable income encouraged the first generation to indulge in the representation of self.[95] John Vanderlyn, who early established himself as a painter of classical

historic scenes, wrote his nephew in 1825 that he should join the ranks of
itinerant portraitmakers, noting the buoyant prospects for someone "moving through the country." "It would besides be the means of introducing a
young man to the best society," Vanderlyn noted, and if "wise might be the
means of establishing himself advantageously in the world."[96]

Other artists found patrons for their landscapes, genre pictures, and
historic scenes, or, like Anna Claypoole Peale and Jane Stuart, both daughters of famous painters, they did miniatures. Painting also had a strong
component of recording in these years. Titian Ramsay Peale and Samuel
Seymour got commissions to accompany Long's expedition to the Rocky
Mountains in 1820, sketching and painting landscapes and Indians, an
undertaking pursued with more intensity by Charles Bird King and George
Catlin. Catlin, lured away from his law career by the sight of Indian chiefs
on the streets of Philadelphia, anticipated the field of ethnography, completing over six hundred portraits of Indians engaged in work, games, and
religious ceremonies. A number of women became lithographers and
many artists, working as engravers and illustrators, became part of the
burgeoning world of print.[97] Bass Otis, who made the first lithograph in the
United States in 1818, entered his profession after being apprenticed to a
coach painter, while Samuel Finley Breese Morse, of Morse code fame,
pursued his career as an artist while applying himself to inventions like the
telegraph. John James Audubon was both amateur scientist and artist, and,
like Catlin, let his love of rambling through the wilderness painting the
birds of America distract him from more profitable pursuits.[98]

And then there was preaching. Just as the Revolutionary War had emboldened men and women to break through the layers of imperial authority to assert their will against British rule, so the religious revivals that
undulated through American towns and villages twenty years later gave
ordinary men and some extraordinary women the courage to claim the
eminent position of clergyman. The established New England churches
with their college-educated ministry fought bitterly over traditional Calvinist dogmas while Baptist and Methodist societies sprang up like daisies in a
June meadow. With simpler preparation for their ministers, the evangelical
denominations were much better able to carry Christianity to the
unchurched communities of the frontier. Local revivals yielded a rich harvest of young men, who once touched by God were ready to join the ranks
of circuit-riding preachers that the Methodist Church organized. Evangelical leaders, especially in the South, recruited heavily among these "young
gifts."[99] Baptists of various kinds also flourished, their congregational struc-

ture making it easy to form new societies out of local prayer meetings, many of them held in the homes of the converted.

In the 1790s, 1800s, and 1810s a ministerial career could begin with spontaneous praying through exhorting to preaching, sometimes with nothing more formal than a "laying on" of hands. Over time the heightened concern with doctrinal exactitude promoted clerical education, though preaching ability remained the prime qualification for a clergyman. Andover Theological Seminary, founded in 1807 by those Congregationalists who eschewed Unitarianism, provided the template for preparing ministers. Within forty years thirteen different Protestant denominations maintained fifty seminaries in seventeen states.[100] Mindful of the poverty of most of their clerical candidates, the Baptists moved slowly towards educational requirements and, when they did, founded institutions like New York's Madison College, which recruited indigent young men.[101] Half of all men attending seminaries had their tuition and board paid for by organizations like the American Education Society, begun in Massachusetts in 1815.

Like many a young man of the early republic, Charles Finney, who became the most famous evangelical preacher in America, tried out several careers before settling on the church. Brought up on the New York frontier, he recalled that neither his parents nor their neighbors professed Christianity. An able learner, Finney was teaching school by the age of fifteen because, as he later explained, "the new settlers, being mostly from New England, almost immediately established common schools." They also had "very little intelligent preaching of the Gospel," according to Finney, who returned to his Connecticut birthplace when he was twenty. He became a lawyer and drew increasingly close to religion. Once converted, a sense of urgency seized him, so much so that he once told an importunate client, "I have a retainer from the Lord Jesus Christ to plead His cause and I cannot plead yours."[102]

According to Finney, his conversion stirred up a lot of excitement in the village, sparked in part by his telling the Princeton-educated pastor of their church that the doctrine of predestination was absurd. Finally ordained, Finney became a missionary preacher for the Oneida Female Missionary Society, beginning his labors in the town of Le Ray, New York, where he discovered a number of deists among the principal men of the community. Already drawn to analyzing preaching, Finney saw that the elevated style of the clergy of New England's Standing Order quickly lost them their audiences; something, he believed, lawyers would never do "when addressing the jury box."[103] Finney combined the qualities of a pastor, an organizer, and an innovator. He also influenced theology with his insistence that revivals came from the people, not God. Finney's career etched an American trope, filled with experimental initiatives, self-confident forays into new territory, and practical shortcuts to complicated goals. At the peak of his powers, Finney threw in his lot with the radical Congregationalists at Oberlin, where he founded and edited the *Oberlin Evangelist* and presided over Oberlin College while it pioneered co-education and integrated schooling for black and white young people.

Christianity flourished among African Americans, enslaved as well as free. Powerful conversion experiences led African-American men to the ministry, and turned women, black and white, into preachers, if not actually ministers. Richard Allen became the first black bishop in 1816 when he was chosen to head the newly organized African Methodist Episcopal Church. Allen laid the religious foundation for black Methodists both in Baltimore and Philadelphia. The testimony against slavery among Baptists, Methodists, Quakers, Episcopalians, Presbyterians, and Congregationalists weakened over time, but their commitment to evangelize among African Americans fared better than their stand on slavery.[104] The most remarkable black religious figure was probably John Stewart, a free-born Virginian who established the first Methodist mission for Indians among the Wyandotts in the Northwest Territory. Sparking a revival there in 1817, Stewart was accused of performing marriages and baptisms with an Exhorter's License, but the presiding Methodist elder rejected the charge.[105] Another African American, Jacob Bishop, actually served as the pastor of the white Baptist Church in Portsmouth, Virginia.[106]

Gifted preachers from the black community evoked surprise from prejudiced white Americans. Their moral and intellectual leadership bore witness to the abilities of African Americans during the critical early decades of the nineteenth century when white Americans hotly debated the subject of their innate capacities. The antislavery activist, Sojourner Truth, took that name as acknowledgment of her calling as an itinerant preacher following a spiritual transformation.[107] Jarena Lee became a licensed Methodist exhorter after a decade of mystical experiences that convinced her of her calling as a preacher. Forced to defend a woman's right to the vocation, she produced a cogent argument that found its way into print. Once permitted a public career in the church, Lee traveled several hundred miles each year, preaching in homes and churches to slaveholders as well as slaves, North and South. Convinced that her life was God's work and would be an inspiration to others, Lee paid for the publication of her autobiography, setting an example for Zilpha Elaw, another black woman exhorter who teamed up with Lee for several rounds of transient preaching after their husbands had died.[108] More radical in her religious practices, Rebecca Jackson, a free black seamstress, learned to write in order to leave an account of her spiritual life, helping later to found a black Shaker community in Philadelphia.[109]

Protestant women responded passionately to the ferment of the revivals, flouting the commands dictating women's role in the church. Martha Howell spoke from Baptist pulpits throughout the western district of New York in the first decade of the century. Deborah Pierce urged women of the Baptist faith to "rise up ye careless daughters . . . for ye have not harkened to the voice of God yourself."[110] Nancy Towle, wife of an Exeter physician, set off in 1822 with the Bible as her "only companion" on a hundred-mile journey through the South. An experienced preacher by 1827 when she visited Great Britain, she drew people from far and wide to hear that "woman from America."[111] The biblical injunction, "Let your women keep silence in the churches," confined most American churchwomen in this cohort to supportive roles in their congregations, but Lee, Towle, Lydia Sexton, Abigail Roberts, and Harriet Livermore argued vociferously against the ban, claiming an inconsistency in scripture.[112]

Reared an Episcopalian in a prominent family in Portsmouth, New Hampshire, Harriet Livermore sought a spiritual home during the years that she taught school until, nearing the age of forty, she abandoned teaching for preaching, taking the name of "the Pilgrim Stranger." Her *Scriptural Evidence in Favor of Female Testimony in Meetings for the Worship of God* made a strong case for women's useful role in bringing people to God. In 1826 Livermore became the first woman to address Congress, accepting an invitation from President John Quincy Adams and later another from Andrew Jackson. Stirred by her conviction that Native Americans came from Jerusalem, she traveled alone to Fort Leavenworth, Kansas, where the Bureau of Indian Affairs denied her request to enter. Prompted by faith in her own prophecy, Livermore spent the next sixteen years in the Holy Land.[113]

Ann Hasseltine Judson became a Christian heroine when she sustained her husband during long years of imprisonment in Burma. Before his incarceration, she had shown remarkable initiative in running a school and translating the Bible into both Burmese and Thai while managing an extensive household.[114] Judson also proved herself a formidable fundraiser during a two-year tour of England and the United States from 1821 to 1823.[115]

Frances Mulligan Hill, who accompanied her husband to the Episcopal Church's first foreign mission, begun in 1830 in Greece, conducted a girls' school that acquired an international reputation over her forty-year tenure. Because many of the women in the "foreign parts" where American missionaries toiled remained inaccessible to men, missionaries' wives assumed direct responsibility for reaching them. The American Board of Commissioners for Foreign Missions finally decided in 1827 to send a woman to India as a missionary. At thirty-two, Cynthia Farrar arrived at Calcutta to embark on a spectacular thirty-four-year career as the head of girls' schools in Bombay and Ahmednagar.[116] Conceived as "callings" and "God's work," preaching, editing religious publications, and evangelizing throughout the non-Christian world created thousands of careers as the vitality of American Protestantism intensified in the early decades of the nineteenth century.

⁂

NEW CAREERS had a tremendous impact on the society emerging out of the mixed colonial legacy. Psychologically ready for innovations, the young generation added an anticipatory quality to American culture. More than optimism or hope, expectation of success oriented the first generation to the future and endowed them with the special burden of fulfilling American predictions of progress. Widely accessible, new careers probably engaged as many as 10 percent of white adult men, but because teaching, writing, and preaching were also open to people of color and women, these careers carried the hope—if not the expectation—that doors now ajar would open wider in the future.

The impact of these new careers can be gauged by the recollections written by members of the first generation. "Probably in no enlightened country on the globe," Harriet Cooke observed, "are children more anxious to be esteemed, or earlier permitted to become men and women than in our own." Since adolescence had yet to be conceived of as a special stage of life, girls and boys typically went from being a child to an adult with little fanfare.[117] Physical maturity signaled adult status. As Cooke commented, "it has been with much truth remarked, that in the United States there is no such period as youth; we jumped at once from childhood to fancied maturity."[118] High mortality rates prompted mothers and fathers to push their children towards maturity; religious parents pressed for the recognition of their children's state of sin that went hand-in-hand with adulthood.[119]

James Durand, who joined the navy at eighteen, claimed that he had been punished by ensigns no older than twelve.[120] Charles Trowbridge, one of Michigan's pioneers, looked back with wonder at the responsibility laid on young boys in his youth. At fourteen he was sent 140 miles "to procure the discount of a note for $4,000," and when the note matured he traveled over the same road again with funds to meet it.[121] In a short autobiography appended to his captivity narrative, James Riley described his transition to manhood, also at age fourteen. Being "tall, stout, and athletic for my age; and having become tired of hard work on the land," he wrote, "I concluded that the best way to get rid of it, was to go to sea and visit foreign countries." His parents' opposition gave way before his determination and within five years he had passed through the grades of cabin boy, cook, ordinary seaman, seaman, and second and chief mate.[122]

The economic and political opportunities opening up to ordinary white boys drew in those who had skills that were still relatively rare. Despite poor schooling, those who prospered mastered the arts of reading, writing, calculating, and speaking in public, skills that in turn distinguished the emerging urban middle class. The freshness of the spectacle of young people making their own way apparently aided only by effort and ambition enthralled contemporaries. Thurlow Weed, who became a prominent New York editor, filled his autobiography with success stories like that of Theodore Faxton, a stage driver who became superintendent of the line before he was twenty-one, moving to great wealth on successive waves of transportation technologies from stage coaches to canal packet boats and on to express lines, railroads, and finally telegraph companies. "The history of Mr. Faxton," Weed concluded, "shows what can be accomplished in our country by young men of industry, intelligence, and integrity." Weed found these traits in the country's "mechanics, its painters, its builders, its hatters, its shoemakers"–just the thing that his hometown of Utica needed.[123] Threadbare now with repetition, these examples of successful rises from obscurity had a freshness for the first generation long before Horatio Alger had turned them into a national stereotype.

Although some urged public support of education and training, private efforts remained the norm. Invoking Francis Bacon's aphorism that knowledge is power, Stephen Elliott, the distinguished Charleston civic leader, told a South Carolina audience that, in a republic, instruction should be universally diffused: "A complete system of national education, is one of the great desiderata of our age." President James Madison shared his opinion, urging the adoption of a national university in his 1810, 1815, and 1816 addresses to Congress. A Kentucky physician, using metaphors appropriate to his calling, celebrated the country's "rapid progress and dissemination of learning and politeness," boasting America's triumph over "those illiberal prejudices, which not only cramp the juices, but sour the temper and disturb all the pleasing intercourse of society."[124] Although Congress promoted education through land sales in the new states, Madison's dream was never realized.

Role models, sponsors, and heroes figured as prominently in the recollections of women as of men. Cooke said that she kept up her spirits during the dark days after her husband's death by "the example of Mrs. Graham, of sainted memory." Isabella Marshall Graham had emigrated in 1789 from Scotland to New York, where she ran a school and promoted relief societies for widows and orphans. Reading a biography of Graham inspired her, Cooke recalled, "with courage when heart and flesh seemed failing."[125] Julia Tevis greatly admired Emma Willard, the founder of Troy Academy. It was her example that gave Tevis the determination to outfit a laboratory so that her young women might learn chemistry and demonstrate the appropriateness of the subject for women, lending substance to her school's name, Science Hill Academy. In both cases, the printed word had carried tales of role models from afar. Sarah Hale, who filled her *Ladies Magazine* with original material for and by women, extolled the idea of "influence— the subtle, unobtrusive type of power that women might exert over others." Although she excoriated the English philanthropist Frances Wright as "a shameless and impious woman" for lecturing to mixed audiences of men and women, she was quick to attack men who demeaned women.[126]

First generation men usually lauded careers that blended the personal with the public. Typical is Gideon Burton's praise of public men for their facilitation of private endeavor, like DeWitt Clinton who rose to fame as the great patron of the Erie Canal, or David Griffin, "a man of great enterprise," who enabled Cincinnati to acquire the beauty of a city like Philadelphia.[127] David Hosack, a distinguished New York physician, called Clinton "the Pericles of our commonwealth."[128] To Samuel Breck, De Witt Clinton appeared "a man of very enlarged views and a statesman of the boldest character, undertaking projects on public account that seemed to common minds infinitely beyond the means of this country; yet by his genius, enterprise and industry have they been accomplished."[129] Clinton and his canal would be remembered much longer "than if he had been a dozen presidents," John Neal maintained, because he had discovered "that money taken out of one pocket and put into another in the same country . . . in works of public utility . . . cannot impoverish a people."[130]

A statue to Henry Clay was raised along the National Road because it was he who as the youngest Speaker of the House had secured its charter. Taking his sons to catch a glimpse of Clay as his boat pulled away from the Philadelphia wharf, Burton told the boys that Clay was the greatest man living because his American system "made our country free from England," adding that "to this day the mention of his name kindles a glow in my heart."[131] In John Bear's case the admiration arose from a personal encounter. After running away from his apprenticeship at a Maryland tavern, he met Clay, who was then a member of the House of Representatives from Kentucky. Clay laid his hand on his head, in Bear's recollection, and "told me that I was too smart a boy to be a servant; he said that I ought to go to a free country where I could get an education and become a man."[132] Interestingly, the first generation's autobiographers displayed an affinity for visionary builders like Clay and Clinton rather than the hugely popular Andrew Jackson, who addressed his contemporaries' resentments and fears.

The young men who joined the mobile bands of restless youth ferreting out opportunities placed great importance upon their early love of books. Levi Beardsley, who later became a president of the New York State Senate, remembered gratefully that four or five families in his frontier home had established a small town library, augmenting his father's two volumes of Dryden's poems with James Bruce's *Travels to Discover the Source of the Nile* and various other histories.[133] The free use of a friend's library figures prominently in the memoir of the John Brown who lies "amouldering in his grave." At age ten, Brown recalled, he "grew to be very fond of the company, & conversation of old & intelligent persons," going on to stress his early ambition to excel in doing anything he undertook to perform. "This kind of feeling" he commended "to all young persons both male & female as will certainly tend to secure admission to the company of the more intelligent; & better portion of every community."[134] John Belton O'Neall carried into old age the recollection of the avidity with which he read his first book–*Pilgrims' Progress*–secured through the library society organized in his hometown of Newberry, South Carolina.[135] The most striking instance of new literacy came from Sequoyau, who completed a

Cherokee syllabary in a labor of twelve years in 1821, and had the satisfaction of seeing thousands of Cherokees learn to read and write.[136]

After his father gave Amos Kendall one of his two shares in a nearby township library in rural Massachusetts, he read every book in the library.[137] George Gilmer bought "Hume's *History* and Ossian's poems" with the wages that his father paid him for picking cotton.[138] William Rudolph Smith remembered learning the names of Robespierre, Danton, Marat, and Dumouriez because each week the children had to read aloud from the newspaper's "domestic occurrences and foreign news."[139] Intelligence, an aptitude for learning, an early gift for reading, a yearning for more schooling, an eagerness to be on one's own—these were the notes that orchestrated the movement from home.

While books played on the youthful imagination of those with access to them, family visitors more often served as the harbingers of change and carriers of vital information about new careers. Displays of aptitude in children often attracted a patron—perhaps an older brother or uncle, arriving like some *deus ex machina* at a propitious moment to urge more schooling, provide credit, or pluck a likely lad from the indifference of his family.[140] The uncle of the religious leader Elias Smith precipitated a protracted family debate over his schooling. Smith's father, a poor tenant farmer, wanted him to learn some arithmetic while his uncle insisted that he should study grammar, arguing the importance of grammar if Smith were called into public life. "Ah," Smith's father replied, "that he nor I may never calculate upon," to which his uncle retorted, "you do not know what he may be." When his father relented, his uncle rejoiced, claiming that his consent would be "worth more to your child than all your farm."[141] Smith's uncle astutely had seized on the critical difference between his and his nephew's generation—learning, opportunity, and ambition would serve them as a family farm had served his father.

⁂

THE CREATION of a personal identity forged during that difficult middle passage from aspiring youth to established adult emerges from the first generation's reminiscences. The dramatic intensity of their stories arises in part from the readers' awareness that the unformed boy and girl were moving into an equally unformed social environment. While descriptions of the quality of life and of emotional satisfactions in childhood varied greatly, few expressed regret about life's choices—certainly none for having left behind the unremitting toil of farm labor that began when one grew "large enough to handle a hoe or a bundle of rye." Success—and those who wrote autobiographies generally succeeded in some small way—tended to obliterate the memories of the cost of separation from the communities of their youth. Nor do their recollections adequately explain how young people acquired the psychological resiliency and social understanding necessary to perform in a society characterized by mobility, novelty, and highly individuated outcomes.

From individual self-assertion came an admiration for personal effort. Edouard de Montulé captured the sense of practical intelligence honored in the United States in 1817 when he commented that know-how *(savoir faire)* in America was not enough. One needed to do something, he said, emphasizing that fortune, reputation, and pretensions went unappreciated while the capacity to make something of one's life garnered public approval. Even better, he said, it made you a contributor to the resources of the nation.[142] Here is a foreigner's recognition of how careers structured the American self. Pride, satisfaction, sociability, all hinged on the capacity to earn respect as one earned one's way. Fresh in its anti-authoritarian spirit and its disdain of privilege, the American work ethic provided the moral underpinnings for a society of individuals linked psychologically and intellectually to a nation while they moved in and out of its communities.

Montulé's trenchant observation applied, of course, almost exclusively to the Northern states, where Protestant values had deep roots. Careers were much less important than family in the South. The law and its sidebar, politics, excited the most interest among Southerners, few of whom were teachers, physicians, publishers, or civil engineers. Those Southerners who aspired to careers in writing or painting normally had to seek outlets for their talent in the North. Several newspapermen rose to fame, but Southern states had many fewer presses. Only the number of Southern preachers and politicians could have matched Northern ones, both callings of the word in an increasingly print-dominated world. Montulé's comment also suggests that Northern qualities were viewed as "national" while Southern preferences became categorized as regional, a development that the Virginians who initiated the move for the "more perfect union" provided by the Constitution could never have predicted.

Although it took someone to discover the native ability of young aspirants, appreciation for their benefactors is nicely balanced in these men's memoirs by their sense of having been responsive to opportunity. Describing his conduct in his uncle's law office, Chambers affirmed his youthful diligence: "I applied myself with unremitting attention to the business of the office, and at the end of six months . . . was able to do all the duties of the office with very little instruction from anybody."[143] David Dodge attributed his self-confidence to the fact that he had "been obliged to rely almost wholly upon my own resources, and when I had an object in view I had devoted so much consideration to it that I generally obtained it."[144] "By attention and close application I got to be head man of the place," Holmes Hinkley reported of his first job in a machine shop.[145] Matthew Vassar, summing up the success as a brewer that made the endowment of Vassar College possible, proclaimed, "this last act of mine is the result of Industry, Perseverance, and Self-reliance and neither kindred nor friends have reached me an assistant hand," adding "the road I have passed is open for all who will mould their character in honorable pursuits by the same means."[146]

This contrapuntal theme of gratitude and pride conveys an important clue about these men's acceptance of the nation's emerging capitalist culture. Rivalries, at least in retrospect, were muted by a sense of mutuality, envy displaced by admiration. Old competitors before the bar or in commerce were safely folded back into friendship at the end of one's career. The exertions necessary to make one's way appeared as profitable expenditures of time and hope, good investments in a basically worthwhile venture. Independence, touted as a political good, acquired a personal resonance for teenage boys—and a few exceptional girls—who were able to carve out careers for themselves, supplying as well a rationale for throwing off the traditional demands of patriarchal families.

The limited scope of the colonial economy had greatly aided those who wished to maintain a social order of place and prescription. When parents and patricians controlled land and credit, their values had the backing of power. Expanding opportunity in America had just the opposite effect, dealing as mighty a blow to traditional assumptions about social order as had the War for Independence. Success eventually became the great divider, but its impermanence chastened the successful. Failure—or at least temporary checks—dogged men's lives. With easy credit and inexperienced risk-takers, the economy expanded and contracted with the ease of an accordion, squeezing the unlucky and unwise by turns. In these routine defeats a kind of freemasonry of the aspiring took shape, nurtured by the awareness that the risk of failure was the inescapable companion of achievement. In the emotional and intellectual efforts to comprehend these sudden changes in the economic weather, success and failure cemented the attachment to an America conceived of as the locus of ingenuity, effort, and risk-taking. If commerce laid the material footings for a new kind of society in the United States, personal autonomy and freedom of association—all products of hard-fought political campaigns—provided its moral underpinnings.

5

DISTINCTIONS

In *Memoirs of a New England Village Choir*, Samuel Gilman depicts the rough waters of social change that very nearly capsized his youthful hometown. The unlikely site of this turmoil was the meeting house balcony, from which the church choir held forth every Sunday. Far from soothing the savage breast, the liturgical music, its performance and performers, promoted a succession of disruptive wrangles. Cast as a gentle satire, Gilman's *Memoirs* offers a shrewd analysis of the seismic shaking of the old colonial social structure. Although the traditional European hierarchy with its chasm between the gentry and ordinary folk had never been successfully transplanted to the American colonies, the model of a society ordered by status had exercised considerable influence, its forms of dress and address the dominant ones in the colonial era. Challenging these, the Revolution had introduced a political philosophy subversive to distinctions based upon birth, confusing local mores in ways that *Memoirs of a New England Village Choir* neatly captures.

Gilman's story begins when the long-time choir director departed to resettle in Maine, leaving the choir so upset that the following Sunday "not an individual ventured to appear in the singing seats."[1] Thus, does Gilman beguilingly introduce the principal plotting element of his and America's new story line: the volitional character of participation. Choristers could freely choose to mount the stairs to the octagonal pews above the lectern, or they could refrain from singing by remaining downstairs with the congregation, or they could not come to church at all, each of which options various singers exercised over the ensuing seven years of discord. Like the United States as a whole, Gilman's New England village found itself buffeted by free choice, changing standards, and a highly mobile population.

Knowing how to "set the tune" was the only essential qualification for the choir director. Charles Williams, a shoemaker's apprentice with great musical talents, could certainly set the tune, but diffidence immobilized him, so the choir members sought out a different young man to lead them, a newcomer from rural New Hampshire who had recently moved to the village to study with the local doctor. Despite some difficulty controlling his pitch pipe, the doctor's apprentice served the choir well enough until he too departed to set up practice in one of the country's new settlements. Meanwhile young Williams had "increased in years, skill, and confidence"—in short, lost his diffidence. His willingness to lead the choir infused new life into "the whole vocal company." The church bought a large supply of the latest edition of *Village Harmony,* and the choir swelled to fifty members. Williams's personal triumph as choir leader proved, however, to be the choir's undoing. So offensive became the idea of someone with Williams's talents becoming a mere shoemaker that the villagers raised the money to send him to Harvard.[2] At this juncture in the story the narrator of the *Memoir* takes on the duties of director as a stopgap measure, only to find himself embroiled with a young academy preceptor who had joined the choir while courting a local woman.

Exuding the poise of an out-of-town sophisticate, the preceptor called one morning for *Old Hundred,* a tune that only the most venerable vocalists could remember. This was but a foretaste of his campaign to get the village choir to follow "a new and purer taste for sacred music" by eschewing all American tunes in favor of "the slow, grand, and simple airs" that their forefathers sang.[3] This imperious demand tore the choir asunder as devotees of the fashionable new atavism battled those deeply attached to the choir's normal "animated style of singing." Now came into play the choir members' weapon of not coming to church at all. "Pew after pew became deserted," the narrator recounted, "until we found that we were singing, and Mr. Welby preaching almost to naked walls," except for the few families of fashionable pretensions who saw something "aristocratical" in the modish return to *Old Hundred*. The director stood alone in the choir stall until four octogenarians, "laurelled old men," all veterans of the War for Independence, "tottered up the stairs one Sabbath morning . . . and took their places in the seats left vacant by their degenerate grandsons."[4]

Saved by this timely intervention, the singing continued, but the choir fell apart, the narrator-director himself going off to college. When a matron of the village offered her services for the duration of the emergency, the ladies of the choir returned. The resolution of this latest crisis only set the stage for a deeper, more lacerating quarrel. The matron-director, "who knew not, or affected not to know the squeamishness respecting rank," invited Mary Wentworth, who was employed as a maid in the village, to the front seat so as to capitalize on her gorgeous voice. Worse was to come for those who *were* squeamish "respecting rank." The new director, laid low by illness one Sunday, asked Wentworth to direct. The distaff side of choir then deserted their musical posts en masse, leaving the shunned servant to sing with the sole support of the pastor, an obligation that she turned into a stunning demonstration of "the whole blazing extent of her musical powers."[5] Forthwith the men returned to the balcony, and the choir briefly recovered some of its former volume only to run afoul of the male choristers' effort get rid of the new director, in order "to emancipate themselves from the mortifying dominion of a woman."

A doctrinal dispute precipitated the last act in the village choir's drama. A visiting minister, filled with Calvinist zeal, called for a Watts hymn that contained vivid "images respecting the future abode of the wicked." The temporary choir leader that sabbath was a tinplate worker who resisted the minister's request, and leaned over the gallery to say, "You are requested, Reverend Sir, to give out another hymn." Asked for the reason behind this extraordinary response, the tinplate worker replied, "We do not approve of the sentiments of the hymn you have just read."[6]

Fascinated by the confusion that democratic rhetoric had wrought on older ways of thinking, Gilman rehearsed in his mini-history all the questions about status that were bedeviling his generation. Why, he pondered, had the villagers recoiled at the thought of the talented Charles Williams following in his father's shoemaking trade? Europeans, he ruminated, claimed that all Americans were plebians, yet, plebian though they might be, Americans nonetheless had their preferences. A Harvard-educated Unitarian minister himself, Gilman concluded that Americans had chosen to "draw arbitrary lines of distinction between different professions." More important than family, wealth, or even education, he felt, were "vocations." This explained why "certain sets of persons do somehow contrive to obtain an ascendancy in every town and village," but, as Gilman conceded, the whole subject was extremely unsettled, "the Mass is fermenting," and only time would reveal its taste.[7]

The fermenting mass effervesced throughout Gilman's story of changing music directors, for he had adroitly put all the elements of social structuring into play—sex, rank, religion, merit, mobility, and ambition. Only the question of race failed to make an appearance in the New England village, even though it moved the entire social system of Gilman's adopted home in South Carolina, where he served as the pastor of the Charleston Second Congregational Church. The men supported the singing privileges of a servant, but rejected a woman as choir director, while the female choristers could not so easily abandon considerations of rank, but did not balk at directorship by a member of their own sex. Appealing to British standards, the academy preceptor uncovered the persistent appeal of English aristocrats through the simple mechanism of singing *Old Hundred* with "a conscious superiority in taste."[8] Yet the villagers accepted the upward mobility of the talented shoemaker's son and the New Hampshire farm boy studying medicine and presumably tolerated the assertiveness of the tinplate worker with strong convictions about the contents of hell.

Mary Wentworth's brief authority had outraged the female choir members, even though her position as a domestic worker was glossed over by the term, "help." Gilman hailed this novel circumlocution because it admitted into the mind "a sense of independence and a hope of rising in the world," which Wentworth in fact showed that she possessed by leaving town to become a teacher. "Help" did not carry with it the stamp of dependency of "servant," Gilman noted. Less charitably, he called the farmer's son studying medicine "an uncouth personage," but, once his education was completed, he nonetheless went off to a new settlement to enjoy the status of a doctor. Even more shocking—probably downright unthinkable—had been the behavior of the tinplate worker, whose religious convictions had emboldened him to rebuke the minister as he stood in his pulpit. Such personal initiatives threw the defenders of community traditions on the defensive. Like a vestigial organ in the social body, Gilman's village choir tried to avoid infection while being assailed by a sequence of surprises, as unexpected as they were unwelcome.

The egalitarian spirit promoted by the Revolution might have remained a purely patriotic sentiment had not the rush to new lands, the religious revivals, and the prosperity that brought the accouterments of refinement to an ever-widening circle of families strengthened the hand of those who longed for comprehensive social change. Seeking to expand rather than limit the ambit of popular government, they sought to eliminate the traces of a deferential society. The protracted battles between the Federalists and their Jeffersonian challengers had thoroughly politicized the very notion of social superiority. Those who found the jumbling of social place unsettling put up stiff resistance to the move to translate political values into social norms, but other forces conspired to promote parity among white American men. The abundance of public land for sale opened up farm ownership to the majority of those maturing in the first decades of the nineteenth century. The revitalization of American Protestantism through the revivals of the Second Great Awakening undermined old religious hierarchies. At the same time an expanding commercial inventory of commodities added convenience, comfort, and beauty to everyday life, triggering a pervasive yearning for refinement and its handmaiden, respectability. New livelihoods carried an invitation to the sons and daughters of rural America to join the sprawling middle class of teachers, clerks, preachers, proprietors, lawyers, and physicians.

It is difficult to fit the American social structure of the early nineteenth century into the stock categories of class analysis, unless one wishes to rely upon income and wealth distribution independent of their social meaning.[9] Yet it would also be a mistake to label this period as one moving towards egalitarian social norms *tout court*. Not only were there distinctive patterns by region, but the democratization of ambition that undermined a fixed system of status also fueled new forms of differentiation. Neither the assertiveness of servants nor the homogenizing of dress forced a redistribution of income. Americans' reputation for equality of condition was earned through comparisons. Landowning and wealth distribution were much more equitable in the United States than in any other country. Looking at the nation as a whole, very nearly half of the free white men in 1798 owned property, with the top 10 percent controlling almost half of all wealth.[10] Colonial deference patterns had been a casualty of the Revolutionary War and notional acceptance of equality a badge of patriotism, but more enduringly Americans who succeeded in establishing a competence on farms, in trade, or through the new array of urban professions began to shape a new social order around their interpretation of American virtues.

After 1800 a very large rent in the social fabric opened up for people who were ready to walk through it. The justification of independence had offered an explicit defense of political rights, and the Jeffersonians quickly linked democratic governance with equality of respect. Manners, forms, and idle gossip were all drawn into the political battles between the Federalists and Jeffersonians that persisted into the 1820s. Looking back on those days, Martin Van Buren considered the key difference between him and the Federalist patrons of New York to have been his "faith in the capacity of the masses of the people of our Country to govern themselves, and in their general integrity in the exercise of that function."[11]

Talk of an egalitarian society disencumbered by privilege and ranks forced the defenders of tradition to become Cassandras, declaiming on the troubles to be visited upon Americans if they abandoned ancient wisdom about public order. A brouhaha over the Order of Cincinnati—provoked when a group of Continental Army officers formed a society for themselves and their descendents—sounded an early warning that ordinary Americans would oppose any national institutions based on hereditary distinctions. The outcry startled George Washington and seemed sufficient in John Marshall's eyes to argue for the Order's disbandment.[12] Seven years later, John Adams's campaign to find a suitably majestic salutation for the president ended in a rout when the consensus supported addressing the nation's chief executive henceforth as "Mr. President."

Shrewd about the political import of social messages, Jefferson rejected the formality that intimidated ordinary people. At the White House he frequently opened the door himself, receiving guests in his lounging jacket. Diplomatic protocol at state dinners yielded to the simple dictum, "those next to the dining room go in first." Even more significant, at his receptions Jefferson replaced Washington's stiff bow from a dais for the fraternal handshake at ground level. The new custom communicated parity and warmth. As a greeting proper only between men, it also signaled a masculine camaraderie that excluded women to whom one might still bow.

In these tempests in a teapot can be read the leaves of America's social future. What seems overdetermined in retrospect appeared to contemporaries as hanging in the balance. Reading Mary Wollstonecraft, Adams exploded with anger at her expectation that the French Revolution would effect lasting change: "And does this foolish woman expect to get rid of an aristocracy?" "God Almighty has decreed in the creation of human nature an eternal aristocracy among men," he scribbled in the margins of his book, adding for emphasis that "the world is always has been and ever will be governed by it."[13] What neither Adams nor Wollstonecraft could have imagined was that expanded opportunities in politics and commerce along with changing sensibilities in religion would soon blur the distinctions of family, dress, taste, literacy, and access to knowledge–the work horses of social differentiation.

The spirit of high Federalism continued to flourish in many places after 1800. Northern cities became sites of what can now be seen as rear-guard actions against the emerging social ethic. John Pickering, the son of arch-Federalist Timothy Pickering, worried about the Americans' corruption of the English language, quoted with approval an article in the *Edinburgh Review* that appealed to "men of birth and education" to do something about the American idioms that grated on English ears. "America has thrown off the yoke of the British nation," Pickering's British authority acknowledged, "but she would do well for some time, to take the laws of composition from the Addisons, the Swifts, and the Robertsons of her ancient sovereign."[14]

In Philadelphia, Joseph Dennie's *Port Folio* attracted a group of young Federalists intent upon exposing the delusive dangers of the new egalitarianism. With mordant wit, aristocratic elegies–even ribald verses–they detailed the malign influence of the French Revolution upon their fellow countrymen, most notably those carried away by Jeffersonian elan. Slowly these conservatives came to realize that "mysterious energies" were acting upon American society in utterly radical ways. By the time of Jefferson's second election they gave up hope that they could bring Americans back to their senses and conceded that for their country "the sunlit world of peace and order and prosperity it had so recently known under Washington" would not return.[15]

Carried on with varying degrees of intensity, champions of an open society battled the defenders of old ways. At risk were the old markers of wealth, style, and family, now attacked as irrelevant to a democratic ethic pivoting around equality of respect and an appreciation of individual merit. Looking back to her childhood in a New England village, Eliza Lee described the great influence of the pastor before "any sectarians had invaded our parishes."[16] Taking a less nostalgic view, Catharine Sedgwick contrasted the Stockbridge pastors' three-cornered beaver hat of her youth with Henry Ward Beecher's "Cavalier" hat: "the first formal, elaborate fixed; the last easy, comfortable, flexible, and assuming nothing superior to the mass."[17] It was exactly these relaxed ways that concerned Dolly Madison, who arranged for the composition of "Hail to the Chief" to be played at state receptions to rouse people to appropriate respect when her husband, the president, entered the room.

The rambunctious politics of the 1790s disillusioned cultural nationalists like Noah Webster, Charles Brockden Brown, Samuel Latham Mitchill, and David Ramsay. They had expected the free institutions of America to promote literature, science, and scholarship; their nationalist fervor had been nourished by fantasies of American greatness in areas marked out by the high civilization of metropolitan Europe. Despite the Federalists' vigor as journalists and their election to state office through the 1820s, the party died a slow death once ordinary people ceased to defer to their social superiors. As the Federalists painfully learned, maintaining social ranks required consent from below. Deeply offended by the crass self-assertion of common folk, the Federalist elite increasingly turned their refinement into an end in itself, strengthening their ties with the English world from whence they took their values. In New York and Philadelphia, rising real-estate prices sustained the wealth of clusters of intermarrying families of the colonial upper class.[18] Disappointed by politics and the paucity of achievements in the arts, the Federalists became America's first cultural critics. Their laments, however, were those of a spurned elite dispossessed of its admiring following. Reborn politically in the 1820s, many New Englanders with Federalist origins would find their American voice as evangelical reformers.

As Gilman's story relates, the continuities that could once have been taken for granted gave way to the predictability that all was in flux. Distinctions, whether linked to the economic notion of class or left to float as shared preferences in attitudes and behavior, only work when most men and women recognize them and seek to perpetuate them in their public performances and through the lessons they pass on to their children. The traditional deployment of shame and praise had depended upon a code of conformity that was vanishing. Top-down enforcement in colonial communities had helped maintain the order of prescribed behavior, but upper-class moralizing had become unacceptable by the turn of the century. Sustained attacks on the hierarchies of church, state, and family had left the public sphere unpoliced by ministers and magistrates. The nicely-defined ranks of gentry, middling folk, and poor increasingly lost credibility in a world where there were few strongholds for the gentry to command, and new opportunities stirred ambitions throughout the "fermenting mass." Without a consensual base, the ideal of a structured society slowly faded, leaving a welter of organizing principles to vie for public affirmation.

Men and women in various social settings began examining once shared values, asking themselves about American indebtedness to British tastes, the status of women, the connection of piety to respectability, and whether the continuation of slavery undercut the republic's claim to the high ground staked out in the Declaration of Independence. Foreign visitors puzzled over the displays of undifferentiated sociability in the United States and attributed them to American politics. Ludwig Gall thought that politicians had to be ultra-democratic, noting that "in the six months before the election of 1820 the governor of Pennsylvania did his own shopping, appearing in the market with basket on arm." "When there was a public auction," he continued, "his business took him there." All this occurred twenty years before the Log Cabin campaign of 1840.[19]

The Scottish traveler James Flint gave the relationship of manners and politics a more extended critique and decided that universal suffrage and frequent elections strengthened the bonds of American society: "the candidates having no boroughs to be treated with in the wholesale way, and the constituents being too numerous, and coming too often in the way, to admit of their being bought over, expectants are obliged to depend on their popularity, and do not find it their interest to repulse any one." "It is only from these causes," he explained, that he could account for "the affability of manners which are almost universal." In contrast to Britain "where neighbors do not know the names of persons who live in adjoining houses," an American, even in new settlements, will know "almost any person, within ten miles of him." "The symptoms of republican equality are visible in all the members of the community," Flint claimed, for America was not "divided or formed into classes by the distinctions of title and rank, neither does political party seem to form such a complete separation amongst men, and the unequal distribution of property operates much less." Hence, he concluded, the individuals who compose American society "are less mutually repellent to one another . . . and the distinctions formed here are of a more natural kind, such as those . . . that proceed from the sympathies of human nature."[20]

❧❦❧

IN LEGAL THEORY, the common law gave all the autonomous and independent white men command over their wives, children, servants, and slaves to secure order in their domains. In practice, free young men *and* women struck out on their own; death regularly broke up families; slaves liberated themselves; and not all householders were up to assuming their supervisory responsibilities. Prospering in the early nineteenth-century economy often required movement—onto new land, towards urban opportunity, into new types of ventures. The migration of men and families onto the frontier exemplifies this point. The availability of public land for private purchase rapidly increased the number of property-owners. While many of them became dirt-poor farmers, they had got on the right side of the critical divide between independence and dependency, probably the most salient of all social markers in an America that was still preponderantly rural. Their status as the heads of their own farming families enabled thousands of young men and women to replicate the world of their parents, even if the multiplying lawyers and bankers who rose to challenge older authority figures could not immediately fill their places.

Morris Birkbeck, writing for his English compatriots, felt that it was almost impossible to convey the American love of movement. Imagine, he wrote after his 1815 visit, the numerous stages, light wagons, and horseback riders and "you have before you a scene of bustle and business, extending over a space of three hundred miles, which is truly wonderful."[21] People not only moved out; they sometimes moved up as they moved out. This very mobility eroded expectations of enduring status and scrambled the social codes inherited from a Europeanized colonial world. The mobility of young adults leaving the place of their birth, of talent searching for its optimal rewards, or of cash and credit chasing after innovation worked against fixed statuses just as, paradoxically, prosperity made it possible for many more people to ape the consuming tastes of the old colonial gentry. As soon as people subjected social position to analysis, they put it at risk, for truly effective social markers must be communicated subliminally—their identities conspicuous, attitudes unthinking, and behavior automatic.

When annual sales of western land vaulted from a hundred thousand acres in the 1790s to half a million after Jefferson's election, farms multiplied at a rate unmatched since the original settlements.[22] Meanwhile, in older sections, farmer-artisans found new profits in the growing demand for clocks, implements, and furniture. As with so many other developments in the West, these new mores bounced back East, opening communities there to new ways to value themselves, their neighbors, and their servants, as Gilman's village choir so charmingly demonstrated.

The frontier had a different impact on America's enslaved population. What was a white man's main chance often brought misery to black Americans because the profits from the cotton boom promoted a thriving domestic slave trade, separating hundreds of thousands of African Americans from their homes and families in what had been the relatively stable plantations of Virginia and Maryland. Working conditions on the Southern frontier were the harshest on the continent, and occasions for forming new communities to replace the ones left behind in Virginia or Maryland rarely materialized. Economic developments fixed the status of slavery more firmly than ever before; the rhetoric of American opportunity, largely produced in the North, rang hollow for this full fifth of the nation's population.

Nor was white mobility always upward. Bankruptcy was a common fact of life, given the fragility of the country's credit system and the foolhardiness of nascent entrepreneurs. Overspeculation brought down the highest flyers while abrupt financial downturns like Jefferson's embargo or the War of 1812 exposed all borrowers to sharp reversals of fortune. New land undercut the value of the old, especially in the northern frontiers of Vermont and Maine, though the intensification of garden cultivation around cities helped offset this trend.

Popular lore had it that American wealth was never successfully passed down through three generations. John Chambers gave voice to this view when he told his children, "I have yet to see wealth pass by descent beyond the third generation, but I have seen & see every day the second generation who has squandered the labours of their predecessors."[23] Echoing Chambers, Ebenezer Thomas remarked how unusual it was that the family of the Providence East India merchant John Brown "has increased in wealth through three generations—a circumstance which I do not recollect to have occurred before, as it has been almost a universal practice, for the children to squander what the father accumulates."[24] Experiences like those of John Jay Smith's father formed the basis for these generalizations. Heir to prime Philadelphia real estate, he bartered away lot after lot to pay for incidental purchases, allegedly selling property at the corner of Chestnut and Samson streets for a box of linen![25] Even the enormous fortune amassed by the assiduous town developer William Cooper melted away before his heirs could lay claim to it.[26]

Egalitarian rhetoric, mobility, and the absence of great and enduring fortunes tended to promote a social homogeneity that Americans began to take pride in. The prominent Baltimore journalist, Hezekiah Niles, regularly told his readers that a man had more honor being descended from a line of mechanics like himself than from royalty.[27] Even the size of American landholdings seemed relatively uniform in comparison with European norms. Benjamin Latrobe, who was reared abroad, described Mount Vernon as pleasant and modest, the country estate of someone in England, he calculated, who would have an income of £500 to £600 a year. Martha, whom he thought had retained "the strong remains of considerable beauty," had "no affectation of superiority in the slightest degree, but acts completely in the character of the mistress of the house of a respectable and opulent country gentleman."[28] At that time, George Washington then ranked as one of the wealthiest men in the United States.

Equally homogenizing were the names this generation gave to its children. Young adults eschewed their parents' habit of looking for names in the Bible, few calling their children Ichabod, Ebenezer, Sylvester, Elezar, Ephraim, Jehudi, Emmor, Alpheus, Elnathan, Bezaleel, Ezekill, Jedadiah, Zebulon, Ludovicus, Eliphalet, Alpheus, Loammi, Hezekiah, Adoniram, Selleck, Jabez, Erastus, Zadoch, Ashahel, Arphaxed, Zephaniah, Shubael, Zacheus, Zebadiah, Azariah, Amariah, or Kaziah, as they had been named. The expression, "every Tom, Dick, and Harry," could only have meaning after this cohort left a progeny named not for Biblical figures, but instead for the Georges, Thomases, Richards, Johns, and Jameses of the Revolutionary leadership.[29]

American homogeneity extended spatially as well. Accustomed to the dramatic differences between rural and urban life at home, foreign travelers repeatedly expressed amazement at the alertness of farming people. Crossing the Allegheny mountains, Birkbeck reported that what was "most at variance with English notions of the American people, is the urbanity and civilization that prevail in situations remote from large cities," where people "have not for a moment lost sight of the manners of polished life." Americans, he claimed, "are strangers to rural simplicity: the embarrassed air of an awkward rustic, so frequent in England, is rarely seen in the United States." He went on to say that this was doubtless "the effect of political equality, the consciousness of which accompanies all their intercourse, and may be supposed to operate most powerfully on the manners of the lowest class."[30] Gall found that country wagoners dressed much like city folk. Flint was impressed that farmers "who own but small properties, keep one horse gigs" that their "ladies drive dexterously."[31]

The number of people living in villages with more than one thousand people only increased from 10 to 16 percent between 1790 and 1830, a statistical reminder that the United States remained a rural society throughout the first half of the century, but with an abundance of enterprising rural artisans and mechanics, country folk could buy the same wares as those in the city, and in fact their taste for stenciled chairs, painted barns, and family portraits accelerated the commercialization of rural life.[32] Country readers' eagerness to get news sustained rural newspapers in most country towns, contributing to the homogeneity of sophistication. When Philadelphia publishers assumed that country folk would buy the books scorned by city dwellers, rural customers showed them how wrong they were and successfully demanded the titles that they wanted.[33]

Explorer Henry Schoolcraft thought that the mixing of western settlers from half a dozen states "must destroy provincialism, and do much to annihilate local prejudices."[34] Pickering, the collector of Americanisms, considered American diction more uniform than in England because of the "frequent removals of people from one part of our country to another." Even beggars conformed to an American style. According to Charles Janson, though rare, these "republican beggars generally profer their requests in the same manner as a person would ask a loan," specifying the sums they expected to be given.[35]

Women, children, and blacks could be assigned a fixed place in society because they were easily identified. The case became more complicated with white men. Unwilling to claim prestige through sartorial distinction, many upper-class men dressed negligently, adopting a kind of social camouflage that foreigners found perplexing. When knee breeches and buckled pumps gave way to long pants and laced shoes, the male body carried fewer signs to be read for social status, especially as the expanding ranks of clerks and storekeepers added to the number of men in conventional town garb. Close attention to clean linen and proper style became a matter of importance to those aspiring to move up. Interlopers—men like James Guild, a Yankee farmer turned peddler and calligrapher—invested in clothes to win respect from strangers. He became furious when the stratagem failed.[36] But, of course, in a real sense there were no interlopers in a society that had opened the gates so widely to the aspirations of the young.

Servants—white servants, that is—wreaked the most havoc on traditional social arrangements in America. Their aversion to the social stigma of dependency manifested itself in what Flint declared a genuine Americanism: the new rubric of "help," which Gilman had praised. Remarking on the reluctance of young women to go into house service, Flint recalled hearing from a Philadelphia manufacturer that he had no difficulty finding "females to be employed in his work-shop; but a girl for house-work he could not procure for less than twice the manufacturing wages." He also noted that throughout the West agricultural laborers were never called "servants," but always "hired hands." When manufacturing jobs came to New England, young women voted with their feet, rarely going "out to service" when they could do factory work.[37] The genteel heirs of Cooperstown founder William Cooper despaired of ever finding proper servants. Those in the local pool failed to show respect for their employers who, for their part, disliked displays of independence. Mary Ann Morris Cooper, James Fenimore Cooper's sister-in-law, crowed in her diary when she succeeded in finding a girl "free from Yankee dignity and ideas of Liberty," which she labeled "insolence only."[38]

The acerbic Charles Janson counted "one of the greatest evils of a republican form of government" the loss of "that subordination in society which is essentially necessary to render a country agreeable." Indeed, Janson feared his European audiences would not believe the arrogance of American servants without some proof, which he furnished in the form of a dialogue that he himself had engaged in at the front door of an acquaintance: "Is your master at home?"—"I have no master."—"Don't you live here?" "I *stay* here"—"And who are you then?" "Why, I am Mr. ____'s *help*."[39]

In nineteenth-century America the behavior of servants loomed large in daily life, for almost every household—down to the poorest farm—had one or more. To be really poor was to live without a servant. Lydia Sigourney, in one of her many didactic writings for young women, warned them of the scarcity of good household help and, like foreign visitors, linked the shortage to American political mores: "In our state of society, where equality so visibly prevails . . . servants faithful, and thoroughly trained in their several departments, are not always to be found."[40]

If servants resisted a servile attitude, ordinary farmers in New England disdained the efforts of their superiors to dictate taste in matters of architecture and landscaping. Upper-class reformers longed to preserve rustic scenes from some imagined agrarian past, when simple cottages festooned with roses and bordered with verdant fields and orchards dotted the countryside. Instead the farmers, who often carried on trades in their garages, poured their profits into outbuildings, which sprawled awkwardly across the landscape.[41] Secure in their property rights, these enterprising husbandmen ignored the lofty prescriptions for bucolic beauty.

Rarely discussed in writings of the first generation were the hopelessly poor, whose poverty denied them respectability and respect, but two physicians writing about their city's medical advances inadvertently disclosed how each one's region treated its lowest stratum. In the South the poor comprised that entire third of the population that was held in slavery; in the North, indigents and those at risk of indigency—probably 10 percent of the population. Both groups were deemed suitable as patients upon whom doctors might freely experiment. A promotional piece announcing the 1823 opening of the Medical College for Charleston outlined the advantages of a "Southern School of Medicine" by pointing to its unique capacity to study the diseases of "the Negro and Mulatto race." Nowhere else in the United States, the brochure continued, would students have "similar opportunities for the acquisition of anatomical knowledge, subjects being procured from among the colored population, in sufficient number for every purpose . . . without offending any individual." Alongside this research bonanza was laid the fact that a local education removed "the danger to our youth from the impressions they may imbibe, during their collegiate course abroad, ungenial to our peculiar modification of society."[42]

Daniel Drake, the founder of the Medical College of Ohio, similarly promoted the availability of pliant patients for his institution, only in Cincinnati they were the city's paupers and immigrants. Their illnesses could be turned into an asset when visitors paid lecturers' fees for lessons drawn from their medical problems, Drake explained. "It is an unquestionable fact," he had printed in italics, "that these wretched people, who at present subject us to the heaviest contributions, would, if an infirmary were provided, become a source of profit and prosperity to the city," doing "in sickness, what they did not perform in health—support themselves." Stirred by his own alchemy of turning dross human material into gold, Drake enthusiastically went on to suggest that a "Poor-house, with shops and gardens might be made a part of the same establishment."[43] Both promoters demonstrated a striking callousness towards the vulnerable in their midst. One offered slaves' bodies as the means for acquiring useful information for planters about slave illnesses, while keeping planters' sons at home for their schooling; the other touted the potential contribution of wasted lives to the prosperity of a thriving western city.

The dethroning of older, invidious social distinctions opened the way for new standards, many successful Americans writing about their country as the locus for exchanges of talents and riches. Productive, inventive individuals were presented as powerful nodes of attention and admiration, their lives serving as models of innovation in a society losing all desire to replicate past ways of doing things. This functional, future-oriented social blueprint replaced the older picture of communities unified around a stable social order. The personal qualities of intelligence, honesty, commitment, and enterprise came to be seen as animating the social whole.

Intelligence was the word contemporaries used to characterize those who succeeded in their midst, but it took a specific kind of intelligence to pry open the opportunities in the United States. The demand for those who could read, write, calculate, and speak was higher than the supply; the commercial opportunities depending upon literacy were expanding more rapidly than the human output of the primitive schooling system. Fitting into the beckoning commercial world also involved a willingness to move to where the jobs were. Those who prospered from these changes were the disciplined, hard-working sons and daughters of farm families who tailored their talents to society's demands, not the few scions of America's wealthy families. Because there were thousands of able young people to fill the positions of a developing society, employers no longer needed to rely upon the old system of sponsored promotion; the fit between talent and task could be made quickly as young people found their ways to opportunity. Lying in the future was the industrial order with its hierarchies of workers and owners, blue collars and white collars, wage-earners and managers. A "pattern of informal leniency," it has been noted, marked even factory relations until Irish and French Canadian mill workers arrived in great numbers in the 1840s. When displaced, American-born artisans tended to go to other skilled jobs, leaving unskilled work for the new arrivals.[44] With such upward mobility for native-born, white Americans, it was difficult to institutionalize a strong class consciousness, but invidious distinctions of foreign birth soon joined that of race.

For a significant proportion of the population, being saved was an even more potent differentiator than intelligence. The three decades of successful evangelizing across the hamlets, villages, towns, and cities of the United

States pushed humility, charity, and faith to the forefront of public consciousness. Commitment to the true Christian life exercised a powerful hold upon hundreds of thousands of Americans, encouraging them to rework their old selves into new and better ones. The conversion experience released enough reforming energy from those touched by the revivals—probably a quarter of the population—to reshape American public life. Intensely personal, the revivals replaced the ceremonialism of the older churches with the unabashed emotionalism of the Baptists and Methodists, leaving those converted with a heightened sense of the difference between the saved and the unsaved, the spiritually alive and spiritually dead—distinctions that further challenged old hierarchies.

Methodists, Baptists, and Presbyterians, like the Quakers, announced their new devotion by spurning fancy clothes, lavish entertainment, and slaves, enjoining their members to wear plain clothing and avoid frivolities. They kept a strict watch over each others' public behavior.[45] Displaying their religious convictions through their dress, evangelical Christians often provoked reactions from the less religious. Julia Tevis, a bride traveling west with her husband, a Methodist circuit-rider, was humiliated when a farmer refused them the conventional hospitality of the road. So unexpected was this, she explained, that its denial had to be taken as an insult. Sensing her distress, the son of the house explained, "It's the broad brim and straight coat that made him do it . . . You see, we're going to have a dancing party tonight."[46] Censorious, the revivalists stirred the ire of those with more relaxed standards or none at all.

Because the revivalists successfully challenged the religious hegemony of the Anglican and Congregational churches, the Second Great Awakening contributed to both the social homogenizing and democratizing of American society. Its social ideals complemented the republican equality spread by the Jeffersonians, even though many revivalists came from stern New England Federalist stock. It may be counted one of the ironies of the age that the public space opened by political outsiders who were often hostile to revealed religion soon was filled by a new crop of outsiders—fervent evangelicals. And both political and Christian radicals attracted the same kind of critics. Arthur Singleton, a New England travel writer, sketched in acid a camp meeting he visited in Kentucky: "the ministers are a species of without-method Methodists; happy compounds of illiterateness and fanaticism . . . With most of these apostles, the text is but a pitching of the tone to the nasality," he continued, "for, altho they name a text when they commence, that is commonly the last you hear of it."[47]

Christiana Tillson gave a similarly sharp appraisal of the Methodist circuit riders who visited her frontier Illinois settlement once a month, "singing and ranting." "If preachers had come among the people meekly, and with an earnest desire to do a good to the souls of men—however weak and ignorant they might have been," she stated, "I could have respected their effort . . . but their whole manner evinced so much arrogance and self display and such unblushing impudence as to repel me."[48]

More charitably, Timothy Flint, a New Englander turned champion of the West, analyzed the revivals' social power when he explained:

> The ambitious and wealthy are there, because in this region opin-
> ion is all-powerful; and they are there, either to extend their
> influence, or that their absence may not be noted to diminish it.
> Aspirants for office are there, to electioneer, and gain popularity.
> Vast numbers are there from simple curiosity, merely to enjoy a
> spectacle. The young and the beautiful are there, with mixed
> motives, which it were best not severely to scrutinize.[49]

In the end those who cherished the learned Christian tradition had to yield to the success of the revivalists and imitate their style.[50] In turn the revivalists learned to accommodate the refined and educated tastes that were surfacing among their members. Like earlier religious reformers, they confronted the tension between the disciplined application to work and the enjoyment of the material fruits of such effort. Their parishioners' pursuit of refinement too was a snare for evangelical preachers, appearing as a diversion to the pious life, but it could also be interpreted as offering the road to respectability that preserved good family morals. In the end refined tastes cloaked as respectability triumphed, and material success once more crowned the religious devotion of Americans.

THE BUOYANCY of the early national economy put money in pockets that had formerly carried stones, apples, string, and scraps of paper. And these coins inspired fantasies of self-fashioning that would have been laughable to an older generation—perhaps were laughable, if shared, at the time. Refinement, once closely associated with the style of a royal court, became an integral part of the aspirations of ordinary men and women in the first decades of the nineteenth century. Where earlier gentility had been the quest of those in the upper reaches of colonial society (one thinks of George Washington laboriously copying injunctions from English etiquette books), the early nineteenth century witnessed a popular surge towards the elusive goals of good manners and refined taste.[51] Linoleum floors, stenciled furniture, pianos—even painted barns and walled-off bedrooms—announced a more genteel, capacious way of life. Country stores expanded their inventories in response to the demands of country folk, stocking more and more household comforts and decorative items.[52]

Fashion too began to encourage a more honest, direct, and simple presentation of self. Elihu Shepard remembered well his shock at finding his teacher "the morning star of fashion," unrecognizable at the beginning of the term in 1800 when "she had caused her long hair to be trimmed short like a young girl's" and had also abandoned the fashionable dress of 1798 for "comely and informal attire." He went on to muse that it was a time of fashion change. "Gentlemen of taste laid aside their sharp-toed shoes and books, their knee and shoe buckles, their long stockings and short breeches, their long vests and ruffled shirts, their single-breasted coats and broad-brimmed cocked hats." Censored by many, the new fashions, he noted, brought "great zest and pleasure to the young."[53] From the 1790s through the 1820s women's fashion, aping the classical style adopted in France, were simple and light, conveying nonchalance through the appearance of uncorseted waistlines and minimalist draped skirts. Cut to permit easy movement, the empire dresses could also be cheaply produced, as Shepard's teacher no doubt discovered.[54]

In this as in so many ways, Jefferson took the lead, renouncing powdered wigs and taking up the humble shoelace. Benjamin Silliman, who seems something of a young fogie and certainly disliked Jeffersonian innovations, connected the new fashions with "new philosophy," claiming that women's exposure of their persons excited passion, but extinguished respect. He also expressed hope that "no cold-hearted, ferocious philosophy" would attempt to substitute "that masculine robustness of character, which Mary Wollstonecraft inculcates, in the place of that delightful tenderness, which adorns every female action," a comment that elicited one of the few discussions of Wollstonecraft's *Vindications of the Rights of Women* in the American press.[55]

Displaying book learning, holding office, and having a house with more than two rooms no longer set a few people off from the great majority. The brisk circulation of news about fashion and manners brought the elements of refined living to an ever-expanding audience. As new consumer commodities found their way into homes and onto bodies, they became fresh social markers. Carpeting not only indicated the money and desire to purchase it, but signaled as well that those who trod on it had learned to wipe their feet. Still the grungy work and long hours of ordinary laborers militated against adoption of much in the way of home furnishings, even if their labor remained the lodestar of American patriotism—its energy, inventiveness, and intelligence furnishing the proof that the American experiment in democracy was working.

Pleasurable in themselves, the new comforts were implicated in a way of life long associated with the upper strata of society. American democratization involved two mildly contradictory developments: the elevation of all white Americans to a plateau of significance and an extension of refined tastes to an increasing number of families that differentiated them from the poor and the dissolute. Most Americans exulted in their abandonment of European snobbery even as they copied European forms of gracious living that enabled them to feel superior to those who had not. Having rejected most aspects of a tiered society with its regimented distances, many ordinary Americans went on to embrace the ideal of refinement. Where people could afford an extra room, parlors became centers for domestic conviviality. The market linked chauvinism to gentility. By 1823, people were able to purchase the first piano produced entirely in the United States from Jonas Chickering.

Refinement involved far more than purchasing embellishments for self and home; it entailed a demanding set of avoidances—not slumping, shuffling, or gaping—along with mastering a range of skills. The popularity of etiquette books detailing courtly codes of behavior gave proof that economic success whetted the appetite for genteel self-fashioning and the careful cultivation of appearances. Abel Bowen advised young women to learn about mineralogy, conchology, entomology, embroidery, writing, painting, music, dancing, archery, riding, and ornamental artistry.[56] Handwriting became a prized accomplishment as calligraphy instructors sprang up like dandies at a cotillion. Holding short-term classes in towns up and down the eastern seaboard, itinerant teachers brought the beauty of cursive script to thousands of eager self-improvers. James Guild, a particularly raffish purveyor of refinement, claimed to have attracted forty scholars in Norfolk simply by advertising "to teach writing, and painting miniatures."[57]

New England moralists feared that the western settlements would foster the same leveling tendencies that alarmed them at home. In this they were correct. Rebecca Burlend noted that every man was called "sir, however

The young woman drawing at her table in this illustration for the 1801 juvenile story, *The History of a Pin*, reflects the new ideal of cultivated tastes for female accomplishment. Courtesy, American Antiquarian Society.

slender his pretensions to knighthood, or how long soever the time since his small-clothes were new." Women, she said, were "in like manner honoured with madam." Birkbeck found the frequent invocation of the word "elegant" a source of amusement, as in "elegant mill, an elegant orchard— used everywhere that is inappropriate in English language." He added that he hadn't heard "taste" referred to, assuming it to be "as foreign to them as comfort the French."[58] Margaret Dwight, a granddaughter of Jonathan Edwards, similarly disdained the diction of those she encountered traveling West in 1810. "We stopt at noon, at a dismal looking log hut tavern," she recorded, where "the landlady (I hate the word but I must use it,) talk'd about bigotry, bigotted notions, liberty of conscience," adding patronizingly that "she did not look as if she knew the meaning of conscience, much less of bigotry."[59]

The contradiction of gentility spreading through a society proud of its democratic ways did not go unnoticed, but most writers who attacked snobbery were inclined to look backwards to family pretensions. John Chambers, a frontier political leader, excoriated "the arrogance of poor stupid wretches who founded their claims for notice, if not for distinction, upon the wealth of some ancestor or relations, or perhaps worse, upon the accidental possession of it in their own persons."[60] Equally indignant, America's first professional architect, Benjamin Latrobe, mocked the folly of loving rank, particularly army titles: "Captains, majors, colonels, and generals elbow a man out of all hopes even of this country."[61] Social arbiters like Catharine Sedgwick tried to square the circle by promoting egalitarian refinement, an oxymoron that nicely captured the split personality of American society, with its yearning for the manners of the better sort and appreciation of the vernacular culture of ordinary folk.[62]

Although the revolutionary zeal for change stopped at the threshold of the "castle," where the master reigned supreme over his household, its transforming potential could be seen in everything from the institution of slavery to the conduct of youth. Few American women emerged to urge a redress of laws affecting property, divorce, or child custody, yet the generation coming of age after the Revolution began to grapple with the question of women's status because their lives began with a severe rupture in established understandings. It was difficult to keep talk of freedom from spilling over the formal channels of law and spreading to informal and private areas. Little was done to change the legal restrictions affecting women's control over their lives, but the outpouring of writings, mostly from men, forced fresh thinking about women's schooling, the examples set by their mothers, and the erotic appeal of feminine incapacity.

George Tucker, one of Virginia's most prominent authors, addressed the subject of women in his imaginary tale of the Okalbia of Happy Valley, where girls grew up "under few restraints" and were taught "all the speculative branches of knowledge" along with instruction "in cookery, needlework, and every sort of domestic economy; as were the young men in the occupations which required strength and exposure."[63] Thomas Branagan, a contentious Irishman who emigrated to Pennsylvania, vacillated in his writings between commiserating with women over their lot in life and condemning them for committing "intellectual assassination at their teaparties." Too many mothers, Branagan charged, brought up their girls "as if they merely intended them to be playthings for our sex," acknowledging that it was "a tyrannical maxim . . . commensurate with Turkish barbarity . . . that women are only to be seen, not heard." Branagan, reared as a Catholic, drew upon his adopted Methodist faith to argue for women's inherent dignity. "Will you then," he asked rhetorically, "let the prejudice of education, the tyranny of custom, or the usurpation of our sex rob you of your crowns, and bereave you of your celestial rewards in a coming world."[64]

John Neal, probably the most unconventional writer of the entire period, wrote an inflammatory pamphlet, *The Rights of Women,* which began with the provocative statement that American women "are not *free–free,* in the sense that Men are *free,* according to any definition of liberty." "Whether the women of this country are *slaves* or not," Neal decided, depended upon one's definition of slavery. Referring to the fact that women voted in New Jersey, Neal explained derisively that the legislature there had settled the constitutional question "by declaring that the word '*inhabitants,*' meant *free white males!*" He might have added that the Jeffersonian champions of universal rights had denied both women and free blacks the vote in the same legislative stroke. For his part, Neal resolved that if women were part of the people, they were "entitled to *participate* in their *legislative council:* and not being represented, have a right to legislate for themselves."[65] Samuel Knapp, a lawyer, author, and popular speaker, more glumly bemoaned the fact that women "in this business-doing country" have incomparably more leisure for literary pursuits and yet in matters literary had accomplished "Nothing! literally *nothing!*"

Like Branagan, Knapp blamed both mothers and men—a rather powerful mix of forces in a young girl's life—for "a misjudged and defective system of education." While vigorously protesting their "mis-education," Knapp despaired of change because of the congruence between "the frivolity of that sex, and the silly part of our own." Probing beneath the surface a bit, he explored the consequences of there being no inducements for women of wealth or fame to liberate themselves from a destination confined to marriage. "So long as men are pleased with toys and play-things," he concluded, "they cannot blame females" for neglecting their minds. He went on to concede that he was only speaking of women who did not have to work for their living. Knapp showed considerable sympathy for young women's situation when he discussed the fear of becoming an old maid that was implanted in women, deploring as well that girls in their early teens were forced into courtship, leaving "young women whose minds are just coming to maturity, crowded out of circles that they would adorn and animate, to make room for frivolous children—who have watched the silent operation of anxiety and neglect on a lively and ingenuous mind, and marked its gradual transition from gaiety and animation, to placid dejection and cheerless indifference."[66]

The neglect of girls' education and their premature involvement in the frivolity attendant upon courtship bothered lots of people, but women writers were significantly more timid than men when discussing this subject. Mary Tyler, the strong-willed wife of playwright Royall Tyler, demurred only slightly from contemporary mores when she wrote that even if mothers must guard the complexions of their daughters there was no reason not to let them run and enjoy themselves in full liberty for a few hours every day. Showing obeisance to the misogynist discourse that held likeness to a woman the worst fate of a man, Tyler entreated mothers "to reflect upon what manner of men you will wish to see your sons become," threatening effeminacy and pusillanimity if mothers instilled "into their tender minds the love of dress and show."[67] Thus conventional morality swiveled in a round of fears about depriving girls of their hopes for intellectual growth and men of their virile development.

Perhaps nothing challenged gendered prescriptions more than the issue of women's education. The vibrancy of urban culture found expression in lecture series, scientific demonstrations, and a heightened appreciation of learning. Some young women clearly benefited from these developments, even though their intellectual tastes clashed with the eroticizing of frailty and innocence. John Griscom, a self-taught chemist, organized a course of lectures on natural philosophy exclusively for females in 1817. More than a hundred young women "from the most respectable families of the city" attended, he claimed, his editor going on to hail "his efforts to extend the benefits of scientific knowledge among the masses."[68]

Elizabeth Levick remembered attending lectures on botany with other young women at the American Philosophical Society in 1815. "This was considered a great innovation, and by not a few we were regarded as very strong-minded young women," she noted. Describing doubts as to "the propriety and the delicacy of our conduct," Levick went on to affirm how interesting and instructive the lectures proved to be. "I was at that time a member of the House of Industry, and growing out of these lectures a committee of us was appointed to collect herbs . . . for the poor."[69] Other women contrasted their education with that of their parents' era: "girls were not much esteemed in those days," Olive Cleaveland Clarke commented dryly. Between the two generations, the literacy gap between women and men in most of the North was closed, though literacy for both sexes remained lower in the South. Women's careers as missionaries, writers, preachers, and school proprietresses revealed a range of female talent that prevented closure on the subject of women's education.

Foreigners were particularly astute in analyzing the gendered etiquette of the new republic. John Melish thought that women had a good deal of influence in the United States.[70] While commenting on the promiscuous mixing of millionaires and swindlers in public conveyances, Frederick Marryat, a British officer traveling through the United States, commented on the "universal deference and civility shown to the women, who may in consequence travel without protection all over the United States without the least chance of annoyance or insult." "Let a female be ever so indifferently clad, whatever her appearance may be," Marryat explained, "still it is sufficient that she is a female; she has the first accommodation, and until she has it, no man will think of himself." More grumpily Charles Janson concurred, complaining that women were "generally indulged" with the best seat on the typical twelve-place American stage coach.[71]

Sigourney's essays "to young ladies" revealed a society in flux, where women could be enjoined alternately to preside gracefully in the parlor or to meet stoically any eventuality. As Sigourney so perceptively saw, refinement could be women's ally without challenging the critics of her aspirations. For the majority of middle-class women, the cultivation of conversational skills was liberating, enabling them to turn their parlors into centers of sociability and cultivation. Refinement effected a number of changes in the American social scene. The successful effort to make public space safe for women meant that they could move freely outside their homes. The goal of being refined also created an incentive for both sexes to acquire the knowledge and taste that made for lively and agreeable exchanges between them. Subtly the range of acceptable feminine qualities expanded, pushing as it did against entrenched misogynist views of women's capacities.

Adverting again to the theme of America's egalitarian mores, Sigourney asserted that the United States had produced a society in which "the grades of rank and station" were not very clearly defined, yet the expectation of defined social tiers continued to underpin her observations, as when she commented that "the lower classes sometimes press upon the higher." And then again she affirmed democratic values, as when she concluded that in the United States "all should be willing to pay some tax for the privilege of a government, which admits such an high degree, and wide expansion of happiness."[72] Sigourney's concept of upper-class indulgence in lower-class

"Return from a Boarding School," an engraving by John Lewis Krimmel, was reproduced for the November, 1802 issue of *Analectic Magazine*. It depicts the sociability and expense of the new American parlors with their pianos, pets, tea sets, and decorative ornaments on walls and mantels. Courtesy, American Antiquarian Society.

aspirations conveys both an openness to fundamental change and the condescension of a social superior.

This same spirit of bracing ambivalence about social status can be found in contemporary novels. Authors routinely excoriated snobbishness and expressed indignation that anyone would be judged by family or wealth. Spirited speeches against snobbery were a favorite motif in American novels, like the one Samuel Woodword gave to his heroine in *The Deed of Gift*. When her father forbade a marriage to a man without fortune, she insisted on her rights because "on this point alone our sex can claim a prerogative."[73] Although memoirs were much more likely to praise actual women for their intelligence, fortitude, and reverence, fiction romanticized the feminine virtues of delicacy, modesty, and refinement. Even Maria Gowen Brooks, who had to fend for herself after her father died bankrupt, eschewed reality for fantasy in the stories of her exquisite heroines. Others, like Phoebe Hinsdale Brown, grappled with the question of women's changing status as when she gratuitously commented that her heroine had received a great education "at a time when female education was far from being understood and valued as it is at the present day."[74]

Readers could judge just how far and fast American mores had diverged from English ones through Jane Austen's novels, to which the women in Eliza Susan Quincy's family became addicted. "They were first mentioned to us by Judge Story, to whom they were recommended by Judge Marshall," Quincy confided in her journal.[75] Far more numerous than American ones, English romances were enormously popular, those of Walter Scott resonating strongly in the South, no doubt because they affirmed and romanticized the past with its hierarchies of class and sex.

Southerners no less than Northerners were affected by the tendencies of American independence to subvert the old colonial order, for the Revolution had dealt Southerners two blows: it exposed the freedom-seeking zeal of enslaved men and women, and it turned slavery into a sectional institution. Because many slaves ran to the British lines during the War, it was no longer possible to believe that they accepted their enslavement. The response of Northerners to the emancipatory spirit of the Declaration of Independence signaled the beginning of an international crusade against slavery. Forced for the first time to provide a moral defense of their now peculiar institution, Southerners turned increasingly to an idealization of kith and kin, honor and gracious living. African Americans, they argued, benefited from the contact with Christian religion and white civilization, even if their savage nature prompted them to flee.[76] Evangelical preachers inveighed against the sin of slavery, but by the 1820s most Baptists and Methodists had ceased their denunciations, acquiescing in the planters' moral code, which stressed the beneficence of slavery, the duties of submission, and the paramount authority of fathers and masters. Effective as an internal socializing mechanism, this creed further differentiated Northerners and Southerners, this time along the axis of their interpretation of Christianity.

When Virginia settlers originally fixed upon race as the defining characteristic of their legal slaves in the seventeenth century, they made the black body a mobile sign of social distinction. The Northern abolition movement challenged the fit of skin color and slave status, as it simultaneously increased the number of free blacks, some of them enjoying the status of citizens. Even in the South antislavery had its advocates, but the handsome profits of the post-1793 boom in cotton unified white Southerners while making Northern beneficiaries complicit as well. An economic development with profound social impact, cotton-growing spun gold for those who controlled the land and labor for its cultivation. The richest planters drew yearly revenues of $40,000–$50,000 from the labor of their slaves at a time when 160 acres of uncultivated land could be bought for two hundred dollars and casual workers earned seventy-five cents a day.[77]

Charles Ball, a self-liberated slave, considered the disparagement of work to be the key difference between the two regions. Drawing upon a youth spent in Maryland, Georgia, and South Carolina, Ball remarked on the lack of family pretensions in the Northern and middle states, stressing that such attitudes strictly controlled the options of white Southerners: "every kind of labour is as strictly prohibited to the sons and daughters of the planters, by universal custom, as if a law of the land made it punishable by fine and imprisonment." "The white man, who has no property, no possession, and no education," Ball continued, "is in Carolina in a condition no better than that to which the slave has been reduced; except only, that he is master of his own person, and of his own time, and may, if he chooses, emigrate and transfer himself to a country where he can better his circumstances." The contempt in which cottagers are held, "to be comprehended, must be seen," he asserted, contrasting poor white Southerners with "the respectable and useful class of day labourers" of the North.[78]

There were other particularities of Southern society. Upper-class Southerners did not confront the sauciness of servants nor the surliness of workers because planters or their surrogates strictly patrolled public places. Forced to be vigilant over the slave population, Southern masters informally policed poor whites and blacks alike, stopping and interrogating them if they were out on the road. Despite the evident race prejudice of poor Southern white men and women, they were often treated with as much disdain as slaves by members of the planter elite. The democratization of politics did not spread to social norms.[79]

Southerners maintained social distances everywhere, even at sea. Alfred Lorrain, a Kentucky lad who became a sailor, remarked on the familiarity between the officers and men on board Northern ships, an informality that, he said, would not have been tolerated on Southern ones.[80] White cottagers were never hired to work on plantations because they wouldn't work in the same fields as slaves, according to Ball, and the planters feared "any illicit traffick to form from mingling poor whites and slaves." Similarly, Southern slaveholders opposed common schools, anticipating dangers from teaching either slaves or yeoman farmers how to read.[81] Christiana Tillson, living among Southerners on the Illinois frontier, was astounded by her neighbor's dismissive attitude towards learning, especially for women, and their disapproval of her unwillingness to perform tasks like hoeing or milking.[82]

The great divergence between rich and poor in the South fed the elite's sense of superiority, a posture that shaped the sensibilities of all Southerners. The number of middling families of farmers, clerks, master craftsmen, storekeepers, merchants, and professional men who formed the dominant social group in the North and West grew slowly in the South. Literacy was less common there, particularly among women, yet a mother's literacy enhanced her child's learning, a form of "cooperative endeavor" reverberating down the generations.[83] The lack of reading and writing skills among ordinary Southerners leaves a silent clue; it is the absence rather than the presence of records that speaks to us. The scramble for land and slaves on the Southern frontier ended with a residue of losers whose lack of options forced migration out of the "black belt." The successful new planters then replicated the ostentation and oppression that characterized the old South. Only in the pine barrens did poor farmers thrive, trading the comforts of settled areas for the independence of the hill people.

When the Marquis de Chastellux visited him in 1785, Jefferson created a table to display the differences of personal qualities cultivated in the two regions:

In the North they are	*In the South they are*
cool	fiery
sober	voluptuary
laborious	indolent
persevering	unsteady
independent	independent
zealous of their own liberties, but just to those of others	jealous of their own liberties, but trampling on those of others
interested	generous
chicaning	candid
superstitious and hypocritical	without attachment or pretentions in their religion . . .[84]

Jefferson's mixture of good and bad qualities suggest a capacity for affectionate regard and self-criticism that eroded in subsequent years. Increasingly, Southerners construed the habits of industry as nothing more than distasteful Northern attributes compared to their own open, free-spending, impulsive, honor-observing ways. For their part, Northerners used the rhetoric of liberty to shame the South. The list of differences grew longer, sharper, more invidious. Soon Northerners and Southerners thought of themselves as the carriers of opposite qualities, a tendency that distorted their own self-image: the South as a resort for the vanishing virtues of aristocracy; the North as a haven of equality.[85] In fact Northern Federalists had shared many of the planters' ideas about family, hierarchy, and order, but slavery and the attitudes towards work that its presence promoted drove a gulf between them. Southern planters clung to their alliance with Northern Jeffersonians while the Federalists became part of new political coalitions.

NORTHERNERS OF English descent pondered the ethnic component of their nation, using "race" to refer to people with different national origins and religion, as well as skin color. In fact the foreign-born portion of the population was just 3 percent until well into the 1830s, the largest part of that being Africans brought to the states during the resumption of the slave trade from 1788 to 1808. In 1820, the first year of keeping statistics, 8,385 European immigrants entered the United States. By the 1840s, there would be a thousand a week.[86] The middle states had long had a mixed population of Europeans with substantial numbers of Native Americans and Africans. The white population of Southern states was predominantly of British descent; Africans came from a broad band of ethnic groups around the Bight of Benin. New England had remained remarkably homogenous since its founding, which perhaps explains the perplexity of President Dwight of Yale University when he pondered how New York City could possibly form a common character with its thirteen different ethnic groups.[87] The Irish in the midst of her beloved New England prompted Catharine Sedgwick to express concerns to a young niece: "The result of this new experiment in the world of a distinct race, with marked characteristics and a religion of their own, living among us with the full benefit of equal rights and privileges, you, my dear Alice, may live to see."[88]

In fiction Americans addressed the even more troubling fears of "mongrelization" that fluttered just beneath the surface of public comment. Catharine Maria Sedgwick's historical novel *Hope Leslie* introduced a beautiful Pequot princess to lecture the first generation on ethnic prejudices.[89] James Fenimore Cooper showed just how complicated the mixtures in America could be in *The Last of the Mohicans*.[90] Ostensibly about the French and Indian war, the novel sought the safety of an historic setting to probe the human pain and social damage of mixing races and cultures. When Cooper's protagonists, Cora, a white carrier of Negro blood, and Magua, a discredited Huron chief, plunge over the precipice at the story's end, they seemed to dash all hope for a new dispensation for human difference in the New World. No more than Jefferson could Cooper, born forty-five years later, conceive of a truly mixed society.[91]

Viewed from the outside, the United States looked like a polyglot country, noisy and chaotic with its cacophonous voices and disparate customs, but on the inside white Americans were acquiring the capacity not to see other skin colors. Dwight left African Americans out of his census of New York City even though they formed a quarter of the city's workers. Blacks and native Americans were often treated as invisible, unless they or some champion like William Apess or David Walker spoke out on their behalf.[92]

Still there were enough references to interracial possibilities to suggest that racial attitudes had not yet congealed, as when the distinguished New England biblical scholar, William Jenks, spoke of American character as "a mixture of Dutch phlegm, the sanguine complexion of the Englishman, French choler and vanity, Irish rapidity, German sensibility and patient industry, Negro indifference, and Indian indolence." There was food, he went on to say, "for any plant whatever."[93]

Jenks's racial inclusiveness startles the reader accustomed to thinking of the implacable American exclusion of those descended from Africans. His literary flourish also underscores the fluidity of thinking about social relations during a period when white men and women coming of age after the Revolution plumbed, tested, and sorted their feelings. Despite a wide range of conflicting and contradictory positions staked out on race, all but a very few rose above didactic expressions of Christian charity to engage the core emotions of prejudice. For their part, free blacks—most of them drawn to Christian themes of redemption and brotherhood—had to puzzle out the hostility displayed by white subscribers to a gospel of love. Still, openness to a different racial regime remained a possibility, however slim, before the tight lines around whiteness were drawn.[94]

During the first decades of the nineteenth century, the rejection of European aristocratic norms and experimentation with equality of respect had created an alternative American tradition.[95] Decisions made in deference to Revolutionary hopes showed that political ideals could influence the terms of social life; in the United States equality impinged upon considerations of both status and race. The Northern Jeffersonians and Jacksonians pushed against class distinctions, but they tolerated—even promoted—racial divides. The more elitist Federalists, like the later Whigs, fielded the most ardent opponents of slavery and little tolerated restrictions on the civil liberties of free blacks. Their inclusive gestures towards African and Native Americans deposited a deep but narrow vein of tolerance in the social sediment, while egalitarian familiarity remained the hallmark of relations among whites. Race, respectability, and refinement slowly gained momentum as the new arbiters of social place, but the affirmations of the first generation guaranteed that the move towards greater inequality would exist in tension with the natural rights tradition that they had expressed in their politics, taught in their schools, and propagated through their manners.

6

INTIMATE RELATIONS

At age twenty-eight, William Meade lost his wife. He consoled himself by composing a "Brief Notice of Mrs. Mary Nelson Meade." Another sixteen years passed, and Meade's second wife died. Again he eased his grief by writing a memoir, this time "Brief Notices of Mrs. Thomasia Meade." The author of many published sermons and a vernacular history of Virginia, Meade poured out his heart in these pieces, celebrating in rapturous prose the intimacies he had enjoyed with two much beloved wives. Comfortable with this evidence of his feelings, Meade left a clause in his will giving his heirs permission to publish the two manuscripts. He evidently became impatient, for three years before his death, he had them printed.[1]

Meade praised his first wife for her wonderful smile and her "modest, retiring, unostentatious" ways. "She was not beautiful in the worldly acceptation of that term, though not the reverse," he made clear, "even as the gay

Alexander Anderson's engraving of "The Happy Family" served as the frontispiece for Donald Fraser's *Mental Flower Garden*, published in 1807. The frontispiece depicts a familial scene distinguished as much for its gentility as its affection. The artist's rendering of the children as little adults reminds us that childhood is as much a cultural creation as a physical fact. Courtesy, American Antiquarian Society.

world would decide," going on to explain that she had cultivated her mind since childhood, something far better than beauty. They had shared many happy moments admiring good poetry; she had even learned Latin as a teenager in order to teach a younger brother. The Meades read Virgil together and worked on his sermons. "Ph! what a sight it was," Meade exclaimed, recalling the birth of their first baby. "I was then too earthly happy. How I would gaze upon the wife, the mother, and the child." He told how she had taught their children to kiss them and each other, acknowledging that his temper, "shown even to her," formed the only blight on their married harmony.[2] It was during these years that Meade—that rare bird, an Episcopal revivalist—became Bishop of Virginia, leading his church out of the slump that followed its disestablishment in the 1780s.

Thomasia Meade elicited even more adulation than Mary Meade. "She was one whom the Author of our being had cast in his finest mould, and endowed with the most interesting qualities," Meade wrote. He described waiting three years to remarry, fearful of disturbing his children with a stepmother. "I loved my children dearly," he explained, but more revealingly admitted that he also "had an indescribable dread of domestic unhappiness."[3] Meade dwelt on the sensuality of his relationship with Thomasia. "Her salutation with a soft but impressive kiss, can never be forgotten," he confided, adding "still less can I forget when we were first alone, after a long absence, she would throw her arms around my neck, and kiss me again and again, and lay her face on my neck or cheek, and say how *much* she wanted to see me." Reveling in these remembered erotic pleasures, he detailed her terms of endearment: "My dear, my darling, my creature were the names by which she called me, and oh! how deeply did they penetrate into my heart." Unusual in his frank discussion of physical affection, Meade sounded more like a woman of the time than a man when he wrote that he never got tired of hearing her speak, invoking an invidious comparison between the Bible's "busy Martha" and his adored Thomasia.[4]

The emotionally-charged accounts of Meade's two marriages stand as unique homages to intimacy, but writings about relationships figured prominently in the books, pamphlets, and journals that the first generation produced. Like so many other aspects of life for them, the freedom from earlier restraints on the expression of emotion opened up the possibility of crafting new cultural forms. The ease of getting writings published and the avidity of Americans for reading material of all kinds turned intimacy—or at least writings about it—into a public good to be studied, weighed, and evaluated. Magazine articles ran to didactic pieces prescribing norms for spouses and parents while novels explored the gamut of emotions—love, hate, envy, jealousy, and admiration.

People who wrote diaries rarely confided their feelings there, filling them instead with laconic notations on the prosaic details of family life and work routines. For the devout, daily journal entries provided a surrogate companion on the rugged trail of their spiritual journeys. Correspondence, particularly between loved ones, became an important adjunct to intimacy; men and women developed a vocabulary of affection to give vent to the yearnings and sadness punctuating separation. Unlike diaries and letters, autobiographies were crafted as literary backward glances—at once artful and reflective, often introspective and sometimes quite compelling. Some experts believe that women typically hid their role as narrator in their reminiscences, depicting life as a flow of experiences rather than as the high drama of one's own life. The autobiographies of this cohort do not bear this out. Those women who had careers—running schools or writing for publication—wrote autobiographies with the strong story lines characteristic of men's, punctuated by the unforeseen break with childhood expectations, the wonder of a new life prospect, and the moral lessons life taught.[5]

The memoir form that Meade used combined recollections and celebration. Earlier, memoirs had been rare and then almost always written to honor public figures like Washington or Lafayette. Their popularity grew exponentially in the early nineteenth century as men and women rushed to pay tribute in print to beloved relatives, admired colleagues, and shining examples of Christian piety. There was something in these homely tributes that appealed, for their number mounted, going from a total of twenty-seven in the last decade of the eighteenth century to 270 in the first decade of the nineteenth. Memoirs also served didactic purposes, for their subjects rarely had the qualities that led to dissipation—"There was not in him any of that frivolity of character which leads young men to engage in the fashionable amusements of life," disappointment—"In a mixed world, it is delightful to meet an example of high endowments, undebased by the mixture of unworthy habits and feeling," or indifference to God, country, and family—"She early showed a disposition to honor and please her parents in all she did."[6] While it is easy to spoof the high seriousness of early nineteenth-century rhetoric, it would be a grave mistake not to note how powerfully these popular memoirs argued for a gravity, rectitude, and piety that were genuinely admired.

Alongside the earthly attachments that men and women in this cohort described lay the intense feelings aroused by thoughts of God. The concerted effort to place religious worship at the center of American life stirred the deepest passions of all, and ruminations about divine power found expression in all contemporary literary forms. Directed to arousing the slumbering spiritual longings of Americans, the revivals, when they were successful, awakened people to the Christian message of love and change. In pamphlets and articles, memoirs, diaries and autobiographies, men and women addressed the liminal experience of conversion and the joy of having achieved worthiness in God's eyes. Forming an intimate relation with God unloosed the tongue and pen of thousands of otherwise silent people who learned to describe in evocative detail their steps towards holiness. To the God who assuaged the guilt of success and the shame of failure, they felt transports of delight and paroxysms of anguish, creating as they wrote of these experiences a powerful discourse.

Taken altogether, these documents of the self offer a window—if clouded—onto the emotional landscape peopled by friends, husbands and wives, parents and children, and God. What can be viewed is the redeployment of those passions that were once attached to the lineal family and community of birth onto new plains of affection and disaffection. The thousands of Americans churning through new settlements as migrants, adventurers, travelers, or sold slaves had been cut off from the emotional matrix of their childhood. Habit and custom could no longer channel their feelings. New experiences provoked new emotional reactions. Mothers earned long-lasting reverence from adolescents thrusting towards an early autonomy, while sons often turned against the fathers who obstructed their personal ambitions. Husbands and wives drew closer together in communities of strangers; slaves found comfort, as did many others, in the promises held out by those who claimed Jesus as their Lord.

Often older brothers or uncles became the carriers of the worldly knowledge that those left back home desperately needed, taking the father's place as life's guide. The printer Joseph Buckingham remembered affectionately a seafaring brother returning with copies of *Gulliver's Travels, The History of Pirates,* and *Robinson Crusoe*. Another brother brought him *The Vicar of Wakefield, Tristam Shandy, Letters of Junius, The Book of Common Prayer,* and the eighth volume of the eighteenth-century English periodical, *The Spectator*.[7] In a world where books were precious keys to mysteries about distant mores, such gifts were the food of youthful imagination. The older brothers of John Chambers and Samuel Foot were the ones who spotted their talents and arranged for the schooling that enabled each of them to leave the family farm and embark on legal careers.

Few writings from this period address sexual desire directly, but a handful of men left sensitive accounts of their marriages. These present a sharp contrast to those autobiographies in which the author's marriage pops up in the text as part of a reference to a move or a death in the family whose existence had heretofore gone unmentioned. Almost always composed after the loss of a wife, the tender reminiscences appear as efforts to extend the duration of the happy marriages or to provide consolation to the bereft survivor. Discretion evidently restrained commentary on bad marriages, so the written record is biased in favor of the happy ones. Clearly there was in people's minds, before they took up their pen, a sense of propriety about their personal lives. A censor worked below the level of consciousness, but it was not a social norm, for the range of disclosures varied widely from none at all to introspective explorations of those affections deemed suitable for sharing with that elusive audience, the public.

"We began the world in love and hope and poverty . . . were cojoined on principles of equality." Daniel Drake announced in a remarkable 214-page manuscript entitled "Emotions, Reflections, and Anticipations." Written after his wife's death brought their eighteen-year marriage to an end, Drake's memoir examined this precious relationship independent of the life story that he composed for his children. Drake married Harriet Sisson when she was twenty and he twenty-two, having returned to Cincinnati after studying medicine in Philadelphia. He was then ready to embark on a career that would take him well beyond his practice as a physician to distinction as a community builder, medical educator, and scientific writer. Looking back he exulted at the prospect life had held for them at the moment of their union: "It was all before us, and we were under the influence of the same ambition to possess it; to acquire not wealth merely, but friends, knowledge, influence, distinction."[8]

A major theme in Drake's text concerned his wife's intellectual awakening. Her favorite authors, he reported, were Elizabeth Hamilton and the Edgeworths, father and daughter, Samuel Johnson and Francis Bacon; they both loved Homer and Milton. "We had equal industry and equal aspiration," he recalled. She criticized the first drafts of his writings "with taste, judgment, severity, and love," he commented, noting with evident nostalgia that they were always in each other's company. While he made house calls she waited in their carriage reading. In a paean to their mutual devotion, Drake made vivid the singularity of his commitment: "I had no separate social or sensual gratifications, no tavern orgies, no political club recreations, no dissipated pleasures nor companions." "Society," he affirmed with evident pride in his fidelity, "was no society to me without her presence and co-operation."[9] Drake was left with five children whom he reared alone, dying himself twenty-seven years later.

The motif of a wife schooled by her husband also appears in the reminiscences of two distinguished writers, Sarah Buell Hale and Caroline Gilman. Hale's description of studying with her husband has none of the sentiment that Drake invested in his story, but she credited her husband, David Hale, a scholarly lawyer, with completing the education that her mother and a brother had begun:

> We commenced immediately after our marriage a system of study, which we pursued together, with few interruptions . . . The hours we allotted for this purpose were from eight o'clock in the evening till ten. In this manner we studied French, botany—then almost a new science in this country, but for which my husband had an uncommon taste—and obtained some knowledge of mineralogy, geology, chemistry, besides pursuing a long and instructive course of miscellaneous reading.[10]

Hale's husband died suddenly after seven years of marriage during which five children had arrived. She then embarked on her career as a writer and editor with the confidence of a well-educated person.

Caroline Gilman made the disparity of knowledge between a bride and her husband the dramatic focus of *Recollections of a Housekeeper,* which was part memoir and part novel. In this account of the early months of a marriage, Gilman's heroine despairs of ever getting her husband's attention because each night he brings his legal business home, keeping her waiting by the door to his study. Too ashamed to complain, her secret comes out when an observant little boy reports to her husband how she angrily attacked his books when he was absent. Hearing this, he effected an immediate reform, and, as Gilman explained to her readers: "From that period his deportment at home had a perpetual view to my happiness and improvement. He brought books to read to me, calculated to interest while they elevated my literary taste. He referred to me for opinions, and by sounding the depth . . . of my intellect, found, that under his guidance there were occasions when even my advice might avail him."[11] Another New Englander, Eliza Follen, composed a charming memoir of her marriage.[12] More rapturous was Harriet Newell's report of her husband to her mother: "with him my days pass cheerfully away—happy in the consciousness of loving and of being loved. With him contented I would live, and contented I would die."[13]

The cohesive force of shared intellectual interests appears again in the autobiography of Eber Howe, who married Sophie Hull after a six-year courtship. As children of New England Revolutionary veterans growing up on the New York frontier, the Howes displayed the same Yankee restlessness when they became pioneers in Ohio. Howe, writing after his wife's death, claimed forty-three years of "connubial felicity" in passages that celebrated his wife's political activism. "Her first sympathies were called out in 1825–26, in behalf of the Greeks in their struggle for independence," he recalled, detailing how she had been instrumental in collecting and sending off several boxes to "that distant and suffering people." She had been among the first to join the anti-slavery movement and worked, he said, "in season and out of season to assist the future from bondage," keeping "a station on what the slaveholders called 'the underground railroad.'"[14]

George Gilmer, writing while his wife was still alive, included a very romantic account of their courtship and marriage in the personal recollections that he tucked into his *Sketches of Some of the First Settlers of Upper Georgia*. Already a member of Congress, Gilmer had been writing to a distant cousin whom he hadn't seen for twelve years. "In this written intercourse, I had said nothing about marrying," he explained while confessing to a great curiosity to see her to learn "whether we would fancy each other upon sight, as we had on paper." He described the scene as though it had happened the day before, starting with his finding Eliza Grattan in the sitting room:

> As I opened the outer door the door from the passage into the sitting room was opened by Eliza Grattan. When I knew what I was about, my arm was around her waist, and I was pressing her lips; a position which I have been constantly taking ever since, and ever with renewed pleasure. Eliza Grattan and myself settled the matter most interesting to us in a very satisfactory way, agreeing that after the session of Congress was over, we would take each other, for better, for life. During my attendance on the first

session of Congress, I wrote to her by every direct mail. During the next session after our marriage, whilse we were separated for three weeks (the longest time we have ever been apart), I wrote to her twice a day.

Gilmer later reflected that his marriage was not only the happiest event in his life, but "the only one of any really great importance to myself," this in the context of a distinguished political career at the center of Democratic politics in Georgia. "Time has never dragged," he affirmed, adding, "We can never be without matters to interest us whilst we are spared to each other."[15]

Sometimes only a single passage in an autobiography conveys the intensity of the emotion aroused by a spouse. Phineas Price lost his wife to consumption after eight years of marriage. "It seemed," he wrote in retrospect "like tearing the flesh and bones asunder to part with her."[16] Elijah Iles's wife died after forty-two years of marriage, calling forth from him the poignant lament: "She was my superior in intellect, and I never realized her worth until she was gone, gone, gone from me forever."[17] Peter Cooper's wife died on their fiftieth anniversary. She was, he reflected, the "day star, the solace, and the inspiration" of his life.[18] Of his wife John Paxton wrote, "God . . . made us a comfort and blessing to each other."[19] John Francis spoke not of his own marriage, but rather of the happy match between Peggy Dow and the famous evangelical, Lorenzo Dow, when he commented that "A reciprocal union of heads and hearts seemed to bind them together." John Tevis's laconic autobiographical sketch commented approvingly, if briefly, on the importance of his wife's work running a boarding school for 230 girls while raising their seven children.[20] James McBride died ten days after his wife of forty years, because, as his eldest daughter explained, he "appeared to lose all interest in his life and its surroundings."[21]

Although the Revolution created the occasion for reexamining the patriarchal structure of family life, few American men or women rose to challenge the assumption that women should submit themselves to their husbands' wills and confine their self-improvement to projects that would make them more pleasing to men.[22] Instead Americans shared in the heightened emphasis placed upon marriage in their larger Anglo-American world, republishing English novels and popular sermons that elaborated feminine models. What the early decades of the nineteenth century brought was not an intellectual assault upon the sanctity of the home and the wife's duties within it, but rather new occasions for women to demonstrate their talents. Through their fund-raising for voluntary associations, teaching school, mobilizing moral reform movements, writing in various genres, and even preaching, women in this generation supplied the empirical evidence for the campaigns of the next. Political activities swept up women too, as Sophie Hull Howe and her more famous contemporaries, Lucretia Mott and Sarah Grimke, attest. In their admiration men breached the social separation of male and female spheres, as when Joseph Storey said of a beloved sweetheart that she had "excellence which would add grace to the best of men."[23] As with so much else in this period, a changing array of opportunities led to the new experiences needed to uproot venerable assumptions about men and women.

Judging from the recollections of those born after Independence, the relationship between fathers and sons was the most vexed of all of their intimacies. While some fathers were remembered with affection, no more vivid personality emerges from the pages of autobiographies than that of the unsympathetic patriarch trying to block the exit of his sons. Before the Revolution, the scarcity of land had conferred upon most parents an attenuated command over their grown children, who had few alternatives to farming. While waiting for a gift or bequest of land, if not the family farm itself, they were often forced to hew the parental line. The opening of fertile new acres in the national domain greatly lessened that bond that the expectation of a valuable inheritance had forged between the generations. Opportunities to teach school or become a peddler further enlarged the scope of action for restless sons, whose restlessness often precipitated family conflicts. Leaving home at the onset of manhood was more than an economic decision; a strike for personal autonomy involved an emotional struggle as well, intensifying the normal tensions between generations with anxiety and guilt about separation.

John Chambers drew a particularly bitter picture of his father, a man to whom he ascribed "very remarkable vigor of intellect." Left in reduced circumstances after the Revolution, Chambers's father moved the family from Pennsylvania to Kentucky. "I was now fourteen years old and my education had been sadly neglected," Chambers wrote, but his father took so little interest in his son's education that Chambers remembered having to ingratiate himself with his father by taking over the care of his corn field just to secure a roof over his head while he went to school. Chambers's dislike of his father—described as extremely ill-tempered—retained such a vivacity that the editor of his autobiography excised those passages in which he had summed up his father's character.[24]

Like Chambers's family, David Dodge's lost money in the Revolution. After the war his parents bought a succession of farms, downgrading in size each time in hopes of escaping the burden of debt that dogged them in their mature years. Dodge recalled that his father's "spirit of enterprise seemed to be crushed, by hard service and misfortune," and rigid economies followed "to free themselves from debt." He depicted himself as "an ambitious lad of about sixteen" who wanted his parents to sell their farm and move to western New York to "grow up with some rising village." When they declined, he set out on his own. Though still a teenager, Dodge began teaching school, provoking his father's opposition when he sought a better-paying teaching post in a nearby school district. This became, as he recalled, "quite a trial as I felt it my duty and desire to comply with his wishes, except in such things as affected my future life."

In a similar drama, Elias Smith's father, described by his son as a poor tenant farmer, mightily resisted Smith's ambition to learn grammar, an attainment of little use in farming, but essential to further education. When his father relented to the extent of allowing him to read by the light of the fire at night, Smith assiduously pursued his studies, in time winning a teaching job. His father strongly opposed his taking it, on the grounds that Smith "didn't know anything."[25] John Thompson remembered his father, an Irish privateersman, as lazy and erratic, making his sons do all of the work. "He never corrected us," Thompson said, "except when he was in a passion, and then sometimes out of reason."[26]

The parents of Matthew Vassar, seeking to escape the tithes of the established church, bought a farm near Poughkeepsie and started a brewery in 1801. Faced with an irksome apprenticeship to a tanner that his father had arranged, Vassar left home, returning three years later with savings of $150 from three years of "drudgery" on a farm. The family business had fallen into ruins, he claimed, whereupon he took charge and they prospered. Vassar, like Chambers, charged his father with negligence: "To sum it all up between my own temper, and Fathers severity and indifference to give me an Education I got none—Scarcely to read and write."[27] Peter Cooper also rescued his father, who did poorly successively as a hat manufacturer, retailer, and brewer. Coming back home after four years on his own, Cooper discovered the family in distress, so he assumed some debts and "stood surety" for others so that, as he wrote, his father would never have "the mortification of failing in business." The remembrance prompted Cooper to comment that so "far from ever having failed in business, I do not remember the week or month when every man who has ever worked for me did not get his pay when it was done."[28]

A number of men—often very successful ones—left pictures of fathers as pleasant failures. Martin Van Buren described his as "an unassuming amiable man who was never known to have an enemy," but also "utterly devoid of the spirit of accumulation." His father's property, "originally modest, was gradually reduced until he could but ill afford to bestow the necessary means upon the education of his children."[29] Thurlow Weed's father appeared to him in retrospect as kind-hearted and hard-working but without luck and so impecunious that Weed himself began working at the age of eight. His bad luck landed him in debtors' prison, but Weed, at ten, carried away happy memories of family outings on his father's Sunday release: "[O]n those days of jubilee I used to roam with my enfranchised father down to the Point, over to the shad fishery with a deep sense of gratitude that he was permitted, one day in the week, to walk God's earth."[30] Chester Harding sketched his father as a pleasant, but improvident man who moved his large family from New England town to New England town as he tinkered with his perpetual motion machine.[31]

Stephen Tyng's struggle with his father had more complexity than that of other sons not only because his father cared deeply for him, but also because the occasion for their disagreement was Tyng's sudden desire to become a clergyman. As the son described it:

> He could not enter into my convictions of duty. He considered
> the proposal to be a mere sudden And unreasoning impulse . . .
> he could not consent to my wish. He remonstrated with me
> against any change, saying that my business prospects were the
> finest of any young man in Boston . . . He thought I had no
> talents or qualifications for the ministry, and said: "You will spoil
> a first-rate merchant to make a very poor parson."

Tyng construed his father's opposition as a test. Having to support himself while preparing for the ministry and simultaneously enduring the distressed reactions of family members provided the kind of travail that confirmed for him the seriousness of his calling.[32]

Somehow the young acquired the psychological resiliency to enter the entrepreneurial vanguard of America's developing economy or, like Tyng, to thwart the plans of their parents and follow their heart. These displays of early independence juxtaposed against paternal weaknesses or disapproval indicates that some family traditions had depended in part upon fathers' control of their children. Other forces were at play. The disruptions caused by the Revolution probably sapped parental authority; poor parents have never enjoyed the same respect as those with financial penalties to exact for insubordination. Poverty eroded filial compliance in addition to offering a repellent contrast to the imagined fortunes that might be garnered elsewhere. The families themselves were often on the move, and death threw many children into the unwelcome control of guardians. Less easy to measure is the importance of the early signs of intelligence that aroused the attention of outsiders who often helped negotiate the break with home.

The remembered hostility towards fathers is all the more arresting in that many of these autobiographies were written when the defiant sons were themselves old men. The opportunity to quit the family farm appeared then as a deliverance; no regret or nostalgia is expressed. Moving on meant moving out to a larger world. Fathers are so frequently resisted in retrospect that one cannot help but feel that rebelling against domestic tyranny had already emerged as an important cultural theme in America, the private move mirroring the public drama. Where their fathers and grandfathers had participated in the Revolution that created the nation, these men personalized the concept of independence, giving it a social and psychological resonance. The political independence that endowed most white men with the privileges of citizenship merged imperceptibly in popular sentiments with the right for each to blaze his own trail. The critical stance some took towards their fathers—whether cast as resentment or disappointment—worked rhetorically to vindicate their own youthful rebellion and enhance their subsequent accomplishments.

In contrast to some sons' representations of their fathers, Julia Hieronymous Tevis, Lydia Marie Sigourney, Sarah Grimke, Catharine Sedgwick, and Emma Hart Willard praised their fathers for supporting their intellectual development. With varying degrees of commitment, fathers of talented daughters had acted against the oppressive ideology of the day to instill in them a sense of the worth of their gifts. Although many American fathers continued to exercise patriarchal authority over grown children, a counter-image was being scripted. Casting off dependency like a snake's old skin, teenagers were turning fatherhood into a transitional relationship. Simultaneously, the evangelical spirit coursing through America's churches emphasized the religious affections, placing the heart over the head as a guide in human relations. The role of the stern patriarch was losing its ideological underpinnings, not solely because of the uncoupling of fathers and their grown sons, but also through a reworking of the supreme authority figure, God.

Leaving home in late adolescence disconnected sons, as well as some daughters, from the round of filial obligations and cut the ties in that dense network of associations that had slowly accumulated in mature settlements. Many passed over the threshold to love and marriage in communities that they themselves had chosen. This unanticipated foreshortening of parental command left a lot of emotion to be redistributed. In the domestic drama prompted when sons of seventeen and eighteen announced their intention of striking out on their own, the role of mothers was also refashioned. While fathers in the sons' memoirs became the stern, implacable barrier to be pushed aside, mothers were remembered as bestowing affectionate support. Perhaps finding in the awkward assertion of a maturing son's ambition the sure signs of success and responding to the promise rather than the performance that fathers found wanting, they buoyed up the fragile confidence of their adolescent boys. Against the father's caution, even competition, the mother's reassurance acted as a bridge of love and hope for the son as he crossed over to a precipitate manhood. Perhaps too there was a hint of excitement about the son's adventurous spirit, contrasting, as he must have, with the dispirited spouse.

One can read appreciation for maternal support in the sons' remembrances. Subject to seizures, John Chambers's mother went to live with a daughter, but as soon as the twenty-year-old Chambers got his license as a lawyer, he brought her to his home, succeeding, he claimed, "in making her more comfortable than she had been for many years." "This was a source of great gratification to me," he explained, "for I loved & venerated my mother beyond all others of Gods creation, and the arduous & suffering struggle she had made to raise her children and keep them together when young, and impress correct principles upon their minds, entitled her to all, and much more than all, I was ever able to do to make her happy."[33] Morgan Dix recalled the wrenching pain he felt when his mother died. Contrasting his happy memories of the last year of her life with her sadness during that period, he later realized that she "was sorrowing for the child from whom she was about to part, and not for the one she was so soon to meet."[34] Thomas Hart Benton, whose wealthy father died in Benton's infancy, credited his mother with preparing him to take his place "among the historic men of the country," a reflection that led Benton to conclude that the destiny of many men "may depend upon the early cares and guidance of a mother."[35]

John Ball remembered "the wonderful ability" his mother showed in giving family prayers when his father was absent. "My mother had never been to school at all, but she could read and was very fond of reading, when she could obtain a book and had the time," he recalled, stressing that she had "naturally a fine mind, and was ever curious to learn all that could be, within her very limited means." "With her aspirations her life was truly hard," he concluded.[36] Samuel Foot recalled with affection his mother's coaxing him to study the Bible "through" and learn the Westminster catechism.[37] Bronson Alcott believed himself the favorite of his mother, who was a "congenial spirit . . . to whom I could speak my whole soul."[38] Matthew Vassar gratefully recorded that his mother had alerted him to an unwanted apprenticeship, even helping him run away once convinced of his determination. They "both wept tears abundantly," he recalled, when he left home to seek his fortune with sixpence in his pocket and "two coarse East India Muslin shirts, a pair of woolen Socks, Scow Skin Shoes, all tied up in a Cotton Bandana Handkerchife."[39] Chester Harding described his mother as a noble woman: "in all the trials of poverty, she managed to keep her children decently dressed, that they might go to meeting on Sunday, and make a respectable appearance among other boys."[40]

Allen Trimble left a heroic account of his mother during the family's passage through the Cumberland Gap. They were with a party of five hundred moving West in military formation under the tight discipline of a former Continental Army officer. Almost all the women were armed with pistols, as of course were the men. His mother led the party as it crossed the Clinch River. "Plunged into the boisterous mass of water," as her son reconstructed the story from family lore:

> She found it impossible to turn her spirited horse, and with a presence of mind, which she had beyond most mortals and which never forsook her, she gave this splendid horse the rein, caught her little son, not three years old, who rode behind her . . . brought him to her lap . . . where I, a feeble infant, eleven months old, was reposing; grasping both of us with her left arm, and her

horse's mane with her right hand, and thus adjusted for the fearful adventure . . . Amid loud exclaims of "She's lost!" "Turn back!" "Oh! Save her" she made it to the other side.[41]

Devout women, whether mothers or friends, figured prominently in men's lives, particularly when stirrings of religious conviction isolated them from their families and friends. Samuel Rogers extolled his mother-in-law as "altogether the most pious and godly woman I ever knew." Her example and conversation had a great influence upon his life, he claimed, going on to say that she had a "strong mind and retentive memory, possessed fine colloquial powers, and being well versed in Scriptures was quite ready in an argument."[42] Two female cousins brought Stephen Tyng to an older Methodist woman when friends thought that he had become a fanatic, and she was able to ease his anxious spirit by explaining his religious turmoil.[43] John Paxton credited his mother with discovering his vocation as a clergyman when she startled him by asking if he had "any thought of preparing for the ministry."[44] Elijah Martindale, born into a South Carolina Baptist family, also claimed that his mother had pointed him towards the ministry: "to her: more than any earthly means am I indebted for that influence which made me a Christian. I now believe that the admonitions, warnings, exhortations and prayers of a faithful mother seldom if ever fail to bring her children under the saving power of the Gospel."[45]

Stepmothers fared less well in reminiscences. Referring to his, Josiah James Evans frequently spoke to his mature acquaintances of "the causeless aversion to her" he felt when he was a boy.[46] Catharine Sedgwick's mother had bouts of insanity. After she died, her father married a Boston widow considered by Sedgwick's family as unsuitable. "Like most second marriages where there are children," Sedgwick commented with finality, "it was disastrous."[47] Emma Hart Willard, who married a much older man, struggled for a decade to gain the trust of her stepchildren.[48] Margaret Dwight, a great-granddaughter of Jonathan Edwards, lost her father when she was six and went to live with her grandmother when her own mother remarried, an indication that the tensions between stepparents and children were openly recognized.[49]

Without the legal structuring of the free world, the intimacies of slaves operated in a strikingly different environment from that of white Americans, but the feelings displayed were remarkably similar. In their recollections, those who had been enslaved described a richer set of experiences—both more cruel and less routinized—than the depictions found in the apologetics of Southern planters or the denunciations of abolitionists. The domestic slave trade that flourished after 1807 placed a Damoclean sword over every family living in slavery, terrifying husbands and wives, parents and children with the hideous threat of separation. Spouses might learn to moderate their feelings, but children had no choice but to feel the full brunt of a loss that they could not possibly prepare for. This painful reality figures in most slave narratives.

Sojourner Truth's father, a New York slave, had lost two wives to sales as well as all of his children except the youngest two. Sojourner herself used the New York emancipation law to gain her freedom, turning to the courts to appeal for the return of her five-year-old son, who had been sent to Alabama in contravention of the law. She successfully brought him back, but not before he had been cruelly treated in his new home.[50] Charles Ball carried with him the poignant memory of having been wrenched from his mother's arms as she implored his new master to buy her as well; the death of his master had precipitated the sale of his mother and all his siblings. Instead of yielding, the man quickened his pace, pulling Ball behind him, trailed by her cries. "At length they died away in the distance," Ball recalled, "and I never again heard the voice of my poor mother."[51] William Hayden had a similar story—taken from his mother when he was five, being sold again when he was seven. Twenty-five years later they were reunited after he had bought his own freedom.[52]

Even without the imminent break-up of families, enslaved men and women had to strike a balance in their intimate lives between the demands of their masters and their own traditions. In almost all cases, masters had to grant permission to new matches and, on many plantations, couples who wished to marry sought the approval of esteemed members of their own community as well. Denied legal marriages, slaves elaborated their own ceremonies to mark the joining of husband and wife, with masters sometimes participating in the solemnizing of the event. Both men and women could and did marry free blacks, although masters feared the scope of liberty such unions entailed. They also entered into marriages outside the plantation, which strengthened the role of mothers in the lives of separated families, since the children always stayed with her as part of her master's property.[53]

Confined in their physical movements and forced to work long hours, enslaved men and women created strong emotional ties, their shared suffering encouraging a sense of kinship that quickly embraced new members of the community. With slave sales increasingly breaking up married couples and dividing parents from their children, the larger extended families in slave communities came to play a more important role in the intimate lives of black Americans at the same time that their influence was diminishing among white Americans. With masters preferring matches within their own work force, the slave population on larger plantations became an intricate network of cousins, aunts, and uncles. Compelled to endure intrusions into every aspect of their personal lives, slaves needed each other more than free blacks or whites. Slaveholders, whether qualifying as good masters or not, had difficulty acknowledging the full scope of passions and attachments in their slaves, leaving a discursive tradition that stressed the ease with which slaves forgot pain and distracted themselves through song and dance. Such indifference to the multiple offenses of slave-owning left slaves bereft of compassion within their country, although there were always a few sympathetic white Americans whose insistence upon talking about the conspicuous cruelties of slavery kept their humanity before the public.

❧❀❦❀❧

A PUBLIC THAT now had access to the intimate feelings and ruminations of strangers came to expect such emotional fare and demanded to know something personal about its heroes. When Joseph Delaplaine brought out his much-publicized *Repository of the Lives and Portraits of Distinguished Americans,* two different critics assailed him for not including the details of the domestic lives of these "distinguished Americans," one claiming that behavior "in the private circle, and with his family by the fire-side" revealed much more of character "than catalogues of public actions ever could."[54] There was an abundant source of intimate details to be found in English and American novels, which accounts in part for their popularity.

America's clergymen regularly reminded readers that novels had a degrading effect upon morals; worse, their departure from the truth enabled them to play promiscuously with the imagination.[55] In their censorious campaigns, ministers especially targeted women, who were presumed to have less experience and hence be more susceptible to the titillation of reading fiction. While granting that Christ had used parables to excite curiosity and awaken sympathy, one clerical writer catalogued the evils of novels as "the omnipotence of *love* over all obligations" and "the extravagance of sinful passion represented as the effect of amiable sensibility." The

— 178 —

worst thing about novels, he thought, came from their mingling of virtues and vices in the human character, but arguably it was their growing popularity that bothered him the most.[56]

Both fiction and memoirs structured emotional patterns for this generation. With courtship a common focal point of plots, novels provided a language for talking about the coded gestures, changing proprieties, social implications, and permissible passions of romancing. Novels not only fed the imagination, they set examples of acceptable behavior in a domain no longer as strictly patrolled as in the colonial era. In the early decades of the nineteenth century, characters displayed emotion and affection with ease.[57] Castigated by moralists as a waste of time and a distraction from duty, novels broached taboo subjects, as in *Emily Hamilton, A Novel "By a Young Lady of Worcester County,"* in which the heroine hangs herself with the ribbon her lover had given her after he confesses his married state and offers her fifty dollars and the promise never to forget the favors she has conferred upon him.[58]

Some moralists realized the power of such imaginative brushes with sin and despair and often found it wiser to imitate their rivals. Starting with Mason Weems and his doctoring of George Washington's youth, religious writers popularized a kind of story that purported to be true while embellishing whatever truth might have been there to begin with. Catering to a taste for intimacy, they cast their lessons in narratives vivifying the temptations as well as the wages of sin. Writing like novelists, Weems' successors flooded the presses with tarted-up morality tales, in which drunks violated their sisters; rogues seduced unwary virgins; vamps provoked dangerous passions; and anger led to unbridled violence. Enlisting sensationalism in the service of virtue, this brand of religious realism slowly bridged the gap between the novel and the sermon while whetting the appetites of readers for hearty emotional fare.[59]

The ruptures in settled family life that marked the early nineteenth century meant that everywhere in America, men and women, black and white, used common interests to cement new ties. In countless towns and all the major cities, gregarious people formed literary clubs for edification and amusement and to cultivate an attractive refinement. Often it took a guiding spirit to bring people together into associations of affinity and affection. Samuel Goodrich evoked such a one when he described Lydia Huntley's arrival in Hartford in 1814: "noiselessly and gracefully she glided into our young social circle and ere long was its presiding genius." Coming as a single schoolteacher, Huntley remained to acquire a reputation as Mrs.

Sigourney, one of the country's most prolific writers. "Few persons living have exercised a wider influence," Goodrich said, concluding that "no one that I now know, can look back upon a long and earnest career of such unblemished beneficence."[60] Mary Anne Hooker remembered that Sigourney gathered friends into an informal literary coterie that met for seventeen years.[61] In rural communities, library societies, usually started in order to provide a pool of money for purchasing books, acted as the catalyst for acquaintances, based on common interests, to blossom into friendship.

Informal gatherings and organized associations provided companionship with strong emotional overtones among friends of the same sex. Here the prescriptive literature defining separate spheres for men and women intensified the feelings of closeness, particularly for women whose designated sphere was a diminished and restricted one. Sigourney commemorated such friendships in a pamphlet that described four women who wanted to establish a convent but settled for a secluded mansion. Something of a humorous piece, *The Square Table* presents arguments for "single blessedness" along with advice to men on "How to Obtain Celibacy," from the resident wit who, we are told, enjoyed "mocking others and keeps them all laughing at midnight when they should be sleeping but in fact have their best conversations."[62]

Less pretentious were the gatherings of single women in Methodist societies. Given the seriousness with which people, especially clergyman, took attentiveness to religious duties, these meetings offered precious space for women to commune with one another, uninterrupted by other obligations.[63] Women participated in greater numbers in the evangelical revivals and represented the working skeleton of most religious bodies. Their avenues to grace became highways to close bonds with those sharing their communion or seeking counsel on spiritual matters. Similarly, the outpouring of writings on women's virtue and refinement created the ideological frame for cultivating friends as one cultivated tastes. In philanthropic organizations, like the "Juvenile Band" to which Elizabeth Levick belonged —eighteen Philadelphia girls who regularly got together to make garments for poor children—the rounds of charitable activities provided the routines for sustaining closeness over many years.[64] Teachers too formed tight bonds with one another, often following friends from school to school or in some cases running establishments as partners. Unmarried working women enjoyed a social freedom denied those in the middle class that enabled them to weave a web of affectionate regard through shared amusements.[65]

Men found male companionship in fire companies, masonic lodges, political clubs, and business ventures.[66] In several of the country's major cities—Boston, New York, Philadelphia, Baltimore—groups of talented men entered into long-term associations publishing journals. Boston could boast the Anthology Club, whose twenty-some members produced the *Monthly Anthology* and founded the Boston Athenaeum, later inspiring the celebrated *North American Review.* Both journals aspired to the standards set by the British critical reviews, and they drew their editors and authors from the same close circle of friends. Baltimore's knot of talented and ambitious writers and editors—John Neal, Paul Allen, Robert Walsh, George Tucker, and Henry Marie Brackenridge—seemed more competitive than companionable whereas Philadelphia's Joseph Dennie exerted the kind of personal charisma that acted as both magnet and synthesizer of friendships.[67] Timothy Dwight commented that Boston was "sufficiently great to ensure all the benefits of refined society, and yet so small as to leave the character of every man open to the observation of every other."[68] While such scrutiny might have a dispiriting effect on intellectual vitality, the intricate connections of these closely watched lives made for a strong sense of a community. For the small minority of white men who attended college, living together away from home sustained many close associations, as exemplified in Sidney Willard's tribute to his Harvard Class of 1798.[69]

Reforming passions also solidified friendships. The brilliant Scottish educator William Russell drew together a group committed to improving New England's schools when he emigrated to Boston. Russell began the *American Journal of Education,* in which he discussed the experimental school of Bronson Alcott, a close associate. Alcott's roommate, Josiah Holbrook, started the Lyceum system, whose traveling lecturers became a feature of American life for the next half-century. Still practicing law, Horace Mann became part of this yeasty cluster of reforming spirits whose cultural initiatives covered museums, libraries, kindergartens, public lectures, and experimental schools. Joseph Dennie's Philadelphia group of young men replicated an early gathering of like-minded friends he had drawn together in Walpole, New Hampshire, both bound in part by their strong Federalist sympathies. Publishers of the *Port Folio,* the most successful literary journal of the period, Dennie's friends included President Adams's sons, John Quincy and Thomas, John Sergeant, Horace Binney, Robert Hare, and the banker, Nicholas Biddle. Formalized into the Tuesday Club, Dennie's associates directed their literary and philosophical shafts at the Jeffersonians whose very popularity they took as an indictment of American taste.[70] Still closer were three Philadelphia brothers-in-law, Thomas Sergeant, George Mifflin Dallas, and Richard Bache, who formed the "family party" that tied together a tight knot of intermarrying political figures, including William Rawle and Peter DuPonceau, all sons of famous fathers.[71]

In New York, Washington Irving and his brothers, Peter and William, were part of an unmarried set of dandies and writers that called themselves variously the Nine Worthies, the Ancient Club of New York, or the Ancient and Honorable Order or the Lads of Kilkenny. Flourishing in the first decade of the century, they met at taverns, drinking champagne and composing satirical pieces for the journal *Salmagundi,* while cultivating an aristocratic sophistication. When Gouverneur Kemble, a manufacturer of cannon balls and later a congressman, acquired a mansion on the Passaic just above Newark, the *bon vivants* dubbed it Cockloft Hall and started meeting there.[72] The members of New York's Friendly Club, among them Charles Brockden Brown, Anthony Bleecker, William Dunlap, and Samuel Miller, gathered almost nightly at Hocquet Caritat's bookstore; they also published a journal. For the people in these social circles of the major eastern seaboard cities Europe figured prominently as a model for gentlemanly behavior. Containing the seeds of an urban elite quite distinct from America's sprawling middle class, these groups of men were self-conscious social critics in the British mode. Their studied sophistication contrasted profoundly with the earnestness of recent evangelical converts who abounded in the first decades of the new century, alienating them from the exuberant enthusiasms of ordinary Americans.

The most passionate feelings that men and women in the first generation expressed in print came when they wrote about their relations with God. In memoirs, published sermons, poems, and autobiographies, ordinary people shared their intimate secrets, confided the sins that filled them with self-loathing, and described the freshets of hope with the shattering return of doubt that marked their religious pilgrimages. Americans had been telling stories about their struggles with self-indulgence, carnal longings, and material distractions since the seventeenth century, for the Puritans, Baptists, and Quakers had planted a strong tradition of experiential religion in the colonies. Equally strong had been a rationalist strain of Protestantism along with the upper-class expectation that established churches would inculcate orderly behavior. From the 1790s through the 1830s these political and rational aspects of religion receded from public prominence, pushed into the shadows by a round of local revivals that created the momentum for a national movement to reinvigorate Christian devotion in the United States.

Wildly successful, the evangelical reformers broke through people's normal inhibitions and unleashed a torrent of zeal among a full quarter of the adult population. First the Methodists and Baptists, followed by their imitators among the mainstream Congregational, Presbyterian, and Episcopal clergy, tapped into a deep popular yearning for religious outlets that swept many into realms of exuberance and ecstasy. The older churchly task of fostering the learned Christian tradition took a backseat to the recruitment and training of those who could best deliver the gospel injunction to open one's heart to God and let the joy of salvation pour in. Filled with holy zeal, evangelical Protestants intruded into the intimate lives of those about them, the grandiosity of their goals giving them warrant for breaking down normal social barriers.

When the evangelicals came to the hamlets, villages, and towns of the country, they had a differential impact on the people who gathered to listen. Unexpectedly, the most attentive members of their audiences were women. At first tilting towards the desirability of celibacy, the Methodists changed their position when it became apparent how powerfully women responded to their message. The homes of female converts became the centers of new societies that carried on the religious work when the circuit riders passed on. Prominent women like the sisters of Patrick Henry and Edward Livingston, who often first heard of revivalist preaching from their servants, offered entries into powerful families. Rich or poor, women provided the sustenance and shelter for visiting preachers; many of them risking conflict within their marriages to do so. Fired up by their new devotion, women turned out to be the most effective fundraisers, especially in finding the money to train new ministers. Methodists kept careful records that show that women formed the majority—frequently a large majority—in their societies: a full half of the husbands of Methodist women did not share their wives' beliefs while only 15 percent of the wives of converts remained outside the church.[73]

The intensity of women's religious ardor put particular stress upon the family and relations between the sexes. Where the older churchly denominations with settled ministers and multi-generational congregations stabilized families through support of fatherly authority, the Methodists and Baptists played havoc with families, setting wives against husbands, brothers and sisters against each other, and most threateningly, the young against their elders. Doctrinal disputes over baptism brought this conflict out into the open. Traditional religions baptized infants, bringing them into the organic community of families that many Congregational churches represented, but Baptists stressed the drama of conversion in which the adult casts off his or her unregenerate self and enters into communion with the saved through adult baptism, often by total immersion in a stream or river. Ruptures and discontinuities became important markers of a religious conversion, the escalating need for evidence of faith often working at cross purposes with the requirements of social order.

Successful revivals of religion left converts struggling with spouses and parents, children, friends and neighbors who had not been similarly touched. Nothing if not demanding, the itinerant preachers taught that Christ must come first and opposition from parents or spouses must be faced down. In the South, the evangelicals' capacity to move individuals often led to a gulf between those touched and their unawakened friends and family, a development exacerbated by the converts' tendency to display their faith publicly by rejecting showy clothes and everyday luxuries. With their reformed demeanor acting as a reproach to others, these gestures setting the godly apart from others became a matter of great concern.[74] Evangelical preachers taught that Christ must come first and that the supplicant had to confront directly any parental or spousal authority aroused against a religious awakening. Sometimes the rhetoric of religious communion impinged upon the loyalties implicit in family life, suggesting that sacred practices might replace the natural family with a religious fellowship. More threatened by these challenges to the family than their Northern neighbors, Southern householders insisted that the evangelical ministers uphold the authority of the father and master, and they succeeded in this demand, changing the dynamic of the original evangelical effort.[75]

A different kind of challenge came from the responsiveness of African Americans, whom the revivalists appealed to with assertions that all were equal in the eyes of God. While a backlash against antislavery preaching forced most churchmen to back away from the subject, the converted slaveholders, in a momentous opening for Christianity, usually allowed ministers to preach to their slaves.[76] Enslaved men and women responded in greater numbers than white Americans, nurturing gifted preachers, both male and female. Through the camp meetings of the Upper South, preachers like the "Sons of Thunder" among Kentucky Presbyterians deliberately exhorted their listeners to express their religious ecstasy in energetic displays of singing and dancing. Black converts who attended white revival meetings but usually worshipped separately fused "African aesthetic elements with Christian forms to create their own distinctive religious rituals, which were at once Christian and African."[77] Free black clergymen began as exhorters in the Methodist church, many passing into full ministerial status. In New York and New Jersey, two remarkable women, Sojourner Truth and Jarena Lee, carried the evangelical message into the lives of the newly-freed African Americans.[78]

The Methodists and Baptists built their churches into the country's largest denominations, but it was a Presbyterian lawyer from frontier New York, Charles Finney, who became America's most famous evangelical clergyman. More than anyone else Finney was able to evoke the passions that moved men and women towards conversion, using—perhaps manipulating—an intensely personal approach that built upon his listeners' emotional anguish at the death of a loved one or the alarming conviction of personal sin. Writing his memoirs from the perspective of his great success, Finney reported that his friends had been greatly ashamed of his preaching, finding his use of common language unbecoming because, as he said, "I aimed not at all at ornament, or at supporting the dignity of the pulpit."[79] Finney left the law to take his dramatic exhortations about salvation from town to town in the North and West. He created the device of the "anxious bench" upon which sat those who felt the first stirrings of faith, thus ratcheting up the tension of spiritual indecision.

The ministers in what is called the Second Great Awakening relied on effective preaching like Finney's to gather new members, reaping their harvest of souls among the disaffected and those who had grown up without religion. Implicitly criticizing existing practices in their peace-shattering sermons, revivalists sought to energize their listeners by making them discontented with a complacent faith. Unlike the more sedate preaching style of conventional ministers, the evangelicals directed their messages to the hearts of those assembled before them, dwelling on the need to awaken to a state of sin and reach for Christ's redemptive love. Both men and women threw themselves into Methodist "love feasts," experiencing raptures and visions and hungering for communal gatherings. It would have been hard during these years to have escaped the urgent appeals to throw off the old man and accept rebirth in Jesus.

Presbyterian synods in Kentucky experimented with camp meetings that met days on end with round-the-clock exhorting and praying sessions. One itinerant Baptist boasted of holding "protracted meetings" day and night for ten-week stretches.[80] James Finley left a memorable description of the great Cane Ridge camp meeting of 1801 that came to epitomize the entire succession of remarkable revivals from the 1790s through the 1830s:

> Here a scene presented itself to my mind not only novel and unaccountable, but awful beyond description. A vast crowd, supposed by some to have amounted to twenty-five thousand, was collected together. The noise was like the roar of Niagara. The vast sea of human beings seemed to be agitated as if by a storm. I counted seven ministers, all preaching at one time, some on stumps, others in wagons, and one . . . was standing of [sic] a tree which had, in falling, lodged against another. Some of the people were praying, some crying for mercy in the most piteous accents, while others were shouting vociferously.

Watching all this, "a peculiarly-strange sensation" seized Finley himself. "My heart beat tumultuously, my knees trembled, my lip quivered, and I

This illustration from Frances Trollope's *Domestic Manners of the Americans,* published in 1832, shows worshippers at an Indiana camp meeting in various attitudes of excitement. Such impromptu revivals, with their hastily-erected pulpits, began with the 1801 gathering, which attracted more than 10,000 people to Cane Ridge, Kentucky. Courtesy, American Antiquarian Society.

felt as though I must fall to the ground," he reported, casting the ensuing struggle as one between wounded pride at his manliness assailed and the power of the Lord.[81]

The conversion experience stood at the core of the individual's religious awakening, made particularly acute by the conviction that one could know if one had been saved. Grappling with a sense of sin and filled with a desire to extricate themselves from its staining presence, men and women usually became deeply introspective when they first felt the stirrings of religious conviction. Harriet Newell, the young missionary's wife whose *Memoir* became an early favorite with the American reading public, poured her tumultuous thoughts into her diary: "I should be willing to have every thing for God; willing to be called by any name which tongue can utter, and to undergo any sufferings, if it would but make me humble, and be for his glory." In the ensuing years, she wrestled with the logic of Calvin's predestination: "Although God is under no obligation to save one of the apostate race of Adam, and it would not derogate from his justice were he to send all to eternal torments; yet to display the riches of his grace he determines to save a few. Why should we say, what doest thou? The children of God are, or ought to be, lights in the world. But I fear that I shall be a stumbling-block to others." And still later, she reported, "My soul is enveloped in a dark cloud of troubles. Oh that God would direct me; that he would plainly mark out the path of duty, and let me not depart from it."[82] Descriptions of headaches and insomnia and pledges to avoid frivolous companions punctuated these ruminations of a teenager obsessed with her spiritual condition.

Sarah Grimke said that she had "never experienced any feeling so terrific as the despair of salvation." "My lips moved in prayer, my feet carried me to the holy sanctuary," she wrote, "but my heart was estranged from piety. I felt as if my doom was irrevocably fixed, and I was destined to that fire which is never quenched . . . My soul still remembers the wormwood and the gall, still remembers how awful the conviction that every door of hope was closed, and that I was given over to death."[83] Frequently described as the "dark night of the soul," those in its grips felt the ridicule or pity of others, who had trouble comprehending the turmoil that tormented them. Some had mystical experiences or heard voices. After one particularly powerful religious service, Charles Finney sought the quiet of the woods for prayer and had a vision of Christ. "It seemed to me that I saw Him as I would see any other man." Later, while at prayer in his kitchen, he felt God's spirit entering in "waves and waves of liquid love" flowing through him while he was fanned by the beat of "immense wings."[84]

Aroused to the crucial importance of the sacred, some seekers went from spiritual home to spiritual home. Harriet Livermore began life as an Episcopalian in a prominent family in Portsmouth, New Hampshire. She longed to join the Society of Friends—indeed she was immortalized in Whittier's "Snow Bound"—but her temper repelled them. Always assiduously studying the Bible, Livermore became a Methodist Perfectionist, next a Farewell Baptist, then, after a conversion experience, she joined the Congregational Church, only to return to the Baptists, before finally discarding that faith for her own solitary path towards Christian truth.

Ebenezer Francis Newell, first a Congregationalist, passed through Methodism before settling as a Universalist while Elijah Martindale longed to join the Methodists but was held "back to sin" by his father's prejudice against them.[85] Martindale finally found comfort with the Seventh Day Baptists only to have them decide that he was really a Cambellite. Ray Potter's religious passions were stoked by his guilt at having once preached the "Arminian system of Doctrines" while Jacob Knapp, who found little comfort within his family's Episcopal faith, fled to the Baptists, after waiting in vain for his father's permission to do so. The most remarkable story of an evolving faith is that of Adoniram Judson, who was turned into a Baptist while reading the Bible on the boat that was carrying him to Calcutta as a Congregational missionary.[86]

A strong subtheme of the doctrinal perfectionist was the joy of overthrowing a constricted Calvinism. Asa Wild recounted how from infancy he felt the striving of the holy spirit, but had been taught that there was nothing he could do about it because of the doctrine of "unconditional election and reprobation." Living as one of "the greatest adepts in wickedness," he became convinced of the error of the "soul-destroying doctrines of Calvinism," which he decided were "more to be dreaded and deprecated than the poisonous effluvia, the malignant vapour, and the destroying pestilence."[87] The congregational church structure of most denominations permitted changes of faith when the minister and flock were in agreement. Asa Mahan, who became the first president of Oberlin College, stayed with his Congregational membership, but rejected the various Calvinist interpretation of necessity.[88]

Theodore Clapp took New Orleans' First Presbyterian Church into the Congregational fold from whence both he and his church switched to

Unitarianism. Like Wild, he retained his dismay that in "the nursery, the school room and the pulpit," he had once been taught that all mankind, including infants, had lost communion with God and were "under his wrath and curse, and so made liable to . . . the pain of hell for ever."[89] For others like Bronson Alcott, revulsion at the doctrines of original sin and human depravity carried them past all formal religions. The philosopher of the classroom, Alcott described the old religion as "not sufficiently rational, spontaneous and social . . . "too much an affair of another life, teaching men how to die rather than to live."[90]

✦

DEATH WAS omnipresent in the lives of the first generation when the new diseases of tuberculosis, yellow fever, and cholera pushed mortality rates to new highs, hitting all age groups and, like bad luck, tending to concentrate in families. The period of the greatest mortality was from birth to two years old, but even for those who survived until age ten, life expectancy declined from fifty-seven to forty-eight years in the early nineteenth century.[91] It was the exceptional boy or girl who kept both parents through childhood. The virulence of disease could carry off several members of a family at once, and childbirth continued to take its toll. So appalling was the death rate from tuberculosis among young women that Lydia Sigourney published a hundred-page essay detailing the deaths of her former pupils, concluding that of eighty-four of them, twenty-six were no longer living.[92] Clapp passed through twenty epidemics in his thirty-five years in New Orleans, retaining a lively sense of the "fury of those autumnal hurricanes," "of the sudden transition to death," "of looking out and seeing a robust young man or woman in congregation, only to preach at their funeral next day."[93]

Understandably the nagging fear of death and the wrenching sadness of losing a loved one colored intimacies and affected the personal trajectory of religious affections. John Fetterhoff remembered being "under conviction" from the age of seven, after his mother's death. His father, he reported, knew nothing of "inward religion," but the fear of dying while unprepared consumed his son. "My father tried to sooth me, but no man could comfort my soul." Hired out to a turnpiker on the Baltimore and Pittsburgh pike, Fetterhoff recoiled at the roughness of life with the Irish workers and sought out a Mennonite family to live with. Nominally a Lutheran, he found himself going to hear any itinerant preacher passing through the area, driven, as he was, by a lively sense of hell. People, Fetterhoff said, were always enticing him "to go with them to apple pealings and corn huskings" where they ridiculed religion, but finally he found relief in the conviction of his faith and become a Methodist circuit rider.[94]

Jacob Knapp believed that from his earliest years his mind had been "deeply impressed with divine truth" expressed in "seasons of secret prayer, and of deep anxiety about the future welfare" of his soul, but it was not until his mother died when he was thirteen that he turned to regular Bible reading and church attendance, praying constantly—"day, night: in the barn, in the woods" to relieve his distress of mind. Phineas Price, brought up a Presbyterian in New Jersey—though his father made "no profession of religion"—turned to prayer and the Methodists after the death of a brother plunged him into depression.[95] Levi Hathaway's mother died, leaving thirteen children who were then, he said, "scattered abroad," causing him and his brother to become "exercised about religion" and worried about the world coming to an end. Edward Hicks, the Quaker painter of the many "Peaceable Kingdoms," described with self-pitying pathos his mother's death, "leaving her poor little feeble infant under the care of her colored woman, Jane, who had been a slave in the family, and being left to shift for herself, took me with her like her own child," because, as he explained, "my father was now broken up, having no home of his own, or any business by which he could support and keep his children together."[96]

Dying became the supreme act of sacrifice, the innocence of the dying cleansing the corruption of the living, the regenerate summoning the unregenerate to take stock of their souls. So construed, the frequent deaths of children and their mothers could be redeemed in their imitation of Christ. Death received an importance that transcended the loss involved if it could be linked to the imperative to change one's life—for the unsaved to court salvation, for the devout to redouble their devotions. Where death had once been used to emphasize the fleeting nature of life, in deference to an afterlife, the emphasis in the early nineteenth century subtly shifted to its sounding a call to engage more seriously with one's life. By the 1830s the presumed persuasive power of a deathbed scene for promoting conversions had created a genre of memoirs, almost all of them streaming off the presses of the American Tract Society, Massachusetts Sabbath School Society, or American Sunday-School Union.[97] Accepting a providential explanation of events, many tormented supplicants interpreted their sickness or the deaths of loved ones as signs to guide them in their personal pilgrimage towards salvation.

Death figured so prominently in people's lives that stories of it became a kind of investment capital in the emotional economy of the day. The tenderness, awe, and loss evoked by the death of a loved one resonated with contemporary readers, stirring up empathy and abating fear. While often formulaic in their descriptions of the piety of dying Christians, some memoirs conveyed well the intimate emotions shared at the sick bed. Death also offered an opportunity to praise the qualities of the deceased. While fewer than thirty memoirs were published in the last ten years of the eighteenth century, ten times as many appeared in each of the next two decades, many from professional groups honoring colleagues or families paying tribute to a cherished member.[98]

The impetus behind the writing of many a memoir, death was the muse for many poets. Probably at no time in the United States have so large a portion of the people written—and even published—poetry.[99] Newspapers, journals, pamphlets, and slim little volumes spread amateur creations widely, undoubtedly encouraging others to compose. Bishop Meade wrote two poems to his late wives in addition to his memoirs. Deaths of public figures stirred the imaginative nerve. Nicholas Biddle claimed that Eliza Townsend's poem, published in *Port Folio* after the untimely death of Joseph Dennie, was the best ever written in the United States. William Cullen Bryant is but the most famous of the period's poets writing on death, his "Thanatopsis" appearing in 1817. Short of death, infirmity could inspire creativity. Cynthia Taggart introduced her book of verse by detailing the crippling disease that had driven her not to distraction but to poetry. "In what agony, in what excruciating tortures, and restless languishing the greater part of the last nine years has been passed," she exclaimed to an audience that read her poems posthumously, wrapped in the vicarious sensation of her bodily pain.[100]

Since almost all intimacies led to death—sooner rather than later—melancholy became a part of the emotional palette of the age. Its somber colors fit well with the self-reproaches that preceded acceptance of God's redeeming grace and the stifling of desire that followed it. Revivals might wax and wane, bringing "dead times" in the wake of arousal, but they never left room for complacency. Most congregations kept a careful watch on their members, disciplining them when it was felt necessary. While men and women could escape scrutiny by moving away or changing denominations, they were usually too serious to trifle with the sacred demands placed upon them. Conversions might inspire kindness to loved ones, servants, and slaves, and frequently they led to marked changes in personal habits, like the avoidance of personal display and the adoption of a simplicity of address reminiscent of the Quakers. For most, this virtuous living confirmed belief in one's salvation. Yet however spontaneous the burst of grace or ecstatic the emotion it aroused, neither spontaneity nor ecstasy became the order of the new day.

FIXED ON A powerful concept and mediated by a full lexicon of feeling, emotions for the devout flowed through and around thoughts of the divine, spilling over into personal intimacies. Carefully channeled, they were available for raptures on the created universe, even on the human potential contained inside each person. Americans developed a language for talking about their inner lives just as they had found the words to describe their love for others. And as the selves in the country followed different trajectories, so the language stretched, curved, split, and became tied to other concerns. Anxieties about salvation masked worries about success and failure that were frequently generated in the country's fierce competition for suitors, jobs, and farms. Absorption with the suffering of Jesus eased the more intimate pain that the afflictions of one's own or a loved one caused.

Methodist love feasts, Unitarian concepts of the Godhead, Baptist experimentalism, and Quaker pietism also challenged the Calvinist doctrine of predestination, emphasizing instead how sinners could contribute to their own salvation by throwing off their thoughtless ways. Like other dynamic elements in American society, many possibilities of belief and worship opened up to be explored under the personal initiative of a seeker. Again responsibility had been returned to the individual, whose character was often shaped decisively by the struggles that clarified the dimensions of human will. Most converts developed inner resources in their encounter with vital religion, experiencing it as both isolating within its internal conflict and companionable through the proffered Christian fellowship. An intensely subjective experience became the crucial test of religious worth. An old Protestant ethic stressing rationality and order was superceded by an emotional version of the Christian doctrines of signs, optimistic in its hopes for salvation, but full of despair for natural virtue.[101]

Changing circumstances reconfigured the emotional patterns within many families, as young men detached themselves from stern or disapproving fathers and conferred lifelong devotion on the mothers whose support had eased their passage over the threshold of adolescence. Pulling away from the rationalism and skepticism that marked eighteenth-century thought, young parents urged their children to consult the heart when making decisions. Because husbands and wives were so frequently separated from the families of their birth, they were thrown upon each other for moral support and emotional sustenance, a fact that makes the frequency of death particularly poignant.

In this crucible a recognizable American type took form, confined to a substantial minority of men and women, but powerful beyond its numbers because it involved a mastery of self and a prompting to good works. Earnest, intrusive, passionate, and disciplined, evangelical Christians eagerly made their affirmations those of the nation at large. While responses to the turmoil in the lives of the first generation were by no means uniform, the one most often vocalized was the seeking of surcease from pain in an acceptance of God's divine rule. Since the path towards redemption possessed its own self-contained drama of pledges of good faith, lapses, back-sliding, assurance, and denials of comforts and luxuries, the pious not only lived a rich emotional life, they also possessed a sense of their importance as human beings, however fallen their original condition. Conversion provided these awakened Christians with a moral compass, an instrument of rare utility in a society with so much uncharted terrain. The participatory politics and free association claimed by radicals in the 1790s set the stage for reformers of the 1800s who would direct American attention towards the moral ends of nationalism.[102]

7

REFORM

THE OPPOSITION CAMPAIGNS of the 1790s unlocked the enormous organizational energy of the generation coming of age. Yet the rhetoric of free choice might have faded with the memory of Jefferson's election had democratic bombast not yielded to new cultural forms. As they set about founding voluntary associations to do the work once shouldered by church, state, and family, Americans demonstrated their gifts of inventiveness. The most powerful nexus between the personal and the public, the intimate and civic, became exemplary individuals who inspired a thousand imitations: the committed Christian reformer, the public-minded man of business, the benevolent angel of mercy. Ready to supply with persuasion the deficit of coercion, undistinguished men and women turned the realm of voluntary action into a field of common purpose, merging their interests with those of the country. Taking advantage of the expanding transportation and communication systems developing alongside a population on the move, new civic leaders knit their local associations into national net-works, revealing the full potential of voluntary efforts in a society in which there was neither an upper class that assumed that it should lead nor a central government that jealously guarded its authority.

In England a sophisticated, urban middle class had forced the state to make room for civil society; in the United States, the public sphere formed itself in a void, growing lush from the fertilization of religious and political controversies as its signature forms spread rapidly from city to town and town to village. In the ensuing decades, the public realm became an arena of initiatives and experiments, religiously-inspired reform movements and heated political contests. Would-be authorities lost control because no group could police all the entrances into the animated world of voluntary action, self-improvement, and social betterment undertaken by the novices and amateurs who shaped American public life at the beginning of the nineteenth century.

Colonial society had been formal; as people performed in it, they confirmed their prescribed roles. In the years after the Revolution men and women abandoned formality, easing the entry of newcomers into civic life by honoring intrinsic over extrinsic qualities. Jefferson replaced the solemn bow with a friendly handshake, and President Madison's wife made the country smile as they spoke familiarly of "Dolly."[1] There was a new gravity as well. The thrust for independence—nationally and personally—had in-curred a sobering load of responsibilities that bound together those who took up the burden of meeting them. While only a substantial minority of American men and women were committed Christians, their influence radiated well beyond their numbers. Although not a complete overlap, the supporters of vital religion and of popular politics shared a suspicion of traditional authority and a respect for common people that played a criti-cal role in shaping the cultural innovations of the first generation. Over time they changed the country through the sweep of their philanthropic efforts and their willingness to open civic space to all comers who pos-sessed virtue and merit in their eyes.

Voluntary associations were not new to Americans, but in the early nineteenth century their reform agendas and organizational reach were. The zeal for self-improvement found outlets in debating and study clubs, a particular favorite among young adults. There were associations of me-chanics and manufacturers in most New England towns; fire societies mul-tiplied with the growth of cities. Masonic lodges attracted ambitious pro-fessionals; 100,000 men joined Masonic lodges between 1790 and 1840.[2]

African American men in Philadelphia had their African Literary Society, the Demosthenian Institute, and the Library Company of Colored Persons. African American women fostered an appreciation of literature through the Edgeworth Society, the Minerva Literary Association, and the Female Literary Association.[3] Women were unusually active in this new associational life, demonstrating a marked capacity for fund-raising while providing care, goods, and money to those suffering from neglect and illness. Almost every town had its Female Domestic Missionary Society and its Home for Friendless Women.

The formation of new voluntary associations was only limited by the reigning social imagination. There was an Association of American Patriots for the Purpose of Forming a National Character, started in 1808. Outraged by Jefferson's Embargo, which kept hundreds of American ships in their harbors, Federalists created two hundred Washington Benevolent Societies between 1809 and 1812.[4] So indefatigable a projector as to be dubbed the "Benjamin Franklin of Cincinnati," Daniel Drake single-handedly inspired the Western Museum, Cincinnati College, the Humane Society, the Library Association, the Cincinnati Manufacturing Company, the Lancasterian Seminary, and the Society for the Promotion of Agriculture in his adopted Ohio home. Another zealot for civil society, Josiah Holbrook, an itinerant science lecturer, started the popular American lyceum for community education; its local associations formed themselves into a national organization with annual conventions by 1827.

It is a significant feature of these voluntary clubs that their members invariably wrote constitutions. Sometimes that was the only thing that they did. They often published their constitutions as well. Jesse Torrey, an unflagging improver, published the constitution of the Juvenile Society for the Acquisition of Knowledge in order "to provide a form for others to copy."[5] Timothy Claxton's Methuen Social Society for Reading and General Inquiry accepted a constitution at its first meeting of forty male and female members who identified themselves as mechanics.[6] Some associations had constitutional provisions for disciplining members who did not seek mediation before going to court. This passion for specifying group objectives and rules of conduct in a written document represented more than mimicry of state and federal governments; more subtly, it denied the power of government to regulate such aspects of people's lives. Writing constitutions familiarized ordinary men and women with the modes of political construction, a skill that enhanced their effectiveness in shaping the public realm.

During the first decades of the nineteenth century, the Second Great Awakening gathered momentum, drawing its strength from hundreds of local revivals, all evangelical in their proselytizing zeal. Successful in directing Americans' attention beyond pride in their political establishments to concern for their moral state, the drive to revitalize Christianity supplied the impetus for a network of religious associations that enlarged and energized the political field seeded by the Jeffersonians. Nothing if not ambitious, the revivalists and their converts sought the transformation of America into the redeemer nation and set out to wrest from all whom they touched a commitment to shape their lives according to the word of God. The "mushroom candidates" ridiculed by the Federalists had their analogues in the sectarian preachers who emerged from the people. As profound an influence on the character of the nation as the toppling of upper-class political control, the Second Great Awakening derived much of its energy from attacking the religious establishments that had survived the Revolution.

Like the actualization of popular sovereignty in national politics, the surge of vital religion overpowered both the leaders and the forms of religious leadership in the first two decades of the nineteenth century.[7] The same anti-institutional bias evident in politics fueled successful challenges to the old church establishments. Independence sheared the Anglican Church of its official recognition and state support, turning it into the American Protestant Episcopal Church, another voluntary association that appealed to those who loved its Old World liturgy and formality. Meanwhile the Methodists, who had constituted an evangelical group within the Church of England, separated from both the mother church and American Episcopalians and launched a highly successful drive for members. In New England public support for the Congregational churches continued for several decades more, but the venerable Calvinist Standing Order of the colonial era had already been rent asunder by the Unitarians, whose rational and humane faith captured Harvard University along with many congregations in Massachusetts.

Struggling to adjust to a world of voluntary religious associations, none of the old establishments could meet the religious needs of the country, for none had the means to carry Christianity to the new settlements that by 1810 claimed a third of America's population. Into this breach poured revivalist preachers—most of them Baptists and Methodists—who proved astoundingly successful in planting religious convictions among the unchurched and awakening many others from their spiritual lethargy. New

Christian denominations proliferated under the nourishing influences of lay enthusiasm, most of them carrying the rallying cry of "No creed but the Bible." A host of artisans, farmers, even slaves and women, discovered that their religious ardor had the power to stir others. Casting aside their normal work to take up a preacher's calling, thousands of poor men of the cloth roamed the countryside as part of a voluntary and seemingly spontaneous campaign to revive American Christianity.

Many associated the revivalists' success with their attacks on the Calvinist doctrines of predestination and damnation. Here was another form of liberation for ordinary Americans who responded by deserting the old churches and flocking to the evangelizers. As one contemporary explained it, the old Calvinists were "at least a century behind the rest of the world," having fallen in the rear "in all that relates to taste, manners, feelings and information."[8] Yet several of the successful new denominations and revivalist Presbyterian congregations emphasized sinners' dependence upon an inscrutable God, and the burgeoning Baptist faith had many overtly Calvinist congregations within its fold. What better discriminated the evangelicals from others was their insistence upon an intense, personal relationship with God, to be expressed in the daily enactments of living.[9] Jefferson's strictures against elite rule may have resonated powerfully among them, but they also sought the kind of uniform public piety that Jefferson himself had found so distasteful in organized religion.[10]

A cohort of youthful revivalist ministers succeeded in invigorating the flagging religious affections of post-Revolutionary America, nurturing the people's spiritual longings while spreading lessons about personal strength that echoed the Republicans' political message. The revival leaders made self-reliance the basis of liberty and worked to undermine people's dependence upon authorities, be they in the pulpit, the legislature, or the surgery. The preachers' zeal for empowering ordinary men frequently gave a Lockean cast to religious exhortations, and the expectation of a morally elevated society encouraged reformers to use a millenarian vocabulary.[11] Radicals in both religion and politics supported the constitutional separation of church and state—"the wall of separation"—that Jefferson announced when he refused to proclaim a national day of thanksgiving. Battling the established churches, evangelical ministers warned their congregations that an aristocracy of Calvinist clergy was trying to control the soul of the nation and crush the simple congregational freedom of ordinary worshippers.[12]

Self-conscious outsiders, the Methodist circuit riders and itinerant preachers of all denominations scrutinized established religious doctrine for evidence of upper-class prejudice. Spurning the formal religious routines of the learned clergy, the revivalists brought sinners to Christ and, once won, left them with confidence in their own ability to discover Christian doctrine unaided. In their sermons, the radical preachers attacked hierarchical ecclesiastical structures as well as the Calvinists' preoccupation with damnation. Despite the well-advertised religious skepticism of Jefferson, many revivalists supported him because of his famous—or notorious—opposition to both precedent and privilege. The old established religions had augmented the authoritarian rule of an upper class; now the flourishing sects enhanced the appeal of limited government and voluntary efforts. With ministers drawn from common folk, no costly physical plant to maintain, and an emphasis upon ardent proselytizing, the revivalists had the flexibility and directness to reach a new generation, but ironically in their very success they pulled away from the Jeffersonian spirit of free inquiry.

Within two decades the revivalists had transformed American civil society, driving the irreligion of the Revolutionary era out of the public space. By the time that Thomas Paine returned to the United States in 1802, the notoriety of his religious skepticism obliterated the memory of *Common Sense*, which is to say that he returned without honor or attention, remembered, as John Francis wrote, as "the notorious author of *The Age of Reason*."[13] Despite the prominence of rationalist thinkers among the Revolutionary elite, the issue of revelation versus reason had not been publicly debated. Rather the revivalists—helped here by conservatives in the old denominations—had structured the discussion around dreaded outcomes: belief in the sufficiency of human reason to answer questions of ultimate meaning led to infidelity and infidelity to corruption and to the eventual dissolution of the whole society. Isaac Chandler, traveling in America in 1822, observed that "instances of openly avowed deism are rare," adding shrewdly that people who hold such opinions "either keep them to themselves, or veil them under the garb of flimsy hypocrisy."[14] The new consensus endorsed liberty and rejected free thinking. As long as there was no hint of infidelity, the shared goal of clearing space for competitive persuasion cemented the alliance of political and religious democrats.

John Ball is rare among the autobiographers of his age in complaining about the evangelical cleansing of the public sphere. Although raised in a strict Calvinist congregation in Vermont, Ball sprinkled critical remarks about the new public piety throughout his memoirs. "In spite of my prior instruction," he wrote, "the thought would arise in my mind, as to the utility of churches, ministers and all those things." He described as a "wild religious reformation" the Methodists' arrival in his hometown with their "frequent day and night and all-night meetings, where all took part in exhorting, singing, weeping and groaning." Explaining that he was a Jackson man, and his law colleagues in Michigan were Whigs, he remembered being advised by a friend "to take a seat in the Second Presbyterian Church, as it would aid my business, but it was always repulsive to me to mingle sacred and secular things."[15] David Hoover made a more oblique tribute to free thinking when he announced that in politics "I profess to belong to the Jeffersonian School," noting his dedication to political and religious liberty and his conviction that Jefferson was "decidedly the greatest statesman that America has yet produced."[16]

The quickening of religious interest in the country did not end controversy. Protestant clergyman not only faced the challenge of finding support for themselves and their churches through voluntary contributions, they also had to contend with flocks that did not act like docile sheep. Revived religion had created a lively interest in Christian doctrine. Awakened to spiritual issues, both lay people and clergy began scrutinizing the Bible in efforts to reconcile divergent views of Christian dogma about infant depravity, adult baptism, the sequential steps towards salvation, inherited grace, justification, sanctification, and their proper ordering in Christian life. Church-goers, now attuned to the subtleties of Protestant doctrine through exposure to competing preachers, readily switched denominations within the Protestant fold, a fluidity that placed a particular burden on the shepherd. As Joseph Tuckerman, founder of the Unitarian ministry to Boston's poor, explained in an ordination sermon, a Protestant minister in America could only lead his people by force of character, having "no sanctions, ecclesiastical or civil, with which to maintain his influence."[17] Alexis de Tocqueville, who visited the United States in 1831, remarked wryly that every time he was told he was to meet a man of the cloth, he met a politician.[18]

Francis Asbury, the founding bishop of the American Methodist Church, estimated that in 1811 over 3 million Americans attended camp meetings—more than a quarter of the total population. Reacting to their success, the Presbyterians and Congregationalists in 1801 formed a "Plan of Union" to combine resources for evangelizing in the West, where the revivals had followed the trail of frontier families. Adopting the revivalists' techniques, leaders in the old churches brought the evangelical spirit back to rekindle religious enthusiasm in the East. Revival fires burned brightly in Hartford and Philadelphia in 1800; in Beaufort, South Carolina in 1803; in North Carolina throughout 1804; in the smaller towns of Connecticut and Massachusetts in 1808; and in Georgia and South Carolina in 1810. In the 1820s Charles Finney returned to the "Godless" frontier he had left as a youth, scorching the parched lands of religious indifference so thoroughly that western New York acquired the name of "the burned over district."[19]

In just a few years, a dozen splinter groups had broken off from the old blocks of Congregationalists, Presbyterians, Baptists, Methodists, and Quakers with enough force to give permanent form to their own versions of the gospel message, usually under the impetus of charismatic leaders like Lorenzo Dow, Barton Stone, Joseph Smith, and Alexander Campbell. The new term "denominations"—with all its antiseptic parity—became the preferred designation for the array of American churches now vying for members.[20] There were Seventh Day Baptists, Six Principle Baptists, Antimission Baptists, and Free Will Baptists; Smithites and Campbellites; Disciples of Christ, Hicksite Quakers, Mormons, Unitarians, and Universalists. America's religious smorgasbord astounded foreign visitors. James Flint took note of fifty-three churches in New York of "seventeen religious sectaries." Philadelphia, he said, had thirty-four places of worship representing eighteen religious sects: three Swedish churches, three Quaker, one Free Quaker, three Episcopal, one Baptist, two Presbyterian, four Catholic, two German Lutheran, two German Calvinist, one Associate Reformed Church, one Associate Church–Antiburgher, one Moravian, one Presbyterian Covenanter, four Methodist (two for blacks; two for whites), one Universalist, one Unitarian, one Independent, and two Jewish synagogues, which with Philadelphia's population of 63,802 worked out to a place of worship for every 1,876 men, women, and children.[21]

In their many successes, the revivalist clergy revealed not only the power of their preaching but also the brilliance of their organizing skills. The Methodists had been able to put into operation a mobile army of ministers riding prescribed circuits through rural America with nothing but Bibles in their saddlebags. Organized into proselytizing bands, they and the Baptists joined a motley assortment of preachers of diverse religious societies—all adding to the explosive revivalist force. National organizers paid their traveling ministers very little, expecting them to rely upon relatives, generous church members, and their own exertions as farmers or writers for supplementary income. Local in their origins, the multiplying

Protestant denominations and voluntary associations built national networks, the Baptists alone gathering 2,633 congregations into a national body. Often working together, the national associations raised money for missions, religious publications, and Sunday schools, establishing in these decades the ethic of private support for public worship.

Few records exist to make precise the revivalists' gains, but John Frost, a Presbyterian minister in western New York, took a religious census of 211 families in his frontier community before the aggressive efforts of the evangelicals and discovered that almost 60 percent of the families contained no church members and among those that did, less than 20 percent comprised whole families.[22] More generally, the number of clergymen per capita increased threefold from one in 1,500 at the time of the Revolution to one in 500 thirty years later. By 1820 the Methodists and Baptists had overtaken the traditional churches in the number of adherents, the Freewill Baptists alone equaling the number of Episcopalians and the Antimission Baptists outnumbering both the Lutherans and the Roman Catholics, who had yet to experience the influx of Irish and German communicants. American Christianity had been democratized and evangelized, which is to say Americanized, by the time most in the first generation reached maturity.

The Second Great Awakening can also be credited with bringing African Americans, both slave and free, into the evangelical Protestant fold.[23] While white Christians had proselytized among slaves earlier, the great conversion of African Americans came after the Revolution, when itinerant Baptist and Methodist preachers, many of them outspokenly opposed to slavery, refused to recognize any spiritual barriers between blacks and whites as they carried their gospel message through the South. The pioneering American Methodist bishops Francis Asbury and Thomas Coke, both Englishmen, had petitioned the Virginia legislature for the abolition of slavery, calling it "this grand Abomination." When Maryland planter Freeborn Garrettson converted to Methodism, he freed his slaves and, as an itinerant preacher, carried blank manumission papers with him in the hope of arousing the consciences of other planters.

Southern revivalists sought out the company of black men and women to share their most precious cultural gift—the Gospel message of salvation. The high tide of religious enthusiasm either convinced or cowed slaveowners into accepting preaching among their slaves with all the entailments of ecstatic worship, regular slave meetings, and the intermingling of blacks and whites as spiritual equals. For several decades, black Christians could worship in biracial congregations of Presbyterians, Episcopalians, Lutherans, Roman Catholics, and Methodists, but a majority of them preferred their own Baptist congregations, finding a spiritual solidarity in their understanding of the Bible's story of expulsion, exodus, revilings, and the peace that passeth understanding.[24] A crucial resource for forging an American identity among slaves and free blacks, the Great African-American Revival signaled a break with African culture, though blacks carried into Christian services many of their song and dance traditions.[25] While bringing slaves and free blacks closer to their American destiny, conversions to Christianity also forced them to confront the ambivalence and hypocrisy in white Americans' religious and political protestations.

The Methodists soon ran into resistance to their antislavery stand in the South, their very success leading them to retreat from the high ground of emancipation and drift towards segregated worship.[26] Moderating their views of slavery was the price they paid for moving from the fringes of Southern society to its center. Informal segregation became the custom of the country. Flint called "the degradation" imposed on people of color "one of the greatest inconsistencies among a people professing liberty and equality." Maintaining that the aversion to blacks could be seen everywhere, even among the Philadelphia Quakers, he said that he looked in vain for a black face "in the church of the most popular preacher in New York."[27] Free blacks who had moved North, such as Moses Grandy and David Walker, found the segregation in churches and theaters that Flint reported. Grandy acknowledged that Northerners had helped him gain his freedom, but reported that he had been made "to feel severely the difference between persons of different colors."[28] Most white Christians chose not to inspect their racial prejudices, preferring to concentrate on the material measures of their success.

Bishop William Meade, who was responsible for the Episcopal revival in Virginia, believed that the whole world was watching to see if religion prospered in America once the established churches had been forced to give up their public support. The results spoke well for the experiment, he thought. "None can deny what all should rejoice to see," Meade announced before his church's 1828 convention, "that there is a great and generous movement of heart and hands in the Christian world," noting that the revenues of the Church were up, even if small compared "with the wants of a ruined world."[29] The indefatigable Charles Ingersoll estimated that the 10 million people in the United States had eight thousand places of worship and five thousand ecclesiastics with twelve theological seminaries "all self-erected and sustained by voluntary contributions." He also claimed that even the Catholic and Episcopalian churches, normally dependent upon an establishment, had "endowed more dioceses, founded more religious houses, and planted a stronger pastoral influence, than in any other part of the globe." African American worshippers were far less well provided, but the swelling numbers of black exhorters and preachers impressed contemporaries. If "this unequalled increase of churches and pastors, and worshippers, attest the prosperity of religion," Ingersoll concluded proudly, "we may rest assured of its welfare without tythes or political support: and we need not fear its decline from the ascendancy of republicanism."[30]

The extraordinary popularity of the revivals produced the curious irony of a proliferation of denominations in the face of a mounting Protestant orthodoxy, albeit an orthodoxy more cultural than doctrinal.[31] Evangelical Protestants had converged on the same values. They all sought a Christian America awakened to its missionary destiny and promoted a common set of qualities in their converts; they all wanted piety expressed in virtuous habits and good works. Alfred Lorrain remembered that the arrival of the Methodists in his hometown of Petersburgh, Virginia brought a sharp decline in horse-racing, the "gander-pulling and cock-fighting" that had enlivened his youth.[32] Protestant leaders also wanted conversions to produce disciplined lives and self-mastery, the personal traits that made the revitalization of religion compatible with limited government and economic enterprise. The character-building that the revivalists sought and often achieved in their highly personalized preaching provided the invisible framework for the market, dependent as it was on an internalized standard of honesty and promise-keeping. The pious entrepreneur became as American as the Christian civic leader. The unexpected responsiveness of the generation born after the Revolution to the revivalists' summons to a new life in Christ brought some measure of order to America's mobile society.

THE SECOND GREAT AWAKENING differed from its colonial predecessor by surviving the controversies it generated. It also shifted the initiating center of revived religion from God to individual Christians. Those who felt themselves to have been touched and cleansed by God's power became powerful evangelists to others. In creating vast pools of proselytizers—preachers, exhorters, lay readers, prayer-meeting organizers—and designating the entire society a missionary field, the evangelical Protestants, particularly in the North, encouraged social activism. Bringing people to Christ through a particular denominational path was but one part of their concern; the society as a whole had to be redeemed for the strict observance of the sabbath, the conversion of pagans, the spread of religious education and, above all, sobriety. Once converted, men and women found ways to express their new-found spiritual awakening by getting government policy, public morals, and private lives to conform to biblical prescriptions.[33] The evangelicals' many commitments to social betterment invested public life with a portentousness and gravity that had been absent earlier.

Sabbatarian, antislavery, and temperance campaigns disclose the main currents and moral conflicts in the reform movements that the revivals inspired; they also mark out the fault lines in the evangelical terrain. Although as one English traveler observed, free thinking had been driven underground, church membership never composed a majority of the population. So, like politicians, the evangelicals could never ignore public opinion, nor could they afford to push too hard against the interests of their communicants, as the Methodist campaign against slavery in the South revealed. Still they plunged ahead with proselytizing zeal, taking soundings of sentiment as they went along. Their rhetoric about temperance and sabbath-keeping tended to present dichotomous choices: dissipation or abstinence, reverence or blasphemy, but antislavery opinions were presented in less cataclysmic packaging in the early decades of the century, suggesting that white Americans who were concerned about the issue were groping towards a coherent position.

Temperance was the generation's great success. Contemporaries called it a second American Revolution in which the grandchildren of the founders liberated themselves from a tyranny worse than Britain's.[34] In the campaign to curb the excessive drinking of their generation, the evangelical reformers scored their greatest victory, because, as personal testimony reveals, individuals independently moved to rid their lives of alcohol. While temperance activities eventually came together in a highly effective national movement, the discrete, personal initiatives of a variety of people—unbeknownst to one another—laid the movement's groundwork.

In embarking on a crusade to banish alcohol from American social life, individual temperance advocates were taking on a major task. Drinking had long marked the daily routines of work and the celebration of most public and professional events, even though contemporaries repeatedly noted its conspicuous cost. Both those living at the turn of the nineteenth century and those looking back a few decades later affirmed the public problem of drunkenness. Federalist jurist Samuel Dexter wrote in 1814 that "the quantity of ardent spirits . . . surpasses belief."[35] Freeman Hunt, the editor of *Merchants Magazine,* noted dolefully that "our ancestors were extensive consumers of all descriptions of intoxicating fluids."[36] A backward glance could not convey the vitality of customs that had enlivened the monotonous round of human activity, but challenges to their venerable status uncorked the memory of those growing up after the Revolution.

Leonard Wood counted forty ministers in New England's Congregational establishment "who were drunkards, or so far addicted to drinking" as to be embarrassments. He also recalled an ordination in which he saw "two aged ministers literally drunk, and a third indecently excited."[37] William Wirt, drawing on his experience as a Virginia planter and political leader, thought that heavy drinking had "produced more vice, crime, poverty, and wretchedness in every form, domestic and social, than all the other ills that scourge us combined."[38] The irrepressible Americanophile William Cobbett, after spending two years in the United States, named drinking "the *great misfortune* of America!"[39]

More liquor was drunk in the early nineteenth century than ever before or since. The annual per capita consumption of spirits by those fifteen or older in 1820 was four times that of today.[40] Many in the general public thought of drinking as healthy. Considering the state of the drinking water, perhaps it was. Harrison Hall, the author of the popular manual *The Distiller,* artlessly characterized "ardent spirits" as being "so useful . . . so important an object of commerce . . . so influential on the health, habits, and happiness of the human race."[41]

The memory of the hard drinking of soldiers in the Revolutionary War had created a moment for temperance when Philadelphia's great physician, Benjamin Rush, wrote a tract denouncing the effects of alcohol. Rush's pamphlet caught the attention of some gentlemen who formed the Massachusetts Society for the Suppression of Intemperance, an association of the well-meaning rich to improve the morals of the unruly poor. It met annually for a sermon, followed by a good meal and some wine. Early in the

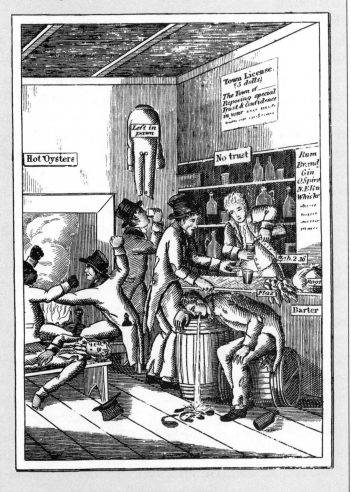

An early temperance broadside of 1826 elucidating the four stages of "The Drunkard's Progress on the Direct Road to Poverty, Wretchedness & Ruin" shows stage two, the bad company drunkards keep in "The Grog Shop." Courtesy, American Antiquarian Society.

century a group of farmers took a pledge not to drink until the harvest was in, but little more was heard about moderation or abstinence, and the old routines continued.

John Marsh remembered election days in Hartford as great gatherings of the state's clergymen, well-oiled with good bottled cider, his mother's currant wine, and spring beer. "The drawing of corks afforded great merriment," Marsh wrote in his memoirs, as he who performed the ceremony was "in danger of a smart shower on his new black coat." "At freemen's meetings, . . . ordinations, and other clerical gatherings, a rich display of decanters with stronger liquors (usually furnished by some generous parishioners) covered the sideboard and were resorted to by all without any sense of wrong doing," he recounted, "though not in all cases without results which were the subject of much private conversation. In my boyhood," Marsh said, "Flip, a drink made of small beer, a glass of spirits, and sugar with nutmeg, made warm by a red hot poker, was a usual drink on the Sabbath, in the winter months, on returning from church. Well do I remember crying in meeting from the cold (there were then no stoves), and holding on to my chair after drinking the Flip till my head became steady."[42]

The association of drinking with harvest was particularly strong. In his otherwise nostalgic reconstruction of life on the Kentucky frontier, Daniel Drake grimly appraised the drinking at corn-husking time: "as they assembled at night-fall the green glass quart whiskey bottle, stopped with a cob, was handed to every one, man and boy, as they arrived, readying themselves for the contests that ended the day," he remembered. "It was there that I first learned that competition is the mother of cheating, falsehood, and broils," Drake commented, going on to set the scene for what he wryly called his autumnal school: "The oft-replenished whisky bottle meanwhile circulated freely . . . Either before or after eating the fighting took place, and by midnight the sober were found assisting the drunken home."[43] Clearing was too hard for the single laborer, the New York editor Thurlow Weed explained—hence the logging "bees" when seasons of hard work were rendered exciting and festive by the indispensable gallon bottle of whiskey.[44] The drunkenness and fighting in the harvesting fields of Pennsylvania left a lasting impression on Ezra Michener.[45]

In their recapitulation of the drinking habits of their youth, few sentimentalized community events. Typical is John Marsh's censorious description of house raisings: "The liquor was free and abundant, and the jugs and demijohns were well emptied." Raisings were great times for drunkards and hard drinkers, he concluded, but awful scenes for Christian communities. "A raising was one of the devil's harvests, and not a few were the distressing accidents then occurring." As a lad in the summer Marsh had had the responsibility of supplying the hayfield with the daily bottle of New England rum, "from which the mowers and others took copious draughts; showing soon how perfectly it unfitted them for continuance in labor." His town, like most in Connecticut, Marsh maintained, had been settled by hard drinkers, many of whom found their way to a drunkard's grave.[46]

Most liquor was sold in country stores and in fact represented the most significant item in their inventory. D. N. Prime recalled that when he had kept a store, the most prominent article was ardent spirits, especially rum, which was rolled in hogsheads and sold in immense quantities by comparison with all else. Later in life, he looked back with astonishment on his morning ritual of drinking bitters.[47] But if country stores were the principal point of purchase, taverns threw a spotlight on drinking itself. The Quaker Edward Hicks worked for a tavern and remembered with great distaste the "apple frolics, spinning frolics, raffling matches, and," he added, "all kind of low convivial parties, so peculiarly calculated to nourish the seeds of vanity and lies."[48]

Artisans were no less prone to drink than farmers. The usual custom was to break for liquor twice a day at 11 A.M. and 2 P.M., the youngest apprentice being sent out to get the bottle. Nathaniel Bouton recalled this routine as an adolescent test. Working in a pottery with fifteen hands when he was thirteen, the responsibility for going out for the jug fell to him, but his resistance to joining in the drinking provided the occasion for daily harassment.[49] Joseph T. Buckingham recalled that the youngest apprentice in his first job in Walpole, New Hampshire, was forced to treat the entire print shop and compelled to drink brandy along with the others. His duties also entailed looking out for the master while the others continued drinking.[50]

To a striking degree, people could not escape the presence of liquor in the first decades of the century. Michener, a much respected Quaker physician, came to temperance by way of a childhood addiction. His mother had given him alcohol as medicine for the colic. Childhood exposure to such medication, he claimed, had left him with an appetite for drink that in "more than four-score years of abstinence has hardly abated its intensity." Excoriating "mints, cordials, cherry bounce" that passed as medicine in his youth, Michener noted that such potions were helpless to prevent the return of pain, and present relief was paid for by lifelong appetites and cravings "for alcoholic liquors, which too surely lead the possessor down to ruin and a drunkard's grave."[51] Charles Kirk, reflecting on the death of his mother, recalled that doctors "depended almost wholly upon stimulants," using wine and brandy in large quantities.[52] Even healthy pastimes became opportunities for imbibing. A. V. Green, who crowned a lifetime of heavy drinking with a career as a popular temperance speaker, explained that not only was liquor pressed upon one at every turn, but conviviality was withheld if one refused; one couldn't find a first-rate young woman without a name "as a fine, friendly, go ahead free hearted young man."[53]

If children missed contact with drunks at home or in the harvest field, there was always the classroom. The schooling of Humphrey Howe Leavitt, a prominent Ohio lawyer, came to an abrupt end when it was discovered that his New England schoolmaster, "the accomplished pedagogue" who was to save the frontier children from illiteracy, had become "a victim to a habit of intemperate drinking, and almost unperceived by his friends and patrons had already plunged deeply into this burning abyss." In a replay of the same melodrama, the parents of Georgia leader Lott Warren withdrew him from his first school because the excessive drinking of the schoolmaster offended them, both pious Baptists.[54] Henry Clarke Wright remembered vividly a drunken teacher who had sent the older boys in his New York frontier school to the whiskey shop for his liquor.[55] More vivid was Eber Howe's recollection of a schoolmaster that "would frequently get 'half seas over,' vomit upon the floor, and take a 'quiet snooze' in the school room." "In those days," Howe added soberly, "intemperance was not considered an insurmountable disqualification for a good teacher." George Gilmer, who later became governor of Georgia, recalled that his first master had been a deserter from the British army, followed by a yearly succession of "wandering, drunken Irishmen [who] were the only class of the frontier people who had the leisure and requisite knowledge for teaching."[56]

Teachers had to cope with a culture that encouraged adolescent boys to drink. John Marsh, who at twelve attended an academy in Bethel, Connecticut, with thirty students drawn from the North and the South, described a Fourth of July bacchanal at his school: "At nightfall, the prostrate and pitiable condition of more than half the school aroused the wrath of our instructor" who forever expelled "the wine cup from his school and all its festivities," but the next year at Yale Marsh witnessed another such scene on the Fourth of July, and this time he joined the wretched and retching group.[57] Sidney Willard, son of Harvard's president, Joseph Willard, re-membered commencements in the 1790s as gatherings of "men, women, and boys, white and black, many of them gambling, drinking, swearing, dancing, and fighting from morning to midnight." In short, according to him, they were "exhibitions of depravity which would disgust the most untutored savage," and they continued, he noted, until a revulsion of public opinion effected a reform.[58] Dr. Richard Carter, a Virginia physi-cian, was more poetic:

> It is proven to a demonstration, that the immoderate use of ardent spirits, is more baneful to our commonwealth than devas-tation and war. For drunkenness is the annoyance of modesty, the trouble of civility, the spoiler of wealth, the destruction of reason . . . It is also the brewers agent, the ale-house-keepers benefactor, the beggars companion, and the officers perplexity. A drunkard is a wife's woe, his children's sorrow, and resembles more the brute than the man.[59]

Certain professions stood out for being particularly prone to drunken-ness, printers leading the lot. Thurlow Weed claimed that far too many journeyman printers "were impoverished by habitual dram-drinking, more or less intemperately," adding that "the printing house habits condemned by Dr. Franklin had not yet been reformed."[60] Another distinguished news-paperman, Massachusetts' Joseph T. Buckingham, tried to redeem printers by pointing to their miserable wages, which left them dying with "little more than enough to pay the joiner for a coffin," but despite this apology he filled his pages with abundant evidence of those he characterized as the "victims of the invisible spirit of wine."[61] In addition to drunken printers, there were alcoholic medical men. Dr. David Hosack estimated that in New York City in 1830 forty out of one hundred physicians were drunkards. Dr. Joseph Speed of Richmond, Virginia, writing to Rush two decades earlier, reported, "I often hear the people saying that they scarcely know of a single sober doctor but myself."[62]

What these remembrances convey with great vivacity is the difficulty of avoiding drinking. Marsh described the struggle among his parishioners in the Haddam, Connecticut Congregational Church "whose labors were in shipyards, coasting, fishing, quarrying and farming; labors in which at that time, ardent spirit was a daily ration at eleven and four, as regularly as food was provided at other hours." Some farmers, he noted, "planted themselves on the doctrine of total abstinence, and they would not give strong drink to those they employed, but it was viewed as a singular freak, and they had but little influence." His own strong stand against drink, stated in Sunday sermons, became the "subject of merriment among the young men, and more was drank the next day in the ship-yards and quarries than before." Only during revivals did he reform hard drinkers, who came to realize that "giving up the cup" was part of "submission to the Gospel."[63]

Against these powerful social mores, men and women began to stop drinking, construing their decision as a deeply meaningful experience. For many of them, the heavy drinking of their youth had proved to be a snare. Anson Jones detailed in his autobiography how failure had dogged him as he went from Massachusetts to New York and then to Louisiana trying to establish a medical practice, but finding each effort undermined by his own dissipation. In desperation to escape the fashionable gambling and drinking in New Orleans, he went to the Texas frontier, an odd place to clean up one's act. But Jones did, becoming the chief rival of Sam Houston and the last governor of the Lone Star Republic.[64]

Others threw themselves into a variety of imaginative efforts to demonstrate the possibility of doing without drink. Michener recalled how he and his friends took an oath not just to stop drinking, but to stop offering drink to visitors at a time when "it had become an established custom to give them something to drink." Next he and his friends formed the Guardian Society in Chester, Pennsylvania to prevent illegal sale of liquor at auctions.[65] Ichabod Washburn, a budding Massachusetts manufacturer, recorded with great satisfaction his decision to see if he could build his house without providing "the stimulus of spirits" to the carpenters. "I attempted to do what had not been done" in Worcester—have "a house-raising without rum!" Even his own employees jeered at the undertaking, but he finally found builders who would accept his bill of fare of "lemonade, crackers, and cheese, with small beer." About the same time in Connecticut, Marsh celebrated another "dry water raising" of the house he was building, commenting in his memoirs that "this was an unheard-of thing."[66]

Joseph Bates, a seafaring man of Plymouth, was even more ambitious in his temperance enterprise after making a personal pledge in 1822 to stop drinking. Bates imposed a ban on liquor once he got his own ship, forbidding profanity and the use of nicknames as well. He introduced daily prayer meetings and also had the idea of preparing a semi-weekly paper for the crew while at sea, reporting proudly that "their interest in the paper continued throughout the entire voyage." With even more pride Bates reported that "temperance and religious principles on shipboard were new, and, of course, objectionable to all around us; but still they were constrained to admit that we enjoyed peace and quiet on board our vessel that they in general were strangers to."[67]

Charles Kirk recorded another temperance milestone, the decision of his family not to serve wine for his sister's wedding, the first without intoxicating beverages that he knew of.[68] Another early temperance advocate, Heman Bangs, introduced prayers at the metal-working shop where he first went to work and fought the lure of the nearby tavern, a "real devil's den," by getting his fellow employees to stop drinking. Henry Marie Brackenridge remembered that his grandfather, long before the establishment of temperance societies in western Pennsylvania, "shut up his distillery from a conviction that he could not conscientiously manufacture a liquid which tempts so many to destroy their health and morals."[69]

Richard Stone, who moved to Oxford, Massachusetts to teach, became a captain in the militia, where drinking was the highlight of muster days. Believing that drinking made his men unfit for service, he secured an agreement first with his company and then at the brigade level to get rid of liquor, "though it was two or three years before any temperance society was formed in the county." Stone later became a Congregational minister. Deeply affected by his experience of presiding at the funeral of a man who had died of intoxication at age thirty, he preached an abstinence sermon which, he claimed, led to several pledges of temperance, having never before "at any funeral of a similar character, spoken so plainly."[70]

Methodists, Baptists, and Quakers had long deplored the drinking of intoxicating beverages among their ranks, and groups like the Free African Society of Philadelphia had barred drinkers from membership, but it was not until 1826 that advocates founded the American Temperance Society along with *The National Philanthropist*, the country's first temperance journal.[71] Under the leadership of the country's most famous Presbyterian minister, Lyman Beecher, the society, which claimed a million and a quarter members by 1834, shifted its focus from the hopeless drunkard to the social drinker and replaced moderation with abstinence as the movement's goal.[72] With inventive genius, temperance workers sent former imbibers out on the lecture trail with "the wagon" for converts to jump on. They saw to the elimination of thousands of acres of apple orchard to reduce cider production, introduced the pledge to dramatize the individual resolve to give up booze, and founded an entire genre of literature in their temperance tracts. By the 1840s, support came from a new source, a group of working-class men in Baltimore who called themselves Washingtonians and campaigned to secure state laws prohibiting the sale, manufacturing, and consumption of alcohol, garnering a membership of half a million in three years.[73]

While some succumbed to dissolute habits and others made their way without moral bootstrap efforts, a significant number of American men faced the demon rum in an epic replay of Jason fighting the harvest of dragon's teeth. Their personal triumphs gave strength to the national movement. From such sources grew a mighty tide that washed drinking from the public sphere. As the widespread approval of Benjamin Rush's anti-liquor pamphlet of 1784 demonstrated, there had always been a voice of protest against intemperance, but American drinking habits had not changed. In fact they got much worse in the next three decades, in part because domestic whiskey offered a cheap alternative to imported rums and brandies. The precipitous decline in per capita drinking instead must be attributed to the hundreds of private battles against self-indulgence. Employers like David Dodge who held prayer meetings on the second floor of his textile mill undoubtedly wanted a sober work force, but Dodge's own evangelical zeal suggests that his factory's output played second fiddle to his desire to bring young men to God.[74] Attesting to the personal nature of commitments to temperance, whole families took the pledge, a trend that gave domestic life a central place in temperance literature.[75]

Temperance changed the forms of public conviviality, making worldliness sufficiently conspicuous to create a recognizable divide between the devout and the negligent. The success of the temperance movement owed something to the New England clergy's efforts to rally their parishioners for a war against evil, but most of the individual struggles against drinking seem to have started unaided by employers or ministers. Turning sobriety into a social virtue was more the work of individuals who craved a reformed society than of clerical inveighing against drunkenness. The Lyman Beechers without the Ichabod Washburns and Joseph Bateses would have represented yet another example of leaders without followers in a democratizing America. Arriving at a moment when hundreds of thousands of American men were ready to sober up, the temperance crusaders presided over a great sea change in public mores; consumption was cut in half between 1830 and 1845. The Washingtonians scored a legislative success in Maine, where selling liquor was outlawed; elsewhere heavy drinking was turned into deviancy, an amazing reversal of traditional mores.[76]

THE FIERCE INTENSITY of committed Christians introduced an urgency into public discussions of values and behavior that blurred the line between religion and politics. Where the Jeffersonians in the 1790s had fought to clear a space for public debate on matters of high government policy, "the Benevolent Empire" of the evangelical reform associations set up camp for an extended siege against the forces of evil. In quick succession, they mobilized a foreign missionary movement aimed at converting the entire pagan and Catholic world, an indication that Samuel Mills and his fellow seminary students had carried the day with their elders.

Local campaigns to reclaim the sabbath as a day of rest and reverence rallied around the goal of halting Sunday mail deliveries. Episcopal Bishop William White founded the first Bible Society in the United States in 1808; by 1824 representatives from fifteen states gathered in Philadelphia to launch the American Sunday School Union.[77] Several independent spirits like David Dodge, William Channing, Henry Clark Wright, William Ladd, and Thomas Smith Grimke converged on the importance of turning people against war and founded the American Peace Society—the first of its kind in the world. Dodge wrote *War Inconsistent with the Religion of Jesus Christ* in 1808 and Ladd, a Maine sea captain turned farmer, organized the pacifists to petition Congress and the state legislatures to set apart an annual day for peace prayers.[78] Campaigns against corporal punishment in the schools and the use of flogging in the dispensing of criminal justice also took shape.

The career of Louis Dwight reveals the synergetic quality of American reform. Dwight's travels through the country as an agent for the American Bible Society exposed him to a slice of life he had never seen before. Shocked by conditions in the country's jails and prisons, he became a leading crusader for the penitentiary system, designed—as its name suggests—to turn criminals into penitents. Reform also brought together Americans in alliances that cut across racial, sexual, and class lines. When Catherine Ferguson, an emancipated slave in New York, began gathering black and white children in her neighborhood for instruction on Sundays, she soon attracted the patronage of the distinguished philanthropists Isabella Graham and Divie Bethune who transferred her school to a nearby Presbyterian Church. Middle-class women in cities and towns everywhere raised funds for the seminary tuition of poor boys with a talent for preaching. In Philadelphia, Boston, and New York, wealthy philanthropists like Edward Delavan, Gerrit Smith, and Arthur and Lewis Tappan opened their pocketbooks to dozens of people with concrete plans for social betterment.

A typical American seeker in the early republic was Elias Smith, who began his career as a Calvinist Baptist in Connecticut, but soon rejected those doctrines like predestination that he could not find in the New Testament. Smith's father wanted him to learn arithmetic instead of grammar, and told him that he was not smart enough to teach school. Outwitting parental predestination, Smith saw that the communication network could liberate plain people from the patronizing instruction of their social superiors, so he turned himself into a veritable publishing machine, producing pamphlets, tracts, songbooks, and sermons, undeterred by the respectable clergy's view that his writings constituted "the most wretched trash that ever issued from the press." Wishing to broadcast his radical ideas for simplifying Christianity, he started the first religious newspaper in

This illustration of a classroom, distributed by the American Tract Society, represents a gathering of boys and girls for Sunday-school instruction, which became increasingly popular in Eastern cities. Courtesy, American Antiquarian Society.

1808, the fortnightly *Herald of Gospel Liberty,* from which he attacked "relig-ious intolerance, 'priestcraft,' ecclesiastical authority, theological seminar-ies, and opulent meeting-houses."[79] A blend of Jeffersonian liberalism and doctrinal questing—a fusion of political and gospel liberty—earned him a circulation of 1,500, with outlets in New England, Pennsylvania, Virginia, and Kentucky.

A severe critic of any form of religious authority—theological seminar-ies, missionary societies, clerical associations—Smith traveled extensively in the South, his adherents calling themselves Smithites. Like Barton Stone and Alexander Campbell, who founded the Disciples of Christ, Smith did not want to found another denomination, but rather to bring people back to the simplicity of Christ in one comprehensive church. However benign this goal, his ideas were not universally approved. He once caused a riot and, as he later reported, men with guns went after him. To get free of the debts from his *Herald,* Smith became an agent for the botanical medicine of Samuel Thomson, a man who disdained medical elites as Smith did clerical ones. Thomson urged Smith to join the Universalists, who denied the existence of the devil and eternity of hell and, as their name suggests, believed in salvation for all. Smith complied, only to return to his Chris-tian Connection sect, before rejoining the Universalists.[80]

Smith was but the first in a long line of evangelical publishers to exploit the printed medium. Seeing its potential to reach, hold, and direct con-verts, they became innovators of genres and formats, indirectly contribut-ing to the intellectual integration of the country as they scoured its byways for subscribers and contributors. As the editors of the *Adviser* commented in their maiden issue of October, 1809, Vermont could certainly support one religious periodical among the fifty-six political works published each month. This hope came fortified with an attack upon the churches' other print competitor, novels. Religious publishers soon learned to emulate the emotional appeal of novels in the memoirs of pious Christians that poured off the presses in the 1820s, 1830s, and 1840s.[81] Like the Jeffersonian Repub-licans in their campaign against the Federalists, America's many denomina-tions turned to printed material to maintain their organizational networks. In many ways intellectually incompatible, the political and religious re-formers used comparable techniques for arousing the public.

As with politics, publications strengthened and extended denomina-tional communities, creating careers for religious writers while reaching prospective donors in a widening circle of subscribers. More than anything else, this rain of the printed word on thirsty readers distinguishes eighteenth- from nineteenth-century popular movements, replacing the episodic and local with sustained communication through a national community of readers. Reform journalism flourished alongside and often within the magazines and pamphlets that the evangelicals used to build their mass movements. In quick succession appeared the *Christian Advocate, Christian Disciple, Christian Examiner, Christian's Magazine, Christian Messenger, Christian's Watchman,* and *Christian's Spectator,* the later offering to pay contributors five dollars a page. By 1827, thirty religious newspapers were sending 7 million issues annually to 60,000 households.

Doctrinal disputes spurred occasional pieces, like the exchange of Thomas Everard and John Watson over Methodist "errors."[82] The split between Congregational liberals and the Calvinist loyalists in New England kept alive many journals, but the most productive animus came from Protestant attacks on Catholics, whose numbers were beginning to grow, soon to be swollen by the potato famine exodus from Ireland of the 1840s. The *United States Catholic Miscellany,* started in 1822, devoted most of its space to answering rampant anti-Catholic charges.[83] Lyman Beecher's famous *Plea for the West* explicitly urged Protestants to check the spread of Catholicism, but more potently the Protestant press contributed to a discourse of national identity that defined as American the qualities of liberty, free choice, and resistance to formal authority, all presumed to be absent from the Catholic mindset.

Few stood outside this publishing mania. The Cherokee Council in Echota, Georgia, began the *Cherokee Phoenix*—the first Indian newspaper—edited by a Cherokee named Elias Boudinot. In New York City, John Brown Russwurm and Samuel Cornish started *Freedom's Journal,* the first African-American newspaper. The American Tract Society had distributed over 5 million tracts by 1828, one for every three people in the country (a figure comparable to 90 million today). During the same period the Bible Society was issuing 300,000 copies of the Old and New Testaments annually.[84] Other voluntary associations added stories, memoirs, songbooks, tracts, and printed sermons to the cascade of newspapers and books pouring down on the American public. The French philosophe Pierre Samuel Dupont noted that a large portion of the American public read the Bible, but all of the nation "assiduously peruses the newspapers; the fathers read them aloud to their children while the mothers are preparing the breakfast."[85] The juxtaposition of the Bible and the newspapers should not be taken as a conventional differentiation of religious and secular reading publics, for it was exactly their interaction that created a new identity for the nation. Every revival left a cluster of new societies in its wake just as every reform campaign led inexorably to the mobilization of voters.

⁂

WHAT NEEDS TO be put into the picture of American reform is the darker side of American freedom in the half-century after Independence. Real social problems fueled reforming engines as they added combustible material to the evangelical fires that were burning across the American landscape. Those who weren't reformers usually needed reforming. The decline of traditional ordering mechanisms exposed the deteriorating standards of personal behavior. The repeated defeats of the Federalists at the polls undermined social authority in many communities. Not only drinking, but gambling and ritualized violence, such as duels and staged fights, figured prominently in public life. Anti-black riots disfigured Boston in 1826; Providence in 1823 and 1831; Cincinnati in 1829; Philadelphia in 1829, 1834, and 1835; and Hartford in 1832, 1833, and 1836.[86] The lightly-governed, newly-settled communities in the West had their urban equivalent in the older cities, where the decadal doubling of population created entirely new neighborhoods. In settled areas people might be hauled into court for blasphemy, but such exactitude required a moral consensus that took years to form. Clergymen of all denominations attempted to fill the void of community authority, but they also were dependent upon popular support.

The churning population of post-Revolutionary America contained a disproportionate number of young men, always a group at risk in matters of social order. Geographic mobility offered cover to those fleeing from family and creditors. The liminal trial for teenagers was the temptation to self-indulgence, a strong narrative theme in the autobiographies of the first generation. Samuel Foot had the most dramatic encounter with vice when he discovered that his benefactor, his "kind, warm-hearted, generous, and talented brother" was addicted to gambling. Co-signing his brother's notes, Foot ended up in debtor's prison when his brother's early death left him saddled with his obligations. Clearly a searing experience for him, Foot interpreted his struggle with "the forgiveness of debt" in the language of his new-found Methodist convictions. John Chambers, who attracted the attention of General William Henry Harrison during the War of 1812, scornfully described the other officers in the unit as "drunken lawyers who having ruined themselves by their intemperance took shelter from starvation by enlisting." Drunkenness and gambling figured as the sinister lures to a degraded life in his mind. Even his wife's early suitors, we are told, ended up "before middle age in great poverty and perfectly besotted."[87]

The ebullience of the American economy, the mobility of its people, and the intense passion of religious revivals roiled emotions that the customary constraints of a more ordered society would have contained. With many old institutions discredited and replacements just emerging, men and women often had to find their way alone, the families of their birth not being of much help, so swiftly had change come. Margaret Dwight, a great-granddaughter of Jonathan Edwards, stayed at taverns on a trip to Ohio in 1810 and recorded in her journal that the filth was only exceeded by the debauchery, as first one drunken wagoner put his arm round her neck and another came into her room at night and lay down beside her before he could be coaxed away.[88]

The ever-watchful English traveler James Flint saw a young man buy a "dirk" with a pointed blade of four or five inches, having already noted the number of these weapons exhibited in jewelers' shops. "The advocates for private arms openly declared that they were for defence," a line he apparently rejected, for he added that, "the dissipated, the passionate, and the freebooter, urge a similar pretext for carrying the stiletto." Hypothesizing that Americans acquired their taste for concealed weapons from the Spanish [certainly not the English!], he declared that "quarrels must be conducted in a dangerous form; and murder must be made a prelude to robbery, amongst a people who use concealed arms."[89]

Levi Hathaway, moving to the West from his native New England in 1810, recoiled at seeing a fight in Pittsburgh: "they were the first two men that I ever saw fight; and to me the sight was awful." His memory highlights the differences among regions that travelers observed. Travelers in the South, for example, reported on the brutality of fights there with some frequency.[90] The enforcement of the law also produced violent scenes. Nathaniel Prime's hometown of Newburyport, Massachusetts retained a whipping post in the first decade of the century at which he saw prisoners stripped to the waist and beaten by the sheriff with his cat-o-nine-tail: "the old fellow would let them have it, until their backs were literally drenched with blood."[91] Yet as early as 1784 Pennsylvania eliminated capital punishment, except for first-degree murder, and Virginia pared down its capital crimes twelve years later.

Each reform was devoted to raising the American standard of living—morally. For some the severity with which children were treated had to be changed. Although formal efforts do not emerge until the 1830s, autobiographies provide a glimpse of their local origins. Sidney Willard, who reported that his home had been devoid of any punishing implement, remembered his schoolmistress reaching every child in a semicircle with her rod. From the distance of seventy years, Nathaniel Prime recalled a teacher in his winter school who would "knock us about rather severely." On the other end of the stick, young people who turned to schoolteaching were caught off guard when their punishments were challenged.[92]

John Griscom told of disciplining a lad who had defied his authority. "I was not conscious of having exceeded the bounds of discretion . . . [but] his father, being a man of high spirit, threatened me with a legal prosecution." Although "the ferule was in requisition" in Massachusetts schools in 1818, when Richard Cecil Stone punished a disobedient boy, his "grandparents and half a score of uncles and aunts came to school and complained," demanding one dollar or one month's schooling. Stone refused and was subsequently acquitted by the Court of Common Pleas, which heard the case. Julia Tevis retold a triumphal story of subduing a ten-year-old girl—"noisy, indolent, and impatient under restraint"—to whom she gave "the well-merited punishment with my slipper, the first she had ever had in her life," leading to "terrific screams and an awful silence in the school-room . . . as I led her back."[93]

The campaign to honor biblical injunctions about keeping the sabbath rallied the most distinguished group of reformers, clergy, and laymen from New England's Standing Order. In most towns, a customary silent sabbath reassured people of the spiritual ends that justified the previous six days of earthly cares, but the building of the Erie Canal shattered the tranquility of frontier New York towns when rowdy boatman wrecked havoc with Sunday peace. Rochester, the heart of "the burned-over district" of revival fires, became the hub of a national reform network, the General Union for Promoting the Observance of the Christian Sabbath, in 1828. Repeating earlier petition drives to halt the Sunday delivery of mail, the campaign to keep the sabbath holy struck a vital chord among the clergy, but not without creating disharmony. Something of a failure in comparison with temperance, the sabbatarians' attack on Sunday mail stirred popular resentment as a top-down effort that had threatening overtones of clerical intrusion into politics.

Congress precipitated a showdown—inevitable in a society that was becoming more commercial as it became more evangelical—by passing a law requiring mail to move seven days a week. Between 1810 and 1828, the number of post offices had tripled from 2,300 to 7,651. On Sundays they served as a kind of male retreat for conviviality and the exchange of news. By insisting that post offices remain open and the stages bring in the mail, Congress was affronting the municipal authorities who had put sabbath-observation laws on their books. At a higher level of abstraction, the issue raised questions about the separation of church and state, a connection that the Massachusetts clergy fought off vigorously, insisting, not very convincingly, upon the difference between a national religious establishment and "legislative protection of an institution, appointed by the benevolent Sovereign of the universe, for the happiness of the whole family."[94]

Never far from sight was the competition that ministers encountered from the world where Mammon ruled. The outraged editors of the important evangelical journal, the *Panoplist,* complained that people mobbed the post office for up-to-date information, allowing newspapers to supplant the pulpit, "even on Sundays when the Word of God should have silenced all others."[95] The sabbatarian crusade evoked vigorous, even strident, opposition, much of it from the libertarians of the old Jeffersonian coalition. Boatlines, ferries, taverns, theatres, and stores stood to lose from Sunday closings, much as the temperance movement had hurt brewers and distillers. The sabbatarians urged the public to boycott offending proprietors; they even established their own six-day-a-week Pioneer Stage Line.[96]

Resistance to this clerical revolt against commercialism came from a variety of sources. Biblical purists demanded a scriptural warrant for the sabbatarian position. Ezra Michener, whom we have met as a Quaker temperance advocate, challenged the Presbyterians to find a reference to Christian sabbath-keeping in the Bible. The irrepressible Anne Royall, who later pioneered investigative reporting in her Washington newspaper *Paul Pry,* feared the movement as an effort to reestablish religion in the country. Soon there was an anti-sabbatarian organization, supported by a coalition of affected businessmen and working men who feared the growing strength of the Benevolent Empire. One critic went so far as to claim that the sabbatarians wished to drive nonevangelical presses out of business in order to "subject the public mind to sectarian views."[97] Although an informal respect for Sunday quiet existed among all religions, the Baptists, by now the country's largest faith, opposed, as part of its historic tradition, the linkage of church and state that laws enforcing a religious observance suggested.

The most effective opposition to the sabbatarians came from Richard

Johnson, chair of the Senate Committee on Post Offices and Post Roads, who had achieved fame as the man who killed Tecumseh at the Battle of Thames. Johnson wrote two reports on the issue, the first ingeniously putting forth the proposition that since Jews and Seventh Day Adventists thought that the sabbath was Saturday, Congress's closing the post offices could be interpreted as an attempt to resolve a religious controversy through legislative means. "Because such a power had been 'wisely with-held' from the federal government—a mere 'civil institution,' wholly desti-tute of religious authority," Johnson concluded it would be unwise to go further, noting that "all religious despotism" starts in a similar way. Noth-ing if not bold, he compared sabbatarians to such famous traitors as Benedict Arnold and Judas Iscariot.[98] In the end, the mails continued to be delivered on Sundays, the sabbatarians won informal compliance in most towns, opponents of the evangelicals found an issue to rally around, and Congress held one of its few debates on the implications of the first amendment. The luster added to Johnson's reputation from these reports earned him the vice-presidency on the Democratic ticket in 1836.

ANTISLAVERY EFFORTS differed from all the other moral campaigns of the early nineteenth century in its divisive impact on reformers, not to men-tion the nation as a whole. Northern abolition had transformed a high-minded discourse into concrete social practices. Despite their gradualness, the laws and judicial decisions enacted between 1780 and 1804 disconnected Northerners from an odious institution at variance with their religious and political precepts. Not only had Northern legislatures demonstrated demo-cratic power, but they formalized a division between free and slave labor that would vex American politics for the next sixty years, not to mention the rancor caused by new regulations that affected Southerners when they traveled North with their slaves.

Most white Northerners considered themselves at the end of the anti-slavery trail after their states had passed abolition acts, but a vigorous minority—its will stiffened by the persistence of the Quakers—turned its attention to arousing the sleeping Southern conscience and thereby rid-ding the country of its most odious institution. The generation that came of age after the Revolution produced many of the most abiding foes of slavery—Sarah Grimke, William Goodell, James Birney, Beriah Green,

Joshua Leavitt, Samuel May, Hosea Easton, Garret Smith, Arthur and Louis Tappen, David Walker, William Jay, Benjamin Lundy, Henry Clarke Wright, John Rankin, Margaret Mercer, and Sojourner Truth. Unlike the Garrisonians of the 1830s, however, these activists followed half a dozen false leads before arriving at the conclusion that only immediate abolition would lance the festering wound of slavery.

After the Revolution, hundreds of antislavery societies sprang up, some surviving in the South until the 1820s. Their members lambasted the slave trade, sending a steady stream of petitions to Congress. These efforts kept alive the principle that slavery was a matter of national concern, a position inimical to Southern insistence on regional diversity. Representative William Loughton Smith of South Carolina told the first Congress that Quaker remonstrances would lead to slave revolts. Such hostility exposed a rift between the representatives from the lower South, who wished to turn

An antislavery broadside from 1836 publicizing "the facts" about slavery features the Slave House of J. W. Neal & Company in one of its nine illustrations. Courtesy, American Antiquarian Society.

antislavery advocates into pariahs, and the Virginians and Marylanders who supported citizens' rights to petition Congress.[99]

Many white Americans "voted with their feet" on the issue of slavery, assiduously avoiding Southern frontiers or, if already residing below the Mason-Dixon line, they opted to move to the states and territories where slavery had been prohibited. When the Constitution was drafted, Virginians expected to sustain their population advantage, not imagining that Southern families would cross the Ohio to settle in the Northwest Territory. Jefferson's young neighbor Edward Coles was but the most prominent of antislavery Southerners to seek refuge in the North, leading the successful battle in 1823 to keep Illinois from legitimating its clandestine slavery.[100]

Personal memoirs are filled with commentary on the slave issue, made portentous by later events. George Gilmer, who became governor of Georgia in 1829, remembered a wonderful teacher whose efforts to enforce South Carolina laws against trading in slaves made him so unpopular that he removed to Ohio. Allen Trimble detailed the arrangements that his father had made with the slaves he carried with him when the family moved from Kentucky to Ohio territory. If they agreed to five years of service in the new home, he would manumit them, providing in the meantime for education of their children with his own. Stephen Tyng wrote his father that he was leaving his Maryland parish for a Philadelphia one because of "the dreadful evil of slavery."[101] Southern Quakers, like Levi Coffin and John Rankin, moved to the free territories in droves, eventually making the Indiana Society of Friends the largest in the country and a major station of the underground railroad.

The English immigrant Morris Birkbeck described an afternoon in Petersburgh, Virginia in 1815 when rain stopped the horse races, sending a sizeable crowd into the tavern, where, he said, "Negro slavery was the prevailing topic—the beginning, the middle, and the end—an evil uppermost in every man's thoughts; which all deplore, many were anxious to flee, but for which no man can devise a remedy." The churches fared no better than the disappointed race track–goers in Petersburgh. After years of debate, Methodists, Baptists, and Presbyterians backed away from their early antislavery positions with hand-wringing statements characterizing slavery as a "moral dilemma." In the case of the Baptists, their congregational structure and historic commitment to the separation of church and state worked against imposing a ban on slave-holding. Local churches resisted the interference implicit in resolutions passed at General Committee meetings and, because Northern abolition had been achieved through legislation, Baptist ministers could and did say, when asked for advice about slavery, that they could only provide counsel on religious matters.[102]

Southerners got tangled in their churches' ambivalence about the South's peculiar institution. John Paxton, a Presbyterian minister in Virginia, faced the issue when he inherited some slaves from his wife's father. In consultation with her, he arranged for their passage to Africa. Sharing the common opinion "that slavery was wrong," Paxton admitted difficulty in deciding how to act on this conviction. As he wrote in his *Letters on Slavery,* "I was feeling it out myself" when he was forced to deal with the seventy slaves owned by his Presbyterian church whose labor, hired out, paid for the pastor's salary. Paxton's agitation to rid the congregation of these slaves provoked the community against him, forcing him to give up his church and move to Illinois. George Bourne, a much less timid English-born clergyman, outraged his Presbyterian congregation by advocating the expulsion of slaveholders from the church, a stand that cost him his pulpit and prompted his departure from Virginia as well.[103]

Those without the albatross of slavery around their necks could speak out more freely, transmogrifying slavery from an institution into an issue. Free blacks began petitioning Congress on such issues as North Carolina's legal strictures on manumission, further discomfiting Southerners who insisted that the Africans in their midst were too savage to understand the nation's political traditions. The Northern press was available for antislavery writings, many coming from the pens of African Americans. The testimony of ex-slaves and free blacks acted as sledgehammer blows to the planters' pretense to know "their people." As the shrewdest observers realized, nothing could stop the spread of this knowledge to the slave population. "Unless you put down the newspaper system, abolish magazines, journals, and reviews, burn the histories of the revolution, banish all books of travels and close the whole concern of printing," it was only a matter of time before African Americans everywhere became familiar with the abolitionist campaign, one Southern critic of slavery maintained.[104]

Older Southern leaders had deferred to Northern views by condemning slavery while asking for time to effect its termination, but those born after Independence had less of a moral investment in the political ideals of the Revolution. Spokesmen for the South began talking about the place of slavery in the embedded hierarchies of age, status, sex, and race in an organic society. When Elihu Embree sent Mississippi's governor, George

Poindexter, a copy of his *Emancipator,* Poindexter returned it with a note saying that the "same Providence which has permitted African slavery . . . will point to the period of its happy termination." Sounding the same quiescent theme, a young Thomas Dew intoned, "there is a time for all things." Edward Brown stressed that slavery had been the stepping ladder for all people to pass from barbarism to civilization. The Manumission Society of North Carolina reported that the "gentlest statement" or "slightest hint" of antislavery opinion produced explosive local resentment. What John Quincy Adams called "the cement of common interest" strengthened Southern solidarity, simultaneously making the South more alien to the rest of the country, which was still wrestling with racial hostilities in the midst of a swelling population of free blacks.[105]

Other obstacles appeared in the path leading to abolition. Slave revolts in Haiti, Virginia, and South Carolina brought home the dangers of antislavery agitation. The cotton boom created riches unimaginable in the Revolutionary era. After the African slave trade ended in 1808, many Virginia and Maryland planters profited from a flourishing new trade supplying slaves to the frontiers of the deep South, further fortifying opposition to the state's antislavery societies. On top of all this, the growing number of free blacks raised the possibility that the United States might become a biracial society in spirit as it was in fact, a proposition that most white Americans—North and South—found distasteful.

Free blacks presented white Americans with an uncomfortable anomaly. Unlike Spain's colonial empire, in which enslavement was a legal status, British colonists had fixed on race as a permanent and visual mark of an enslaved condition. For many Southerners the phrase "free black" was an oxymoron.[106] Northerners faced a different conundrum. They increasingly identified themselves as the defenders of natural rights, but clung to the ties of race, language, and tradition that connected them with Europe's high civilization, paying the price of hypocrisy for their failure to confront the contradiction. Feelings of racial difference proved stronger than either religious or political precepts for the majority of Northerners. Both sections produced men and women who were prepared to abandon the historic hobble of racial hostility, but most people, North and South, longed for a white America, Thomas Jefferson prominently among them. Yet by 1820 the country had 300,000 free African Americans, the beneficiaries of Northern emancipation, Southern manumissions, and their own bids for freedom. Southerners feared that free blacks would undermine slavery and corrupt white labor; Northern workers disliked the labor competition from African Americans. Other whites feared miscegenation, a new word for an old practice.[107]

The idea of colonizing free blacks in the West, in Haiti, or in Africa had been bruited about for many years, appealing to a mixed group of African Americans, white friends of African Americans, and Southerners who recoiled at living alongside ex-slaves. In 1816 Robert Finley, a Presbyterian clergyman in Princeton who later became president of the University of Georgia, formed the American Colonization Society (ACS). The society specified as its goal the founding of a settlement for free American blacks in West Africa. While Southerners hostile to the increase of free blacks played a prominent part in the colonization movement, the roster of its antislavery members is impressive. John Brown Russwurm, the distinguished Jamaican émigré who started the *Freedom's Journal*, went to Liberia in 1829 to serve as superintendent of its public schools, as did the antislavery missionary Samuel Mills and the free black leaders of Richmond, Lott Cary and Colin Teage. Benjamin Lundy, the most ardent Quaker foe of slavery, traveled widely in the West to find a location for a free black colony, agitating for colonization in his *Genius of Universal Emancipation*.

Enthusiasts pinned their hopes on getting a federal subsidy, and in this they were helped by Henry Clay, Speaker of the House of Representatives and an ardent colonization advocate, who managed to get $100,000 for the establishment of Liberia on the west coast of Africa. An air of idealism surrounded the scheme, which many construed as a providential implementation of God's plan to bring Africans to America so that they might return to Christianize the heathen population left behind. When Samuel Mills was asked if there was anything in Providence that linked the "elevation of the African race" to the "new order of things" since the Revolution, he replied "unequivocally . . . the evidence is truly astonishing." Over the course of forty years, the ACS relocated 3,600 African Americans, a number so infinitesimal when compared to the millions being added to the slave population as to blatantly advertise the wishful thinking behind colonization schemes. Still, the society maintained a membership of thousands scattered in auxiliaries throughout the country; it continued to garner supporters, including a young Illinois politician named Abraham Lincoln.[108]

Many antislavery activists later rethought their position on colonization, becoming suspicious of Southern support for the resettlement of free blacks who themselves had begun to voice alarm at the proposal. The 1820s were a watershed for free blacks who consciously moved away from an identity with Africa in order to establish their claims to full citizenship in the United States. The Massachusetts General Colored Association meeting of 1826 denounced the ACS, demanding immediate emancipation and racial equality.[109]

"Immediatism" found increasing favor in antislavery circles. William Jay, whose father, John Jay, had worked for New York emancipation, capitulated after reading *Immediate, Not Gradual Emancipation,* a powerful tract by the English Quaker Elizabeth Heyrick. Two years later, Frances Wright, a British philanthropist, established a plantation in western Tennessee to demonstrate the capacity of freed slaves. Ardent in her embrace of emancipation, she took to the lecture circuit in America. Lafayette, her great friend and defender, commented wryly to a friend, "Judge the success that she will have in the United States . . . she preaches to them about the reform of society, in which she sees only three fundamental evils: religion, property, and marriage." More significantly "immediatism" provided the basis for collaboration between Northern black and white antislavery leaders. Both groups believed that respectability was a better discriminator among people than race and worked to propagate their vision of interracial collaboration to smooth the rough edges in the society as a whole. Paradoxically these initiatives and growing evidence of black middle-class progress triggered even more violence against blacks, exposing the chasm of sentiment and principle separating Northerners as the 1820s drew to a close.[110]

The voices discussing slavery may have produced cacophony, but at no time did silence enwrap the issue. All knew that something could be accomplished—had been accomplished—by those opposed to human chattel. Unlike the rallies behind the sabbath and sobriety, antislavery advocates were taking aim at the practices of a whole section of the country. Slavery had been obliquely recognized in the Constitution; the rhetoric of union honored regional differences; and violent opposition lurked just below the surface of speech. The antislavery fires—stoked by evangelical fervor—could not be quenched by pragmatic concerns, but the road ahead was littered with obstacles. For the first three decades of the nineteenth century, those eager to cleanse the United States of all trace of slavery tried various stratagems to effect that end. Learning from these initial forays, they finally stopped cajoling Southern slaveholders and began haranguing their complacent Northern neighbors in a momentous shift that cut a tenuous connection between the two sections.

Increasingly those in the antislavery vanguard focused on race prejudice as the stumbling block on the road to abolition. Sarah Grimke, who left her home in a South Carolina plantation to become a antislavery activist, clearly saw the need to awaken Northerners to its baleful influence. Northerners like Josephus Wheaton developed complex arguments about environmental influences to illustrate the equality of mankind. "Thought, memory, reason and imaginations, volition, affections and passions," Wheaton argued, "are common to men in all nations, whether civilized or savage—whether christian or barbarian." He concluded his tract more polemically with the observation that the phrase, *"republican slave holder* was a solecism." Tapping into the sentiments aroused by corporal punishment, antislavery writers increasingly drew attention to the cruelty and violence slaves suffered at the hands of their masters.

Jesse Torrey, a Philadelphia physician, alluded to the atrocities perpetrated by cruel masters and mistresses, highlighting his own agitation at seeing a coffle of slaves while attending Congress by describing the surrounding federal buildings standing gutted after the British rampage through Washington the previous year.[111]

The issue of race prejudice perplexed Northerners not otherwise given to reform. Benjamin Silliman, scion of a distinguished New England family, indulged in a great deal of snobbish commentary in his European travels, saying of the working class, "most of the men are said to be drunkards, and the women dissolute," but the muted racial consciousness in Europe impressed him. "An ill dressed or starving negro is never seen in England," he noted, and added his surprise at seeing bi-racial couples. "As there are no slaves in England," Silliman reasoned, "perhaps the English have not learned to regard negroes as a degraded class of men, as we do in the United States, where we have never seen them in any other condition." Reflecting on the superior free blacks of the Ohio valley, he exclaimed in an untypical outburst of passion, "it is a foul dishonor, it is a crying iniquity, it is a most glaring inconsistency, that we tolerate slavery."[112]

Nothing white antislavery speakers said matched the ferocity of David Walker's excoriation of white racial hostility. Totally rejecting all colonization schemes, Walker dug deep into the psychology of racism, urging blacks in *An Appeal to the Coloured Citizens of the World* to combat those forces that contributed to self-hatred and disunity within their ranks. Walker's detailing of European brutality towards Africans lent great rhetorical power to his affirmation of revolt, a position that Denmark Vesey might have suggested to him, since Walker had been living in Charleston during the six years that Vesey plotted his uprising. Black seamen circulated copies of Walker's *Appeal* in the Southern ports. Although the document resonated among African Americans, Walker's unwillingness to condemn violence split the free black community as the Abolitionists' immediatism did the white one. In reaction to the uproar, Southern legislators voted to put a price on Walker's head and made it a crime to teach slaves to read and write. Their ire would certainly not have been mitigated had they known that Walker named his newborn son after William Lloyd Garrison.[113]

The antislavery agitation of the first generation presents an anomaly. Tackling a far more insidious evil than other reformers addressed, the foes of slavery watched while most of their evangelical allies wilted in the face of Southern intransigence. They garnered nowhere near the support of temperance and sabbath-keeping, even though deploying similar agents, publications, and lecturers. Born of the same revivals that inspired missionary expeditions, Sunday schools, and tract societies, antislavery agitators had wrapped themselves around a complex social wrong. To combat this matrix of malevolence required exposing people's shameful prejudices, deriding the conceits of Southern apologetics, challenging the primacy of the Constitution, confronting the complacency of typical Northerners, and championing a people whom many held in contempt. As the pressure from Southern opposition grew, men and women outspoken in their indictment of slavery became fewer and fewer, but their witness to the crime of human chattel proved to be enough, because neither it nor they went away.

AT AN INTIMATE level, slavery disturbed Americans because it involved the denial of their most precious inheritance—liberty. It also touched upon the issue of self-possession. Nineteenth-century Americans chose such terms as self-respect, self-cultured, and self-educated to express their strong confidence in the power of the individual. For the devout, the individual had to be free to wrestle with the torments of the damned; for those more inclined to a secular view of life, individual power came from disciplined work and cautious risk-taking. That quintessential leader of the first generation, Henry Clay, coined the potent phrase "self-made," but his generation's stories were not about rises from rags to riches, but about the self made into a vehicle for constructive action. Methodists encouraged other Methodists to write life stories that charted the path to self-control, self-improvement, and personal fulfillment. Much later, the Baltimore mechanics that formed the Washington temperance societies had tens of thousands of people recounting "experience narratives," which one witness called the "sublime testimony that they could govern themselves."[114]

Women occupied a social penumbra from which they could admire the self-possession of men. Denied an independent status, they readily exploited their access to the press. Their organizational and fund-raising virtuosity gave them a new scope for influence. Sarah Hale told her readers that self-control "in every station and to every individual is indispensable," urging women to retain an equanimity of mind that is "the essential of contentment and happiness." Testimonials to the virtues of the awakened self were legion. William Ellery Channing lectured Boston's young working men on self-culture, calling broad participation in politics "the people's university." Matthew Vassar highlighted "Industry, Perseverance and Self-reliance" when summing up the success that made it possible for him to endow Vassar College. Charles Ingersoll concluded his speech before the American Philosophical Society by extolling "SELF-GOVERNMENT" as "the best patronage of religion, science, literature, and the arts" that man can achieve.[115]

Not all reformers were evangelicals, nor all evangelicals reformers, but the two groups shared a common belief that society was flawed and human beings were the means of repairing it. They were also willing to expend enormous energy convincing others that this was the case. The evangelical movement had its most persistent cultural impact in encouraging uneducated men and women, particularly the young, to act on behalf of their convictions.[116] By relying upon the self-knowledge of a conversion experience, revivalist preachers unknowingly filled ordinary men and women with a sense of their spiritual importance and their religious competence unfiltered by clergy or doctrine, generating self-respect for the part they played in the moral rearmament of the nation. The revivalists taught that the awakened Christian belonged to God, but not in the Calvinist sense "that we are not our own; we are God's." Nineteenth-century evangelical Protestants frequently transmuted dependence upon God into liberation from dependence upon others. Conversion stiffened the will to follow the dictates of conscience, as the conscience became a magnet for nineteenth-century reform impulses.

In all social transformations there is a selective mechanism at work. Some are ready for the change, prepared by their own discontent with existing arrangements, or fortuitously endowed with the qualities called forth by the reform. Others resist novelties, and often find themselves unexpectedly on the margin after a new page has been turned. This became apparent with the temperance movement's success in driving drinking from work sites and public occasions. The hard-drinking workers at the house-raisings and corn frolics that teetotalers excoriated once figured as hardy, brave, and impulsive men. The artisans who importuned young apprentices to drink were acting as carriers of a venerable shop tradition, performing the important cultural work of recruiting for their values. In the South, conviviality implied horse races, cock fights, barbecues, weddings, and balls—all occasions for heavy drinking and evangelical censure.[117] Drinking was an act that signaled and substantiated manliness; temperance vows required repudiation of that model. The new ethic with its psychological muscularity in restraining passions resonated mainly with those who were already moderate in their habits and looked to temperance to create a supporting milieu—a social ambience to mirror their decorum.

Underneath the bustling confusion of a thousand different routes to self-improvement, we can see a new set of male ideals in the making as well as the psychological and intellectual strategies for shifting loyalties from home and habit to self and progress. Before temperance became a norm, it separated the person from the group in a test of private will. Only when this experience had become common could behavior that had once been approved be turned into an object of opprobrium. The reformers' success in expunging the lingering components of a traditional agrarian society like the admired masculinity of the hard-drinking, physically powerful man stands as a modern benchmark. It also attested to the capacity of individual choice to push aside entrenched traditions if supplied with a cultural vehicle like moral regeneration. Temperance narratives supplied the details for a collective romance in which virtue found the strength to slay a corrupt masculinity, now portrayed as a deformation of the true man. Old timers' descriptions of the pervasive debauchery in their youth signaled their amazement at what temperance had wrought in their lifetime.

The new social imperative to pull away from the convivial norm and cultivate one's self-direction became inextricably bound up with economic developments that put a premium on self-discipline. That these new habits were conducive to an emergent modern order only enhanced the attractiveness of temperance. A fascinating, if painful, coda to temperance's victory played itself out when Irish and German Catholic emigrants arrived in the United States in the 1840s, bringing with them an Old World nonchalance about drinking. Sober Americans viewed with alarm the emigrant families picnicking in public parks with kegs of beer, convinced that deficient moral standards distinguished Catholics from Protestants, having forgotten the drinking of their own elders.

While witnesses from the South are rarer, those that exist attest to the same reform of the public sphere. A New England friend asked the South Carolina planter William Grayson to reflect on transformations in "manners and morals" during his life. Complying, Grayson reported that he was "compelled to confess that the change for the better was immense. Religion had revived. The churches were filled . . . the riotous sensuality of the old times had disappeared." His experience, Grayson maintained, "is that of every man whose memory runs back as far as sixty years, when every public day was a day of drinking[,] disorder and fighting throughout the country," adding reflectively that if immorality still existed "it was at least deferential enough to conceal itself from the public eye."[118]

These changes should have helped cement the states and probably would have had slavery not worked silently and steadily to differentiate the motives and mores of men and women in the North and South. The Northern capacity for cooperation across the barriers of religion, sex, and wealth—even sometimes race—underpinned the vibrant public realm that the first generation brought into being. Through voluntary associations Northerners defined themselves as a nation of entrepreneurs and reformers. Initially swept up in the prayer meetings, love feasts, and religious societies of the revivalists, Southerners who had earlier displayed an enthusiasm for participation, slowly retreated from the activists' round of parades and rallies, scared off by the antislavery potential in Northern reform efforts. Politics became the province of the planter elite; literacy received little encouragement; and the printed materials that itinerant salesmen brought south carried with them the strong smell of Northern cant. What earlier had been welcome now looked like unwarranted intrusions.

In 1794 George Washington, worried about the raucous public displays of partisan groups, lectured Congress about the dangers issuing from "certain self-created societies." He spoke then for a class, the revolutionary gentry that created the United States. His verbal volley fell to the ground because groups of younger men, less identified with the colonial elite, insisted on their right to form political clubs. Their challenges to elected officials caused the Federalists much anguish, not to mention incredulity when they realized that many people did not just want to vote; they yearned to experience full social participation—gathering in quasi-public meetings, debating matters of policy, mobilizing fellow citizens, and forming associations based on the affinities of conviction.

Less than thirty years later, Charles Ingersoll, scion of a distinguished colonial family, could not give "self-created societies" too much credit:

> I am within bounds in asserting, that several hundred thousand persons assemble in this country every year, in various spontaneous convocations, to discuss and determine measures according to parliamentary routine. From bible societies to the lowest handicraft there is no impediment, but every facility, by law, to their organization: And we find not only harmless but beneficial, those various self-created associations, which in other countries give so much trouble and alarm.

Setting aside their political influences, Ingersoll zeroed in on the likely effect on the individuals involved, asserting that the tendency was "to sharpen their wits, temper their passions, and cultivate their elocution," adding that "the mode of transacting business is nearly the same in them all, from the humblest debating club to Congress in the capitol."[119] The new civic spirit had found its champions, even in the upper class.

In another era, Samuel Mills, racing from his canvass of religion in the American West to the resettlement of America's free blacks in Liberia, might have appeared a windmill-tilting zealot. In the first three decades of the nineteenth century he seemed but an unusually energetic representative of his generation's activists. Evangelicalism normalized ardor like his, not just by reviving religion but in summoning converts to be public witnesses to virtue. Women flocked to the churches, where they found activities inspired by high-mindedness and an authority greater than their husband's.[120] Young people turned their clubs into surrogates for the families that many had left behind. Affinity became the great cement when ties of family and community frayed. Reformers were passionate; their imagery appealed to the sentiments. With words they created a solidarity among lovers of justice and dispensers of sympathy. Toiling in the field of virtue created bonds of affection and support.

Among foreign travelers were those shrewd enough to see that it took an austere morality to enjoy, as Americans did, an expansive liberty. This anomaly rested on the paradox that those who acted voluntarily claimed a scope of authority that Americans had denied their government. They were permitted to rage at sin, name the vicious, and declaim against old, relaxed ways of sport and merriment. By no means a majority of adult Americans, they garnered prestige that more than made up for their minority status. Their zeal alone silenced many of their less religious neighbors. The disestablishment of the Anglican and New England churches in America had produced an unintended but profoundly religious consequence. Without the moral and financial support of government, America's voluntary congregations took it upon themselves, as the Baptists, Quakers, and Methodist Societies always had, to discipline their members, making the simple manners and chaste behavior of the sects a standard of conduct for the society as a whole.

The unexpected eruption of confrontational politics, the sweeping success of religious revivals, and the extended reach of communications were highly interactive in the first decades of the nineteenth century and their effect cumulative, even though they emanated from different popular sources, sometimes working at cross purposes. They focused upon the same people—literate, undistinguished men and women open to redeeming a secular society after first dismantling the traditional hierarchical order. Never firmly transplanted to America, that order was politicized in the 1790s, its benign intentions impugned, its eternal verities mocked, its most trusted handmaidens—church and state—democratized. The model citizen of deferential politics—the man who respects what has already been established—was replaced by the assertive individual who bends every effort to make his own way, both socially and intellectually, and reads his own reform as a sign of the possibilities for society at large.

Despite their demanding gospel message, the competing evangelical congregations worked to strengthen the self-importance of their members. Through their wooing, the proselytizing organizations of the early republic fostered self-reliance. Simultaneously appealed to as voters, candidates for salvation, prospective club members, and journal subscribers, ordinary men acquired a sense of their worth. Their individuality was promoted by repeated calls to form personal judgments, choose goals, and make their own decisions. Even without the vote, many women found their organizational and fund-raising skills in great demand, experiencing, as ordinary men had, an expanding sense of personal value. Selective belonging with its sociability of shared beliefs and its adhesion of like-mindedness replaced the once uncontested membership in a family network or settled community. Encouraged to act in the public realm, those who joined the new political clubs, evangelical churches, and reform associations ended up restructuring American society.

Elite families did not cease to exercise extraordinary influence in public life. Rather it was the case that the respect given to lineage, education, and the civilized display of wealth—what we might call the social capital of gentlemen and women—depreciated while the common stock rose. Like Barton Stone's Christian movement, which set out to unite America's faithful in one church and ended up spawning yet another new denomination, upper-class efforts to uplift the common folk through sponsored societies only added to the proliferation of voluntary associations. Americans had created a highly developed political society, independent of the state and frequently in opposition to established authorities. Americans' reluctance to let their government take the lead in philanthropy and education left the poor dependent upon the charity of the better-off, casting the needy upon the mercy of the charitable. The protracted fight against attitudes of superiority had politicized snobbery, firming up a distaste for condescension among ordinary Americans.

The assault on slavery drove a wedge between Northern activists and Southern planters who correctly recognized that American public-spiritedness fostered values inimical to slavery. Censoriousness about drinking and Sunday games aggravated tensions between those targets of reform who remained unreformed and their would-be reformers. The proliferating popular initiatives did not produce a coherent body of democratic thought so much as a *modus operandi*. A Vermont editor described knowledge as "the standing army of Republics."[121] The metaphor is apt when opinions, learning, and information are mobilized to activate a citizenry. It helps explain the militancy of American reformers and the fact that, even with shared characteristics and the national reach of their organizations, they did not unify the nation. The like-minded organized, but their associations only advertised the fullness of the interests and causes seeking unity. Americans had created so many identities from religious denominations and social preferences that the national aspiration captured in the motto *e pluribus unum* moved out of range.

Only the method for expressing the diverse social impulses offered common ground for national identity, and then only in the parts of the North where they were appreciated. Commitment to the free circulation of information, spontaneous social action, and individual empowerment stood in for the ends they were designed to attain. Without the cutting edge of converging purposes, the means themselves were sharpened into tools for discriminating Americans from other people. More self-conscious than others about national cohesion, America's self-appointed architects exemplified the vitality of an ebullient democracy even when their tangible goals eluded them. They generated both solidarity and exclusion along an axis set by the first generation.

8

A NEW NATIONAL IDENTITY

URING THE LAST MONTH HE SPENT in the White House, Jefferson
received a letter from the Westward Mill Library Society of New
Brunswick County, Virginia, inviting his patronage. "Our society," the secretary reported "is composed of farmers, mechanics, Justices of the Peace,
ministers of the Gospel—Military Officers, Lawyers, School masters—merchants—postmasters, one member of the Assembly & one member of Congress. Our present president," the secretary continued, is "a substantial &
respectable farmer." He then gave the names and a description of the Six
Directors for the year 1809: two planters, "a naturalized citisen," an elder in
the Methodist Church, a deacon in the Baptist Church, and "a Major in
the Militia of Virginia." In closing his letter to the president, the secretary
posed an arresting question: "Will such an heterogeneous body ever firmly
. . . coalesce?"[1]

Here in microcosm was the macrocosmic problem of the first generation of Americans: the intensely felt need to create a union from the disparate groups that formed their country. Americans knew that the ideal of a commonwealth was one king, one church, and one tongue. The Revolution had offered patriots the rhetorical opportunity to treat America's social diversity as a summons to a new kind of nationhood, but a successful War for Independence did not supply the shared sentiments, symbols, and social explanations necessary for an integrative national identity. That would take fresh experiences and opportunistic experiments—not the "mystic chords of memory" that fifty-four years later Abraham Lincoln summoned to the cause of the union, but rather the rooting out of sensibilities acquired in a colonial past. What seems remarkable in retrospect is that so many members of the first generation deliberately reflected upon their situation. From News Brunswick, Virginia to Walpole, New Hampshire to Lexington, Kentucky, men and women thought and wrote about the nation as their concern, its future their responsibility.

The familiarity with which these strangers addressed their president shows how easily Americans had sloughed off the skin of monarchical forms, abandoning entirely the formality that marked petitions to royal officials. The secretary's sweeping reference to a membership of farmers, mechanics, merchants, magistrates, lawyers, militia officers, and schoolmasters announced as well an egalitarian sociability among independent householders. The mingling of designations—planter, assemblyman, naturalized citizen, church elder—suggests also that there were many ways to earn acceptance in this rural community.

Noteworthy too is the purpose of the society. Each member paid two shillings a year to create a fund for book purchases. Such a pooling of purchasing power meant that the major in the militia, the Baptist deacon, and the member of Congress felt that they shared enough intellectual interests to benefit from a group collection. The mingling of Baptists and Methodists in the Westward Mill Library Society surprises, as well as the presumed compatibility of all of their reading tastes. Both sides of an earlier cultural divide had moved to the common ground of mutual accommodation. Venerable demarcations between the saved and the damned, the learned and the vulgar, the authorized and the unauthorized, had dissolved into a freemasonry of the tolerant and the self-improving. The intellectual ambitions that were once the hallmark of the free thinker were now embraced by Baptists and Methodists, who had earlier viewed with deep suspicion those who displayed book learning. They had all become people of the book, but the book could be David Ramsay's *History of the American Revolution* or Jedediah Morse's *American Geography* as easily as the Bible.

This document does not explain, but it does epitomize the qualities in American life that gave shape to a new national identity. There is first of all this exercise of initiative. A group of undistinguished men form an association for personal reasons and unselfconsciously take on the responsibility for thinking about social cohesion. Matters of state—that once jealously guarded preserve of gentlemen, magistrates, and ministers—had been breached, the line between the public and private blurred. The neighbors in rural Virginia were also using the market in a way that strengthened the commercial linkages between country and city, no mean consideration in a society still predominantly agricultural. By pooling their money to buy books, these library societies—and there were hundreds of them all over the country—were stimulating the economy as they registered their consuming tastes. Their members' penchant for reading helped fuel the expansion of a print culture that itself became an integral part of a national identity rooted in the free and aggressive exchange of opinion. As they consumed the pamphlets and books that came from Philadelphia and New York, they were also taking in the views of those who took it upon themselves to articulate values for the country as a whole.

The letter to Jefferson was as likely to have come from Chillacothe, Ohio as Utica, New York. That it came from a southside county in Virginia reminds us of the similarities that might have drawn the country together in 1809 had differences over slavery not intensified with each passing decade. The question, "will such a heterogeneous body ever firmly coalesce?" makes salient what Americans confronted when they thought about their union. Could a people split into a dozen religions, shedding the social forms that separated mechanics from militia majors, divided between native-born and naturalized citizens, ever unify? And if so, on which and whose terms? Could Americans will themselves into a national culture as they had willed themselves into a War for Independence?

Questions about American nationalism have engaged the attention of pundits, politicians, and scholars for over two hundred years. It has simmered beneath the surface of this study. In my summing up of the public experiences of the first generation of Americans, three interconnected conclusions emerge. The statutes providing for the gradual abolition of slavery in the Northern states sealed the identity of the South with its peculiar labor system while the burden of rationalizing human chattel had been lifted from the Northern conscience. At the same time, successive Jeffersonian victories at the polls opened the public realm in the North to a host of new men and women who took this opportunity to mobilize public opinion in the interest of their causes, many of them anathema to those who had first championed popular participation. The campaigns to abolish slavery became the "earnest money" for a sustained reform commitment that animated the Northern public and repelled Southern planters. Adopting a defensive strategy, Southern leaders retreated from the national enterprise that their own leaders had earlier launched, and the innovating newcomers and zealous reformers of the North, sensing the power of their views and virtues, appropriated for themselves the task of speaking for the nation as a whole. Active participants in the newly democratized world of print, they composed a powerful account of enterprise, success, and progress that dominated Americans' self-evaluations for the rest of the century, leaving Southerners bereft of a national narrative that included them.

Looking at these outcomes sequentially throws into high relief their unexpectedness. Neither Northern abolition, the displacement of the colonial elite, the cotton boom (which tightened Southern planters' attachment to slave labor), nor the cultural inventiveness of a group of middle-class aspirants in the North could have been predicted at the conclusion of the Revolution. Their manifestation demonstrates both the irony of unintended consequences and the invisibility of a society's latent possibilities that lie ready to be acted upon when all the predisposing forces are in place.

The alienation of Southern leaders from the "national panegyric" elaborated in the North is ironic, for Virginia's James Madison and George Washington had been at the forefront in creating the "more perfect union" of the United States Constitution. Southerners also pushed for continental expansion, the major national policy goal of ordinary farmers, when many Northerners, fearing the dispersal of the American people, opposed the Louisiana Purchase. The developing rift between the regions took decades to become salient. Southern nationalists like Charleston's Stephen Elliott continued to speak of the luster that "the rising generation . . . will give to national character," and a succession of Southern leaders occupied the White House even as younger planters gravitated towards John C. Calhoun, who pointedly declared, "I never use the word Nation. We are not a nation, but a Union, a confederacy of equal and sovereign states."[2]

The absence of slavery in the North mattered just as much as its presence in the South for erecting walls of distrust between the two sections. The cacophony of opinion that enlivened Northern public life grated on

Southern sensibilities, particularly after it became associated with a zealotry to reform social institutions. Northerners' straightforwardness seemed graceless, their assertiveness in argument strident. Contentious politics and moral reform campaigns found few parallels below the Mason-Dixon line. Defending against anti-slavery polemics, Southern spokesmen articulated a set of atavistic values. They employed a nostalgic imagery and an elegiac tone in their reflections while Northern entrepreneurs and activists imagined a future transformed by their efforts, aided by science and a general receptivity to change. The potency of this one distinction grew exponentially in the first decades of the nineteenth century. A passive difference in labor systems became dynamic when charged with the ideological fervor of conflicting attitudes to good and evil, truth and honor, past and future.

Northerners even changed the significance of work, the touchstone of slavery. Once tied to the drudgery necessary for survival, work became a part of a new discourse about inventiveness, opportunity, self-improvement, and progress. Writers rehabilitated wage labor, long considered debased by its implicit dependence upon a wage-giving master, by connecting it to economic development.[3] The foes of slavery dramatized the connection between pride and productivity when they lamented the personhood denied African Americans who could not work to improve themselves. Northern spokesmen attached disciplined labor to the expanded realm of freedom. Productivity demonstrated the benefits of democracy. What in an aristocratic society announced the badge of servility, democratic enthusiasts elevated to personal achievement.[4]

By contrast, Southerners viewed their way of life as genteel, warm, and stable just because they did not engage in the hard bargaining and unremitting application to business that characterized for them the Yankees' way of life. Although they participated in a capitalistic economy, Southern planters eschewed the culture of capitalism taking shape before their critical eyes up North. Slave labor created great fortunes for a small number of planters, who used their wealth to embellish themselves, their families, houses, and hospitality. Publicly active, they competed in politics as gentlemen, serving their neighbors as justices of the peace and vestrymen and their region as forceful advocates in Congress. The acceptance of the intrusion of commerce into all facets of Northern public life shocked Southerners, who used an almost biblical language to describe the rounds of work on their plantations. Recoiling from the crassness of Northern enterprise, Southern planters cultivated the courtly manners of an earlier era and celebrated the past for the intrinsic beauty of tradition.

The bulk of the Southern white population was composed of small farmers whose eagerness for political reform was as strong as that of Northerners, but owning slaves formed a part of the small farmers' plans for success, linking their concerns with large slaveholders, a bond that proved far stronger than shared interests with Northern farmers.[5] However intense their drive for personal success, their white supremacist views compromised their political allegiances. The hierarchical values that proved most effective in justifying slavery embarrassed their efforts to achieve the equality of esteem that their counterparts in the North acquired. While both regions saw a great deal of social mobility on the frontier, the succession of cotton booms in the Southwest quickly divided a few winners from the bulk of the aspirants, whereas in the North more diverse opportunities in farming, manufacturing, and trade sustained ambitious men of little property. The slave economy maintained an entrenched elite at the top of Southern society; their political influence outlasted the democratic momentum of the 1820s and 1830s.

Living arrangements differed in the two sections. Northern states, east and west, were honeycombed with towns, villages, and hamlets, unlike the South, where gatherings of more than a hundred people were likely to take place on the great plantations. The dispersal of population aided prominent Southern planters. The market had brought power to a large group of new men in the North who challenged elite preferences in matters of taste, values, and decorum, whereas the self-made planter fitted himself into the fully-scripted role of planter and master.[6] With fewer openings in leadership, patronage exerted a stronger influence in the centers of Southern life; newcomers more successfully competed for profitable positions in Northern states. Taking up frontier farms, plying novel trades, developing inventions, harnessing the water power of rivers and streams for hundreds of new enterprises, ordinary New Englanders laid the foundation for a progressive economy, even though Southern profits from cotton produced the largest share of the country's income.

Models of masculinity diverged as well. One astute observer claimed that no pastime could flourish among Georgians that did not partake of danger or risk, a comment that helps explain the frequency of duels.[7] For Southerners, autonomy meant the absence of restraints on one's behavior, a state fully realized by having slaves of one's own. Only if one were clearly identified as being religious could a Southern gentleman reject a challenge without loss of honor. The popularity of dueling in the North demonstrates the pervasiveness of these masculine ideals of honor, courage—even audacity—that Southern planters embraced and embodied. Yet commercial and religious developments in the North were bringing forth a new manly type—one that celebrated sobriety, restraint, dignity, and self-control—the mirror opposite of the impulsive masculine ideal embraced in the South by planters and hill folk alike.[8]

Even in their response to the evangelical Protestant revivals, the two regions differed. Although both Northerners and Southerners were deeply affected by this popular religious movement, they did not take equally to the possibilities for social action from a revived Christian piety. Salvation as surcease figured more prominently in the spiritual economy of South-erners, while Northerners who threw off "the old man" of spiritual indiffer-ence girded their loins for battle against society's many sins.[9] Northern evangelicals, freed of the moral complications of slavery, actively partici-pated in the voluntary societies and print campaigns of an ecumenical reform program. Women throughout the country furnished the glue for the religious sociability that took the place of the ceremonial life of the more formal churches. North and South, they provided the essential time and organizational skills for the new denominations that were utterly de-pendent upon converts for material support, but in the North piety pro-duced expansive, even grandiose, reform campaigns that gave women an opportunity to cash in their social assets.

The Second Great Awakening reshaped American Christianity, pulling ordinary people, black and white, into the dense circuitry of meetings and services of the proselytizing denominations while reinvigorating men's and women's religious affections through vernacular preaching about the an-guish of individual sinners. African Americans, both enslaved and free, joined the Methodist and Baptist congregations in great numbers. In their initial thrust into the South, evangelical preachers counted slavery among the sins for which God was punishing wayward Americans, but within two decades the planter patriciate had succeeded in containing evangelical fer-vor. Southern conservatives forced denominational leaders to back away from their antislavery commitments, blocking the momentum for spiritual awakening and inducing an otherworldliness that bordered on fatalism.[10]

Differences that were once merely the subjects of interesting observa-tions became crucial factors in the evolution of two distinct social orders. A plainer style of living mediated the relations among diverse groups in the middle states and New England. A mutual respect based upon literacy, morality, and appreciation of work took the edge off disparities in wealth, rendering the Southern gentlemen's obsession with honor more and more archaic to those Northerners cultivating a shared rectitude. Northerners relied more on books than talk for their information, committing considerable resources to schooling and publishing. If Northerners were becoming the people of the printed word, Southerners remained the masters of public oratory and convivial conversation, the gifted performers in the theatrics of governing.[11]

In their trade, the two regions were completely compatible, even if their differing roles in the Atlantic economy promoted different trade policies. Southern leaders enunciated a *laissez faire* philosophy, but some Northerners began to articulate a national economic program, reflecting the fact that the South specialized in a single, export staple in great demand and the North produced a diversity of processed and manufactured goods along with foodstuffs. Still, the Northern textile factories needed Southern cotton just as much as planters needed markets for their crop, despite the presence of a major consumer of raw cotton in Great Britain. Northern and Southern congressmen fought over legislation for tariffs and internal improvements, but compromises were always possible on these policy issues. What could not be brokered was mutual respect and diverging concepts of justice.

One of Jefferson's granddaughters, Ellen Wayles Randolph Coolidge, struggled to comprehend why the Northern and Southern states were moving so quickly apart. Having married a Bostonian, Coolidge had ample opportunity to observe the bustle of a thriving commercial center and finally conceded that New Englanders deserved the prosperity that had been denied the Old Dominion. But still it was a puzzle. How had it come about, she pondered, that Virginia—the largest and wealthiest of the states, supplying four of the first five presidents to the republic—fell behind its Northern neighbors in enterprise, improvements, and innovations. The difference, she perceptively saw, was not a matter of profits, but of spirit, of raw energy and confidence about the future.[12]

While Southern planters and professional men supported education through private academies—many for women—ordinary Northern farmers taxed themselves for country schools, subscribed to newspapers, and gave their time and money to a vast array of self-improving projects. With such an arsenal for organizing and exchanging opinions, Northern reform campaigns sparked Southern concerns about the possibility of unwarranted interference, particularly in matters affecting slavery. Northern energy, viewed from the Southern vantage point, did not signal public vitality, but the threat of a detested imposition of will. From religious sensibilities to attitudes towards work and trade, Northerners and Southerners differed. More grave, developments in the early decades of the nineteenth century funneled a variety of distinct qualities into a set of ominous dichotomies.

By the 1820s regional differences had hardened into bitter animosity. When Missouri, the first territory to be carved from the Louisiana Purchase—Jefferson's Empire for Freedom—asked Congress for admission to the union as a slave state, Northern critics of slavery not surprisingly believed that they could and should do something. New York's James Tallmadge offered an amendment calling for the gradual emancipation of Missouri's slaves patterned on similar Northern state statutes. Passed by the House, only the South's power in the Senate checked the success of this bold act to cleanse the West of the hated institution. Tallmadge, a Democrat, called slavery a "monstrous scourge," ratcheting up the rhetoric in a debate that drew on the Founding Fathers, the Declaration of Independence, and Old Testament prophets before both houses passed the famous compromise bills that allowed Missouri to enter the United States as a slave state but barred slavery from the rest of the area. The debate in Congress over the admission of Missouri offered a dress rehearsal for the positions that would drive the Southern states to secession, congressmen voting along strict geographic lines for the first time.

The defeated Tallmadge amendment clarified the official Southern position. Slavery was not a dying institution, but a growing one, its proponents very much intent on future expansion, a fact confirmed by the 1820 census that showed that the number of slaves had nearly doubled since 1800. Two years later, the aborted insurrection of South Carolina blacks led by Denmark Vesey stirred new anxieties about racial warfare. Vesey compared himself to George Washington as the liberator of his people, a claim that aggravated sectional tensions. Northern foes of slavery wailed that they had been deceived by Southern condemnations of the evil institution while Southerners stormed at zealous fanatics that threatened their lives and homes and impugned their honor.

Officially Southern sentiment was again canvassed in the mid-1820s. The Ohio legislature passed a resolution in 1824 proposing a federal law to free all slaves born after its enactment at age twenty-one—if they would agree to foreign colonization. The next year, nine Northern state legislatures called for emancipation at federal expense, advertising the Northern position that slavery was a national issue.[13] Both proposals were summarily rejected by the Southern states after a flurry of formal exchanges among the state legislatures.

Even though Congressional leaders had worked out a compromise to admit Missouri as a slave state, slavery was an issue that would not disappear. The South Carolina legislature passed laws forbidding negro seamen from leaving their ships when they docked in Charleston, which precipitated a diplomatic wrangle when Great Britain vigorously protested the restrictions on the freedom of movement for its black citizens.[14] The racist component in the Southern stance became salient when Southern senators objected to President John Quincy Adams's sending delegates to the Panama Congress called by Simon Bolivar in 1826 lest Americans be forced to mingle with Negro representatives from Haiti, one of the newly-formed independent countries of Latin America. With the passing of the Revolutionary generation of Southerners who had condemned slavery, the shared understanding of why human chattel contradicted American values died too. Sentiments expressed in Fourth of July orations also signaled a Southern disengagement from the country as a whole.[15]

In 1823 Gerrit Smith, a wealthy New York foe of slavery, summarized a widely shared view when he referred to their being an almost "national difference of character between the people of the Northern and the people of the Southern States."[16] What he didn't say was that Northerners imaginatively thought of their "nation" as the United States, leaving the South with its peculiar institution and a particular regional culture. An aging Thomas Jefferson perceived the situation and began urging Virginia leaders to support local colleges and academies. Harvard, Princeton, Columbia, and Penn were no longer proper for Southern or western students, he thought. Estimating that there must be "five hundred of our own sons, imbibing opinions and principles in discord with their own country," Jefferson declared that "the times admonish us to call them home." "If knowledge is power, we should look to its advancement at home," he wrote in a letter to James Madison, rather than trust "to those who are against us in position and principle, to fashion to their own form the minds and affections of our youth."[17] Prophetically, John Adams insisted that "we must settle the question of slavery's extension now, otherwise it will stamp our National Character and lay a Foundation for Calamities, if not disunion."[18]

With the retreat of the Federalists from public prominence, responsibility for defining American character had passed down the social ladder in the Northern states. Where the educated elite had wished to establish national identity upon the basis of America's distinctive contributions to established realms of achievement, America's undistinguished citizens—the ones who voted the Federalists out of office—sought affirmation of their values in the celebration of what was distinctively American in their eyes. To them America's departure from English norms had enormous appeal, for it played to their strengths. Taking up land in the national domain could be viewed as spreading democratic institutions across the continent. American abundance could be attached to the virtue of hard work, infusing the independence and hardiness of America's farming families with civic value and generating patriotic images that could resonate widely without evoking the curse of slavery.

For ordinary men and women, the country's greatness emerged in a set of lusty qualities—open opportunity, an unfettered spirit of inquiry, personal independence—the threads reform-minded Europeans had already plucked from the tapestry of American life to weave into an Enlightenment picture of a new dispensation for mankind.[19] Those who struck out on their own, whether in business endeavors, reform efforts, or reviving Christian zeal, expressed a different sense of nationhood. For them the United States represented a new kind of social existence in which the public prospered because of personal initiatives. Having rid themselves of a powerful upper class inherited from the colonial era, the public found that self-appointed leaders and organizers throughout the North were only waiting for an opening. Optimism about concerted efforts to eliminate slavery, correct the treatment of the insane and criminal, reorganize charity, and raise the tone of public morals became a part of their idea of American character.

The vision of America as having a special destiny for the human race provided the raw material for creating a national myth, an elaboration of enlightenment themes, or what might be called the poor person's enlightenment, directed as it was to liberating ordinary men from the flagrant injuries of inherited privilege. The merger of this goal with the loftier Enlightenment preoccupations with free inquiry, scientific knowledge, and political liberty enabled ordinary and elite reformers to move in tandem. Sharing an ideological commitment to change, the real distances in wealth, education, and opportunity could be rendered a matter of rhetorical, and perhaps even emotional, indifference. Thinking no further than the evils they could perceive, these male reformers had little sense of how women would soon use their philosophical arguments to expand the scope of universal rights.

The aspirations of Northern activists cohered around an imagined enterprise of improving the material environment, reforming a flawed people, and putting the United States in the vanguard of history. Here the imperatives of nationalist rhetoric abraded sectional differences. Southerners embraced wholeheartedly the ideal of individual liberty, but recoiled when it was attached to a vision of social activism. Southerners neither shared Northern enthusiasm nor their optimism. Nor was everyone in the North swept up in these programs, but the elan they sparked stifled rival discourses.

⁂

NOTHING WAS MORE striking in these years than the accommodation of American Christianity to the imperatives of commercial enterprise. Many of those brought into the new evangelical denominations actively pursued profitable careers, and they tended to prosper after their conversions.[20] For Christian leaders to embrace the very worldly aspirations evident in the larger culture involved a number of adjustments. Most of the evangelical preachers had been born into ordinary rural homes, making them particularly likely to judge the prosperity of plain folk as part of God's bounty, especially since their own opponents in the established clergy sprang from the old colonial elite. "The people of the United States have more reason to be thankful to God than any other people; for he had not dealt so with any nation," the Methodist leader James Finley explained, adding that "the pious mind can not fail to see a Divine hand overruling and conducting the whole."[21]

America's free churches, like its free men, appeared to thrive on expanded choices, personal autonomy, and ardent striving. Having reached new converts by preaching a very personal message about sin and redemption, evangelical ministers found it easy to look to individual success as a sign of divine approval. Since the Second Great Awakening had fragmented American communities, it was harder to see signs of God's work in the society as a whole.[22] Better it was to find cohesion in higher levels of abstraction, as when Gardiner Spring, an eminent Presbyterian clergyman, hailed America as a "land of freedom, peace, wealth, and privilege."[23]

There were larger intellectual forces at work in the early nineteenth century. The conviction that God's will could be read in the structure of the natural world relocated the sources of religious authority. Both secular and religious theories naturalized human action. By the end of the eighteenth century, most Protestant leaders in America had accepted the fundamental premise of a free market—the morality of individuals making private decisions about their resources, including the free use of their time and talents. As the particularity of Calvinist ideas of salvation yielded to the universality of natural law assertions in public discourse, churches gradually acknowledged that individuals were to be regulated by an internalized understanding of moral principles. Disciplinary bodies within the churches focused more on sexual transgressions and alcohol consumption than on dubious moral standards in economic practices.

A more dramatic intellectual shift took place when thinkers started looking for God's will within the human lifetime rather than fixing exclusively on future rewards and punishments. The secular concept of progress fused with old millennial hopes.[24] As Charles Finney stressed, Christians were enjoined by God to revive religion themselves. No longer considered something of divine origin, revivals became the responsibility of the clergy and their lay followers. It was up to popular initiative to keep the spiritual fires burning. By ignoring conservative wisdom, taking risks and prospering, many Americans had demonstrated the power of independent thought and action. In response, ministers preached to their rich followers about the capacity of their wealth to serve God in the world, leaving to them the decisions about how to make their money.[25]

The permeation of business enterprise with lay religious activism can be found in the lives of a remarkable trio of brothers: Benjamin, Lewis, and Arthur Tappan. Pillars of reform establishments in New York and Ohio, they supported evangelical churches and progressive colleges and gave unstintingly to the cause of anti-slavery, even as they pursued successful careers in law, politics, and publishing. Lewis Tappan's "Mercantile Agency" supplied the first formal credit ratings in the United States and Arthur's *New York Journal of Commerce* helped stabilize New York's volatile business community. Devout Christians, they displayed in their inventiveness, zeal, and patriotism the potent synergy of virtue and know-how that strengthened the American public realm in both its commercial and religious sectors. Risk-taking infused all their endeavors, including Arthur and Lewis's initial support of William Lloyd Garrison's fiery abolitionist journal, *The Liberator*. Except in the eyes of purists like the Hicksite Quakers, the worldly connections of evangelical benevolence appeared among its greatest strengths.[26]

The underside of Northern enterprise was raw avarice. Among all the charges Southerners leveled against their Northern compatriots, none resonated quite as fully as the accusation that Northerners had become money mad. Disturbed themselves by the swiftness of the commercial penetration of their society, many agreed with Sarah Hale's excoriation of "this bank-note world" with "its mundane values, materialism, competitiveness, and acquisitiveness."[27] Washington Irving coined the phrase "the almighty dollar," and even that booster DeWitt Clinton noted defensively that Americans would have to lean "for literary support upon Europe" since everyone seemed to be busy accumulating wealth.[28]

Foreigners—many of whom published travel journals—frequently converged on the same repellent qualities in their American travels: the promiscuous mixing of social classes, the confident forwardness of American women, and the crassness of incessant money-making, all testifying to the distance white Americans had moved from their Old World origins.[29] Benjamin Latrobe chronicled the lamentable influence of personal avidity on society in New Orleans after Louisiana became part of the Union. "The opportunity of growing rich by more active, extensive, and intelligent modes of agriculture and commerce has diminished the hospitality, destroyed the leisure, and added more selfishness to the character of the creoles," he concluded sternly, adding that Americans' "business is to make money," "they are in an eternal bustle." Latrobe continued with a graphic summary: "their limbs, their heads, and their hearts move to that sole object. Cotton and tobacco, buying and selling, and all the rest of the occupation of a money-making community, fill their time and give the habit of their minds."[30] Less censoriously, James Hall concluded that Arithmetic "comes by instinct among this guessing, reckoning, expecting, and calculating people."[31]

William Austin caricatured American money madness in *Peter Rugg: The Missing Man*, the story with which this book opened. His hero, that manic colonial who survived mysteriously into the nineteenth century, returned to Boston in time for the auction of his property, which had reverted to the state. The auctioneer, eager to scotch the weird story of a still-living heir, ridiculed anyone who believed the rumor, warning how such credulity could check the spirit of enterprise and "bid farewell to all mercantile excitement." Your surplus money, he told the gathering, "instead of refreshing your sleep with the golden dreams of new sources of speculation" would cause a nightmare, for "a man's money, if not employed, serves only to disturb his rest."[32] The spirit of speculation had haunted Americans ever since the Revolution. E. S. Thomas called the rush for soldiers' notes in 1788 "a scene of *legal* robbery, such as the history of civilized nations can scarcely produce a parallel to." According to him, mechanics and journeyman carpenters made fortunes, the more enterprising participants in the race for unearned profits setting up relay horses from Albany to Boston for news of the New York ratification of the Constitution because they considered the mail stages too slow.[33]

There is evidence that even the clergy got caught up in the passion for making money. William Neill, a Presbyterian minister educated on scholarships at Princeton, acknowledged in taking a new pulpit that he had "yielded to considerations, which, I fear, have, in many instances too much influence on such occasions, such as a more ample support." Regretful that he had never been able to pay into the fund from which he benefited, he invested an unexpected gift of 750 dollars in a real estate scheme instead.[34] Money intruded into prayer requests. Charles Kirk, a Quaker elder, made a covenant with God when he got married "that if I ever acquired a home worth ten thousand dollars I would be fully satisfied, and not covet any more."[35]

The rate of growth in the early republic was largely set by ordinary men and women whose propensity to move, to innovate, to accept paper money, and to switch from homemade goods once commercial ones were available paced the expansion of farming, commerce, credit, and information.[36] The steady elaboration of the national market also depended upon many of them leaving the place of their birth, trying their hand at new careers, and using their imagination to make commercial connections. Frederic W. Lincoln, Jr., a self-made instrument-maker in Boston, celebrated the process through which capitalists were produced: "the laborer of to-day is the capitalist of tomorrow, and the son of the man who yesterday rolled in affluence, is today working for his daily bread. Every man stands upon his own merits,— upon his own habits of industry and frugality;— industry in acquiring, frugality in expanding the fruits of his labors. The fact that he may become a capitalist, is a spur to exertion to the very news-boy in our streets."[37]

In the first generation a society oriented around the free market economy took shape in America, its materialism plain to all. At odds with traditional mores and aesthetics, the market had a scope of social influence in the United States that was unparalleled. Its opportunities unleashed ambition; its cues drew the rapt attention of those attracted to the novel connections that knit the country into an ever-expanding network of trade ties. By no means absent in the colonial period, the market intensified and rewarded an array of personal characteristics, most of them masculine: alert self-interest, promise-keeping, pleasure deferral, attention to distant communication, commercial imagination, the capacity to initiate trade relations. There was also in the independence fostered by personal engagement with market schemes an accompanying acceptance of the setbacks of commercial failures. These were the qualities necessary for a free-market system to flourish; they were also the ones that the system fostered. A later generation would call it the school of hard knocks.

The economy in the United States has never stopped changing; major transformations have marked each generation. Through the early nineteenth century Americans still had a producer's economy in which most people lived off their own exertions and those of family members, but by the 1820s, small-scale merchandisers and manufacturers had added to the rich mix of farmers in most Northern counties. The entrepreneurial values of the first generation ensured that there would be little serious opposition to industrialization. Americans were convinced, as public commentary would suggest, that inequalities were promoted not by capitalist development, but rather by the political privileges of an aristocracy.[38] More important than capital to economic development was the readiness of American women and men to move to improve their lot; they responded as well to the innovations that promoted material advances. Few cultural restraints to individuals' investing their wealth as they saw fit—regardless of its impact on the moral or physical environment—emerged to socialize this profound economic transformation, and the flood of immigrants, starting with the Irish in the 1840s, provided the factory fodder that enabled native-born Americans to ignore the cruelest forms of exploitation that industrialization brought.

Few understood the linked phenomena of economic change. Those who did try to discern its secret springs were almost always prompted by their commitment to a national policy; usually one that was being contested. Hezekiah Niles and Daniel Raymond analyzed the economy in terms that made high tariffs reasonable, yet Stephen Elliot offered a very sophisticated grasp of the blessings of free trade.[39] In their works we can see that the prod of sectional interests produced both capably imagined recommendations for facilitative legislation as well as effective arguments for restraining government interference. More important than an appreciation of economic theory to most Americans was an understanding of the character of the economic agent, the man—usually white and Northern—who committed his energy and talents to some productive enterprise.

Joseph Caldwell, recounting a harrowing tale from his youth, offered a revealing glimpse of the personal dimension of endeavor. One warm summer day he and a fellow Princeton divinity student decided to walk to a nearby pond to refresh themselves with a swim. When his friend realized that he could not touch the bottom of the pond, he panicked, calling frantically for help to Caldwell, who hesitated to go to the rescue lest he become trapped in the wild gyrations of a drowning man. Torn between his conscience and his desire to regain the shore himself, Caldwell did return to help his friend, who immediately seized him as he had feared he would. Breaking free from the grasping hands, Caldwell swam with all his might to the shore, only to discover that his drowning companion, desperate to grab him again, had actually followed him to safety.[40]

At first blush this seems a strange story to include in the memoirs of a highly successful career. Caldwell had left his native New England to teach mathematics at the University of North Carolina, where he remained to become the university's first president and a leading spokesman for educational reform. Why would he wish to appear uncaring, maybe even cowardly? The answer must lie in the moral lesson to be extracted from the incident: strike out on your own, don't look back, set a strong example, and let others follow and learn.

Caldwell's story also conveyed metaphorically those elements of contemporary life usually excised from the personal narratives of his generation: the panic that could be triggered at being in over one's head and the desperate wish to find support from others. Fear of drowning in debt stalked almost all who set out to secure a frontier farm, set up a store, start a newspaper, or launch a professional career. The aspirations of Caldwell's peers rarely had the backing of savings, experience, or guidance. Failure was just as likely as success, and losses from death, economic downturns, endemic sickness, and industrial accidents abounded. Almost everyone had relatives or acquaintances whose dissolute habits or mental instability brought them low. In such a social environment, the sudden shift of tenor in a day's outing could take on the qualities of a parable, particularly when personal strength and intuitive good sense saved both men's lives.

Only in the United States did the decisions that individuals made about their lives play so large a part in shaping the character of public institutions. In the absence of an acknowledged upper class, an established church, or a highly regulatory government, personal undertakings did the work of authority. Once the discipline of the market had been internalized, its workings appeared natural, a perception that discouraged purposeful intervention.[41] To be sure government—particularly state governments—dispensed licenses, bounties, and articles of incorporation while enforcing contracts and selling land with an abandonment that would have shocked Hamilton.[42] These benefits moderated the risk of enterprise, but they did not alter the fact that private persons devised and executed economic schemes, mobilizing on their own the necessary money and labor. The rewards and punishments from economic effort gave people the cues to direct their work lives, making economic information a necessity. In a society with few safety nets, most people were both vulnerable and free, exposed to market exploitation while being animated by thoughts of gain.

What needs to be considered is how potentially disruptive this general, pell-mell pursuit of personal ambitions might have been had those who lost in the scramble turned against the system that failed them. That such patterned hostility did not develop suggests the presence of a powerful and pervasive explanation of the individual engagement with opportunity. Successful Northerners wrote about their country as the locus for beneficial exchanges of talents and riches. This functional, future-oriented social blueprint replaced the older picture of communities unified around a stable set of precepts. The age-old concept of a structure with divisions of ranks was supplanted by that of a machine with interacting parts and interchangeable participants.

Repeated in orations and pamphlets, by mechanics in their association meetings and merchants in their economic treatises, the truths about a perpetually improving social engine were hammered home: farmers who produced agricultural surpluses could buy better tools; manufacturers who reinvested the profits from selling those goods expanded output; merchants who sold the farmers' crops and the manufacturers' goods enhanced the size and efficiency of the market.[43] Important here was the recognition of the interdependence of the productive sectors of the economy. Society divided among rich, poor, and middling gave way to one in which representatives of occupations—farmers, lawyers, schoolteachers, manufacturers, and merchants—interacted to create general prosperity. That writers and speakers elaborated these imaginative reworkings in the years when many farm workers and artisans were moving into factory employment helped mask their simultaneous disinvestment of hope.

Easy access to print guaranteed that the distilled experience of the first generation would fix ideas about ambition, success, effort, discipline, and responsibility. Enterprising Americans became objects of their own curiosity; they constituted themselves as objects of discourse because they were doing new things. Selectively construing liberty as the chance to strike out on one's own, writers and speakers narrowed their interest to a few archetypes, cultivating an avid interest in the successful. Within the image of an improving America, intelligence, honesty, determination, and enterprise came to represent the personal forces animating the social whole. Accordingly, energetic, productive, inventive individuals became powerful nodes of attention and admiration. Their lives served as models of innovation in a society losing all desire to replicate past ways of doing things. Narrative accounts of their successes set forth in eulogies, testimonials, autobiographies, and memoirs formed a kind of cultural capital accumulating in the country alongside the savings from industry. In the division of ideological labor, life stories supplied the empirical evidence to validate sanguine assertions about American destiny. The easy access to opportunity, the just reward of virtue, the irrepressible pluck in the face of adversity—so simply depicted in the first person accounts of America's charter entrepreneurs—sank deep into the public consciousness.

This vision of a society of mutually accommodating functions no doubt appealed to a vast number of ordinary men and women because it leveled their social superiors and refurbished an egalitarian rhetoric. As Samuel Latham Mitchill explained, since all citizens are equal, the only inequality that exists arises necessarily from office, talents, or wealth and as the road "is open for every one to aspire to these, it is by the exercise of one or more of his rights that a man acquires these means of influence."[44] John Watson retailed the glories of American prosperity in his *Annals of Philadelphia* by crediting free institutions with the country's conspicuous material advances:

> Here human life is not wantonly wasted in ambitious broils for sovereignty; we therefore behold our population quadrupled in a term of forty years . . . and our hardy pioneers subduing the soil, or advancing their settlements, from the Atlantic to the Pacific wave. Canals, rivaling in magnitude the boasted aqueducts of imperial Rome are in successful operation. By these and turnpikes, inaccessible districts are brought nigh; mountains charged with metallic treasures are entered, and their deposits of iron, coal, and lead, &c lavished over the land. Cities, towns, and villages, arise in the West, as if by enchantment—Many of their present inhabitants redeemed their soils from a waste howling wilderness . . . Our private law, commercial code, and bold diplomacy, have grown into a matured and learned system. Our inventions and improvements in the arts . . . make us, even now, "a wonder until many;" . . . Here we have no lordly potentates in church, "lording it over the consciences of the people;" no stand-

ing armies to endanger their liberties, no despots to riot on the oppression of the subject. Nay, so exalted are our privileges, as a *self-governing* people, that the fact of our example and happiness is bidding fair to regenerate other nations, or to moderate the rigor of despotic governments throughout the world.[45]

In Watson's encomium one can see how the visible changes in the landscape predisposed the imagination to thoughts of progress, no small feat within a culture that had long looked back to the glories of Greece or the perfection of the Garden of Eden as acmes of human attainment.[46] Not the lofty achievements of genius, but the humble efforts of manual laborers, farmers, and engineers produced the towns in the West, arising as if "by enchantment." Watson's reference to Americans redeeming their soils from a "howling wilderness" signaled the common justification for dispossessing the indigenous people who once roamed the "waste" that had been replaced by fields of golden grain. Others echoed Watson in making the tangible signs of prosperity an American signature: Dr. Richard Carter claimed that "the rapid progress and dissemination of learning and politeness" distinguished "the inhabitants of these United States" from all others. Even when Americans were talking about something else, as in William Prescott's *History of the Reign of Ferdinand and Isabel,* they could not resist making invidious comparisons. Writing a narrative that turned Spain into America's antithesis, Prescott attributed his country's enthusiasm and "bold commercial spirit" to the absence of Spanish despotism and religious bigotry.[47]

Many men and women of the first generation succeeded in creating their own myths as they analyzed what was going on in their experimental democracy. Extraordinarily self-conscious about the way that their lives fit into the whole, they demonstrated the power of the press to purvey attitudes as well. The individual stories of striving and succeeding poured into one large narrative. It was not the first generation's only story, but it was the one gaining the most momentum by the end of their lives. The repetition of themes in these texts exerted an adhesive, if not a coercive, force that pulled the collective imagination towards a few emblematic dramas. Expanded political participation, an unexpected free black population, novel economic and social opportunities, a revitalization of Christian piety, and a veritable folk movement onto the national domain in the West filled people's lives with novelties demanding reflection and explanation. The proliferation of all kinds of printed material assured that published views would get a wide circulation. While few people were able to construct original interpretations, they at least conferred approval or disagreement with the ones advanced.

∼⊛∼

COMPELLING AS Northern interpretations of American successes were, they could not dissolve the very real tensions that divided the country. A sequence of wrangles about intensely-felt oppositions—slave and free, native-born and immigrant, black and white, male and female, saved and depraved, respectable and degraded, national and local, successful and failed, educated and superstitious, refined and vulgar—worked against the actual unity that the rhetorical consensus inferred. Differentiated as they were by region and religion, most white Americans after independence charted their course in life with two vivid and negative referents: those of savagery and aristocracy. Savagery lurked within and without, evoked readily by the presence of enslaved Africans in the South and the indigenous tribes west of the Appalachians. Aristocracy represented the British ruling class scorned by the colonists in their act of rebellion.

Savages in the American imagination were indolent and sexually permissive, living a hand-to-mouth existence that left few traces of *homo faber,* man the maker, for posterity. Aristocrats too were seen as lazy, self-indulgent, and sensual beings. They also appropriated the work of others and, more provocative of indignation, they defended their wealth as necessary to the very civilization that differentiated white Americans from blacks and American Indians. Both were atavistic—the one inexplicably neglected by the author of human progress and the other immured in feudal traditions of hereditary privilege, hierarchical authority, and overweening presumptions of superiority. Measuring their values against both savagery and aristocracy, the self-conscious shapers of American values spoke for a meritocracy in which merit was defined by ordinary talent, effort, and risk-taking. In embracing the virtues of personal autonomy and individual responsibility, they rallied around qualities with wide appeal across the spectrum of classes, faiths, families, and even races. The range of human potentialities engaged by this model of excellence was narrow, but widely shared.

Most Native Americans lived outside the reach of America's new liberal prescriptions, coming into contact with the United States, if at all, when purchases or treaties expelled them from their ancestral lands. The continent's indigenous population makes only a brief appearance in the United States Constitution, confined to a section granting Congress the power to regulate commerce "with the Indian Tribes."[48] Most policymakers shared in the settled, silent, self-fulfilling conviction that Native Americans would soon become extinct. Thomas Lorrain McKenney, Superintendent of Indian Trade and Commissioner for Indian Affairs, began collecting American Indian artifacts during his tenure from 1816 to 1830, and artists and ethnographers like George Catlin and Henry Schoolcraft promoted the study of Native Americans in a way that emphasized their remoteness. Under a War Department Commission of 1821, Charles Bird King painted the Kansas, Omaha, Pawnee, and Missouri American Indian delegates to Washington, producing in the next decade 139 studies of American Indians, including those of the southeastern tribes before Indian Removal, all on display in the department's Indian Gallery.[49]

Real American Indians were memorialized after they had died or had been defeated. The greatest American Indian leader of the era, the Shawnee chief Tecumseh, was old enough by the end of the American Revolution to perceive the threat that America's migrating families posed to the many tribes that he collected into a grand alliance. Brilliant as an intertribal organizer, Tecumseh was perhaps the one Native American capable of negotiating some kind of an accommodation with the United States, but Army victories in the War of 1812 felled him and defeated his allies, opening up the upper Northwest to American settlement. Through the ritual cleansing of print, Tecumseh quickly became an American hero, praised in death as highly as he had been feared in life.

Tecumseh's fate found an echo in the other leaders who organized opposition to the onslaught of American families. Osceola rose to power among the Seminoles for opposing the Treaty of Payne's Landing that negotiated their removal across the Mississippi. Treacherously arrested under a flag of truce, he died at Fort Moultrie. Elias Boudinot, an important Native American editor, was murdered for his part in agreeing to the removal of the Cherokees. Black Hawk disavowed the cession of Sauk ancestral lands and fought unsuccessfully to repossess them, composing an autobiography that has become an American classic. Like Black Hawk and Boudinot, William Apes wrote to keep alive the memory of American Indian greatness in what could be considered an ironic variation of approval for the "dead Indian."[50]

Although the plight of Native American tribes elicited some sympathy, the fate of African Americans aroused much fiercer passions. Northerners took great pride in their emancipation laws. Not only had these gradual abolition statutes demonstrated to the world that an ancient institution could be deconstructed through legislative power, it also gave the force of action to the ringing phrases of the Declaration of Independence. Henry Adams noted that slavery "drove the whole Puritan community back on its Puritanism."[51] What he didn't say was that it also reanimated the rule of the Elect, a fact that Thomas Jefferson intuited when he became incensed by Northern efforts to check the entrance of Missouri as a slave state. Owning or not owning slaves became a political statement for those residing in Washington, D.C., even as the expanding free black population plumbed the depth of white hostility to blacks, North and South.[52]

Some Northerners took up the cause of black education and enjoined their neighbors to follow up emancipation with full citizenship for African Americans. Struggling to accommodate the racism around them with the Christian principles that white Americans professed to hold, black leaders looked for hints of change as signs of America's regeneration. Most white Christians straddled the issue—disavowing slavery, but allowing race prejudice to compromise their commitment to a higher law of political and social behavior.[53] Those who hoped that white Northerners might build a bi-racial society underestimated their fellow citizens' capacity to live with the tension of affirming natural rights while tolerating the denial of justice to blacks. A strong minority of white men and women felt keenly the injustices even as many resigned themselves or encouraged the degradation of African Americans in their midst. People sought answers to why blacks were not fully integrated into white society in new theories about race.[54] It was easier to talk about slavery than black civil rights.

Northern abolition had delivered an unexpected reproof to Southern planters. A sense of mutual betrayal soon complicated relations among state leaders. Antislavery Northerners thought that white Southerners shared their belief that slavery was evil and were asking only for time to end it, not taking into account the fact that a new generation of Southern planters was rushing to expand rather than contract slave labor. For their part, fully convinced of the hypocrisy of Northern antislavery sentiments in the presence of pervasive racial hostility, Southern leaders assailed Northern interference as a breach of the original political understanding, embracing states' rights as the only doctrine that could preserve a union of such dissimilar regions. Neither group could see what hindsight reveals: that each was reacting to changes in the other's section of the country and to differing attitudes towards change. Southerners had fewer incentives to embrace social and economic innovations, and ordinary Northerners had found in the lexicon of progress, novelty, and advancement the language of liberation.

Virtue too played a different role in the emotional economy of the North. Having dismantled hierarchical authority among white males, Northerners relied upon internalized character traits, implanted in boys and girls alike, to supply the deficiency in external monitoring. Parents, employers, and religious leaders subscribed to the pedagogy that "as the twig is bent, the tree will grow" and instilled the principles of honesty, effort, self-reliance, and accountability in the young. Northerners had accepted a less ordered society as the price for being able to move freely, to express their own opinions, to seek economic gain, and to worship God as they wished. Government agencies still existed to police public spaces and facilitate legitimate endeavors, but the watchful censors of staid communities no longer enforced personal morals.[55] Adults had many options. Those who wanted to live within tight communitarian structures could find them, but others could as easily escape into cities or the heterogeneous settlements of the west.

America's founding fathers, the men who engineered a constitutional convention and drafted a new form of government for the loosely-joined states in 1787, succeeded through the force of personal authority. They did not act in response to popular sentiments in favor of a stronger union, but out of their informed conviction that, with peace and independence secured, the people in the states would immure themselves in local concerns and leave the eleven-year-old union perilously exposed to foreign intrigue. Because political union preceded the formation of a national identity, the first generation was forced to imagine the sentiments that might bind the nation together. If the Federalists had succeeded in institutionalizing their political upper class, American nationalism would have followed a trajectory more recognizably akin to European models, more conspicuously imitative of Great Britain. Or one could speculate further that if Southern leaders had used the new avenues of communication—circuit speaking, published speeches, newspapers—to contend with those Northerners who began speaking for the nation, they might have compelled respect for local mores and adherence to tradition.

Instead a virtual nation materialized out of the repeated messages about effort and accomplishment, virtue and autonomy, national prosperity and universal progress. Like a magnet, this imaginative construction of what it meant to be an American drew to it the filings of conforming views, anecdotes, and homilies. Those who shaped opinion as candidates, office-holders, organization leaders, editors, ministers, writers, and speakers obscured the heterogeneous nature of American life when they spoke of uniform impulses and universal goals. Ironically the self-conscious pursuit of national unity exacerbated the tensions created by its absence. The country's partisan institutions, rival newspapers, and conflicting evangelical societies enticed most adult white men into the public realm while simultaneously politicizing the entire culture.

The sequence of social developments in America also proved crucial in the transmission of precedents from one generation to the next. Modernization—as measured by literacy, social mobility, enhanced wealth, and participatory politics—ran well ahead of industrialization in the United States, a fact of considerable importance considering the hierarchical order that would later be imposed in factories.[56] The capacity of industrial capitalism to concentrate economic power and forge a new elite could not have been predicted in the decades after the Revolution. Commercial advance served as all-purpose evidence of American sagacity, acting as a moral and material handmaiden to the first generation's construction of a democratic and liberal society.

While commercial prowess was a source of pride to Americans, the market throve on three discordant forces: competition, the indulgence of material wants, and the cultivation of self-interest—all of them at variance with political ideals of personal autonomy and religious commitments to neighborly love. Many lamented the creative destruction that Joseph Schumpeter called an inevitable accompaniment of the free enterprise economy, but the new goods, careers, and frontiers promoted by commerce had unleashed a thousand fantasies that distracted men and women from their losses.

Predisposed towards reform and resistant to radicalism, Americans in this first cohort promoted attitudes that still retain their vitality. Even their blind spots have survived. Successful in new ways, they often interpreted their accomplishments as the unique product of a free society and in doing so created a divide between the perpetually successful nation of the imagination and the sections and people who did not share their triumphs, values, or optimism. National identity might well have been built upon a pluralist appreciation of a nation that protected diversity. One journalist wrote in 1816, no nation on the face "of the habitable globe" contains within its "expansive bosom a greater variety of individuals under the same species," going on to instance "the polished European, the tawny Asiatic and the sun-burnt Africans." More frequent were claims about the universal qualities that the nation embodied, leaving those who didn't conform culturally disenfranchised.[57]

Appealing as the American ethos is in its formal inclusivity, its self-congratulatory themes have discouraged a skeptical self-interrogation that could have challenged its unspoken assumptions. Rather than probe the nature of their economic and political systems, American writers acted as though they had discovered the secret spring of human effort—the desire to be free of external restraint in order to act on one's own. In truth, the release of human energy has been remarkable, a renewable resource of effort and inventiveness, but it has also demanded conformity to a strict set of rules of social engagement, inculcated by families and reinforced through didactic repetition. The broad support of the market system and the personal liberties that uphold it inhibited class formation, yet exposed the vulnerable to a form of ideological ostracism.

In 1824, the Greek struggle to gain independence from Turkey gave American leaders a chance to reflect on the role in the world of their path-breaking democracy. Throughout the Western world, people pressured their governments to help the Greeks, whose cause had been ennobled by association with the Golden Age of antiquity. In America, men and women—soon dubbed hellenophiles—raised funds, held public rallies, and memorialized Congress to do something for the brave defenders of Greek liberties. Obligingly, the House of Representatives engaged in an extended debate on whether or not to pass a resolution enabling President Monroe to send a mission to the Greek rebels expressing America's sympathy. The proposition created the occasion for Representatives to excoriate monarchs and despots who held their people in thrall, to express support for lawful resistance, and to attribute their own country's "rapid and irresistible" prosperity to its self-governing liberties.[58]

Despite the forensic flourishes of Daniel Webster and Henry Clay among others, those who did not want the United States to act like "the renowned Knight of La Mancha" prevailed. The resolution was defeated. What America had to offer, Congressman Silas Wood of New York explained, was "the moral influence of its example." The United States presented to the world "a model by which the rights of men may be secured, and the benefit of good government may be obtained, with the least sacrifice to individual independence," he said.[59] Having kept up their flagging spirits in the long haul of nation-building with boasts about democracy's power, this truth turned the country into a metaphorical beacon. A year shy of the nation's fiftieth anniversary, a consensus had emerged. America was special not for what it preached but for what it was. Americans need only continue on course to be a force in the world.

As this congressional debate reveals, inheriting a revolutionary tradition had thrust upon an entire generation of Americans the responsibility for explicit articulation of what the United States stood for. Impossible to ignore, the bequest of the founders catapulted radical philosophical propositions into the center of American public debate, giving every group excluded by prejudice and custom from citizenship potent arguments for their inclusion. Reason and justice were expected to explain social arrangements, an expectation baffled by formal institutions of slavery and common-law traditions that bolstered the authority of white householders over family and employees. Natural law affirmations of liberty and equality gave the union the moral glue it badly needed while promoting a rift between those states that found a way to abolish slavery and those that did not. These contradictions and the conflicts they engendered paradoxically enhanced openness in government, popular political participation, a vibrant print culture, and inclusiveness in public life. Americans seemed to shed old conventions like a snake its skin, coming through with colors brighter than ever.

A flood of European visitors had come to the United States as they would to a zoo, to observe the only democratic society in captivity. Their commentary heightened many Americans' self-consciousness about their democratic experiment and induced a rush to interpretation. Not totally adventitious, the country's stellar growth in people, inventions, buildings, acreage, and goods produced and sold suggested that liberty and prosperity went together very much like the horse and carriage. Eager to draw attention away from their country's deficiencies in the arts and sciences, writers and speakers used this connection to explain American particularities as portents for humanity's future, invoking the statistics of conspicuous development like a mantra to ward off doubt.

The first generation guaranteed that America's revolutionary tradition would be celebrated as a successful one. Both in Indian country and throughout the South, the Revolutionary War had taken on the brutal ferocity of both an invasion and a civil war, yet the prize of Independence had been won and the price could be forgotten.[60] If, as it is said, victory has many fathers, it could be added that it tempts those triumphant fathers to silence discordant voices. Having pushed to include most white men and a few black ones in the citizenry, political radicals rested on their oars early in the century, leaving a different set of reformers to infuse their Christian morals into Americans' public and personal lives.

From the springs of ardor and enthusiasm issued a powerful myth about America that metamorphosed ordinary labor into extraordinary acts of nation building. It also attached personal virtue to a narrative about human progress and claimed for liberty the protean capacity to sustain economic development and maintain democratic vigor. In the simplicity of this national narrative there was little room for alternative constructions of reality, no place for failures, scant concern for diverging truths, and insufficient attention paid to prophetic voices. Only one division could not be printed and papered over—that between the Northern and Southern states that was leading inexorably to dividing the house that had gone into escrow at Philadelphia.

The American Revolution had not produced its own reactionaries. The Southern gentry had applauded the break with Great Britain with even more fervor than Northern leaders. What they disdained to share was the interpretation of America's revolutionary heritage as a call to innovation, enterprise, and reform. The success of Northerners in fashioning this understanding of their joint inheritance led to a new North that spoke for the nation and an old South that clung to values that pushed them apart. What was happening in the United States in its first fifty years—the elaboration of democratic institutions, the hardening of racist lines, the openness of opportunity, thinning of intellectual traditions, and reconfiguring of Northern and Southern states into the North and the South—could not be comprehended within a unifying story, yet this did not prevent those in the first generation most conscious of the nation from claiming their story for the whole. Rather than abandon the cherished object of an American truth, they accepted the half loaf of a half truth wrapped in a covering myth about the land of the free.

NOTES

INDEX

NOTES

1 Introduction

1. William Austin, *Peter Rugg: The Missing Man* (Boston, 1908) [originally published 1824], p. 10.

2. Ibid., pp. 49–50, 27–30, 93–94.

3. Gouverneur Morris to John Jay, January 10, 1784, in *The Correspondence and Public Papers of John Jay*, ed. Henry P. Johnston (New York, 1891), vol. 3, pp. 104–105.

4. Duc de La Rochefoucauld-Liancourt, *Voyages dans les Etats-Unis d'Amerique, fait en 1795, 1796, et 1797* (Paris, 1799), vol. 1, p. xi.

5. John W. Ward, ed., *Society, Manners, and Politics in the United States* (Garden City, N.J., 1961 [originally published 1839]), p. 299.

6. Frederick Marryat, *A Diary in America, with Remarks on Its Institutions*, ed. Sydney Jackman (New York, 1962), p. 366.

7. Hal S. Barron, *Those Who Stayed Behind: Rural Society in Nineteenth-Century New England* (New York, 1981).

8. Ichabod Washburn, *Autobiography and Memorials* (Boston, 1878), p. 24.

9. Ibid., p. x.

10. Ibid., p. 43.

11. Ibid., p. 30.

12. [Leonard Woods], *The Memoir of the Life of Mrs. Harriet Newell* (Lexington, 1815).

13. Jonathan Allen, *A Sermon at Haverhill, February 5, 1812* (Haverhill, Mass., 1812).

14. A million and a half in today's dollars; the multiple is fifty.

15. Allen, *A Sermon at Haverhill*, pp. 19–20.

16. [Woods], *Memoir of Harriet Newell*, pp. 191–220, 240–243.

17. Gardiner Spring, *Memoir of Samuel John Mills*, 2nd ed. (Boston, 1829), pp. 23–27.

18. Leonard Woods, *History of the Andover Theological Seminary* (Boston, 1885).

19. Spring, *Memoir of Mills*, pp. 36–41.

20. Ibid., pp. 71–72, 86.

21. Ibid., pp. 116, 237.

22. [Delano A. Goodard], *Biographical Sketch of A. Bronson Alcott* (n.p., n.d.), pp. 4–7.

23. Stephen Aron, *How the West Was Lost: The Transformation of Kentucky from Daniel Boone to Henry Clay* (Baltimore, 1996), pp. 57–64.

24. Daniel Drake, *Pioneer Life in Kentucky* (Cincinnati, 1870), pp. 8–13, 166.

25. Ira Berlin, "The Revolution in Afro-American Life," in Alfred F. Young, ed., *The American Revolution: Explorations in American Radicalism* (De Kalb, Ill., 1976).

26. David Walker, *Walker's Appeal in Four Articles* (Boston, 1830), p. 5. See also Peter P. Hinks, *To Awaken My Afflicted Brethren: David Walker and the Problem of Antebellum Slave Resistance* (University Park, Pa., 1997).

27. Henry Highland Garnet, *Walker's Appeal* (New York, 1848); Sterling Stuckey, *Slave Culture: Nationalist Theory and the Foundations of Black America* (New York, 1987), pp. 115–123, 137; and Harvey Reed, *Platform for Change: The Foundations of the Northern Free Black Community, 1775–1865* (East Lansing, Mich., 1994), p. 27.

28. Erik Erikson, as quoted in Robert Dallek, *The American Style of Foreign Policy* (New York, 1989), p. 249.

29. According to the *Oxford English Dictionary* this definition appeared in an 1802 biography; the definition, "the ground on which a race is run, a race-course" dates from 1580.

30. Elizabeth W. Levick, *Recollections of Early Days* (Philadelphia, 1881), p. 51; Olive Cleaveland Clarke, *Things that I Remember at Ninety-Five* (n.p., 1881), p. 9; and Elihu H.[otchkiss] Shepard, *The Autobiography of Elihu Shepard* (St. Louis, 1869), p. 16.

31. Louis Kaplan, ed., *A Bibliography of American Autobiographies* (Madison, 1961).

32. There is a vast literature on autobiographies. For an overview see Robert Folkenflik, ed., *The Culture of Autobiography: Constructions of Self-Representation* (Stanford, 1993).

33. John Murrin, "A Roof Without Walls," in Richard Beeman et al., eds., *Beyond Confederation: Origins of the Constitution and American National Identity* (Chapel Hill, 1987).

2 Responding to a Revolutionary Tradition

1. The phrase is Alexander Hamilton's. *Federalist No. 85,* in *The Federalist,* ed. Edward Mead Earle (New York, 1937), p. 569.

2. John Ball, *Autobiography,* compiled by Kate Ball Powers, Flora Ball Hopkins and Lucy Ball (Glendale, Calif., 1925), p. 10.

3. John R. Howe, Jr., "Republican Thought and Political Violence of the 1790s," *American Quarterly,* 19 (1967): 147–165.

4. Morton Borden, *Parties and Politics in the Early Republic, 1789–1815* (Arlington Heights, Ill., 1967), p. 51; Jefferson to William Branch Giles, December 31, 1795, as quoted in William A. Robinson, *Jeffersonian Democracy in New England* (New Haven, 1916), p. 53.

5. As quoted in David S. Fischer, "The Myth of the Essex Junto," *William and Mary Quarterly,* 21 (1966): 200.

6. Sylvia R. Frey, *Water from the Rock: Black Resistance in a Revolutionary Age* (Princeton, 1991), p. 241.

7. Marc W. Kruman, "The Second Party System and the Transformation of Revolutionary Republicanism," *Journal of the Early Republic,* 12 (1992): 517.

8. David Montgomery, *Citizen Worker* (New York, 1993), p. 14.

9. See Kruman, "The Second Party System," pp. 516–518.

10. Jon C. Teaford, *The Municipal Revolution in America* (Chicago, 1975); see also Andrew W. Robertson, *The Language of Democracy: Political Rhetoric in the United States and Britain, 1790–1900* (Ithaca, 1995), pp. 50–53.

11. Rachel N. Klein, *Unification of a Slave State* (Chapel Hill, 1990), p. 303.

12. Fifty percent of the population was female; 60 percent was under the age of twenty-one; and 20 percent lacked the property to meet the voting requirements in the North. Additionally, between 40 and 60 percent of the population in the Southern states was enslaved.

13. A long historiographical tradition that Jefferson in fact "outfederalized" the Federalists dates back to Henry Adams's *The History of the United States* (Boston, 1889–1891). For a more convincing interpretation, see Noble E. Cunningham, Jr., *The Process of Government under Jefferson* (Princeton, 1978).

14. Stephen Aron, *How the West Was Lost: The Transformation of Kentucky from Daniel Boone to Henry Clay* (Baltimore, 1996).

15. Carl Prince, "The Passing of the Aristocracy: Jefferson's Removal of the Federalists, 1801–1805," *Journal of American History,* 57 (1970): 563–575.

16. January 13, 1807, in Henry Adams, ed., *The Writings of Albert Gallatin* (Philadelphia, 1879), vol. 1, p. 328; William B. Skelton, "High Army Leadership in the Era of the War of 1812: The Making and Remaking of the Officer Corps," *William and Mary Quarterly*, 41 (1994): 257–260.

17. In 1805, he carried a majority in every state save Connecticut. Only Lincoln's election without a single Southern vote was more sectional than the 1800 election.

18. Fischer, "The Myth of the Essex Junto," pp. 230–235.

19. Marc L. Harris, "Revelation and the American Republic: Timothy Dwight's Civic Participation," *Journal of the History of Ideas*, 54 (1993): 449–468, p. 466; Conrad Wright, *The Liberal Christians: Essays on American Unitarian History* (Boston, 1970), pp. 15–17.

20. Samuel Eliot Morison, *Harrison Gray Otis, 1765–1848: The Urbane Federalist* (Boston, 1969), p. 268.

21. As quoted in Thomas Lawrence Davis, "Aristocrats and Jacobins in Country Towns: Party Formation in Berkshire County, Massachusetts" (Ph.D. diss., Boston University, 1976), p. 321.

22. S. G. Goodrich, *Recollections of a Lifetime, or Men and Things I have Seen: In a Series of Familiar Letters to a Friend* (New York, 1857), vol. 1, p. 85.

23. See Philip Lampi and Andrew Robertson, "The First Democratization Project" (available in manuscript at the American Antiquarian Society), for the most complete figures on candidates, parties, and turnout for the thirty years after 1789.

24. John W. Francis, *Old New York; or, Reminiscences of the Past Sixty Years* (New York, 1850), p. 335.

25. Duane's newspaper bore the name of the *Evening Post* for the first few months. See Andrew Shankman, "Malcontents and Tertium Quids: The Battle to Define Democracy in Jeffersonian Philadelphia," *Journal of the Early Republic*, 19 (1999): 43–72; Richard N. Rosenfeld, *American Aurora: A Democratic-Republican Returns: The Suppressed History of Our Nation's Beginnings and the Heroic Newspaper that Tried to Report It* (New York, 1997).

26. [Samuel Knapp], *Extracts from a Journal of Travels in North America* (Boston, 1818), p. 43.

27. H. M. Brackenridge, *Recollections of Persons and Places in the West*, 2nd ed., enl. (Philadelphia, 1868), pp. 285, 142.

28. George P. Fisher, *The Life of Benjamin Silliman*, 2 vols. (Boston, 1866), vol. I, p. 35. *Reminiscences of James A. Hamilton* (New York, 1869), p. 42.

29. Jeremiah Spofford, *Reminiscences of Seventy Years* (Haverhill, Mass., 1867), p. 15.

30. R. Kent Newmyer, *Supreme Court Justice Joseph Story: Statesman of the Old Republic* (Chapel Hill, 1985), pp. 45–47, and Alan Taylor, *William Cooper's Town: Power and Persuasion on the Frontier of the Early American Republic* (New York, 1995), p. 305.

31. DeWitt Clinton, *An Introductory Discourse, Delivered Before the Literary and Philosophical Society of New-York on the Fourth of May, 1814* (New York, 1815), pp. 14–15.

32. "Pennsylvania Through a German's Eyes: The Travels of Ludwig Gall, 1819–1820," ed. and trans. Frederic Trautmann, *Pennsylvania Magazine of History and Biography*, 105 (1981): 52.

33. Sidney Willard, *Memoirs of Youth and Manhood* (Cambridge, 1855), vol. 2, p. 22.

34. *The Papers of John C. Calhoun, Vol. I, 1801–1817*, ed. Robert L. Meriwether (Columbia, S.C., 1959), p. 287. I owe the recognition of proto-affirmative action to Daniel Howe.

35. Noble E. Cunningham, *The Presidency of James Monroe* (Lawrence, Kan., 1996), p. 111; Irving H. Bartlett, *Calhoun: A Biography* (New York, 1993), p. 93.

36. Jacqueline S. Painter, ed., *The Trial of Captain Alden Partridge, Corps of Engineers* (Northfield, Vt., 1987), pp. 6–7, 88. Partridge's letter appeared in the September 12, 1817 issue.

37. Painter, ed., *Trial of Partridge*, pp. 1–8, 100–103. See also Lester A. Webb, *Captain Alden Partridge and the United States Military Academy, 1806–1833* (Northport, Ala., 1965), pp. 122–123; and the *Daily National Intelligencer*, Nov. 29, 1817.

38. William Arba Ellis, ed., *Norwich University, 1819–1911* (Montpelier, Vt., 1911), vol. 1, pp. 38–46.

39. [Americanus], *The Military Academy at West Point Unmasked or Corruption and Military Despotism Exposed* (Washington, D.C., 1830).

40. R. Don Higginbotham, "The Martial Spirit in the Antebellum South: Some Further Speculations in a National Context," *Journal of Southern History*, 58 (1992): 20.

41. Powel Mills Dawley, *The Story of the General Theological Seminary: A Sesquicentennial History, 1817–1967* (New York, 1969), pp. 39–40.

42. [Samuel Turner and Samuel Farmar Jarvis], *An Account of the True Nature and Object of the Late Protestant Episcopal Clerical Association of the City of New York* (New York, 1820). See also Samuel Hulbeart Turner, *Autobiography* (New York, 1863), pp. 133–143; and Dawley, *Story of the General Theological Seminary*, p. 38.

43. *Plan of the Theological Seminary of the Protestant Episcopal Church*, 2nd ed. (Hartford, 1820).

44. Dawley, *Story of the General Theological Seminary*, pp. 74–76.

45. Emmet Field Horine, ed., *Pioneer Life in Kentucky, 1785–1800* (New York, 1948), pp. xviii–xx.

46. Henry D. Shapiro and Zane L. Miller, eds., *Physician to the West: Selected Writings of Daniel Drake on Science and Society* (Lexington, Ky., 1970), pp. 159–160, xxxvi–xxxvii.

47. Daniel Drake, *Practical Essays on Medical Education and the Medical Profession in the United States* (Cincinnati, 1832), p. xxiv.

48. Horine, ed., *Pioneer Life in Kentucky*, p. xvii.

49. *Proceedings and Correspondence of the Third District Medical Society of the State of Ohio*, 1832; *Dr. Drake's Resignation*, broadside (Cincinnati, 1832). See also John Flourney Henry, *Exposure of the Conduct of the Trustees and Professors of the Medical College of Ohio* (Cincinnati, 1833) and *Inquiry into the Causes that have Retarded the Prosperity of the Medical College of Cincinnati* (Cincinnati, 1835).

50. Drake, *Practical Essays*, pp. 97–98.

51. See Rosalind Remer, *Printers and Men of Capital: Philadelphia Book Publishers in the New Republic* (Philadelphia, 1996).

52. Charles Royster, *A Revolutionary People at War: The Continental Army and American Character, 1775–1783* (Chapel Hill, 1979), pp. 208–211.

53. Joanne B. Freedman, "Duelling as Politics: Reinterpreting the Burr-Hamilton Duel," *William and Mary Quarterly*, 43 (1996); for the one hundred figure, see *The Circular* [Wilmington], May 7, 1824, p. 2.

54. John Chester Miller, *Federalist Era, 1789–1801* (New York, 1960), pp. 102–105.

55. Norman Risjord, *Chesapeake Politics, 1781–1800* (New York, 1978), p. 562.

56. Augustus C. Buell, *History of Andrew Jackson, Pioneer, Patriot, Soldier, Politician, President* (New York, 1904), pp. 158–164.

57. Brenda E. Stevenson, *Life in Black and White: Family and Community in the Slave South* (New York, 1996), pp. 349–354; Hamilton Cochran, *Noted American Duels and Hostile Encounters* (Philadelphia, 1963).

58. *National Intelligencer*, March 14, 1808.

59. Eliza Susan Morton Quincy, *Memoir* (Boston, 1861), p. 127.

60. S. G. W. Benjamin, "Notable Editors," *Magazine of American History*, 17 (1887): 110–114.

61. Jack P. Greene, "The Intellectual Reconstruction of Virginia in the Age of Jefferson," in Peter S. Onuf, ed., *Jeffersonian Legacies* (Charlottesville, 1993), p. 227; "James Cheetham" in Allen Johnson et al., eds., *Dictionary of American Biography* (New York, 1943–1944).

62. Dickson D. Bruce, Jr., *Violence and Culture in the Antebellum South* (Austin, Tx., 1979); Arnold A. Rogow, *A Fatal Friendship: Alexander Hamilton and Aaron Burr* (New York, 1998).

63. Postmus, *Observation on the South Carolina Memorial Upon the Subject of Duelling* (n.p., 1805).

64. Alfred M. Lorrain, *The Helm, The Sword, and the Cross: A Life Narrative* (Cincinnati, 1862), pp. 223–224.

65. June 2, 1807, *The Balance and Columbia Repository* [Hudson, N.Y.], p. 169; *The Christian Observor*, 3 (1804): 514; *The Boston Spectator*, Oct. 22, 1814, p. 172; Samuel Gilman, *Funeral Address for Edward Peter Simons* (Charleston, 1823); *The Christian Advocate*, 3 (1825): 109; and Frederick Beasley, *A Sermon upon*

Duelling delivered to the senior class in the University of Pennsylvania (Philadelphia, 1822).

66. *Portico*, 3 (1817): 132–146, 283–285, 380–383. The quote is from p. 285.

67. *American Law Journal*, Philadelphia, 1808–1809, pp. 7ff.

68. Bruce, *Violence and Culture in the Antebellum South*, p. 27.

69. Martin Van Buren, "The Autobiography of M__V__B__," ed. John C. Fitzpatrick, in *Annual Report to AHA for year 1918*, 2: 27.

70. Shapiro and Miller, eds., *Physician to the West*, pp. xxxvi–xxxvii.

71. Hamilton, *Reminiscences*, p. 41.

72. Risjord, *Chesapeake Politics*, p. 563.

73. November 24, 1808 in *The Portable Thomas Jefferson*, ed. Merrill D. Peterson (New York, 1975), p. 510.

74. Benjamin Lease and Hans-Joachim Lang, ed., *The Genius of John Neal: Selections from His Writings* (Frankfurt am Main, 1978), p. xiii.

75. [John Neal], "Remarks on American writers," *Blackwood's Edinburgh Magazine*, 17 (1825): 194.

76. Amos Kendall, *Autobiography of Amos Kendall*, ed. William Stickney (Boston, 1872), p. 24.

77. Ben C. Truman, *The Field of Honour* (New York, 1884), pp. 378–379.

78. Arthur Zilversmit, *The First Emancipation: The Abolition of Slavery in the North* (Chicago, 1967). See also Leon Litwack, *North of Slavery: The Negro in the Free States, 1790–1860* (Chicago, 1961), pp. 6–8.

79. Litwack, *North of Slavery*, p. 8.

80. Austin Steward, *Twenty-Two Years a Slave and Forty Years a Freeman* (Reading, Mass., 1969 [originally published in Rochester, 1857]), p. x.

81. [Olive Gilbert and Frances Titus], *Narrative of Sojourner Truth* (n.p., 1878), pp. 44–45, as cited in Nell Painter, *Sojourner Truth: A Life, A Symbol* (New York, 1996), pp. 32–35.

82. James Mars, *Life of James Mars* (Hartford, 1867), pp. 33–38.

83. Bureau of the Census, *Historical Statistics of the United States*, (Washington, D.C., 1961), p. 10.

84. Kruman, "The Second Party System," p. 518.

85. Litwack, *North of Slavery*, pp. 31–32.

86. Frey, *Water from the Rock*, p. 224.

87. Jean Baker, *Affairs of Party: The Political Culture of Northern Democrats in the Mid-Nineteenth Century* (Ithaca, 1983); and Henry Mayer, *All on Fire: William Lloyd Garrison and the Abolition of Slavery* (New York, 1998).

88. Anthony Iaccarino, "Virginia and the National Context over Slavery in the Early Republic, 1780–1833" (Ph.D. diss., UCLA, 1999).

89. Frey, *Water from the Rock,* pp. 232–233.

90. Sterling Stuckey, *Slave Culture: Nationalist Theory and the Foundations of Black America* (New York, 1987), pp. 98–100.

91. Lawrence M. Friedman, *Crime and Punishment in American History* (New York, 1993), pp. 88–90.

92. Richard S. Newman, "Prelude to the Gag Rule: Southern Reaction to Antislavery Petitions in the First Federal Congress," *Journal of the Early Republic,* 16 (1996): 576, 398. See for instance Morris Birkbeck, *Notes on a Journey in America,* 2nd ed. (London, 1818); and John Davis, *Travels of Four Years and a half in the United States of America During 1789, 1799, 1801 and 1802,* (New York, 1909).

93. Michael Sagrue, "Correct Political Principles, South Carolina College and the Problem of S.C." Paper given at the Society of the History of the Early American Republic, in Cincinnati, July 23, 1995.

94. *Annals of Congress,* 14th Congress, 2nd Session, 1816, p. 237, as quoted in O. Edward Skeen, "*Vox Populi, Vox Dei:* The Compensation Act of 1816 and the Rise of Popular Politics," *Journal of the Early Republic,* 6 (1986): 258–259.

95. As quoted in Skeen, "*Vox Populi, Vox Dei,*" pp. 262–263.

96. Richard L. McCormick, *The Party Period and Public Policy: American Politics from the Age of Jackson to the Progressive Era* (New York, 1986), pp. 155–156.

97. Skeen, "*Vox Populi, Vox Dei,*" pp. 266–272.

98. Charles M. Cook, *The American Codification Movement: A Study of Antebellum Legal Reform* (Westport, Conn., 1981); Morton J. Horwitz, *The Transformation of American Law, 1780–1860* (Cambridge, Mass., 1977); and Gary T. Schwartz, "Tort Law and the Economy in Nineteenth Century America: A Reinterpretation," *Yale Law Journal,* 90 (1981).

99. Daniel Scott Smith, "Population and Political Ethics: Thomas Jefferson's Demography of Generations," *William and Mary Quarterly,* 56 (1999): 609. See Karen Orren, *Belated Feudalism: Labor, the Law, and Liberal Development in the United States* (New York, 1991), for an exploration of this development.

100. *Considerations on the Abolition of the Common Law in the United States* (Boston, 1809); Carole Shammas, "Anglo-American Household Government in Comparative Perspective," *William and Mary Quarterly,* 52 (1995): 104–144.

101. [Alexander Graydon], *Memoirs of a Life* (Edinburgh, 1822 [1811]), pp. 422–423. See also Stephen Carl Arch, "Writing a Federalist Self: Alexander Graydon's *Memoirs of a Life,*" *William and Mary Quarterly,* 52 (1995): 417–418.

102. *Journal of Vermont Assembly . . . 1828,* pp. 67, 106, 117, 133, 150, as cited in Randolph Roth, "The Other Masonic Outrage: The Death and Transfiguration of Joseph Burnham," *Journal of the Early Republic,* 14 (1994): 43.

103. Birkbeck, *Notes on a Journey,* pp. 113–115.

104. Tim Matthewson, "Jefferson and the Nonrecognition of Haiti," *Proceedings of the American Philosophical Society,* 140 (1996): 26.

3 Enterprise

1. Benedict R. O'G. Anderson, *Imagined Communities: Reflections on the Origin and Spread of Nationalism* (New York, 1991).

2. Edwin J. Perkins, *American Public Finance and Financial Services, 1700–1815* (Columbus, 1994) makes clear what a departure Jeffersonian fiscal decisions represented.

3. Noble E. Cunningham, Jr., *The Process of Government under Jefferson* (Princeton, 1978), p. 107; L. Ray Gunn, *The Decline of Authority: Public Economic Policy and Political Development in New York, 1800–1860* (Ithaca, 1988); and John Majewski, *A House Dividing: Economic Development in Pennsylvania and Virginia before the Civil War* (New York, 1999).

4. Morris Birkbeck, *Notes on a Journey in America, from the Coast of Virginia to the Territory of Illinois*, 2nd ed. (London, 1818), p. 37.

5. John Ball, *Autobiography* (Grand Rapids, 1925), pp. 8, 12–14.

6. Ibid., pp. 52–53, 55.

7. Ibid., pp. 20, 29, 46, 52.

8. Ibid., pp. 60–62.

9. Ball in fact sent an article to Benjamin Silliman then bringing out the first issue of the *American Journal of Science*.

10. Ibid., pp. 133–143.

11. For statistical details of this pattern see David Galenson, "Economic Determinants of the Age at Leaving Home," *Social Science History*, 11 (1987). See also Carole Shammas, "Anglo-American Household Government in Comparative Perspective," *William and Mary Quarterly*, 52 (1995): 137–141.

12. Arabet, Gautier, and Manning handbill (Barcelona, May 18, 1796), File 1215, Miscellaneous Material Regarding Philadelphia Business Concerns, 1784–1824, Eleutherian Mills Historical Library; "An Account of the Grain . . . Imported into Great Britain in Each Year from January 5, 1800 to January 5, 1825," *Parliamentary Papers* (Commons) 227 (1825): xx, 233–267.

13. James L. Huston, *Securing the Fruits of Labor: The American Concept of Wealth Distribution, 1765–1900* (Baton Rouge, 1998), p. 89; Olive Cleaveland Clarke, *Things that I Remember at Ninety-Five* (n.p., 1881), pp. 10–11. This was in 1802.

14. Frey, *Water From the Rock*, p. 280. See also Andrew R. L. Cayton, "The Early National Period," in Mary Kupiec Cayton et al., eds., *Encyclopedia of American Social History* (New York, 1993), vol. 1, p. 100.

15. William J. Baumol et al., *Productivity and American Leadership* (Boston, 1989), p. 53; Clayne L. Pope, "The Changing View of the Standard-of-Living Question in the United States," *American Economic Association Papers and Proceedings*, 83 (1993): 332.

16. Bureau of the Census, *Statistical Abstract of the United States* (Washington, D.C., 1983). For slave fertility see Robert Fogel and Stanley Engerman, eds., *Without Consent or Contract: The Rise and Fall of American Slavery* (New York, 1989), p. 149.

17. Warren S. Thompson, "The Demographic Revolution in the United States," *Annals of the American Academy of Political and Social Sciences*, 262 (1949): pp. 62–69; Cayton, "The Early National Period," p. 88.

18. Allen Trimble, "Autobiography," in *The Old Northwest Genealogical Quarterly*, 9 (1907): 74; Gershom Flagg, *The Flagg Correspondence Selected Letters, 1816–1854*, eds. Barbara Lawrence and Nedra Branz (Carbondale, Ill., 1986), pp. 5–7; Baumol et al., *Productivity and American Leadership*, pp. 34–35.

19. Birkbeck, *Notes on a Journey*, pp. 41–42; Baumol et al., *Productivity and American Leadership*, p. 34.

20. Henry L. Ellsworth, *A Digest of Patents issued by the United States, from 1790 to January 1, 1839* (Washington, D.C., 1840). See also Kenneth Sokoloff, "Inventive Activity in Early Industrial America: Evidence from Patent Records, 1790–1846," *Journal of Economic History*, 48 (1988): 813–850.

21. Chauncey Jerome, *History of the American Clock Business for the Past Sixty Years, and Life of Chauncey Jerome* (New Haven, 1860), p. 8.

22. Daniel P. Jones, *The Economic and Social Transformation of Rural Rhode Island, 1780–1850* (Boston, 1992); for details of these conflicts in Rhode Island see Gary Kulik, "Dams, Fish, and Farmers: Defense of Public Rights in Eighteenth-Century Rhode Island," in Steven Hahn and Jonathan Prude, eds., *The Countryside in the Age of Capitalist Transformation: Essays in the Social History of Rural America* (Chapel Hill, 1985), pp. 25–50.

23. H. Larry Ingle, *Quakers in Conflict: The Hickside Reformation* (Knoxville, Tenn., 1986).

24. Malcolm Rohrbough, *The Land Office Business: The Settlement and Administration of American Public Lands, 1789–1837* (New York, 1968), p. 48 as cited in Cunningham, *The Process of Government*, p. 107. See also Arthur H. Cole, "Cyclical and Sectional Variations in the Sale of Public Land," *Review of Economics and Statistics*, 9 (1927): 50; and Andrew R. L. Cayton, *The Frontier Republic: Ideology and Politics in the Ohio Country, 1780–1825* (Kent, Ohio, 1986) pp. 115–117.

25. Allan Kulikoff, *Tobacco and Slaves: The Development of Southern Cultures in the Chesapeake, 1680–1800* (Chapel Hill, 1986), p. 430; *Recollections of John Jay Smith* (Philadelphia, 1892), p. 32.

26. Trimble, "Autobiography," pp. 13–15, 49–56. See also Stephen Aron, *How the West Was Lost: The Transformation of Kentucky from Daniel Boone to Henry Clay* (Baltimore, 1996), pp. 29–35.

27. W. J. Rorabaugh, *The Alcoholic Republic: An American Tradition* (New York, 1979), pp. 80–82; Stanley Lebergott, *Manpower in Economic Growth: The American Record Since 1800* (New York, 1964), p. 12; Mark Edward Lender and James Kirby Martin, *Drinking in America: A History* (New York, 1982), pp. 47–48; Timothy Flint, *A Condensed Geography and History of the Western States* (Cincinnati, 1828), pp. 227–229.

28. *Encyclopedia of American History*, pp. 131, 137. Stevens and his sons, Robert and Edward, pioneered America's first steam locomotive railroad on a private track in 1826. In 1819 the first United States steamboat crossed the Atlantic.

29. Rorabaugh, *The Alcoholic Republic*, p. 61. See also Merton M. Hyman et al., *Drinkers, Drinking, and Alcohol-Related Mortality and Hospitalizations: A Statistical Compendium* (New Brunswick, N.J., 1980).

30. Christiana Holmes Tillson, *Reminiscences of Early Life in Illinois* (n.p., 1873), pp. 6–17. This has been republished as *A Woman's Story of Pioneer Illinois*, ed. Milo Milton Quaife (Carbondale, Ill., 1995).

31. Birkbeck, *Notes on a Journey*, p. 32.

32. Ibid., p. 80.

33. William Cobbett, *A Year's Residence in the United States of America*, 3rd ed. (London, 1828), pp. 313, 83–84.

34. Matthew Gardner, *The Autobiography of Elder Matthew Gardner* (Dayton, 1874), p. 69.

35. Stephen Cooper, *Sketches from the Life of Major Stephen Cooper* (Oakland, 1888), p. 3.

36. Mark D. Kaplanoff, "From Colony to State: New Hampshire, 1800–1815" (research paper, Cambridge University, 1975), pp. 107–108.

37. Harold Fisher Wilson, *The Hill Country of Northern New England: Its Social and Economic History, 1790–1930* (New York, 1967); Paul Gates, *The Farmer's Age: Agriculture, 1815–1860* (New York, 1960), pp. 25–29.

38. John C. Pease and John M. Niles, *A Gazetteer . . . of Connecticut and Rhode Island* (Hartford, 1819), p. 6.

39. Richard L. Bushman, *The Refinement of America: Persons, Houses, Cities* (New York, 1992), p. 265. See also Gregory H. Nobles, "Commerce and Community: A Case Study of the Rural Broommaking Business in Antebellum Massachusetts," *Journal of the Early Republic* 4 (1984), pp. 288–291.

40. "The Diary of Lucy Fletcher Kellogg" (American Antiquarian Society typescript of a manuscript written in 1879).

41. Richard J. Calhoun, *Witness to Sorrow: The Antebellum Autobiography of William J. Grayson*, with intro. by Eugene Genovese (Columbia, S.C., 1990), p. 43.

42. E. S. Thomas, *Reminiscences of the Last Sixty-Five Years* (Hartford, 1840), p. 36.

43. Roger L. Ransom and Richard Sutch, "Conflicting Visions: The Economic Origins of Sectional Conflict in the United States," paper given at the Russian-American Conference in Economic History, Moscow, June 23–25, 1995, p. 24; Majewski, *A House Dividing*.

44. United States Bureau of the Census, *Historical Statistics of the United States: Colonial Times to 1957* (Washington, D.C., 1961), pp. 7–11.

45. Birkbeck, *Notes on a Journey*, p. 21; see also Brenda E. Stevenson, *Life in Black and White: Family and Community in the Slave South* (New York, 1996).

46. As quoted in Steven Deyle, "The Irony of Liberty: Origins of the Domestic Slave Trade," *Journal of the Early Republic*, 4 (1984): 37; see also Walter Johnson, *Soul by Soul: Life Inside the Antebellum Slave Market* (Cambridge, Mass., 1999).

47. Gavin Wright, *The Political Economy of the Cotton South: Households, Markets, and Wealth in the Nineteenth Century* (New York, 1978), pp. 141–142; Ransom and Sutch, "Conflicting Visions," p. 24.

48. Carl Patrick Burrowes, *Black Christian Republicanism: Selected Writings of Hilary Teage (1805–1854)* (forthcoming).

49. William Hayden, *Narrative of William Hayden* (Cincinnati, 1846), pp. 22–46.

50. Moses Grandy, *Narrative of the Life of Moses Grandy*, 2nd ed. (Boston, 1844), pp. 12–30.

51. Juliet E. K. Walker, *Free Frank: A Black Pioneer on the Antebellum Frontier* (Lexington, 1983), pp. 32–35, 93ff. His name is listed in different U.S. Censuses as Frank Denham and Frank McWorter, the surname of his first owner and probable father.

52. Austin Steward, *Twenty-Two Years a Slave and Forty Years a Freeman* (Reading, Mass., 1969 [orig. pub. Rochester, 1857]), p. x.

53. Charles Ball, *Slavery in the United States: A Narrative of the Life and Adventures of Charles Ball, A Black Man* (Lewistown, Pa., 1836), pp. 5, 219, 293–303.

54. Forrest McDonald and Grady McWhiney, "The South from Self-Sufficiency to Peonage," in *American Historical Review*, 85 (1980): 1107–1110; Charles Sellers, *The Market Revolution: Jacksonian America, 1815–1846* (New York, 1991), p. 273.

55. Theodore Rosengarten, "The Southern Agriculturist in an Age of Reform," in Michael O'Brien and David Moltke-Hansen, eds., *Intellectual Life in Antebellum Charleston* (Knoxville, 1986), pp. 281, 292.

56. Lebergott, *Manpower in Economic Growth*, p. 11.

57. J. S. Holliday, *Rush For Riches: Gold Fever and the Making of California* (Berkeley, 1999), pp. 18–22.

58. Alfred Chandler, *The Visible Hand: The Managerial Revolution in American Business* (Cambridge, Mass., 1977).

59. Elizabeth Blackmar, *Manhattan for Rent, 1785–1850* (Ithaca, 1989).

60. John Denis Haeger, *The Investment Frontier: New York Businessmen and the Economic Development of the Old Northwest* (Albany, 1981), pp. 18–19.

61. Ibid., p. 19. See also Viviana Zelizer, *Morals and Markets: The Development of Life Insurance in the United States* (New York, 1983).

62. Robert F. Dalzell, Jr., "The Rise of the Waltham-Lowell System and Some Thoughts on the Political Economy of Modernization in Ante-Bellum Massachusetts," *Perspectives in American History*, 9 (1975): 239–268.

63. Thomas Dublin, *Women at Work: The Transformation of Work and Community in Lowell, Massachusetts, 1826–1860* (New York, 1979).

64. Claudia Goldin and Kenneth Sokoloff, "Women, Children, and Industrialization in the Early Republic: Evidence from the Manufacturing Censuses," *Journal of Economic History*, 41 (1982): 741–744, 766.

65. Francois Weil, "Capitalism and Industrialization en Nouvelle-Angleterre, 1815–1845," *Annales, Histoire, Sciences Sociales*, (1995): 29–52; Anthony Wallace, *Rockdale: The Growth of an Industrial Village in the Early Industrial Revolution* (New York, 1978); Cynthia Shelton, *The Mills of Manayunk: Industrialization and Social Conflict in the Philadelphia Region, 1787–1837* (Baltimore, 1986).

66. Dalzell, Jr., "The Rise of the Waltham-Lowell System," pp. 235, 161–163. Daniel Tyler, *A Memorial Volume Containing his Autobiography*, ed. Donald G. Mitchell (New Haven, 1883), p. 29, describes the "first coke hot-blast furnace ever built in America," which some of the Boston Associates constructed on a five-thousand-acre tract of land in Lycoming, Pennsylvania.

67. Margaret Newell, *Economic Revolutions: Political Economy, Culture and Development in New England, 1620–1775* (New York, 1996) notes the move of artisans out of Boston as early as the 1750s.

68. Susan E. Hirsch, "From Artisan to Manufacturer: Industrialization and the Small Producer in Newark, 1830–60," in Stuart W. Bruchey, ed., *Small Business and American Life* (New York, 1980), p. 89. The quotation is from Stanley Engerman and Kenneth Sokoloff, "Factor Endowments, Institutions, and Differential Paths of Growth Among New World Economies: A View from Economic Historians of the United States," in Stephen Haber, ed., *How Latin America Fell Behind* (Stanford, 1996), p. 283.

69. Arial Bragg, *The Memoirs of Col. Arial Bragg* (Milford, Mass., 1846), pp. 25, 39, 49. A fine study of the shoemaking industry is Alan Dawley, *Class and Community: the Industrial Revolution in Lynn* (Cambridge, Mass., 1976).

70. Zachariah Allen, *Practical Tourist or Sketches of the State of the Useful Arts and of Society . . . in Great Britain, France and Holland* (Boston, 1832), vol. 2, pp. 153–154.

71. Clarke, *Things that I Remember at Ninety-Five*, p. 9.

72. John Melish, *Travels in the United States of America, in the years 1806 & 1807, and 1809, 1810, & 1811* (Philadelphia, 1812), vol. 2, pp. 387–388.

73. William Darby and Theodore Dwight, Jr., *A New Gazetteer of The United States of America*, rev. ed. (Hartford, 1836), p. 568.

74. James Flint, *Letters from America* (Edinburgh, 1822), in Reuben Gold Twaites, ed., *Early Western Travels, 1748–1846* (Cleveland, 1904), p. 44.

75. Charles Goodyear, *Gum-Elastics and Its Varieties* (New Haven, 1853), pp. 94, 53.

76. Thomas Cochran, "Philadelphia: The American Industrial Center, 1750–1850," *Pennsylvania Magazine of History and Biography*, 106 (1982): 325–328.

77. Allan Pred, "Manufacturing in the American Mercantile City, 1800–1840," *Annals of the Association of American Geographers*, 56 (1966): 307, 314, 337.

78. Hirsch, "From Artisan to Manufacturer," pp. 89–93; Jonathan A. Glickstein, *Concepts of Free Labor in Antebellum America* (New Haven, 1991), pp. 10, 223.

79. Holmes Hinkley, *Holmes Hinkley, An Industrial Pioneer, 1793–1866*, ed. Walter S. Hinchman (Cambridge, 1913), pp. 28–30.

80. Jerome, *History of the American Clock Business*, pp. 16–18.

81. Ibid., pp. 5ff; John Thompson, *Autobiography of Deacon John Thompson* (Farmington, Maine, 1920), p. 60; James Riley, *The Authentic Narrative of the Loss of the American Brig Commerce* (Hartford, 1817), p. 19.

82. Hinkley, *Holmes Hinkley*, p. 22.

83. E.g. Timothy Claxton, *Memoir of a Mechanic* (Boston, 1839), p. 68; Goodyear, *Gum-Elastics and Its Varieties*, pp. 95–96; and James B. Finley, *Autobiography of Rev. James B. Finley* (Cincinnati, 1854), p. 150.

84. Bushman, *The Refinement of America*, p. 265.

85. C. J. Ingersoll, *A Discourse Concerning the Influence of America on the Mind* (Philadelphia, 1823), p. 24.

86. Ibid., p. 27.

87. [Delano A. Goddard], *Biographical Sketch of A. Bronson Alcott*, (n.p., n.d.), pp. 3–4.

88. Thomas Douglas, *Autobiography of Thomas Douglas* (New York, 1856), p. 32.

89. Asa Sheldon, *Yankee Drover: Being the Unpretending Life of Asa Sheldon, Farmer, Trader, and Working Man, 1788–1870* (Hanover, N.H., 1988), pp. 60–83.

90. David Jaffee, "Peddlers of Progress and the Transformation of the Rural North, 1760–1860," *Journal of American History*, 78 (1991): 515–517.

91. Stephen Noyes Winslow, *Biographies of Successful Philadelphia Merchants* (Philadelphia, 1864), pp. 18–20, 96–97, 141–142.

92. In the city directory of Utica, New York in 1817, for instance, 17 percent of the people listed claimed the occupation of merchant, according to Mary P. Ryan, *Cradle of the Middle Class* (New York, 1981).

93. Malcolm J. Rohrbough, *The Trans-Appalachian Frontier: People, Societies, and Institutions, 1775–1850* (New York, 1978), pp. 43–46.

94. Carole Shammas, "Anglo-American Household Government in Comparative Perspective," *William and Mary Quarterly*, 52 (1995): 104–144. This is measured in constant dollars.

95. Richard Sylla, "U.S. Securities Markets and the Banking System, 1790–1840," *Review* (1998): 86; Naomi R. Lamoreaux and Christopher Glaisek, "Vehicles of Privilege or Mobility: Banks in Providence, R.I. during the Age of Jackson," *Business History Review*, 65 (1991): 507–521.

96. Thomas, *Reminiscences*, p. 49.

97. As quoted from the *Sun*, February 11, 1801, in Kaplanoff, "From Colony to State: New Hampshire, 1800–1815."

98. Lamoreaux and Glaisek, "Vehicles of Privilege or Mobility," pp. 502–503. See also Larry Schweikart, "U.S. Commercial Banking: A Historiographical Survey," *Business History Review*, 65 (1991); Cochran, "Philadelphia: The American Industrial Center," p. 327. According to Shammas, "Anglo-American Household Government in Comparative Perspective," p. 135, there was as much land settled by Euro-Americans between 1760 and 1800 as in the previous 150 years.

99. John Farmer and Jacob B. Moore, *A Gazetteer of the State of New-Hampshire* (Concord, 1823).

100. Anna Jacobson Schwartz, "The Beginning of Competitive Banking in Philadelphia, 1782–1809," *Journal of Political Economy*, 55 (1947): 421–431. See also Richard Sylla, "Forgotten Men of Money: Private Banks in Early U.S. History," *Journal of Economic History*, 29 (1969); and Lamoreaux and Glaisek, "Vehicles of Privilege or Mobility."

101. Washburn, *Autobiography*, pp. 31–32.

102. [John Neal], "Remarks on American Writers," *Blackwood's Edinburgh Magazine*, 17 (February 1825): 190; John Neal, *Wandering Recollections of a Somewhat Busy Life* (Boston, 1869), pp. 124–125.

103. [John Neal], "Remarks on American Writers," *Blackwood's Edinburgh Magazine*, 17 (January–June, 1825): 194.

104. *Sketches of the Life of William Stuart* (Bridgeport, Conn., 1854), pp. 40–42.

105. Edwin J. Perkins, *Continuities and Deviations: A History of American Financial Services, 1700–1815* (Columbus, 1994). Charles Buck in his *Memoirs*, p. 42, claims to have negotiated loans in Hamburg in which the United States paid 83 percent interest.

106. Sandra F. VanBurkleo, "'The Paws of Banks': The Origins and Significance of Kentucky's Decision to Tax Federal Bankers, 1818–1820," *Journal of the Early Republic*, 9 (1989): 457–487.

107. "Bailhache Memoir" (typescript dated June 1, 1855, Alton, Ill., in manuscript collection of the American Antiquarian Society), pp. 19–20.

108. Anson Jones, *Memoranda and Official Correspondence Relating to the Republic of Texas, Its History and Annexation* (New York, 1859), pp. 5–6.

109. Samuel Alfred Foot, *Autobiography* (New York, 1872), p. 28.

110. John Chambers, *Autobiography*, ed. John Carl Parish (Iowa City, Iowa, 1908), p. 16.

111. Lucy R. Richards, *Memoirs of the Late Miss Lucy Richards* (New York, 1842), p. 70.

112. Glickstein, *Concepts of Free Labor*, p. 11.

113. In 1811. Charles Francis Adams, ed., *Works of John Adams* (Boston, 1851), vol. 9, pp. 633–634.

4 Careers

1. Richard John, *Spreading the News: The American Postal System from Franklin to Morse* (Cambridge, Mass., 1996).

2. William Gilmore, "Literacy, The Rise of an Age of Reading, and the Cultural Grammar of Print Communications in America, 1735–1850," *Communication*, 11 (1988): 23–46.

3. Rosalind Remer, *Printers and Men of Capital: Philadelphia Book Publishers in the New Republic* (Philadelphia, 1996).

4. John Griscom, *Memoir of John Griscom*, ed. John H. Griscom, M.D., (New York, 1859), p. 47. See William J. Gilmore-Lehne, *Reading Becomes a Necessity of Life: Material and Cultural Life in Rural New England, 1780–1835* (Knoxville, 1989).

5. Timothy Flint, *Recollections of Last Ten Years* (Boston, 1826), ed. Bernard de Voto (New York, 1932), p. xi. See also Timothy Flint, *Francis Berrian, or the Mexican Patriot* (Cincinnati, 1826); *A Condensed Geography and History of the Western States* (Cincinnati, 1828); *The Shoshonee Valley* (Cincinnati, 1830); *Biographical Memoir of Daniel Boone* (Cincinnati, 1833).

6. Timothy Flint, *The Life and Adventures of Arthur Clenning* (Philadelphia, 1828), pp. 9, 36, 43; James Riley, *The Authentic Narrative of the Loss of the American Brig Commerce* (Hartford, 1817).

7. Paul Baepler, "The Barbary Captivity Narrative in Early America," *Early American Literature*, 30 (1995): 95–120.

8. *Logan* (1822), *Seventy-Six* (1823), *Randolph* (1823), *Errata* (1823), *Brother Jonathan* (1825). See also John Neal, *Wandering Recollections of a Somewhat Busy Life* (Boston, 1869), pp. 140–161, 100–102.

9. Neal, *Rachel Dyer*, facsimile edition, with intro. by John D. Seelye (n.p., 1964 [originally published in 1828]), p. xx.

10. [Neal], "Remarks on American Writers," *Blackwood's Edinburgh Magazine*, 16 (July-December, 1824): 304–311, 415–429, 560–574; 17 (January-June, 1825): 48–69, 186–207.

11. Harold Edward Dickson, ed., *Observations on American Art: Selections from the Writing of John Neal* (State College, Penn., 1943), p. xviii.

12. Benjamin Lease and Hans-Joachim Lang, eds., *The Genius of John Neal: Selections from His Writings* (Frankfurt am Main, 1978).

13. Susan J. Wolfe compiled these figures from data derived from the Printers Catalogue at the American Antiquarian Society.

14. Richard Gabriel Stone, *Hezekiah Niles as an Economist* (Baltimore, 1933), pp. 43–58.

15. [Neal], "Remarks on American Writers," *Blackwood's Edinburgh Magazine*, 16 (September, 1824): 309; H. M. Brackenridge, *Recollections of Persons and Places in the West*, 2nd ed., enl. (Philadelphia, 1868), pp. 64, 281ff.

16. *The Writings of Robert C. Sands*, ed. Julian Verplanck (New York, 1834), vol. 1, pp. 3–14.

17. Barbara L. Packer, "The Transcendentalists," in *The Cambridge History of American Literature*, ed. Sacvan Bercovitch and Cyrus R. K. Patell (Cambridge, 1994), vol. 2, p. 356.

18. Remer, *Printers and Men of Capital*.

19. William Charvat, *Literary Publishing in America, 1790–1850* (Philadelphia, 1959). In 1820, Charleston had 37 people in the print trade; Richmond, 51; and New Orleans, 22, compared to Boston's 188, Philadelphia's 234, and New York's 301. See note 13.

20. [Charles Jared Ingersoll], *A Discourse Concerning the Influence of America on the Mind* (Philadelphia, 1823), pp. 16–18.

21. Thomas Jefferson to William Short, November 10, 1804, Jefferson Papers, Library of Congress.

22. Rufus Wilmot Griswold, *The Female Poets of America* (Philadelphia, 1849), pp. 55–58; Nancy Woloch, *Women and the American Experience, Volume One: To 1920*, 2nd ed. (New York, 1994), pp. 99–102.

23. S. G. Goodrich, *Recollections of a lifetime, or men and things I have seen: in a series of familiar letters to a friend* (New York, 1857), vol. 2, pp. 143ff, and vol. 1, p. 125.

24. Gordon S. Haight, *Mrs. Sigourney: The Sweet Singer of Hartford* (New Haven, 1930).

25. See also her fictionalized autobiographies: [Caroline Gilman], *Recollections of a Southern Matron* (New York, 1838) and *Recollections of a Housekeeper* (New York, 1834).

26. Fredrika Teute and Joyce Appleby, eds., *The First Forty Years of Washington Society* (Armonk, N.Y., 2000).

27. Anna Maria Lee, *Memoirs of Eminent Females* (Philadelphia, 1827).

28. Sarah Hale, *Sketches of American Character* (Boston, 1829), pp. 102–106. Hale was also remembered as the author of "Mary Had a Little Lamb."

29. Lydia Huntley [Sigourney], *Moral Pieces, in Prose and Verse* (Hartford, 1815), pp. 73–79.

30. [Lydia Sigourney], *Letters to Young Ladies* (Hartford, 1833), pp. 28–31.

31. Jan Lewis, *The Pursuit of Happiness: Family and Values in Jefferson's Virginia* (Cambridge, 1983), pp. 148–149.

32. Gerda Lerner, *The Feminist Thought of Sarah Grimke* (New York, 1998), pp. 5, 22.

33. Nancy F. Cott, *The Bonds of Womanhood: "Woman's Sphere" in New England, 1780–1835* (New Haven, 1977), pp. 6–9.

34. Lyle Henry Wright, *American Fiction, 1774–1850* (San Marino, Calif., 1969), "Chronological Index," pp. 363–365. See novels of Catharine Sedgwick, Elizabeth Boardman Otis, Louisa Caroline Tuthill, Sarah Savage, Sukey Vickery, Lydia Maria Child, Sarah Hale, Maria Gowen Brooks, Carolyn Lee Whiting Hentz, Eliza Cabot Follen, Hannah Farnham Sawyer Lee, Eliza Ware Farrar, Harriet Vaughan Foster Cheney, Margaret Miller Davidson, Sarah Ann Irwin Myers, Sophia Robbins Little, Susan Ann Livingston Sedgwick, and Margaret Bayard Smith.

35. [Ingersoll], *A Discourse*, pp. 10, 16–18.

36. Bernard Bailyn et al., eds., *The Great Republic* (Lexington, Mass., 1992), p. 328; Allan R. Pred, *Urban Growth and the Circulation of Information: The United States System of Cities, 1790–1840* (Cambridge, Mass., 1973), p. 21.

37. L. Ray Gunn, *The Decline of Authority: Public Economic Policy and Political Development in New York, 1800–1860* (Ithaca, 1988), p. 52.

38. See note 13.

39. Eber D. Howe, *Autobiography and Recollections of a Pioneer Printer* (Painesville, Ohio, 1878), pp. 3–19.

40. Ibid., pp. 3–19.

41. Ibid., p. 27.

42. Howard B. Rock, *Artisans of the New Republic: The Tradesmen of New York City in the Age of Jefferson* (New York, 1979), p. 37.

43. Elihu H.[otchkiss] Shepard, *The Autobiography of Elihu Shepard* (St. Louis, 1869), p. 25.

44. Frederic Trautmann, ed. and trans., "Pennsylvania Through a German's Eyes: The Travels of Ludwig Gall, 1819–1820," *Pennsylvania Magazine of History and Biography*, 105 (1981): 42–48.

45. Ibid., pp. 47–49.

46. [Joseph Caldwell], *Letters on Popular Education* (Hillsborough, N.C., 1832), pp. 8–9.

47. Carl F. Kaestle et al., eds., *Literacy in the United States* (New Haven, 1991).

48. Joan E. Cashin, *A Family Venture: Men and Women on the Southern Frontier* (New York, 1991), pp. 5, 41, 45.

49. James G. Carter, *Letters on the Free Schools of New England*, as cited in [Caldwell], *Letters on Popular Education*, p. 12.

50. John Ball, *Autobiography* (Grand Rapids, 1925); John Chambers, *Autobiography*, ed. John Carl Parish (Iowa City, Iowa, 1908); Humphrey Howe Leavitt, *Autobiography of the Hon. Humphrey Howe Leavitt* (New York, [1893]); John Belton O'Neall, *Biographical Sketches of the Bench and Bar of South Carolina* (Charleston, S.C., 1859); Anson Jones, *Memoranda and Official Correspondence Relating to the Republic of Texas, Its History and Annexation* (New York, 1859), pp. 3–5; Christiana Holmes Tillson, *A Woman's Story of Pioneer Illinois*, ed. Milo M. Quaife (Carbondale, Ill., 1995).

51. Amos Bronson Alcott, *The Journals of Bronson Alcott*, ed. Odell Shepard (Boston, 1938), vol. 1, entry for Dec. 4, 1828.

52. Richard Cecil Stone, *Life Incidents of Home, School and Church* (St. Louis, 1874), p. 76.

53. Julia Tevis, *Sixty Years in a Schoolroom: An Autobiography of Mrs. Julia A. Tevis* (Cincinnati, 1878).

54. Ibid., pp. 50, 81, 184.

55. Ibid., p. 163.

56. Ibid., pp. 479–482.

57. *An Address to the Public; particularly to the Members of the Legislature of New-York, Proposing a Plan for Improving Female Education* (n.p., 1819). From 1825–1827, Boston had supported a public English high school for girls: Jane H. Pease and William H. Pease, *Ladies, Women, and Wenches: Choice and Constraint in Antebellum Charleston and Boston* (Chapel Hill, 1990).

58. Frederick Rudolph, "WILLARD, Emma Hart," *Notable American Women: The Modern Period: A Biographical Dictionary* (Cambridge, Mass., 1980).

59. L. H. Sigourney, *Letters of Life,* ed. Rita Lawn (facsimile reprint, New York, 1980 [New York, 1867]).

60. John F. Ohles and Shirley M. Ohles, *Private Colleges and Universities* (Westport, 1982); and *Public Colleges and Universities* (Westport, 1986).

61. Neal, *Recollections of a Somewhat Busy Life,* p. 15.

62. Carolyn E. DeLatte, *Lucy Audubon: A Biography* (Baton Rouge, 1982).

63. Frederick B. Tolles, ed., *Slavery and "The Woman Question": Lucretia Mott's Diary* (Haverford, Penn., 1952).

64. Bishop [William] Meade, *Recollections of Two Beloved Wives* (n.p., [1857]), pp. 11–12; Jan Lewis, "Mother as Teachers: Reconceptualizing the Role of the Family as Educator," in *Education and the American Family: A Research Synthesis* (New York, 1980); Marilyn S. Blackwell, "The Republican Vision of Mary Palmer Tyler," *Journal of the Early Republic,* 12 (1992): 30.

65. Harriet B. Cooke, *Memoirs of My Life Work: The Autobiography of Mrs. Harriet B. Cooke* (New York, 1858).

66. [Abel Bowen], *The Young Lady's Book: A Manual of Elegant Recreations, Exercises and Pursuits* (Boston, [1829]); John Bidwell, "American History in Image and Text," *Proceedings of the American Antiquarian Society,* 98 (1989): 250; Walter Harding, ed., *Essays on Education by Amos Bronson Alcott* (Gainesville, Fla., 1960).

67. Griscom, *Memoir,* pp. 49, 98–99.

68. A. Comstock, *Autobiography of A. Comstock, M.D.* (Philadelphia, 1857), pp. 10–11, 6.

69. Marian C. McKenna, *Tapping Reeve and the Litchfield Law School,* (New York, 1986), p. 59. William and Mary College and the Universities of Pennsylvania and Maryland pioneered law chairs.

70. Martin Van Buren, "The Autobiography of M__V__B__," ed. John C. Fitzpatrick, in *Annual Report to AHA for year 1918,* 2: 12–13.

71. Samuel Alford Foot, *Autobiography* (New York, 1872), p. 11.

72. Chambers, *Autobiography,* pp. 6–9.

73. Kenneth C. Martis and Gregory A. Elmes, eds., *The Historical Atlas of State Power in Congress, 1790–1990* (Washington, D.C., 1993).

74. O'Neall, *Biographical Sketches of the Bench and Bar,* vol. 1, pp. xv–xviii. See also Robert Ferguson, *Law and Letters in American Culture* (Cambridge, Mass., 1984).

75. Richard D. Brown, *Knowledge Is Power: The Diffusion of Information in Early America: 1700–1865* (New York, 1989), p. 277.

76. Daniel Drake, *Pioneer Life in Kentucky,* ed. Charles Drake (Cincinnati, 1870), pp. v–xv. One can use a multiplier of fifty for current dollars.

77. William Barlow and David O. Powell, "A Dedicated Medical Student: Solomon Mordecai, 1819–1822," *Journal of the Early Republic,* 7 (1987): 382–384.

78. [Ingersoll], *A Discourse,* pp. 41–46.

79. *Philadelphia Medical Museum,* new ser., I (1811); *Medical Repository,* 10 (1807): iii; 13 (1810): iii; 19 (1819): iii.

80. William Darrach, *Memoir of George McClellan* (Philadelphia, 1847), pp. 15–18. Biographical data on the doctors mentioned here can be found in Allen Johnson et al., eds., *Dictionary of American Biography* (New York, 1943–1944). See Chandos Brown, *Benjamin Silliman: A Life in the Young Republic* (Princeton, 1989).

81. Reginald Horsman, *Frontier Doctor: William Beaumont, America's First Great Medical Scientist* (Columbia, 1996); William Beaumont, *Experiments and Observations on the Gastric Juice and the Physiology of Digestion* (Plattsburgh, 1833).

82. George W. Cullom, *Biographical Register of the Officers and Graduates of the U.S. Military Academy, 1802–1840* (New York, 1868), pp. 2–3.

83. William B. Skelton, "High Army Leadership in the Era of the War of 1812: The Making and Remaking of the Officer Corps," *William and Mary Quarterly,* 41 (1994): 254–259, 271–272.

84. Edwin James, *Account of an Expedition from Pittsburgh to the Rocky Mountains* (Philadelphia, 1823); W. H. Keating, ed., *Narrative of an Expedition to the Source of the St. Peter's River* (London, 1825).

85. S. H. Long and William Gibbs McNeill, *Narrative of the Proceedings of the Board of Engineers, of the Baltimore and Ohio Rail Road Company* (Baltimore, 1830), p. 11. For share figures see Milton Reizenstein, *The Economic History of the Baltimore and Ohio Railroad, 1827–1853* (Baltimore, 1897), p. 19.

86. Daniel Tyler (1799–1882), *A Memorial Volume Containing his Autobiography,* ed. Donald G. Mitchell (New Haven, 1883), p. 4.

87. Ibid., pp. 8–27.

88. Chester Harding, *My Egotistigraphy* (Cambridge, 1866), pp. 17–18; Neal, *Wandering Recollections,* p. 108; and Jonathan Israel, *The Dutch Republic: Its Rise, Greatness, and Fall, 1477–1806* (New York, 1995).

89. Harding, *My Egotistigraphy,* pp. 18–19.

90. Ibid., pp. 7–8.

91. Ibid., pp. 22–32.

92. Dickson, ed., *Observations on American Art,* p. xviii.

93. Ibid., pp. xiv–xvi.

94. Harding, *My Egotistigraphy*, p. 31.

95. David Jaffee, "Peddlers of Progress," p. 523, and "One of the Primitive Sort: Portrait Makers of the Rural North, 1760–1860," in Steven Hahn and Jonathan Prude, eds., *The Countryside in the Age of Capitalist Transformation: Essays in the Social History of Rural America* (Chapel Hill, 1985).

96. Jaffee, "Peddlers of Progress," p. 520.

97. [Samuel Knapp], *Sketches of Public Characters* (New York, 1830), pp. 202–204.

98. *Audubon By Himself, A Profile of John James Audubon*, ed. Alice Ford (Garden City, N.Y., 1969 [1897]).

99. Christine Heyrman, *Southern Cross: The Beginnings of the Bible Belt* (New York, 1997), pp. 81–82.

100. Natalie A. Naylor, "The Theological Seminary in the Configuration of American Higher Education: The Antebellum Years," *History of Education Quarterly*, 17 (1977): 20–22.

101. Jacob Knapp, *Autobiography of Elder Jacob Knapp* (New York, 1968), pp. 20–29.

102. Charles G. Finney, *An Autobiography* (New York, 1903), pp. 5–21.

103. Ibid., pp. 47–68.

104. Jan Lewis, "Southerners and the Problem of Slavery in Political Discourse," in David Thomas Konig, ed., *Devising Liberty: Preserving and Creating Freedom in the New American Republic* (Stanford, 1995), and John H. Wigger, "Taking Heaven by Storm: Enthusiasm and Early American Methodism, 1770–1820," *Journal of the Early Republic*, 14 (1994).

105. James B. Finley, *Autobiography* (Cincinnati, 1854), pp. 87–95.

106. Sylvia R. Frey, *Water From the Rock: Black Resistance in a Revolutionary Age* (Princeton, 1991), p. 269.

107. Nell Painter, *Sojourner Truth: A Life, A Symbol* (New York, 1996), p. 5.

108. William L. Andrews, ed., *Sisters of the Spirit: Three Black Women's Autobiographies* (Bloomington, 1986); *The Life and Religious Experience of Jarena Lee* (Philadelphia, 1836); and *Memoirs of the Life, Religious Experience, Ministerial Travels and Labours of Mrs. Zilpha Elaw* (London, 1846).

109. Rebecca Jackson, *Gifts of Power: The Writings of Rebecca Jackson, Black Visionary, Shaker Eldress*, ed. Jean McMahon Humez (Amherst, Mass., 1981), p. 3.

110. James Carnahan, *Christianity Defended Against the Cavils of Infidels, and the Weakness of Enthusiasts* (Utica, 1808), pp. 17, 29; and Deborah Pierce, "A Scripture Vindication of Female Preaching, Prophesying, or Exhortation" (Utica, 1817), as quoted in Mary P. Ryan, *Cradle of the Middle Class: The Family in Oneida County, New York, 1790–1865* (New York, 1981), p. 71.

111. Nancy Towle, *Vicissitudes Illustrated in the Experience of Nancy Towle* (Portsmouth, N.H., 1833), pp. 15, 23, 41, 50–51, 62.

112. The biblical passage appears in I Corinthians, 14: 34. See also Lydia Sexton, *Autobiography of Lydia Sexton* (Dayton, 1885); Abigail Roberts, *Memoir of Mrs. Abigail*

Roberts (Irvington, N.J., 1858); Rebecca I. Davis, *Gleanings from Merrimac Valley* (Portland, Maine, 1881).

113. Davis, *Gleanings from Merrimac Valley*, pp. 8–23.

114. Dana Robert, "Evangelist or Homemaker? Mission Strategies of Early Nineteenth-Century Missionary Wives in Burma and Hawaii," *International Bulletin of Missionary Research* (January 1993), pp. 4–5.

115. Arabella Mary Stuart Willson, *Lives of Mrs. Ann H. Judson and Mrs. Sarah B. Judson, with a Biographical Sketch of Mrs. Emily C. Judson, missionaries to Burmah* (New York, 1855), pp. 115–118.

116. Rufus Anderson, ed., *Memorial Volume of the First Fifty Years of the American Board of Commissions for Foreign Missionaries* (Boston, 1861).

117. Joseph F. Kett, "Adolescence and Youth in Nineteenth-Century America," *Journal of Interdisciplinary History*, 10 (1979).

118. Cooke, *Memoirs of My Life Work*, p. 354.

119. Heyrman, *Southern Cross*, pp. 3–4.

120. James Durand, *The Life and Adventures of James Durand* (Bridgeport, 1817), pp. 45–46.

121. James V. Campbell, *Biographical Sketch of Charles C. Trowbridge* (Detroit, 1883), pp. 6–7.

122. Riley, *Authentic Narrative of the Loss of the Brig Commerce*, pp. 20–21, 27.

123. Thurlow Weed, "Autobiography of Thurlow Weed," ed. Harriet A. Weed, in *Life of Thurlow Weed including his autobiography and a memoir* (Boston, 1883), pp. 30–33.

124. Stephen Elliot, *An Address to the Literary and Philosophical Society of South-Carolina* (Charleston, 1814), p. 15; Richard D. Brown, *The Strength of the People: The Idea of an Informed Citizenry in America, 1650–1870* (Chapel Hill, 1996), p. 96; and Dr. Richard Carter, *A Short Sketch of the Author's Life* (Versailles, Ky., 1825), p. 3.

125. Cooke, *Memoirs of My Life Work*, pp. 63–66.

126. Woloch, *Women and the American Experience*, vol. 1, pp. 102–108.

127. Gideon Burton, *Reminiscences* (Cincinnati, 1895), p. 23.

128. David Hosack, *Memoir of DeWitt Clinton* (New York, 1829), p. 124.

129. *Recollections of Samuel Breck, with Passages from his Note-Books (1771–1862)*, ed. H. E. Scudder (Philadelphia, 1877), p. 255.

130. [Neal], "Remarks on American Writers," *Blackwood's Edinburgh Magazine*, 16 (November, 1824): 565.

131. Burton, *Reminiscences*, pp. 23, 16, 24. See also Emil Pocock, "Popular Roots of Jacksonian Democracy: The Case of Dayton, Ohio, 1815–1830," *Journal of the Early Republic*, 19 (1989): 506–507.

132. John W. Bear, *The Life and Travels of John W. Bear, "the Buckeye Blacksmith"* (Baltimore, 1875), p. 9.

133. Levi Beardsley, *Reminiscences* (New York, 1852), p. 65.

134. *The Public Life of Capt. John Brown, with an Auto-Biography of His Childhood and Youth* (Boston, 1860), pp. 30–36.

135. O'Neall, *Biographical Sketches,* vol. 1, p. 302. See also Wayne A. Wiegand, "'To Diffuse Useful Knowledge and Correct Moral Principles': Social Libraries in the Old Northwest, 1800–1850," in Paul H. Mattingly and Edward W. Stevens, Jr., *'. . . Schools and the Means of Education Shall Forever Be Encouraged': A History of Education in the Old Northwest, 1787–1880* (Athens, Ga., 1987).

136. Johnson et al., *Dictionary of American Biography.*

137. Amos Kendall, *Autobiography of Amos Kendall,* ed. William Stickney (Boston, 1872), p. 4. See also Griscom, *Memoir,* pp. 17–23.

138. George Rockingham Gilmer, *Sketches of Some of the First Settlers of Upper Georgia; and of the Cherokees, and the Author* (Baltimore, 1970 [1855]), p. 184.

139. William Rudolph Smith, "Autobiography of General William R. Smith: Dates and Incidents in My Life, Recorded for the Information of My Children and Grandchildren (1787–1808)" in *Incidents of a Journey from Pennsylvania to Wisconsin Territory in 1837* (Chicago, 1927), pp. 16–18.

140. George Wallace Jones, "Autobiography," in John Carl Parish, *George Wallace Jones* (Iowa City, Iowa, 1912); Burton, *Reminiscences;* Chambers, *Autobiography.*

141. Elias Smith, *The Life, Conversion, Preaching, Travels and Sufferings of Elias Smith* (Portsmouth, N.H., 1816), pp. 49–51.

142. Edouard de Montule, *A Voyage to North America, and the West Indies in 1817* (London, 1821), as quoted in Harry Liebersohn, *Aristocratic Encounters* (Princeton, 1999).

143. Chambers, *Autobiography,* p. 10.

144. David Low Dodge, *Memorial of Mr. David L. Dodge* (Boston, 1854), pp. 47–48.

145. Holmes Hinkley, *Holmes Hinkley, An Industrial Pioneer, 1793–1866,* ed. Walter S. Hinchman (Cambridge, 1913), p. 21.

146. Matthew Vassar, *The Autobiography and Letters of Matthew Vassar,* ed. Elizabeth Hazelton Haight (New York, 1916), p. 7.

5   Distinctions

1. [Samuel Gilman], *Memoirs of a New England Village Choir* (Boston, 1829), p. 2.

2. Ibid., pp. 17, 24–25, 64.

3. Ibid., pp. 68–78.

4. Ibid., pp. 68, 86, 112.

5. Ibid., pp. 123–124, 128–130.

6. Ibid., pp. 139–144.

7. Ibid., pp. 58–62.

8. Ibid., pp. 86, 112.

9. Stuart M. Blumin, "The Hypothesis of Middle-Class Formation in Nineteenth-Century America: A Critique and some Proposals," *American Historical Review*, 90 (1985) reviews the recent literature on the subject.

10. Lee Soltow, *Distribution of Wealth and Income in the United States in 1798* (Pittsburgh, 1989), pp. 232–248. Property owning in Sweden was 29 percent; in England 10 percent; and in Scotland 3 percent.

11. Martin Van Buren, "The Autobiography of M__V__B__," ed. John C. Fitzpatrick, in *Annual Report to AHA for year 1918*, 2: 19.

12. Lester H. Cohen, "Explaining the Revolution: Ideology and Ethics in Mercy Otis Warren's Historical Theory," *William and Mary Quarterly*, 37 (1980): 202.

13. Zoltan Haraszti, *John Adams and the Prophets of Progress* (New York, 1964), p. 201.

14. John Pickering, *A Vocabulary or Collection of Words and Phrases . . . peculiar to the United States of America* (Boston, 1816), pp. 14–15.

15. William C. Dowling, *Literary Federalism in the Age of Jefferson: Joseph Dennie and the Port folio, 1801–1812* (Columbia, S.C., 1999), p. 24.

16. Eliza Lee, *Sketches of a New England Village* (Boston, 1838), pp. 6–7.

17. Catharine M. Sedgwick, *Life and Letters of Catharine M. Sedgwick* (New York, 1871), p. 60.

18. Edith Wharton, *A Backward Glance* (New York, 1934), pp. 7–25, lists the Schermehorns, Ledyards, Rhinelanders, Pendletons, Gallatins, Stevens, Van Renssalears, Cadwaladers, Renshaws, Duers, Rutherfurds, Livingstons, and De Grasses.

19. Frederic Trautmann, ed. and trans., "Pennsylvania Through a German's Eyes: The Travels of Ludwig Gall, 1819–1820," *Pennsylvania Magazine of History and Biography*, 105 (1981): 54.

20. James Flint, *Letters from America* (Edinburgh, 1822), republished in Reuben Gold Twaites, ed., *Early Western Travels, 1748–1846* (Cleveland, 1904), pp. 44, 292–293, 62–63.

21. Morris Birkbeck, *Notes on a Journey in America*, 2nd ed. (London, 1818), pp. 35–36.

22. Malcolm Rohrbough, *The Land Office Business: The Settlement and Administration of American Public Lands, 1789–1837* (New York, 1968), p. 48. See also Arthur H. Cole, "Cyclical and Sectional Variations in the Sale of Public Land," *Review of Economics and Statistics*, 9 (1927): 50.

23. John Chambers, *Autobiography*, ed. John Carl Parish (Iowa City, Iowa, 1908), pp. 30–31.

24. E. S. Thomas, *Reminiscences of the Last Sixty-Five Years* (Hartford, 1840), p. 45.

25. *Recollections of John Jay Smith* (Philadelphia, 1892), p. 18.

26. Alan Taylor, *William Cooper's Town: Power and Persuasion on the Frontier of the Early American Republic* (New York, 1995), pp. 371–372.

27. Richard Gabriel Stone, *Hezekiah Niles as an Economist* (Baltimore, 1933), p. 54.

28. J. H. B. Latrobe, ed., *The Journal of Benjamin Latrobe: Being the Notes and Sketches of an Architect, Naturalist and Traveler in the United States from 1796 to 1820* (New York, 1905), p. 51.

29. Samuel Maunder, *The Treasury of Knowledge and Library of Reference*, 3rd ed. (New York, 1833) published a seven-page list of Old Testament names from Aalar to Zuzima and one page devoted to Christian ones. See also Richard L. Bushman, *The Refinement of America: Persons, Houses, Cities* (New York, 1992), pp. 296–297.

30. Birkbeck, *Notes on a Journey in America*, pp. 37, 108, 98.

31. Ibid., p. 108; Trautmann, ed. and trans., "Pennsylvania Through a German's Eyes," p. 41; Flint, *Letters from America*, p. 42.

32. U.S. Bureau of the Census, *Historical Statistics of the United States: Colonial Times to 1957* (Washington, D.C., 1961), pp. 7, 14; David Jaffee, *The People of the Wachusett: The Town Founders and Village Historians of New England, 1630–1820* (Ithaca, 1999), pp. 51off.

33. Rosalind Remer, "Preachers, Peddlers, and Publishers: Philadelphia's Backcountry Book Trade, 1800–1830," *Journal of the Early Republic*, 13 (1994): 501.

34. Henry R. Schoolcraft, *Western Scenes and Reminiscences of the Red Men of the Forest* (Buffalo, 1853), p. 28.

35. John Pickering, *A vocabulary, or collection of words and phrases which have been supposed to be peculiar to the United States of America* (Boston, 1816), pp. 10–11; Charles William Janson, *The Stranger in America* (London, 1807), pp. 185–186.

36. James Guild, "From Tunbridge, Vermont, to London, England: The Journal of James Guild, Peddler, Tinker, Schoolmaster, Portrait Painter, from 1818 to 1824," *Proceedings of the Vermont Historical Society*, new series, 5 (1937): 307.

37. *New England and Her Institutions* (Boston, 1835), pp. 28–29, as quoted in Nancy F. Cott, *The Bonds of Womanhood: "Woman's Sphere" in New England, 1780–1835* (New Haven, 1977), p. 51.

38. James Flint, *Letters from America* (Edinburgh, 1822), republished in S. G. Goodrich, *Recollections of a Lifetime, or Men and Things I have Seen: In a Series of Familiar Letters to a Friend* (New York, 1857), p. 122; Taylor, *William Cooper's Town*, p. 379.

39. Janson, *The Stranger in America*, p. 87.

40. [Lydia Sigourney], *Letters to Young Ladies* (Hartford, 1833), pp. 28–31.

41. Nora Pat Small, "The Search for a New Rural Order: Farmhouses in Sutton, Massachusetts, 1790–1830," *William and Mary Quarterly*, 43 (1996): 85–96.

42. As quoted in Kenneth Severens, *Charleston: Antebellum Architecture and Civil Destiny* (Knoxville, Tenn., 1988), pp. 49, 53.

43. Daniel Drake, "Inaugural Discourse on Medical Education" [1820], in Henry D. Shapiro and Zane L. Miller, eds., *Physician to the West: Selected Writings of Daniel Drake on Science and Society* (Lexington, Ky., 1970), pp. 159–160.

44. Jonathan Prude, *The Coming of Industrial Order: Town and Factory Life in Rural Massachusetts, 1810–1860* (Cambridge, 1983), p. 156. See also Stephan Thernstrom, "Ur-

banization, Migration, and Social Mobility in Late Nineteenth-Century America," in Barton J. Bernstein, ed., *Towards a New Past* (New York, 1968), p. 173.

45. Curtis D. Johnson, *Islands of Holiness: Rural Religion in Upstate New York, 1790–1860* (Ithaca, 1989), pp. 22–25.

46. Julia Tevis, *Sixty Years in a School Room: An Autobiography of Mrs. Julia A. Tevis* (Cincinnati, 1878), p. 252.

47. Arthur Singleton, *Letters from the South and West* (Boston, 1824), pp. 96–99.

48. Christiana Holmes Tillson, *Reminiscences of Early Life in Illinois,* (n.p., 1873), pp. 78–81.

49. Timothy Flint, *A Condensed Geography and History of the Western States* (Cincinnati, 1828), pp. 207–208.

50. Russell E. Richey, *Early Methodism* (Bloomington, Ind., 1991); William G. McLoughlin, *Soul Liberty: The Baptists' Struggle in New England, 1630–1833* (Hanover, N.H., 1991).

51. Bushman, *Refinement of America,* pp. 242, 273.

52. Carole Shammas, "Anglo-American Household Government in Comparative Perspective," *William and Mary Quarterly,* 52 (1995): 137–141.

53. Elihu H.[otchkiss] Shepard, *The Autobiography of Elihu Shepard* (St. Louis, 1869), p. 19.

54. Diana de Marly, *Dress in North America: The New World* (New York, 1990), vol. 1, pp. 169–173.

55. [Benjamin Silliman], *Letters of Shahcoolen* (Boston, 1802), p. 48. The discussion of Wollstonecraft appeared in the *Boston Weekly Magazine* (Feb. 5, 1803).

56. Guild, "From Tunbridge, Vermont, to London, England," p. 300; and [Abel Bowen], *The Young Lady's Book: A Manual of Elegant Recreations, Exercises and Pursuits* (Boston [1829]).

57. John Bidwell, "American History in Image and Text," *Proceedings of the American Antiquarian Society,* 98 (1988): 250.

58. Rebecca Burton Burlend, *A True Picture of Emigration,* ed. Milo Milton Quaife (Chicago, 1936), p. 46; Birkbeck, *Notes on a Journey in America,* p. 134.

59. Margo Culley, *A Day at a Time: The Diary Literature of American Women from 1764 to the Present* (New York, 1985), p. 83.

60. Chambers, *Autobiography,* pp. 30–31.

61. Latrobe, *Journal,* pp. 15, 24, 26.

62. Bushman, *Refinement of America,* pp. 278–292.

63. [George Tucker] Joseph Atterley, *A Voyage to the Moon* (New York, 1827), p. 201.

64. Thomas Branagan, *The Beauties of Philanthropy* (Philadelphia, 1808), pp. 62–64.

65. Benjamin Lease and Hans-Joachim Lang, *The Genius of John Neal: Selections from His Writings* (Frankfurt am Main, 1978), pp. 241–249. See also Marc W. Kruman, "The Second Party System and the Transformation of Revolutionary Republican-

ism," *Journal of the Early Republic*, 12 (1992): 518. New Jersey disqualified both women and African Americans at the same time.

66. [Samuel Knapp], *Extracts from a Journal of Travels in North America . . . by Ali Bey* (Boston, 1818), pp. 31–50.

67. [Mary Hunt Tyler], *The Maternal Physician; A Treatise on the Nurture and Management of Infants* (New York, 1811), p. 280.

68. John Griscom, *Memoir of John Griscom*, ed. John H. Griscom, M.D. (New York, 1859), pp. 97–98.

69. Elizabeth W. Levick, *Recollections of Early Days* (Philadelphia, 1881), p. 23.

70. John Melish, *Travels in the United States of America, in the years 1806 & 1807, and 1809, 1810, & 1811* (Philadelphia, 1812), pp. 59, 63.

71. Frederick Marryat, *A Diary in America, with Remarks on Its Institutions*, ed. Sydney Jackman (New York, 1962), p. 366; and Janson, *The Stranger in America*, p. 172.

72. [Sigourney], *Letters to Young Ladies*, pp. 29–30.

73. Samuel Woodworth, *The Deed of Gift, A Comic Opera, performed at Boston Theater* (New York, 1822), p. 8. See also Nathaniel Ames, *An Old Sailor's Yarns* (New York, 1835) and *History of Constantius and Pulchera, or, Virtue Rewarded* (Boston, 1821).

74. Maria del Occidente [Brooks], *Idomen; or, the Vale of Yumuri* (New York, 1843), pp. 12–13; Mrs. Phoebe Hinsdale Brown, *The Tree and Its Fruits, or Narrative from Real Life* (New York, 1836), pp. 31–32.

75. M. A. DeWolfe Howe, ed., *The Articulate Sisters: Passages from the Journals and Letters of the Daughters of President Josiah Quincy of Harvard University* (Cambridge, Mass., 1946), p. 46.

76. Jan Lewis, "Southerners and the Problem of Slavery in Political Discourse," in David Thomas Konig, ed., *Devising Liberty: Preserving and Creating Freedom in the New American Republic* (Stanford, 1995) and *The Pursuit of Happiness: Family and Values in Jefferson's Virginia* (New York, 1983), pp. 51–52, 160–162.

77. Janson, *Stranger in America*, p. 358.

78. Charles Ball, *Slavery in the United States: A Narrative of the Life and Adventures of Charles Ball, a Black Man* (Lewistown, Penn., 1836), pp. 219–225.

79. John W. Bear, *The Life and Travels of John W. Bear* (Baltimore, 1875), pp. 14–15.

80. Alfred M. Lorrain, *The Helm, The Sword, and the Cross: A Life Narrative* (Cincinnati, 1862), p. 89.

81. Carl Kaestle, *Pillars of the Republic: Common Schools and American Society, 1780–1860* (New York, 1983), pp. 205–208.

82. Tillson, *Reminiscences of Early Life in Illinois*, pp. 82, 102.

83. Olive Cleaveland Clarke, *Things that I Remember at Ninety-Five* (n.p., 1881), p. 3; Shepard, *Autobiography*, p. 2; and John E. Murray, "Generation(s) of Human Capital: Literacy in American Families, 1830–1875," *Journal of Interdisciplinary History*, 27 (1997): 427.

84. Julian P. Boyd, ed., *The Papers of Thomas Jefferson* (Princeton, 1950–), vol. 8, p. 468.

85. Lewis, *The Pursuit of Happiness*, p. 162.

86. The figure comes from *The New York Times*, March 25, 1995, p. A19. Andrew R. L. Cayton, "The Early National Period," in Mary Kupiec Cayton et al., eds., *Encyclopedia of American Social History* (New York, 1993), vol. 1, p. 100.

87. Timothy Dwight, *Travels in New England and New York,* ed. Barbara M. Solomon (Cambridge, Mass., 1969), vol. 1, p. xxxiv, as quoted in Jane Tompkins, *Sensational Designs: The Cultural Work of American Fiction, 1790–1860* (New York, 1985), pp. 107–108.

88. Sedgwick, *Life and Letters*, pp. 18–20.

89. Catharine M. Sedgwick, *Hope Leslie; or Early Times in Massachusetts* (New York, 1827).

90. I am indebted to Jane Tompkins, *Sensational Designs,* for opening my eyes to this theme, particularly on pp. 106–111.

91. Gary Nash, "The Hidden History of Mestizo America," *Journal of American History,* 82 (1995).

92. Henry Highland Garnet, *Walker's Appeal* (New York, 1848); Barry O'Connell, ed., *On Our Own Ground: The Complete Writings of William Appes, A Pequot* (Amherst, Mass., 1994).

93. [William Jenks], *Memoir of the Northern Kingdom, written* A.D. *1872, by the late Rev. Williamson Jaknsenykes* (Boston, 1808), p. 28.

94. David R. Roediger, *The Wages of Whiteness* (New York, 1991).

95. The phrase originated in J. R. Pole, *The Pursuit of Equality* (Berkeley, 1978). See also Mary P. Ryan, *The Cradle of the Middle Class* (New York, 1981), pp. 142–144.

6   Intimate Relations

1. Meade, *Recollections of Two Beloved Wives*, preface.

2. Ibid., pp. 11–17.

3. Ibid., pp. 31–34.

4. Ibid., pp. 35–41; quotation on p. 38.

5. Mary Gergen, "Life Stories: Pieces of a Dream," in George Rosenwald and Richard Ochberg, eds., *Storied Lives: The Cultural Politics of Self-Understanding* (New Haven, 1992) and Domna Stanton, ed., *The Female Autograph* (Chicago, 1984).

6. Henry William Ducachet, *A Tribute to the Memory of Jacob Dyckman, M.D.* (New York, 1812), p. 14; William E. Channing, *Memoir of John Gallison* (Boston, 1821), p. 3; *Memoir of Mary Lothrop* (New York, 1832), p. 15.

7. Joseph T. Buckingham, *Personal Memoirs and Recollections of Editorial Life* (Boston, 1852), vol. 1, p. 23.

8. Daniel Drake, *Pioneer Life in Kentucky* (Cincinnati, 1870), pp. xv–xvi.

9. Ibid., p. xvi.

10. Rufus Wilmot Griswold, *The Female Poets of America* (Philadelphia 1849), pp. 55–56.

11. [Caroline Gilman], *Recollections of a Housekeeper* (New York, 1834), pp. 55–58. Samuel Gilman wrote *Memoirs of a New England Village Choir,* discussed in chapter 5.

12. Eliza Follen, *Sketches of Married Life* (Boston, 1839). See also Elizabeth Bancroft Schlesinger, "Two Early Harvard Wives: Eliza Farrar and Eliza Follen," *New England Quarterly,* 38 (1965): 157–165.

13. [Leonard Woods], *The Memoir of the Life of Mrs. Harriet Newell* (Lexington, 1815), pp. 174–220.

14. Eber D. Howe, *Autobiography and Recollections of a Pioneer Printer* (Painesville, Ohio, 1878), pp. 30–31.

15. George Rockingham Gilmer, *Sketches of Some of the First Settlers of Upper Georgia* (Baltimore, 1970 [1855]), pp. 217–218, 226–227.

16. Phineas Price, *A Narrative of the Life and Travels, Preaching and Suffering of Phineas Price* (Philadelphia, 1843), p. 109.

17. Elijah Iles, *Sketches of Early Life and Times in Kentucky, Missouri, and Illinois* (Springfield, Ill., 1883).

18. Peter Cooper, *A Sketch of the Early Days and Business Life of Peter Cooper: An Autobiography* (New York, 1877), pp. 19–21.

19. John D. Paxton, *A Memoir of J. D. Paxton, D.D.* (Philadelphia, 1870), pp. 70–71, 298.

20. John Tevis, "Autobiographical Sketch," in Julia Tevis, *Sixty Years in a School Room: An Autobiography of Mrs. Julia A. Tevis* (Cincinnati, 1878).

21. James McBride, *Pioneer Biography: Sketches of the Lives of Some of the Early Settlers of Butler County, Ohio,* ed. Laura McBride Stembel (Bowie, Md., 1991 [originally published in Cincinnati, 1869]), vol. 1, p. viii.

22. Elaine Forman Crane, *Ebb Tide in New England: Women, Seaports, and Social Change, 1630–1800* (Boston, 1998), pp. 208–212.

23. R. Kent Newmyer, *Supreme Court Justice Joseph Story: Statesman of the Old Republic* (Chapel Hill, 1985), pp. 45–47, as quoted in Rosemarie Zagarri, "Romeo, Juliet, and the First Political Parties," paper delivered at the annual meeting of the Society for the History of the Early Republic, Harper's Ferry, Virginia, 1998.

24. John Chambers, *Autobiography,* ed. John Carl Parish (Iowa City, 1908), pp. 6–10.

25. Elias Smith, *The Life, Conversion, Preaching, Travels and Sufferings of Elias Smith* (Portsmouth, N.H., 1816), pp. 50, 89.

26. John Thompson, *Autobiography of Deacon John Thompson,* comp. Josiah H. Thompson (Farmington, Me., 1920), pp. 16–38.

27. Matthew Vassar, *The Autobiography and Letters of Matthew Vassar,* ed. Elizabeth Hazelton Haight (New York, 1916), pp. 26–29, 7.

28. Cooper, *A Sketch of the Early Days,* pp. 2–3.

29. Martin Van Buren, "The Autobiography of M_V_B_," ed. John C. Fitzpatrick, in *Annual Report to AHA for year 1918,* 2: 10–12.

30. Edward Thurlow Weed, *Autobiography*, ed. Harriet A. Weed (Boston, 1883), pp. 1–6.

31. Chester Harding, *My Egotistigraphy* (Cambridge, 1866), p. 20.

32. Stephen Higginson Tyng, *Record of the Life and Work of Rev. Stephen Higginson Tyng*, ed. Charles Rockland Tyng (New York, 1890), pp. 37–39.

33. Chambers, *Autobiography*, pp. 10–11.

34. Morgan Dix, ed., *Memoirs of John Adams Dix* (New York, 1883), pp. 14, 51–55.

35. Thomas Hart Benton, *Thirty Years View* (New York, 1880 [1866]), vol. 1, p. ii.

36. Chambers, *Autobiography*, pp. 10–11.

37. Samuel Alfred Foot, *Autobiography* (New York, 1972), p. 10.

38. Bronson Alcott, *The Journals of Bronson Alcott*, ed. Odell Shepard (Boston, 1938), vol. 1.

39. Vassar, *Autobiography*, pp. 27–29.

40. Harding, *My Egotistigraphy*, p. 11.

41. Allen Trimble, "Autobiography," in *The Old Northwest Genealogical Quarterly*, 9 (1907): 13–15.

42. Samuel Rogers, *Autobiography of Elder Samuel Rogers*, ed. John I. Rogers (Cincinnati, 1880), pp. 14–16.

43. Tyng, *Record of the Life and Work*, p. 38.

44. Paxton, *A Memoir of J. D. Paxton*, pp. 22–26.

45. Elijah Martindale, *Autobiography and Sermons of Elder Elijah Martindale* (Indianapolis, 1892), p. 1.

46. John Belton O'Neall, *Biographical Sketches of the Bench and Bar of South Carolina* (Charleston, 1859), vol. 1, p. 185.

47. Catharine M. Sedgwick, *Life and Letters of Catharine M. Sedgwick* (New York, 1871), p. 38.

48. Alma Lutz, *Emma Willard: Daughter of Democracy* (Washington, D.C., 1929), pp. 23–25.

49. Margo Culley, *A Day at a Time: The Diary Literature of American Women from 1764 to the Present* (New York, 1985), p. 83.

50. Nell Painter, *Sojourner Truth: A Life, A Symbol* (New York, 1996), pp. 11–12.

51. Charles Ball, *Fifty Years in Chains, or, The Life of an American Slave* (New York, 1836), pp. 10–11.

52. William Hayden, *Narrative of William Hayden* (Cincinnati, Ohio, 1846), pp. 26–30.

53. Brenda E. Stevenson, *Life in Black and White: Family and Community in the Slave South* (New York, 1996), pp. 226–232.

54. *Portico*, 2 (October, 1816): 286, 293; and *Analectic Magazine and Naval Chronicle*, 8 (September, 1816): 193–209, as quoted in Scott E. Casper, *Constructing American Lives: Biography and Culture in Nineteenth-Century America* (Chapel Hill, 1999).

55. R. Laurence Moore, *Selling God: American Religion in the Marketplace of Culture* (New York, 1994), pp. 20–23.

56. *Vermont Evangelical Magazine* (1809): 113–116.

57. Laura McCall, "'With All the Wild, Trembling, Rapturous Feelings of a Lover': Men, Women, and Sexuality in American Literature, 1820–1860," *Journal of the Early Republic,* 14 (1994): 88.

58. [Sukey Vickery Watson], *Emily Hamilton, A Novel By a Young Lady of Worcester County* (Worcester, 1803), pp. 45–47.

59. Moore, *Selling God*, pp. 20–27.

60. S. G. Goodrich, *Recollections of a Lifetime, or Men and Things I have Seen: In a Series of Familiar Letters to a Friend* (New York, 1857), vol. 1, pp. 125, 109.

61. *Memoir of Mary Anne Hooker* (Philadelphia, 1840), pp. 9–13.

62. [Lydia Marie Sigourney], *The Square Table* (Hartford, 1819).

63. Dee E. Andrews, *The Methodists and Revolutionary America, 1760–1800: The Shaping of an Evangelical Culture* (Princeton, 2000).

64. Elizabeth W. Levick, *Recollections of Early Days* (Philadelphia, 1881), pp. 36–37.

65. Christine Stansell, *City of Women: Sex and Class in New York, 1789–1860* (New York, 1986).

66. Steven C. Bullock, *Revolutionary Brotherhood: Freemasonry and the Transformation of the American Social Order, 1730–1840* (Chapel Hill, 1996).

67. William C. Dowling, *Literary Federalism in the Age of Jefferson: Joseph Dennie and the Port folio, 1801–1812* (Columbia, S.C., 1999).

68. Timothy Dwight, *Travels in New-England and New-York,* ed. Barbara Miller Solomon, vol. 1, pp. 365–366, as quoted in Lawrence Buell, *New England Literary Culture: From Revolution through Renaissance* (New York, 1986), p. 32.

69. Sidney Willard, *Memoirs of Youth and Manhood* (Cambridge, 1855), two vols.

70. Dowling, *Literary Federalism*.

71. Tony Freyer, *Producers Versus Capitalists: Constitutional Conflict in Antebellum America* (Charlottesville, 1994).

72. R. Jackson Wilson, *Figures of Speech: American Writers and the Literary Marketplace from Benjamin Franklin to Emily Dickinson* (New York, 1989), pp. 72–77.

73. Andrews, *The Methodists and Revolutionary America,* ms. pp. 209–211, 221.

74. Christine Heyrman, *Southern Cross: The Beginnings of the Bible Belt* (New York, 1997), pp. 17–19.

75. Ibid., pp. 145–146, 160.

76. Andrews, *The Methodists and Revolutionary America,* ms. pp. 255–258.

77. Sylvia R. Frey and Betty Wood, *Come Shouting to Zion: African American Protestantism in the American South and Caribbean to 1830* (Chapel Hill, 1998), p. 143.

78. Jarena Lee, *The Life and Religious Experiences of Jarena Lee,* ed. William L. Andrews (Bloomington, 1986); Painter, *Sojourner Truth*.

79. Charles G. Finney, *An Autobiography* (New York, 1903), pp. 47–70.

80. Jacob Knapp, *Autobiography of Elder Jacob Knapp* (New York, 1968), p. 29.

81. James B. Finley, *Autobiography of Rev. James B. Finley* (Cincinnati, 1854), pp. 166–167.

82. [Leonard Woods], *The Memoir of the Life of Mrs. Harriet Newell* (Lexington, 1815), pp. 2–3, 72–77.

83. Catherine H. Birney, *Sarah and Angelina Grimke: The First American Women Advocates of Abolition and Woman's Rights* (Boston, 1885), p. 28, as quoted in Gerda Lerner, *The Feminist Thought of Sarah Grimke* (New York, 1998), p. 8.

84. C. G. Finney, *The Inner and Outer Life of C. G. Finney* (London, 1882), pp. 3–4.

85. Ebenezer Francis Newell, *Life and Observations of Rev. E. F. Newell* (Worcester, 1847), pp. 53–77; Martindale, *Autobiography*, pp. 10–14, 25.

86. Ray Potter, *Memoirs of the Life and Religious Experience of Ray Potter* (Providence, 1829), p. vii; Knapp, *Autobiography*, pp. 15–18; and Arabella Mary Stuart Willson, *Lives of Mrs. Ann H. Judson and Mrs. Sarah B. Judson, with a Biographical Sketch of Mrs. Emily C. Judson, missionaries to Burmah* (New York, 1855), pp. 203–229.

87. Asa Wild, *A Short Sketch of the Religious Experience, and Spiritual Travels of Asa Wild* (Amsterdam, N.Y., 1824), pp. 9–15.

88. Asa Mahan, *Autobiography, Intellectual, Moral and Spiritual* (London, 1882), pp. 41–57.

89. Theodore Clapp, *Autobiographical Sketches* (Boston, 1859), pp. 14–15, 8.

90. Alcott, *Journals*, vol. 1, p. 13.

91. Robert Fogel, *The Fourth Great Awakening and the Future of Egalitarianism* (forthcoming), chap. 2, n34.

92. L. H. Sigourney, "My Dead," in *Letters to My Pupils* (New York, 1851), pp. 205–320.

93. Clapp, *Autobiographical Sketches*, p. vi.

94. John Fetterhoff, *The Life of Rev. John Fetterhoff* (Chambersburg, Penn., 1883), pp. 5–18.

95. Knapp, *Autobiography of Elder Jacob Knapp*, pp. 13–15; Price, *A Narrative of the Life and Travels*, pp. 6, 18, 29.

96. Edward Hicks, *Memoirs* (Philadelphia, 1851), pp. 19–21.

97. Jane Tompkins, *Sensational Designs: The Cultural Work of American Fiction, 1790–1860* (New York, 1985), pp. 126–154; Gary Laderman, *The Sacred Remains: American Attitudes Towards Death, 1799–1883* (New Haven, 1996), pp. 42ff; Elias Smith, *The Life, Conversion, Preaching, Travels and Sufferings of Elias Smith* (Portsmouth, 1816), pp. 50, 89.

98. These figures have come from a survey of the databases of the American Antiquarian Society.

99. Woloch, *Women and the American Experience*, vol. 1, p. 103.

100. Cynthia Taggart, *Poems*, 2nd ed. (Cambridge, 1834), pp. xxxvi–xl.

101. Colin Campbell, *The Romantic Ethic and the Spirit of Modern Consumerism* (New York, 1987), pp. 129–137, 69.

102. John T. Noonan, Jr., in *The Lustre of Our Country: The American Experience of Religious Freedom* (Berkeley and Los Angeles, 1998), pp. 95–115, invents a sister for Alexis de Tocqueville to lecture him on his neglect of the true political import of American religion.

7   Reform

1. Levick, *Recollections of Early Days*, pp. 16–17.

2. Steven C. Bullock, *Revolutionary Brotherhood: Freemasonry and the Transformation of the American Social Order, 1730–1840* (Chapel Hill, 1996).

3. Todd S. Gernes, "Poetic Justice: Sarah Forten, Eliza Earle and the Paradox of Intellectual Property," *New England Quarterly*, 121 (1998): 231–232.

4. Jeffrey P. Brown, "The Ohio Federalists, 1803–1830," *Journal of the Early Republic*, 2 (1982): 270–271.

5. Jesse Torrey, Jr., *The Herald of Knowledge* (Washington, D.C., 1822), pp. 32–33.

6. Timothy Claxton, *Memoir of a Mechanic* (Boston, 1839), pp. 133, 61–62, 8–87, 104.

7. Nathan O. Hatch, *The Democratization of American Christianity* (New Haven, 1989).

8. [Samuel Knapp], *Extracts from a Journal of Travels in North America* (Boston, 1818), p. 19.

9. John H. Wigger, "Taking Heaven by Storm: Enthusiasm and Early American Methodism, 1770–1820," *Journal of the Early Republic*, 14 (1994): 177–179.

10. John Brooke, *The Heart of the Commonwealth: Society and Political Culture in Worcester County, Massachusetts, 1713–1861* (New York, 1989).

11. Hatch, *Democratization of American Christianity*, pp. 14–15.

12. Ibid., p. 174.

13. John W. Francis, *Old New York; or, Reminiscences of the Past Sixty Years* (New York, 1850), pp. 125–137.

14. As quoted in Howard Mumford Jones, *America and French Culture, 1750–1848* (Montreal, 1928), p. 410.

15. John Ball, *Autobiography*, compiled by Kate Ball Powers, Flora Ball Hopkins, and Lucy Ball (Glendale, Calif., 1925), pp. 11–12, 63–65, 129.

16. *Memoir of David Hoover written by himself* (Richmond, Ind., 1857), p. 19.

17. "A Sermon Delivered at the Ordination of the Rev. Samuel Gilman," as quoted in Daniel Walker Howe, "A Massachusetts Yankee in Senator Calhoun's Court: Samuel Gilman in South Carolina," *New England Quarterly*, 44 (1971): 202.

18. Alexis de Tocqueville, *Democracy in America*, ed. Phillips Bradley (New York, 1954), vol. 1, pp. 304–307.

19. Whitney R. Cross, *The Burned-Over District: The Social and Intellectual History of Enthusiastic Religion in Western New York, 1800–1850* (Ithaca, 1950).

20. Sidney Mead, "Denominationalism: The Shape of Protestantism in America," *Church History*, 23 (1954).

21. James Flint, *Letters from America* (Edinburgh, 1822), in Reuben Gold Twaites, ed., *Early Western Travels, 1748–1846* (Cleveland, 1904), pp. 47, 54–55.

22. John Frost, "Families Within the Boundaries of the United Society of Whitestown, April 1813–July 1816," as tabulated in Mary P. Ryan, *The Cradle of the Middle Class: The Family in Oneida County, New York, 1790–1865* (New York, 1981), p. 257. In 20 percent only the wife and children were members; in 3 percent only husbands.

23. Sylvia R. Frey and Betty Wood, *Come Shouting to Zion: African American Protestantism in the American South and British Caribbean to 1830* (Chapel Hill, 1998), pp. 118ff.

24. Ibid., pp. 144–147, 158–161.

25. Jon Butler, *Awash in a Sea of Faith: Christianizing the American People* (Cambridge, Mass., 1990), pp. 129–163.

26. Christine Heyrman, *Southern Cross: The Beginnings of the Bible Belt* (New York, 1997), pp. 67–69.

27. Flint, *Letters from America*, pp. 47, 61, 141.

28. Moses Grandy, *Narrative of the Life of Moses Grandy* (Boston, 1844), p. 42.

29. William Meade, *Sermon at the Opening of the convention, of the Protestant Episcopal Church of Virginia held in Petersburg, 1828* (Richmond, Va., 1828), p. 7.

30. [C. J. Ingersoll], *A Discourse Concerning the Influence of America on the Mind*, (Philadelphia, 1823), pp. 50–64.

31. Sidney Earl Mead, *The Lively Experiment: The Shaping of Christianity in America* (New York, 1963).

32. Alfred M. Lorrain, *The Helm, the Sword, and the Cross: A Life Narrative* (Cincinnati, 1862), pp. 251–278, 441–442.

33. Lois W. Banner, "Religion and Reform in the Early Republic: The Role of Youth, I," *American Quarterly*, 23 (1971).

34. William Breitenbach, "Sons of the Fathers: Temperance Reformers and the Legacy of the American Revolution," *Journal of the Early Republic*, 3 (1983): 78–80.

35. As quoted in Mark Edward Lender and James Kirby Martin, *Drinking in America: A History* (New York, 1982).

36. Freeman Hunt, *Lives of American Merchants* (New York, 1858), pp. 239–245.

37. Lender and Martin, *Drinking in America*, p. 48.

38. As quoted in Stanley K. Schultz, "Temperance Reform in the Antebellum

South: Social Control and Urban Order," *The South Atlantic Quarterly*, 83 (1984): 325.

39. As quoted from *A Year's Residence in the United States* (London, 1818) in A. Gregory Schneider, "Social Religion, the Christian Homes, and Republican Spirituality in Antebellum Methodism," *Journal of the Early Republic*, 10 (1990): 82.

40. W. J. Rorabaugh, *The Alcoholic Republic: An American Tradition* (New York, 1979), pp. 7–8. The average adult man drank eight ounces of hard liquor a day. See also Merton M. Hyman et al., *Drinkers, Drinking, and Alcohol-Related Mortality and Hospitalizations: A Statistical Compendium* (New Brunswick, N.J., 1980).

41. Harrison Hall, *The Distiller*, 2nd ed. (Philadelphia, 1818), p. 2.

42. John Marsh, *Temperance Recollections: Labors, Defeats, Triumphs, An Autobiography* (New York, 1866), p. 9.

43. Daniel Drake, *Pioneer Life in Kentucky* (Cincinnati, 1870), pp. 52–56.

44. Edward Thurlow Weed, *Autobiography*, ed. Harriet A. Weed (Boston, 1883), p. 16.

45. Ezra Michener, *Autobiographical Notes from the Life and Letters of Ezra Michener* (Philadelphia, 1893), pp. 3, 1, 34.

46. Marsh, *Temperance Recollections*, p. 18.

47. D. N. Prime, *The Autobiography of an Octogenarian* (Newburyport, Mass., 1873), pp. 87–88.

48. Edward Hicks, *Memoirs of the Life and Religious Labors of Edward Hicks* (Philadelphia, 1851), p. 35.

49. Nathaniel Bouton, *Autobiography of Nathaniel Bouton, D.C.*, ed. John Bell Bouton (New York, 1879), p. 11.

50. Joseph T. Buckingham, *Personal Memoirs and Recollections of Editorial Life* (Boston, 1852), vol. 1, p. 25.

51. Michener, *Autobiographical Notes*, p. 3.

52. Charles Kirk, *Recollections of Charles Kirk* (Philadelphia, 1891), p. 9.

53. Andrus V. Green, *The Life and Experience of A. V. Green* (Wooster, 1848), pp. 9–10.

54. John Livingston, *Biographical Sketches of Eminent American Lawyers, Now Living, II and III* (April and May, 1852): 406–407.

55. Louis C. Jones, ed., *Growing Up in the Cooper Country* (Syracuse, 1965), pp. 116–117. This is a published excerpt from Wright's memoirs, *Human Life Illustrated in My Individual Experience* (Boston, 1849).

56. Eber D. Howe, *Autobiography and Recollections of a Pioneer Printer* (Painesville, Ohio, 1878), p. 2; George Rockingham Gilmer, *Sketches of Some of the First Settlers of Upper Georgia; and of the Cherokees, and the Author* (Baltimore, 1970 [repr. of 1855 ed.]), pp. 181–182.

57. Marsh, *Temperance Recollections*, pp. 9–10.

58. Sidney Willard, *Memoirs of Youth and Manhood* (Cambridge, 1855), vol. 1, p. 252.

59. Richard Carter, *A Short Sketch of the Author's Life* (Versailles, Ky., 1825), pp. 25–26.

60. Weed, *Autobiography*, pp. 58–59.

61. Buckingham, *Personal Memoirs*, vol. 1, pp. 33–35, 46.

62. As quoted in Rorabaugh, *The Alcoholic Republic*, pp. 138, 279n16.

63. Marsh, *Temperance Recollections*, pp. 16–17.

64. Anson Jones, *Memoranda and Official Correspondence Relating to the Republic of Texas* (New York, 1859), p. 10.

65. Michener, *Autobiographical Notes*, p. 29.

66. Ichabod Washburn, *Autobiography and Memorials* (Boston, 1878), pp. 56–57; Marsh, *Temperance Recollections*, pp. 13–18.

67. Joseph Bates, *The Autobiography of Joseph Bates* (Battle Creek, Mich., 1868), pp. 172, 179, 207–212.

68. Kirk, *Recollections*, pp. 28–29.

69. Heman Bangs, *The Autobiography and Journal of Rev. Heman Bangs* (New York, 1872); H. M. Brackenridge, *Recollections of Persons and Places in the West*, 2nd ed., enl. (Philadelphia, 1868), p. 13.

70. Richard Cecil Stone, *Life Incidents of Home, School and Church* (St. Louis, 1874), pp. 63–64, 92, 146–147.

71. Richard B. Morris and Jeffrey B. Morris, eds., *Encyclopedia of American History* (New York, 1996), p. 101; Donald Yacovone, "The Transformation of the Black Temperance Movement, 1827–1854: An Interpretation," *Journal of the Early Republic*, 8 (Fall, 1988): 281.

72. Richard R. John, "Taking Sabbatarianism Seriously: The Postal System, the Sabbath and the Transformation of American Political Culture," *Journal of the Early Republic*, 10 (1990): 538.

73. Rorabaugh, *The Alcoholic Republic*, pp. 40–46, 191–195.

74. Paul E. Johnson, *A Shopkeeper's Millennium: Society and Revivals in Rochester, New York, 1815–1837* (New York, 1978); Robert Abzug, *Cosmos Crumbling: American Reform and the Religious Imagination* (New York, 1994); and Barbara Leslie Epstein, *The Politics of Domesticity: Women, Evangelism, and Temperance in Nineteenth-Century America* (Middletown, Conn., 1981).

75. Rorabaugh, *The Alcoholic Republic*, pp. 7–8.

76. Ryan, *Cradle of the Middle Class*, pp. 11–16.

77. Jacqueline S. Reinier, *From Virtue to Character: American Childhood, 1775–1850* (New York, 1996).

78. Ronald G. Walters, *American Reformers, 1815–1860* (New York, 1978), p. 112.

79. As quoted in Hatch, *Democratization of American Christianity*, pp. 128–129; Bruce Dorsey, "Friends Becoming Enemies: Philadelphia Benevolence and the Neglected Era of American Quaker History," *Journal of the Early Republic*, 18 (1998): 408.

80. Elias Smith, *The Life, Conversion, Preaching, Travels and Sufferings of Elias Smith* (Portsmouth, N.H., 1816), pp. 49–51, 383–396; Michael G. Kenny, *The Perfect Law of*

Liberty: Elias Smith and the Providential History of America (Washington, D.C., 1994).

81. R. Laurence Moore, *Selling God: American Religion in the Marketplace of Culture* (New York, 1994), pp. 82–84.

82. Thomas Everard, *Some Plain Scriptural Observations and Remarks on what is denominated Shouting* (Philadelphia, 1820); [John E. Watson], *Methodist Error; or, Friendly, Christian Advice* (Trenton, 1819).

83. Ray Allen Billington, *The Protestant Crusade, 1800–1860* (Chicago, 1938), pp. 44–52.

84. Moore, *Selling God*, p. 18.

85. Howard B. Rock, *Artisans of the New Republic: The Tradesmen of New York City in the Age of Jefferson* (New York, 1979), p. 37.

86. Paul Goodman, *Of One Blood: Abolitionism and the Origins of Racial Equality* (Berkeley, 1998), p. 10.

87. Samuel Alford Foot, *Autobiography* (New York, 1872), pp. 11, 21, 27, 31; Chambers, *Autobiography*, pp. 6, 20, 15.

88. Culley, *A Day at a Time*, p. 86.

89. Flint, *Letters from America*, p. 138.

90. Levi Hathaway, *The Narrative of Levi Hathaway* (Providence, 1820), pp. 14–19.

91. Prime, *Autobiography of an Octogenarian*, pp. 37–38.

92. Myra Glenn, *Campaigns Against Corporal Punishment: Prisoners, Sailors, Women, and Children in Antebellum America* (Albany, 1984); Sidney Willard, *Memoirs of Youth and Manhood* (Cambridge, 1855), vol. 1, p. 221; Prime, *Autobiography of an Octogenarian*, p. 62.

93. John Griscom, *Memoir of John Griscom*, ed. John H. Griscom, M.D. (New York, 1859), p. 26; Stone, *Life Incidents of Home, School and Church*, pp. 29–31; Julia A. Tevis, *Sixty Years in a Schoolroom: An Autobiography of Mrs. Julia A. Tevis* (Cincinnati, 1876), pp. 166–168.

94. Zephaniah Swift Moore, "The Sabbath a Permanent and Benevolent Institution" (Boston, 1818), p. 27, as quoted in Jonathan Sassi, "To Envision a Godly Society: The Public Christianity of the Southern New England Clergy, 1783–1833" (Ph.D. diss., UCLA, 1996), p. 311.

95. John, "Taking Sabbatarianism Seriously," pp. 528–529.

96. James R. Rohrer, "Sunday Mails and the Church-State Theme in Jacksonian America," *Journal of the Early Republic*, 7 (1987): 53–78; John, "Taking Sabbatarianism Seriously," p. 547; Bernard Bailyn et al., *The Great Republic* (Lexington, Mass., 1992), pp. 435–439.

97. Michener, *Autobiographical Notes*, pp. 30–31; Hatch, *Democratization of American Christianity*, p. 100; John, "Taking Sabbatarianism Seriously," pp. 526–528, 548–564.

98. John, "Taking Sabbatarianism Seriously," p. 558.

99. As quoted in Jan Lewis, "Southerners and the Problem of Slavery in Political

Discourse," in David Thomas Konig, ed., *Devising Liberty: Preserving and Creating Freedom in the New American Republic* (Stanford, 1995); Anthony Iaccarino, "Virginia and the National Contest Over Slavery in the Early Republic, 1780–1833" (Ph.D. diss., UCLA, 1999).

100. Goodman, *Of One Blood*, p. 14; Paul Finkelman, "Evading the Ordinance: the Persistence of Bondage in Indiana and Illinois," *Journal of the Early Republic*, 9 (1989): 49.

101. Gilmer, *Sketches of Some of the First Settlers of Upper Georgia*, p. 184; Allen Trimble, "Autobiography," in *The Old Northwest Genealogical Quarterly*, 9 (1907), pp. 31–32; Stephen Higginson Tyng, ed., *Record of the Life and Work of the Rev. Stephen Higginson Tyng*, ed. Charles Rockland Tyng (New York, 1890), p. 77.

102. Morris Birkbeck, *Notes on a Journey*, 2nd ed. (London, 1818), p. 17; as quoted in Lewis, "Southerners and the Problem of Slavery," p. 286; James David Essig, "A Very Wintry Season: Virginia Baptists and Slavery, 1785–1797," *Virginia Magazine of History and Biography*, 88 (1980): 183.

103. John D. Paxton, *A Memoir of J. D. Paxton, D.D.* (Philadelphia, 1870), pp. 74–44; *Letters on Slavery* (Lexington, 1833), p. 11; David W. Blight, "Perceptions of Southern Intransigence and the Rise of Radical Antislavery Thought, 1816–1830," *Journal of the Early Republic*, 3 (1983): 141. Rankin later published *Letters on American Slavery* (Newburyport, 1837), which he had written to his brother in Virginia in 1823. Bourne published *The Book and Slavery Irreconcilable* in 1816.

104. Annals of the Congress of the United States, Fourth Congress (Washington, D.C., 1849), vol. 6, pp. 2015–2018; Sixth Congress (Washington, D.C., 1851), vol. 10, pp. 229–230; Paxton, *Letters on Slavery*, pp. 35–36.

105. Blight, "Perceptions of Southern Intransigence," pp. 144–147, 153, 156–157.

106. Ira Berlin, *Slaves Without Masters* (New York, 1974); John B. Boles, *Black Southerners, 1619–1869* (Lexington, Ky., 1983), pp. 133–137.

107. David R. Roediger, *The Wages of Whiteness* (New York, 1991); Alexander Saxton, *The Rise and Fall of the White Republic: Class Politics and Mass Culture in Nineteenth-Century America* (New York, 1990); Gary B. Nash, *Forging Freedom: the Formation of Philadephia's Black Antebellum Community, 1720–1840* (Cambridge, Mass., 1988).

108. Goodman, *Of One Blood*, p. 17; Spring, *Memoir of Mills*, pp. 123–131; Howe, *Autobiography*, p. 46.

109. James Oliver Horton and Lois E. Horton, *In Hope of Liberty: Culture, Community and Protest Among Northern Free Blacks, 1700–1860* (New York, 1997); Goodman, *Of One Blood*, pp. 26–27.

110. Howe, *Autobiography*, p. 46; Lloyd S. Kramer, *Lafayette in Two Worlds: Public Cultures and Personal Identities in an Age of Revolutions* (Chapel Hill, 1996), p. 165; James Brewer Stewart, "The Emergence of Racial Modernity and the Rise of the White North, 1790–1840," *The Journal of the Early Republic* (1998): 195–198. See also Shane White, *Somewhat More Independent: The End of Slavery in New York City, 1770–1810* (Athens, Ga., 1991).

III. Goodman, *Of One Blood;* Lerner, *The Feminist Thought of Sarah Grimke,* pp. 20–21; e.g., Sarah Moore Grimke, *Appeal to the Christian women of the South* (Philadelphia, 1836). Grimke's *Appeal* was publicly burned in South Carolina. Josephus Wheaton, *The Equality of Mankind and the Evils of Slavery Illustrated* (Boston, 1820), pp. 3–5, 11–22; Jesse Torrey, jun., *A Portraiture of Domestic Slavery* (Philadelphia, 1817), pp. 12–13, 32, 47–48.

112. Benjamin Silliman, *Journal of Travels in England, Holland and Scotland* (New Haven, 1820), 3rd ed. [orig. pub. 1809], pp. 105, 272.

113. Sterling Stuckey, *Slave Culture: Nationalist Theory and the Foundations of Black America* (New York, 1987), pp. 122–128; Harvey Reed, *Platform for Change: The Foundations of the Northern Free Black Community, 1775–1865* (East Lansing, Mich., 1994), pp. 27–28. See also Maria W. Stewart's *An Address Delivered at the African Masonic Hall* (Boston, 1833). Goodman, *Of One Blood,* pp. 87, 31; Henry Highland Garnet, *Walker's Appeal* (New York, 1848); Stuckey, *Slave Culture,* pp. 115–123, 137; Reed, *Platform for Change,* p. 27; Stewart, "The Emergence of Racial Modernity," p. 197.

114. Daniel Walker Howe, *Making the American Self: Jonathan Edwards to Abraham Lincoln* (Cambridge, Mass., 1997); Marsh, *Temperance Recollections,* p. 14.

115. Sarah Hale, *Sketches of American Character* (Boston, 1829), p. 53. See also Lori D. Ginzberg, *Women and the Work of Benevolence: Morality, Politics, and Class in the 19th-Century United States* (New Haven, 1990); Richard D. Brown, *Knowledge Is Power: The Diffusion of Information in Early America, 1700–1865* (New York, 1989), p. 221; Vassar, *Autobiography and Letters,* p. 7; [Ingersoll], *A Discourse Concerning the Influence of America on the Mind,* p. 67.

116. Lois Banner, "Religion and Reform in the Early Republic: The Role of Youth," *American Quarterly,* 23 (1971).

117. Heyrman, *Southern Cross,* pp. 17–19.

118. Richard J. Calhoun, ed., *Witness to Sorrow: The Antebellum Autobiography of William J. Grayson* (Columbia, S.C., 1990), p. 65.

119. [Ingersoll], *A Discourse Concerning the Influence of America on the Mind,* p. 36.

120. Nancy F. Cott, *The Bonds of Womanhood: "Woman's Sphere" in New England, 1780–1835* (New Haven, 1977), pp. 6–9.

121. [Orsamus Cook Merrill], *The Happiness of America* (Bennington, Vt., 1804).

8 A New National Identity

1. John Wyche to Thomas Jefferson, March 19, 1809, Bixby Collection, Missouri Historical Society, St. Louis.

2. Stephen Elliott, *An Address Delivered at the Opening of the Medical College* (Charleston, 1826), pp. 11–13.

3. John Ashworth, "The Relationship between Capitalism and Humanitarianism," *American Historical Review,* 92 (1987): 797–812.

4. Eric Foner, *Free Soil, Free Labor, Free Men: The Ideology of the Republican Party Before the Civil War* (New York, 1970).

5. James Oakes, *The Ruling Race: A History of American Slaveholders* (New York, 1982).

6. Kenneth S. Greenberg, *Masters and Statesmen: The Political Culture of American Slavery* (Baltimore, 1985).

7. John Bach McMaster, *The History of People of the United States* (New York, 1888–1914), pp. 4–5.

8. William J. Cooper, Jr., *The South and the Politics of Slavery, 1828–1856* (Baton Rouge, 1978).

9. Bruce Dorsey, "Friends Becoming Enemies: Philadelphia Benevolence and the Neglected Era of American Quaker History," *Journal of the Early Republic*, 18 (1998): 403.

10. John H. Wigger, *Taking Heaven by Storm: Methodism and the Rise of Popular Christianity in America* (New York, 1998); Dee E. Andrews, *The Methodists and Revolutionary America, 1760–1800: The Shaping of an Evangelical Culture* (Princeton, 2000).

11. Drew Gilpin Faust, *The Creation of Confederate Nationalism: Ideology and Identity in the Civil War South* (Baton Rouge, 1988), p. 16.

12. Ellen Wayles Coolidge, "2 Autobiographical Papers," University of Virginia Library manuscripts; Jan Lewis, *The Pursuit of Happiness: Family and Values in Jefferson's Virginia* (Cambridge, 1983), pp. 152–153.

13. Barbara L. Fladeland, "Compensated Emancipation: A Rejected Alternative," *Journal of Southern History*, 42 (1976): 175.

14. Kenneth S. Greenberg, *Honor and Slavery* (Princeton, 1996), pp. 83–84.

15. Michael O'Brien and David Moltke-Hansen, eds., *Intellectual Life in Antebellum Charleston* (Knoxville, 1986), p. 43; A. V. Huff, "The Eager and the Vulture: Changing Attitudes Towards Nationalism in Fourth of July Orations, Delivered in Charleston, 1778–1860," *South Atlantic Quarterly*, 73 (1974): 11.

16. Craig Hanyan with Mary L. Hanyan, *De Witt Clinton and the Rise of the People's Men* (Montreal, 1996), p. 228.

17. Jefferson to Gen. James Breckinridge, Monticello, Feb. 15, 1821, in Andrew A. Lipscomb and Albert Ellery Bergh, eds., *The Writings of Thomas Jefferson* (Washington, D.C., 1905), vol. 15, pp. 313–315; Jefferson to John Taylor, Feb. 14, 1821, ibid. vol. 18, p. 313; and Jefferson to Joseph Campbell, Jan. 31, 1821, ibid. vol. 15, p. 311, as cited in Brown, *The Strength of a People*, p. 97.

18. Joseph J. Ellis, *Passionate Sage: The Character and Legacy of John Adams* (New York, 1993).

19. Joyce Appleby, "Recovering America's Historic Diversity: Beyond Exceptionalism," *Journal of American History*, 79 (1992).

20. Bruce Laurie, *Working People of Philadelphia, 1800–1850* (Philadelphia, 1980), pp. 191–193.

21. James B. Finley, *Autobiography of Rev. James B. Finley* (Cincinnati, 1854), p. 118.

22. Nathan O. Hatch, *The Democratization of American Christianity* (New Haven, 1989), pp. 22, 64.

23. Gardiner Spring, *Memoir of Samuel John Mills*, 2nd ed. (Boston, 1829), p. 27.

24. Ruth Bloch, *Visionary Republic: Millennial Themes in American Thought, 1756–1800* (New York, 1985).

25. Leonard Bacon, *The Christian Doctrine of Stewardship in Respect to Property* (New Haven, 1832).

26. Dorsey, "Friends Becoming Enemies," p. 398.

27. Nancy Woloch, *Women and the American Experience, Volume One: To 1920* (New York, 1994), 2nd ed., pp. 99–102.

28. DeWitt Clinton, *An Introductory Discourse, Delivered Before the Literary and Philosophical Society of New-York on the Fourth of May, 1814* (New York, 1815), p. 17.

29. See, for instance, [Le Baron de Montlezun], *Voyage fait dans les annees 1816 et 1817, de New-Yorck a la Nouvelle-Orleans* (Paris, 1818), vol. 1, pp. 6–17, 54–65; Jean Guillaume, Baron Hyde de Neuville, *Memoires et Souvenirs du Baron Hyde de Neuville* (Paris, 1888–1892), vol. 1, p. 453; Edouard de Montule, *A Voyage to North America, and the West Indies in 1817* (London, 1821); Maria de Las Mercedes Merlin, *La Havane* (Paris, 1844), vol. 1, pp. 80–81.

30. J. H. B. Latrobe, ed., *The Journal of Benjamin Latrobe: Being the Notes and Sketches of an Architect, Naturalist and Traveler in the United States from 1796 to 1820* (New York, 1905), p. 170. An American, Latrobe was born and reared in Europe.

31. Patricia Cline Cohen, *A Calculating People: The Spread of Numeracy in Early America* (Chicago, 1982), p. 4.

32. William Austin, *Peter Rugg: The Missing Man* (Boston, 1908) [originally published 1824], pp. 96–101.

33. E. S. Thomas, *Reminiscences of the Last Sixty-Five Years* (Hartford, 1840), p. 11.

34. William Neill, *Autobiography of William Neill* (Philadelphia, 1861), pp. 26–27.

35. Charles Kirk, *Recollections of Charles Kirk* (Philadelphia, 1891), p. 21.

36. Diane Lindstrom, in *Economic Development in the Philadelphia Region, 1810–1850* (New York, 1978), pp. 11–12, notes the rapidity with which farmers gave up making things when they could buy them.

37. Frederic W. Lincoln, Jr., *An Address Delivered before the Massachusetts Charitable Mechanic Association* (Boston, 1845), p. 20, as cited in Gary J. Kornblith, "Self-Made Men: The Development of Middling-Class Consciousness in New England," *Massachusetts Review*, 26 (1985): 469.

38. Mary P. Ryan, *Cradle of the Middle Class: Oneida County, New York, 1790–1865* (New York, 1981), pp. 10–11; James L. Huston, *Securing the Fruits of Labor: The American Concept of Wealth Distribution, 1765–1900* (Baton Rouge, La., 1998), p. 53.

39. *Niles Register,* 1811ff; Daniel Raymond, *The Elements of Political Economy* (Baltimore, 1823); Stephen Elliott, *Memorial of the Citizens of Charleston, Against the Proposed Increase of the Tariff* (Charleston, 1820).

40. Joseph Caldwell, *Autobiography and Biography of Rev. Joseph Caldwell, D.D. LL.D.* (Chapel Hill, 1860), pp. 47–49.

41. Michael Meranze, *Laboratories of Virtue: Punishment, Revolution, and Authority in Philadelphia, 1760–1835* (Chapel Hill, 1996), pp. 327–328.

42. L. Ray Gunn, *The Decline of Authority: Public Economic Policy and Political Development in New York State, 1780–1860* (Ithaca, 1988).

43. I am indebted to Kornblith, "Self-Made Men," pp. 461–474, for the development of this idea.

44. Samuel Latham Mitchill, *An Oration before the Society of Black Friars* (New York, 1793), pp. 19–20. It is perhaps fitting for a man with the reputed encyclopedic knowledge of Mitchill, living in such a turbulent time, to be called "a chaos of knowledge."

45. John F. Watson, *Annals of Philadelphia* (Philadelphia, 1830), pp. v–vi.

46. See T. H. Breen and Timothy Hall, "Structuring Provincial Imagination: The Rhetoric and Experience of Social Change in Eighteenth-Century New England," *American Historical Review*, 103 (1998).

47. William Hickling Prescott, *The History of the Reign of Ferdinand and Isabella the Catholic* (Boston, 1838).

48. Francis Paul Prucha, *The Great Father: The United States Government and the American Indians* (Lincoln, Neb., 1984), pp. 50–51.

49. Thomas L. McKenney and James Hall, *A Catalogue of Eighty Indian Portrait Lithographs* (Philadelphia, 1836–1844) (introduction from Catalogue of Haffenreffer Museum of Anthropology Exhibition, Brown University, 1990), p. 7. In 1866 fire destroyed all but four of King's paintings.

50. Cheryl Walker, *Indian Nation: Native American Literature and Nineteenth-Century Nationalisms* (Durham, N.C., 1997).

51. Henry Adams, *The Education of Henry Adams* (New York, 1918), p. 48.

52. Rachel M. Varble, *Julie Ann* (New York, 1939), p. 121; Fredrika Teute and Joyce Appleby, eds., *The First Forty Years of Washington Society* (Armonk, N.Y., 2000).

53. Harvey Reed, *Platform for Change: The Foundations of the Northern Free Black Community, 1775–1865* (East Lansing, Mich., 1994), pp. 30–32.

54. Barbara Jeanne Fields, "Ideological Race in American History," *Region, Race, and Reconstruction: Essays in Honor of C. Vann Woodward*, ed. J. Morgan Kousser (New York, 1982); Gary Nash, "The Hidden History of Mestizo America," *Journal of American History* 82 (1995).

55. William J. Novak, *The People's Welfare: Law and Regulation in Nineteenth-Century America* (Chapel Hill, 1996).

56. Robert E. Gallman and John Joseph Wallis, eds., *American Economic Growth and Standard of Living Before the Civil War* (Chicago, 1993).

57. *The Aeronaut* 1816–1819 (AC ser. 2, Reel 49); the term belongs to George Schultz. Naomi R. Lamoreaux and Christopher Glaisek, "Vehicles of Privilege or Mobil-

ity: Banks in Providence, R.I. during the Age of Jackson," *Business History Review*, 65 (1991).

58. *Annals of Congress*, 18th Congress, 1st Session (Washington, D.C., 1824), pp. 1085–1094.

59. Ibid., pp. 1103–1135.

60. See Sylvia R. Frey, *Water from the Rock: Black Resistance in a Revolutionary Age* (Princeton, 1991); Colin G. Calloway, *The American Revolution in Indian Country: Crisis and Diversity in Native American Communities* (Cambridge, 1995).

INDEX

politics, 33–34; and careers, 91; growth of, 99–103; and rural population, 141; and religion, 217–218. *See also* Press

Niles, Hezekiah, 94, 140, 254

Niles' Register, 94

Nine Worthies, 182

North: and African Americans, 17; and free blacks, 17; and civil society, 19; and national identity, 22–23, 242–243, 266; and slavery, 45–47, 48–49, 53–54, 156, 223, 226, 227, 229–230, 241–244, 247–248, 260–261; and manufacture, 76; and newspapers, 102, 103; and education, 104; and parental control, 104; and poverty, 143; and literacy, 153; and status, 155; and work, 156; and attitude towards South, 158; self-image of, 158; and reform, 234, 243, 245, 249; and dueling, 244–245; and African Americans, 260–261; and freedom, 262; and morality, 262

Novels. *See* Literature

Ohio, 68

O'Neall, John Belton, 110, 124

Order of Cincinnati, 134

Osceola, 260

Otis, Bass, 117

Paine, Thomas, 199

Panama Congress, 248

Parents, 2–3, 104, 170–176, 192–193

Partisanship, 20, 27–28, 30–31, 33–35, 41–45

Partridge, Alden, 36, 37–38

Patent, 63

Patron, 125. *See also* Brothers; Uncles

Paxton, John, 169, 176, 226

Peale, Anna Claypoole, 117

Peale, Titian Ramsay, 117

Peddlars, 14–15, 82–83, 84. *See also* Careers

Phelps, Almira Hart Lincoln, 97

Philanthropy, 180

Phillips, Willard, 95

Physicians, 110–112, 211. *See also* Medicine

Pickering, John, 135, 141

Pierce, Deborah, 120

Pinckney, William, 110

Pluralism, 264

Poindexter, George, 226–227

Politics, 26–55; attitude towards, 4–5; and campaigns, 6, 30, 38, 41, 52, 54, 85, 128, 194, 215, 243, 245; and partisanship, 20; and economy, 57, 58–59; and law, 109–110; and status, 136, 137, 160; and race, 160; and Hull, 168; and women, 170; and religious associations, 197; and religion, 215; and reform, 236; and South, 243, 244, 246. *See also* Government

Population, 75, 91, 141, 158–159, 244

Porter, Abel, 79

Postal service, 91, 221–222

Posting, 42

Potter, Ray, 188

Poverty, 143, 173

Powers, William, 60

Preaching, 117–121. *See also* Clergy; Religion

Presbyterian, 225

Prescott, William, 258

Presidents, 6, 52, 134, 136, 239–240

Press: and culture, 18; and West Point, 37; and Episcopal Church, 39; and Medical College of Ohio, 40; and dueling, 42–43; and slavery, 54, 226; and intimate relations, 163–164; and religion, 217–218; and national identity, 241, 242; and progress, 256. *See also* Journals; Literature; Newspapers; Publishing

Price, Phineas, 169, 190

Progress, 251, 256–259

Property, 28, 29, 71, 138

Public realm, 34–41, 42, 43, 123–124, 170, 241, 242

Publicity, 30, 34, 36–37, 40–42, 98

Publishing, 91–92, 95–96, 99

Quaker, 225

Quincy, Eliza Susan, 155

Race, 156, 158–160, 227, 230. *See also* Slavery

Railroads, 113

Raymond, Daniel, 254